WEYERHAEUSER ENVIRONMENTAL BOOKS

William Cronon, Editor

Weyerhaeuser Environmental Books explore human relationships with natural environments in all their variety and complexity. They seek to cast new light on the ways that natural systems affect human communities, the ways that people affect the environments of which they are a part, and the ways that different cultural conceptions of nature profoundly shape our sense of the world around us. A complete list of the books in the series appears at the end of this book.

Kurkpatrick Dorsey

WHALES

& NATIONS

ENVIRONMENTAL

DIPLOMACY

on the

HIGH SEAS

UNIVERSITY OF WASHINGTON PRESS
Seattle and London

Whales and Nations: Environmental Diplomacy on the High Seas is published with the assistance of a grant from the Weyerhaeuser Environmental Books Endowment, established by the Weyerhaeuser Company Foundation, members of the Weyerhaeuser family, and Janet and Jack Creighton.

© 2013 by the University of Washington Press
Printed and bound in the United States of America
Design by Thomas Eykemans
Composed in Sorts Mill Goudy, typeface designed by Barry Schwartz
18 17 16 15 14 13   5 4 3 2 1

UNIVERSITY OF WASHINGTON PRESS
PO Box 50096, Seattle, WA 98145, USA
www.washington.edu/uwpress

LIBRARY OF CONGRESS CATALOGING-IN-PUBLICATION DATA
Dorsey, Kurkpatrick.
Whales and nations : environmental diplomacy on the high seas / Kurkpatrick Dorsey.
    pages cm. — (Weyerhaeuser environmental books)
Includes bibliographical references and index.
ISBN 978-0-295-99311-9 (hardcover : alkaline paper) 1. Whaling—Political aspects—History—20th century. 2. Whaling—Environmental aspects—History—20th century. 3. Whales—Conservation—History—20th century. 4. Sustainable fisheries—History—20th century. 5. Whaling—Law and legislation—History—20th century. 6. Environmental law, International—History—20th century. 7. Diplomacy—History—20th century. 8. International cooperation—History—20th century. I. Title.
SH383.D67 2014   338.3'7295—dc23   2013024193

Contents

Foreword by William Cronon   vii
Acknowledgments   xiii
Preface   xix

Introduction   3

1   A Global Industry and Global Challenges   17

2   The Pelagic and the Political   49

3   World War and the World's Whales   91

4   Cheaters Sometimes Prosper   129

5   Melting Down and Muddling Through   163

6   Save the Whales (for Later)   207

7   The End of Commercial Whaling   243

Epilogue   279

Appendix: Whaling Data, 1904–1965   291
Notes   295
Bibliography   339
Index   347

Illustrations follow pages 82 and 194

Foreword

CREATURES OF THE CONTESTED DEEP

William Cronon

IN 1968, THE BIOLOGIST GARRETT HARDIN PUBLISHED AN ARTICLE IN *Science* that became an instant environmental classic. Entitled "The Tragedy of the Commons," it offered a moral fable about medieval peasants who destroyed their shared pastures by gradually adding more and more grazing animals until the carrying capacity of the land collapsed, with devastating consequences for all concerned. What made Hardin's essay so striking was his claim that the peasants destroyed their own prosperity precisely because their behavior was the only *rational* choice available to them. The crux of his argument was that individual peasants got all the profits from selling each new animal they added to the pasture, whereas the small incremental harm caused by that animal was shared by everyone in common. From an individual's point of view, it made perfect sense to add more animals since their environmental costs were mainly borne by everyone else. Furthermore, if a few enlightened peasants resisted adding animals to the commons in an effort to conserve the pasture, their neighbors would simply add more animals to gain the incremental profits for themselves. Under such circumstances, the only intelligent thing to do was to keep adding animals to earn as much individual profit as possible ... until the inevitable collapse brought the whole weirdly rational game to a catastrophic halt.

Hardin did not originate this important argument, though the evocative title he chose for his essay has associated his name with it ever since. Environmental problems arising from market failures involving property held in common had first been described decades earlier by fisheries economists working on what they called "the fisherman's problem." That story will be familiar to anyone who has read Arthur McEvoy's classic 1986 book of the same title. The puzzle these economists had tried to solve was why fishing fleets seem almost inevitably to overharvest the animals on which their own profitability depends. The answer was essentially the same as for Hardin's peasants. Individual fishers had no incentive *not* to harvest more fish, since if they failed to do so their competitors would just grab those profits for themselves. Rather than limit their catch in an enlightened effort to protect the stocks on which they all depended, fishing fleets harvested with competitive abandon until the resource collapsed. The problem was compounded by the enormous uncertainties involved in estimating fish populations that ranged vast distances beneath the surface of the water, a challenge Hardin's peasants never faced. The only solution to this paradox, the fisheries economists argued, was either to privatize fish by creating property rights that gave fishers incentives to conserve them or to keep the harvest sustainable by imposing government regulations that would limit the catch by size or duration.

McEvoy demonstrated the ways in which this seemingly universal economic model—which everyone now calls "the tragedy of the commons"—does not do full justice to the cultural and historical complexities involved in harvesting fish or any other common property resource. In fact, the "rationality" of overharvesting mainly arises under conditions of uncontrolled market competition, which have been much more the exception than the rule over the sweep of human history. Any number of mechanisms, ranging from cultural norms to religious rituals to state regulations, have been relatively effective in avoiding the fisherman's problem—medieval peasants themselves rarely behaved in the ways Hardin ascribed to them—so that treating the tragedy of the commons as a universal law of human nature turns out to be deeply misleading. It nonetheless offers important insights into the causes of overfishing in the modern era, and the reasons why governments have so often resorted to regulations to protect fisheries.

But there is an additional problem that McEvoy, writing mainly about fisheries in California, did not need to address at length. Wild animals do not honor national boundaries. Moreover, such boundaries are especially challenging to define and defend in the waters of the open ocean, which is why they have so often been a source of international conflict. If the tragedy of the commons is best solved by state intervention—whether through regulation or the creation of property rights—uncertainties about the effectiveness of state power in maritime environments mean that the challenge of avoiding the fisherman's problem is not merely economic, but legal, political, and diplomatic as well.

This is why Kurk Dorsey's book, *Whales and Nations: Environmental Diplomacy on the High Seas*, is such an important contribution, with implications that are as far-reaching as McEvoy's and Hardin's. Dorsey helped pioneer the field of diplomatic environmental history with his *The Dawn of Conservation Diplomacy: U.S.-Canadian Wildlife Protection Treaties in the Progressive Era*, which was published in our Weyerhaeuser series in 1998. Now, he brings his formidable expertise to the story of international whaling in the twentieth century, in an engagingly written book that readers will likely find both surprising and compelling.

I suspect most of us carry in our heads images of this industry that date back to the nineteenth century, when wooden sailing ships traveled for months on end to track down prey, which they then killed with hand-held harpoons thrown from rowboats. It was a dramatic and dangerous way to harvest these enormous creatures, since a harpooned whale in its death throes was more than capable of wreaking havoc for sailors, rowboats, and ships alike before finally giving up its life to be hauled aboard and rendered into oil. Even if we have never read it, *Moby-Dick* still dominates our imaginations when we think of this way of life.

We forget that whaling of this kind was already nearing its end by the time Melville wrote his great novel in 1851. The 1859 discovery of petroleum meant that "rock oil" (kerosene) would increasingly compete with whale oil as a source for illumination. The Victorian inclination to define a woman's beauty by the narrowness of her waist fueled an intense demand for baleen—the narrow strips of cartilage with which plankton-feeding whales strain seawater—that lasted until the first decade of the twentieth century, when brassieres replaced corsets as fashion's preferred tool for reshaping the curves of women's bodies. By then, wooden sailing vessels were largely a thing of the past, and with their disappearance, popular consciousness of whaling receded as well.

But the sheer volume of cetacean biomass was just too tempting an economic reward, and fishing fleets continued to harvest these enormous animals. New technologies made it possible to hunt even the largest whales—the blues and finbacks—which had been off limits because of the greater danger they posed and because their heavier bodies tended to sink before their flesh could be processed. The Norwegian inventor Sven Foynd's perfection in the 1870s of an exploding harpoon fired from a cannon meant that it was now possible to kill such whales much more reliably. Machines for pumping compressed air into a dead whale's body now kept it from sinking. Steel-hulled ships using steam and then diesel had the power needed to maneuver the massive carcasses, and the addition of slipways to the sterns of these vessels made the process of hauling whales on board much safer than when they had to be lifted over the side. Together, these technologies also made it possible for whalers to work the dangerously stormy waters off Antarctica, where these largest of all creatures were most abundant.

Once blubber had been rendered into oil, who wanted it after petroleum had become more cheaply and abundantly available? The answer was simple: human beings couldn't eat petroleum, and whale oil was still a relatively cheap source of animal fat for industrial food processing. With the growing popularity of margarine as an inexpensive alternative to butter, the British company Unilever nearly monopolized the world's whale oil market in the 1930s to assure itself a reliable supply. Whale oil became margarine; whale meat became pet food.

Britain's dominant position led it to join Norway and other interested nations in promoting in 1937 an international Convention on Whaling to control competition and make it more sustainable. But the geopolitics of the pre-war era kept important states from participating. Ominously, just a few years earlier the Japanese—who despite a long history of offshore whaling in the North Pacific had not ranged world-wide in their hunting—gained a foothold in international whaling by purchasing modern ships and hiring Norwegian sailors to learn from them the skills needed to expand. Growing competition before the Second World War led to negotiations that finally created the International Whaling Commission in 1946—a political body whose clear purpose was to regulate the whale harvest so as to avoid the fisherman's problem.

The rest of this story is best left for Kurk Dorsey to tell. Let me close by sketching some of the most important lessons of his fine book. As I've already explained, Arthur McEvoy demonstrated that Hardin's "tragedy of the commons" was too simple an explanation of the reasons why modern human beings so often get into trouble when harvesting common property resources. Hardin was right that individual actors in market economies often compete with each other in unsustainable ways, but he was wrong to universalize that phenomenon to all times and places. Kurk Dorsey complicates the story by reminding us that people bring to markets a host of different backgrounds and values combined with national interests and identities. It is these as much as abstract economic logic that shape their behavior relative to the natural resources they harvest. When an environmental challenge becomes truly international in scope, these different values and national interests must be analyzed in all their subtle intricacies if we are to have any hope of shaping economic and political behaviors that can otherwise frustrate even the most well-intentioned efforts to build more sustainable human relationships with the earth.

In the case of whales, the crucial players during the middle decades of the twentieth century included nation states—Great Britain, the United States, Norway, the Soviet Union, Japan, and several others—as well as the corporations that operated their whaling fleets. Equally important were scientists interested in studying and protecting the marine environment and its largest inhabitants. The work of those scientists, aided by activists and filmmakers, led members of the public increasingly to view whales as animals who were close to human beings in their levels of intelligence, and thus worthy of empathy. Concern about environmental protection after the 1950s combined with a growing animal rights movement to recast whaling as a barbaric assault on sentient beings for the appallingly trivial purpose of turning their brutalized carcasses into margarine and pet food.

The resulting controversy brought an end to commercial whaling in the 1980s—but not quite an end to whaling itself. Certain nations—Japan chief among them—insisted on continuing a "scientific" harvest of whales, though more than just science was clearly at stake. It is here that Dorsey offers one of his most important insights. As so often happens, generalized environmental concerns were in conflict with deeply held convictions. Protecting the environment, in other words, collided not just with national *interests* but also with the cultural traditions and values embodied in national *identities*. The implications of this insight extend far beyond whales; indeed, they reach all the way to that greatest of all international environmental challenges, global climate change. If common property resources—not just whales, but the ocean and the atmosphere—are ever to be better conserved, it will only be by grappling more thoughtfully with what these things *mean* to the people who use them. To see why global sustainability is so challenging, we would do well to understand why so many of the world's most magnificent ocean creatures plummeted toward extinction even as diplomats negotiated agreements intended to keep them alive. The story is more troubling and fascinating than you might imagine, and no one has ever told it better than Kurk Dorsey.

Acknowledgments

AT THE END OF WRITING A BOOK COMES THE MONUMENTAL BUT HAPPY task of counting up the numerous debts accrued over the course of many years of research and writing. With a list so long, where does one even begin?

Although none of them had any direct influence on this book, I realize now more than ever how indebted I am to excellent professors who put up with me as a student and set examples that I have tried to emulate: Walter LaFeber and David Winkler at Cornell; Art McEvoy and Mike Sherry at Northwestern; and Gaddis Smith and Paul Kennedy at Yale. They probably deserve some sort of apology from me more than anything else.

I have been very fortunate to have access to archives around the world. I spent so much time at the US National Archives early in this project that I could have gotten my mail there; many people in College Park, Maryland, were helpful, but I want to particularly acknowledge Milt Gustafson, who took me into the stacks in successful pursuit of a misplaced file. Archivists in Canberra, Wellington, Ottawa, Oslo, and Kew all helped me find things and showed me hospitality beyond their job requirements. The staff at the International Whaling Commission, starting with Martin Harvey and Julie Creek, were gracious and welcoming during a cold January visit. I am still particularly humbled by an Iraqi-born clerk at the Riksarkivet in Oslo who apologized to me for his poor English as he was busily working during his breaks on a pocket Norwegian-Arabic phrase book for refugees.

Several people at the various archives stand out for their efforts. Bill Cox at the Smithsonian Institution Archives took an interest in this bearded fellow who put up with the lumpy chairs in the reading room to read through Remington Kellogg's papers, and one day he brought me a list of entries from the archives' Oral History Project of people who had worked with Kellogg. Graeme Eskrigge, a retired diplomat from New Zealand, was extremely gracious in helping me get access to material from the 1980s and guiding me through his government's policy on using archival material. I am sorry that he passed away before he got a chance to read my manuscript, but Neil Robertson kindly filled his shoes and provided helpful clarifications. Norway's foreign ministry was incredibly hospitable, as Inga Badi-Massoud and her colleagues granted me access to recent documents and the liberal use of a photocopier. Since I neglected to learn Norwegian as a high schooler, that access would have been meaningless without the sharp-eyed assistance of Heidi Engler, who translated hundreds of pages of documents into fluent English. Without her work and the kindness of the Norwegian Foreign Ministry, I would have been unable to get a sense of what the Norwegian government and whalers thought they were doing, and a whaling book without that sense would obviously be incomplete.

Of course, getting permission to use archives in foreign countries means nothing without the resources to get there, and I have been very fortunate to have the support of many offices at the University of New Hampshire. At the earliest stages of this project, Ann Bucklin of the New Hampshire Sea Grant office and Burt Feintuch of the Humanities Center were able to pool resources to grant me a fellowship for a semester free of teaching, which allowed me to take six weeks in Canberra and Wellington without getting fired. The Center for International Education supported that trip with an international engagement grant. Dean Marilyn Hoskin of the College of Liberal Arts was incredibly supportive, approving funds for translation of Norwegian documents and travel to Norway. The Faculty Development Grant also provided support for travel and translation. Near the end of the project, the Humanities Center came through once again with a fellowship to provide writing time. I have also hired undergraduate research assistants over the years, including Jon Rice, Steve Burlinguette, and Courtney Southworth, all of whom found unexpected material and brought good cheer to my unreasonable requests to find things about whaling. My old friends Drew Isenberg and Fred Logevall provided encouragement and letters when needed.

I am grateful to work in an excellent, productive, collegial department at UNH. At faculty seminars, I received welcome feedback at various stages of the manuscript. I owe the biggest debt to Bill Harris and Jeff Bolster, both of whom read the complete draft when it was almost finished and helped it immensely. Having served on many dissertation committees with him, I have concluded that Bill is the best reader of manuscripts I know. In Jeff, I am very fortunate to have an expert on marine environmental history in the department.

I asked two others to read portions of the manuscript. Erika Bsumek immeasurably improved the section on the bowhead whale controversy with her insight and citations. Tim Smith provided important insights over the years during his visits to UNH, as well as access to hard-to-find sources on Soviet whaling data. He gave me good, pointed advice about the introduction and first chapter that made the manuscript much better. Tim also introduced me to Tore Schweder and Lars Walloe, who graciously took time to talk to me about modern Norwegian whaling. Jake Hamblin and Helen Rozwadowski gave the manuscript thorough reviews for the University of Washington Press, and both of them contributed to improving the manuscript. Jake is an old friend and collaborator on several panels, reaching back to the 1990s, and I have learned a great deal from him in particular. Harry Scheiber graciously provided insights and publications early in my research.

The people at UW Press have been just great to work with. I promised the manuscript years ago to Julidta Tarver, and she and Bill Cronon never gave up on it, even as I spent a few years wandering around. While I am sorry that I could not finish it before Julidta retired, all of us who publish in the Weyerhaeuser Series know that Marianne Keddington-Lang has maintained Julidta's strong support and standard of excellence for the series. Her editorial advice on revisions, tone, and images, among other things, has always been spot-on. Tim Zimmerman has been a joy to work with, particularly in helping work out all the details concerning photos and maps to make them as sharp as possible. Denise Clark, Rachael Levay, and Mary Ribesky have all been very helpful in moving the manuscript from a stack of paper to a marketable object. Julie Van Pelt skillfully took on the unenviable task of ferreting out unfortunate jokes, tying up several dozen loose ends, and making me stop treating citations as endangered species to be conserved. The manuscript simply is much better because of editorial advice. Of course, it is impossible to measure the importance of Bill Cronon's guidance on the series as a whole. It is an honor to publish in this series.

The process of gathering photos was a team effort. Mary Markey at the Smithsonian archives found original photos from the 1946 whaling conference; Carolyn Soltau assisted with getting a photo from the *Vancouver Sun* and identified the person in the photo; Bob Meyers helped navigate the wealth of photos in Greenpeace's collections; Øyvind Thurreson at the Sandefjord Hvalfangstmuseet found and delivered several valuable images; Jacky Graham at AccentAlaska helped find a suitable photo and facilitated work with the photographer; and Vishnu Jani at the Hoover Institution Archives turned my somewhat vague requests about the Hubert Gregory Schenck Papers into actual usable images. I would not have had any of the Hoover Institution images without the work of James Mayfield, who went through the Schenck papers in the first place, and the kind permission of Edward Beach and Ingrid Beach to use the photos. Others who helped include Melanie Correia at the New Bedford Whaling Museum, Katy Seppings at Lafayette Photography, Amy Whetstone at the People's Trust for Endangered Species, Veena Manchanda of the UN Photo Library, and Matthew Bailey at the National Portrait Gallery. Special thanks go to my fellow birder Len Medlock, who is famous among New England birders for his spectacular nature photos, for letting me use his shot of the breaching humpback, and to my parents for sending me the photo years ago of whale bones from their much envied (by me at least) trip to Antarctica.

I have published two articles with similarities to the material herein, and I thank the editors: "Compromising on Conservation: World War II and American Leadership in Whaling Diplomacy," in *Natural Enemy, Natural Ally: Toward an Environmental History of War*, ed. Richard Tucker and Edmund Russell, 252–69 (Corvallis: Oregon State University Press, 2004); and "National Sovereignty, the International Whaling Commission, and the Save the Whales Movement," in *Nation-States and the Global Environment: New Approaches to International Environmental History*, ed. Erika Bsumek, David Kinkela, and Mark Lawrence, 43–61 (New York: Oxford University Press, 2013).

Finally, I owe much to my family. Joe and Peg Girard were always enthusiastic about this project and were not above occasional small acts of bribery (Joe, I haven't forgotten the promised whale carving). Anne and Robert Dorsey inspired me to follow their footsteps into academia and they set models for the importance of undergraduate education, even as both are accomplished authors in their own right. They sent me to a summer camp where I became a birder and ran across the game "Save the Whales," and they also impressed upon me the value of healthy skepticism. In the fall of 2000, I went to Kew to figure out what the British government was doing about whaling in the twentieth century, but I found something much better. At the Public Records Office, as it was then known, Molly Girard and I met as she was doing her own research. As anyone who knows us will attest, she is both the brains and the common sense of the operation. She has improved this book with her feedback and insight, but she has improved the author even more. Our two sons, Luke and Nick, are fortunate to have her intelligence, looks, and personality. I am responsible for the rest. I cannot say that our sons have stirred me to write this book, but I have to acknowledge that they have kept me from taking it or myself too seriously. Even as he persuades me to be Gandalf to his Elrond, Nick will not accept that Elrond was not in Moria; nor will Luke rest until he has gleaned every detail of the life of Luke Skywalker. Together they slowed down the book by about two years and in return let me act about thirty years younger—it was a good deal for me. And the trip to London was the best I have ever taken.

Preface

OVER THE PAST DOZEN OR SO YEARS, WHEN I HAVE MENTIONED TO someone that I have been writing a book on whaling, the reply frequently makes mention of Mystic, Connecticut, or New Bedford, Massachusetts, or maybe *Moby Dick* (yes, I have read it; no I don't really recommend it). In most people's minds, whaling still conjures up the allegedly romantic era of wooden ships and iron men cruising the Pacific or nudging into the icy Arctic Ocean. There is nothing romantic about this book (except that my wife and I met while both of us were in London doing research). Instead, this is a book about international efforts to make whaling sustainable in the twentieth century, from the earliest suggestions that regulation was necessary before the First World War, through the signing of whaling conventions in the 1930s and the creation of the International Whaling Commission in the 1940s, to the modern era of the commercial moratorium.

This is also a book with many moving parts. I have attempted to learn how diplomats, whalers, scientists, fisheries regulators, environmentalists, and consumers from a variety of countries valued whales; how they understood the nature of whales and the whales' environment; and, therefore, how and why they responded to one another in formal and informal negotiations. By necessity it is an international history. Nations from each continent were involved, although admittedly South America's and Africa's roles were generally small, and the focus of attention for most of the century was one of the least national places on earth, the seas around Antarctica. Because the seas are open to all, and the southern sea in particular is far from any law, the diplomatic efforts to regulate whaling were complex and slow moving. While I do not devote many pages to discussing the biology and ecology of whales directly, I have kept in mind that nature is hardly static. Ecosystem dynamics alone could wreak havoc with any scientist's or whaler's expectations for a particular whaling season.

The archival sources for this book reflect the different constituencies. Material comes from the national archives, including foreign ministries and fisheries ministries, as well as other agencies on occasion, in Australia, Canada, Great Britain, New Zealand, Norway, and the United States. The foreign ministries in New Zealand and Norway were particularly helpful in allowing me access to fairly recent files that made the last chapter and the epilogue possible. The International Whaling Commission (IWC) in Cambridge, England, also allowed me access to its files. Beyond the organizational records, I relied heavily on the material saved by a prominent scientist, Remington Kellogg of the Smithsonian, and those of the Salvesen whaling firm, housed at the University of Edinburgh. While I did not gain access to Russian or Japanese archives, there has been enough published from both nations, as well as diplomatic correspondence in other nations' files, for me to feel confident that I have captured their positions. It also helped that the Japanese got back into whaling with the help of the US occupation authorities, and those records are all in the US National Archives. As to the environmentalists, they have left their own informal archives in letters to governments and the IWC, innumerable books, and newspaper advertisements and stories.

Ultimately, this book deals with three specific, ongoing concerns in whaling diplomacy: sustainability, sovereignty, and science. From the start of the century, those who knew the history of whaling believed that whalers would always follow a pattern of finding a large stock of whales, ramping up catching, and fairly quickly driving the stock to commercial extinction—too few to bother hunting. Generally, knowledgeable observers wanted to negotiate some sort of agreement that would make whaling rational, by which they meant roughly what in the early twenty-first century would usually be called sustainable: it would not be rational to hunt so many whales that the industry would collapse. Into the middle of the 1970s, the central question about whaling was how much to restrict catching to ensure more catching in the future, and the winners were usually those who wanted fewer restrictions. The unwillingness of whalers and their governments to sacrifice some short-term profits helped set the stage for the rise of an anti-whaling coalition, which eventually concluded that even if there could be sustainable whaling, whaling was itself unethical and hence should end, unless undertaken by aboriginal peoples, and even that right was in dispute.

In deciding that whaling was unethical and should be banned, environmentalists touched on issues of national sovereignty that had never been far from the surface of whaling diplomacy. The core problem of whaling diplomacy was convincing governments to yield control over their whalers on the high seas. From the earliest discussions of the possibility of regulating pelagic, or high-seas, whaling, government officials worried that whalers would simply change their ships' registration if regulations became too onerous. Governments were particularly concerned that the IWC, as a permanent body with the right to make rules for member states' whaling companies, might infringe on a nation's rights. Thus, they agreed to establish the objection system, which allowed a government to opt out of an onerous rule. On many occasions in the commission's first forty years, governments filed objections to protect their industries. Had they been forced to choose between accepting the moratorium or leaving the IWC altogether, certainly some governments would have left. While governments rarely emphasized sovereignty in the same way that they discussed the proper use of whales or science, the principle was present every time negotiators tried to limit whalers' options.

Finally, the negotiations about sustainability and sovereignty were inseparable from debates about science. From the earliest days of discussing whaling regulations, two competing threads dominated the thinking about science: it was necessary to make good decisions, and the amount of scientific knowledge was totally inadequate to make good decisions. Most of the first people to raise the alarm about whaling were scientists, and many of the proponents of taking fewer whales in the present to preserve them for the future were scientists. In 1931, the first whaling convention required member states to contribute data because most observers recognized that there would be no rules without reliable data to serve as the basis for those rules. The convention of 1946, which created the IWC, specifically gave scientists a critical place in making decisions. Yet the data were not strong enough to stand up to those demands, in part because whaling proponents manipulated the data, in part because it simply is difficult to get factual information about whales, and in part because the scientists were hesitant to make specific recommendations. What the scientists did not know or could not agree upon, such as the level of cetacean sentience, would play as important a role in the outcome of the diplomacy as what they did know.

In the end, then, this is a book about the failure of efforts to create a sustainable whaling system. The stocks of great whales in the Antarctic seas that numbered in the hundreds of thousands are gone, reduced to mere remnant populations. This is not a story of missed opportunities, however, for it is hard to imagine whalers and their governments accepting sets of rules that might have curtailed whaling while it was still sustainable. A commitment to saving resources for the morrow was neither wide nor deep while the largest whales were still numerous, the concerns about protecting sovereignty were real, and the science was a slender reed on which to lean.

Whales and Nations

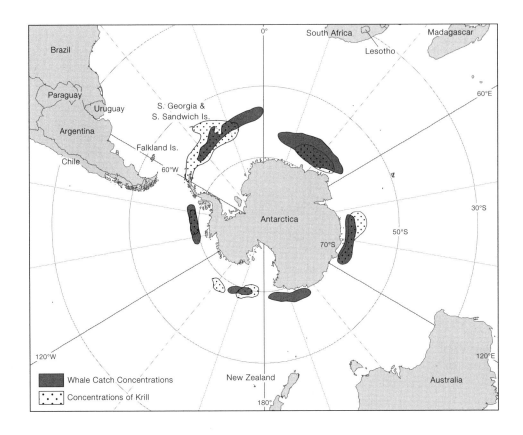

Concentrations of krill and whale catches around Antarctica
(adapted from Connor and Peterson, 1994).

Introduction

HISTORY WAS ABOUT TO REPEAT ITSELF, WARNED SIDNEY HARMER. IN 1913, while serving as keeper of zoology for the British Museum (Natural History), Sir Sidney concluded, "It is impossible to avoid seeing an analogy between what is taking place off South Georgia and the neighboring Antarctic localities and what has happened elsewhere in the world." The history of hunting right whales (which he called Greenlands) around the world showed that "enormous numbers of whales were discovered," and "the industry had a period of great prosperity." The number of ships involved increased rapidly, stripping the population and reducing the whales to a mere remnant. Looking at contemporary whaling, he wrote: "In southern waters, indeed, we are still in the period of prosperity. But, taking into consideration the more deadly nature of modern whaler's weapons than of those which have been almost successful in the extermination of the Greenland whale, it can not be disputed that the present rate of destruction of whales in the south gives rise to grave anxiety."[1]

Harmer wrote these words at the intersection of two trends that would define the politics and practice of whaling in the twentieth century. First, whaling was undergoing a technological revolution that revitalized the industry. After boom years for much of the nineteenth century, whaling had appeared to be a dying industry by the end of the century, with a depleted resource base and an outdated product. But with new means of hunting whales and new uses for whale oil, the Antarctic seas were yielding enormous blue and fin whales and equally large profits. At the same time, voices for conservation in the industrialized world were pushing for restraint in the use of natural resources. In the United States, the most powerful mantra was that uttered by Gifford Pinchot, a utilitarian forester

3

with Theodore Roosevelt's ear: a resource should provide the greatest good to the greatest number for the longest time. This simple framework of sustainable use was meant especially to describe how a renewable resource should be husbanded rather than stripped, whether it was a forest or a fishery. Pinchot's utilitarian maxim was so grounded in common sense that few whalers, conservationists, scientists, bureaucrats, or consumers could possibly have objected to it as a generic statement of goals. The objections came in moving from the generic statement to specific practices—how many whales could be taken? On what basis would the decisions be made? A century after Harmer voiced concern, these are still the central questions.

For as long as people have lived near the sea, they have been thrilled to find a mass of meat washed up on shore, so pursuing small whales was probably one of the first things seafaring people did. Whales provided more than food, as their bones, baleen (or teeth), sinews, and the like could be used for a range of things, and their blubber could provide oil, which was mainly used for lighting. Commercial whaling probably began in the eleventh century in the Basque country of Iberia, but the well-known whalers of the nineteenth century were still doing things much the same, using harpoons to kill relatively slow-moving whales, like bowheads, rights, and humpbacks, as well as sperm whales, which as toothed whales offered a different range of products as well as a more resilient and combative attitude—no right whale could have done what the white whale did to Captain Ahab.

Several factors constrained whalers before the twentieth century. Perhaps most important was the size of the whale; for the hunters, bigger was better up to a point, after which bigger meant more dangerous. Blue whales and fin whales were appealing for their sheer size, but the prospect of trying to kill a ninety-ton blue whale with a handheld harpoon would have given pause to the hardiest whaler. A thirty-five-ton sperm whale was usually enough to satisfy the thirst for adventure and danger for any whaling crew. In addition, some species simply carried more blubber, so relatively thin fin whales were less interesting than the thickly layered bowheads of Arctic waters. Speed was also a factor, as a fin whale could make fifteen knots, leaving even the most powerful rowers gasping in its wake, whereas right whales and bowheads were usually content to move slowly. Some whales had habits that made them easier to hunt.

One expert concluded, for instance, that "the humpback whale, once the chase has started, is an almost certain prey, whilst the pursued blue or fin whale not infrequently escapes even an experienced hunter." Because humpbacks stay closer to the shore and use the same locales year after year, they were especially vulnerable.[2] Finally, some whales float when they die and others tend to sink rapidly, making them more difficult to handle. So even if all whales were evenly distributed, the whalers would have focused on smaller, slow-moving, thickly blubbered species, like rights, bowheads, and humpbacks.

By the middle of the 1800s, the center of the global whaling industry was Massachusetts, especially Nantucket and New Bedford, with major posts in Britain as well. From these locations, whalers set out on their global search for whale oil, focusing on such locations as the northern Pacific and Arctic Oceans for their bowheads and the tropical Pacific for its sperms. Even though whaling was quite risky and ships would sometimes return with empty holds, many New and Olde Englanders made fortunes in the business, and the United States in particular benefited. Three factors conspired to undermine the industry. Most important, the discovery of methods for refining petroleum and making steel introduced serious challenges to the whale oil and whale bone markets. The American Civil War produced Confederate raiders who preyed on US merchant vessels, driving up insurance rates for whalers and ruining their business. Finally, decades of intense hunting added to the problems by making it harder to find whales. Most, if not all, of the most valuable places had been tapped by the latter part of the nineteenth century, and whale oil was fast becoming thought of as a mere seasonal commodity, not nearly as reliable as petroleum products.[3]

Thus the long voyage of Melville became a thing of the past. No longer would scores of wooden vessels head out, sailing wherever history and hope suggested that there might be whales, returning months, if not years, later with holds and deck space crammed with barrels of oil. By the late nineteenth century the industry had been largely relegated to shore stations, where whalers would wait for seasonal migrations to bring their prey close to land. Particularly in the tropics, where humpbacks came inshore for calving, land stations continued to operate with low costs. Because the whales taken were generally thin, and hunting might disrupt breeding and birthing, most disinterested observers found tropical shore whaling to be indefensible. In 1938, British fisheries official Henry Maurice, who was active on whaling matters for many years, nailed the point in a rare fit of garbled grammar: "I think land stations in tropical waters is the most wasteful form of fishing and very dangerous to stock.... It is bad and more bad than anything else."[4] But such whaling was also cheap enough to stay afloat long after the wooden ships were rotting at the wharves.

There is a statue in Tønsberg, Norway, near the central church, of the man who made a whaling revival possible. Svend Foyn, slightly larger than life, looks out over a flower garden toward the harbor, and nearby a chapel and a school bear his name. Foyn earned his statue by designing an exploding harpoon that would kill a seventy-ton fin whale. He was not alone in working to find a more powerful weapon; he was just the most successful. The modern harpoon that one can find outside of museums from Santa Barbara to Sandefjord is Foyn's brainchild—a swivel-mounted cannon modified to fire a heavy iron lance, weighing about 110 pounds and measuring just over six feet, capped with an explosive device timed to go off a few seconds after impact. Just below the bomb, three or four short hooks run alongside the shaft, waiting to unfold and fasten the harpoon into the whale's flesh. A strong rope from the harpoon back to the catcher vessel ensured that the harpooned animal did not break loose. This more powerful weapon made it possible to kill or mortally wound a large whale with one shot and tie it fast to the hunters' vessel.[5]

Foyn's harpoon had to be mounted on a powerful boat. The development of smaller steam engines and steel vessels in the late 1800s made possible the development of the modern whale catcher, which also owed a lot to Foyn's initiative.[6] These vessels were usually about one hundred feet long, could sustain speeds of about fifteen knots, and featured a harpoon cannon on the bow. The old days of rowing after a whale, hitting it with thrown harpoons, and stabbing it with long lances, had passed. In its place were the days of steamships that could run down even the fastest whales and weapons that could stop even the largest. It still was a contest, though. Explorer and conservationist Roy Chapman Andrews reported in 1916 about being on a catcher boat with engines full astern yet still being dragged at six knots by a harpooned blue whale.[7]

Most harpooned whales still sank. Harpooning a ninety-ton whale and tying it to one's whale catcher was a foolhardy act once that whale lost it buoyancy. Unlike the right whales that stayed afloat for days, blues and fins started to sink in just hours, leaving whalers with a small window for getting the body back to a processing station. The simple solution was to fill the carcass with compressed air; once the whale was roped to the catcher, a whaler used a long knife to cut a hole in the blubber, inserted an air hose until the beast ballooned a bit, and then stuffed a heavy rag in to hold the air. This development gave the whalers enough time not only to get leviathan back to the flensers for processing but even to leave a dead whale behind while pursuing more members of the pod, secure in the knowledge that the original trophy would still be bobbing on the surface hours later.

The three inventions of small steam vessels, exploding harpoons, and compressed air helped to revitalize the industry on a local level by bringing the largest whales into the range of possibility. Blue whales in particular carried enormous fat reserves, which for the first time were readily available, and Foyn made his mark hunting the relatively abundant fins off northern Norway, although it appears that he harpooned anything that swam along.[8] In addition, whaling stations, particularly on the islands south of the Falklands, gained economic value because they could employ fewer ships to bring back more and larger whales. Norwegian and British whalers picked up their operations and moved as close as possible to the last great concentrations of whales in the southern seas. Christen Christensen made the family's first southern venture in 1893, teaming up with C. A. Larsen, but Christensen did not send another vessel down until 1905.[9] At islands like South Georgia, whalers found sheltered coves with plenty of freshwater, frequently from glacier-fed streams, and began to build small industrial villages, complete with factories, houses, recreation halls, and chapels. Because whale movements are usually cyclical, whaling stations were in operation for a few months a year, even though some workers stayed year-round to maintain the equipment and vessels. A modern visitor to these sites can find evidence of their success, both in the range of trash left behind and the cetacean skeletons scattered about. Lt. Cdr. John Chrisp, a British whaling inspector in the 1950s, wrote of Salvesen's Leith Harbour on South Georgia, "Never had I seen, side by side, such beauty and such squalor." The "dark, satanic mills" were a blot on the "virgin purity of the Antarctic."[10]

Even before people began to change whale distribution patterns, the populations were heavily skewed toward the Antarctic (and to a lesser extent the Arctic), with its rich marine life. Pre-hunting population estimates will probably always be a source of controversy, but it seems safe to say that blue and fin whales roamed the southern seas in the hundreds of thousands, with humpback, sei, sperm, and right whales mixed in too. The sheer cetacean biomass, drawn by the even more abundant krill, is boggling to consider. If there were about 250,000 blue whales averaging 100 tons each, and 400,000 fin whales averaging 50 tons each, then those species alone accounted for 45 million tons of life finding enough krill and small fish each day for months on end in Antarctic waters. Explorers had reported on the marine abundance in those waters for years, but as long as there were whales to be had in safer grounds, whalers were content to leave the southern seas alone. As one Norwegian whaler put it, after sealing petered out, "The mighty calm of the Antarctic Ocean was left undisturbed."[11] But by the time that Harmer expressed his worry in 1913, people had perfected the exploding harpoon and the steam-powered killer boat that, combined, made it possible to run down the two biggest animals ever, kill them, and drag them back to processing plants on islands.[12]

How much of each whale became marketable material depended on the thoroughness of the workers at the processing plant and the time of the year. With so many whales in the seas, whalers in the early twentieth century were able to skim the cream and throw away the milk. Why waste effort on using every last bit of a whale when a brand new one was right there for the taking? Each species followed a general migratory cycle, heading deeper south as the austral summer warmed up in December and January and the pack ice scattered, although some appear to move east and west along the coast of Antarctica too—in either case, a steady flow of targets came past the whalers on their frigid outposts. With winter, the whales moved north to warmer calving grounds. Hence, when spring returned, a whale might not have eaten for months, meaning that it was quite lean. From a whaler's standpoint, then, the best time to catch an Antarctic whale was March or April, when the animals were at their fattest. A blue whale that might yield less than 100 barrels of oil in October could produce more than 120 by the end of March.[13]

What worried Harmer was that emerging technology like Foyn's finally allowed whalers to crack the defenses of the hundreds of thousands of blue and fin whales that sauntered along at the top of the food web of the incredibly productive waters around Antarctica. As Harmer was writing in 1913, the southern stations were producing oil in abundance by catching whatever happened to swim by. The blue and fin whales in the region had rarely been hunted, and even the humpbacks were frequently numerous. With the powerful harpoon and catcher vessels, the hunters brought in so many whales that they focused on rendering only the best parts, dumping the rest for the sea to carry away. Few people cared about the waste, because it seemed impossible that a few men on a remote speck of land could affect the whale populations of a vast ocean.[14]

That conclusion was largely correct. The whalers' impact was predominantly local, as their vessels sailed only a score or so miles from the islands. Admittedly, the whales they hunted were usually heading somewhere else, so the impact was felt miles away on the calving grounds as well, and there is no doubt that certain island stations' activities hammered certain whale stocks, most particularly the humpbacks around South Georgia. More than 19,000 were taken between 1909 and 1912 by the whalers around the islands in the Antarctic seas, and humpback numbers never recovered (see the appendix for whaling data). But in the expanse of the southern seas, these outposts did not threaten species' existence, and in fact their take was so small that they outlasted the pelagic operations that depended on larger catches.

The slaughter of humpback whales rattled the bones of attentive conservationists. Harmer was just one of several people in Great Britain in the years before World War I who raised concerns about whalers' waste and inability to stop themselves from plowing through the population of whales before the populations were destroyed. Canadian and US diplomats and scientists also expressed concern about whales in a meeting in 1911. But in a world of big problems, it was nearly impossible to generate action to regulate whaling, especially when whaling took place so far from civilization and hence seemed unlikely to live up to the worst predictions, even if it were possible to take action in such remote locales. More common was the perspective of Roy Chapman Andrews, who regretted the decline of whales but still contended that commercial whaling had "contributed to the comfort and welfare of the civilized world for over a thousand years." He even found a silver lining in the expected destruction of whale populations: "It is deeply to be regretted that the wholesale slaughter of whales will inevitably result in their early commercial extinction, but meanwhile science is profiting by the golden opportunities given for the study of those strange and interesting animals."[15] For most of the century, the dominant idea about whales was that they were strange and interesting, but they were first food and energy for humans.

Andrews' silver lining had more tarnish than he acknowledged. Perhaps it was true that scientists were learning about cetacean anatomy and physiology, but they were not getting the information that they really needed to conserve whale populations for sustainable use, which most scientists of the day would have held as a worthy goal. As late as the 1950s, Canadian scientist G. R. Clark, in fighting for a conservation measure, sighed that "Scientific investigation of the stocks of whales is perhaps the most difficult of all fisheries work."[16] Whales did not have the decency to haul out on islands like seals, and dissecting one was not exactly lab work. That most of them by the turn of the century were as remote as possible only compounded the problems of conducting research on them. In the Progressive era in the United States there was a rising faith in the ability of trained experts to make rational decisions about the use of resources. Technical expertise could help society improve rivers or regulate the hunting of migratory birds or manage forests. The United States and Great Britain (for Canada) had cooperated on fisheries (Inland Fisheries Treaty, 1908), rivers (International Boundary Commission, 1909), fur seals (North Pacific Fur Seal Conventions, 1911), and migratory birds (Migratory Bird Treaty, 1916) all while accepting that scientific knowledge would be central in helping to determine policy. Both Great Britain and the United States had promoted conservation efforts, whether domestically or in the empire, and conservation organizations, such as Audubon or the Royal Society for the Protection of Birds, had mobilized citizen support for conservation policies.

It is also worth remembering, in the modern age of global negotiations and the United Nations, that when governments thought about the Antarctic early in the twentieth century they were thinking about making imperial claims to the land and resources that might be there. Whaling on distant islands or Antarctic seas provided a means to stake a claim, as indeed several countries would emphasize. Great Britain made the first claim on the least habitable continent in 1908, followed over four decades by Norway, Australia, New Zealand, Argentina, Chile, and France. There was no reason to predict that Antarctica might become, in effect, an international trusteeship. Nor was there reason to expect a global conference of interested nations to solve the problems of competing for whales. When the first diplomatic conference on whaling convened in 1930, it was moving into uncharted waters. The few precedents included a global oil pollution convention, a British-led effort to protect wildlife in African colonies, and regional wildlife agreements in North America.

So without much scientific evidence about whale populations or a history of multilateral cooperation on resource issues, it was likely that anyone espousing the position that a "rational" whaling system would involve more controls and fewer whales taken would face a substantial challenge. When people involved in the industry used the term *rational*, they implied that it would be irrational to destroy the stocks of whales rather than use them carefully. A related analogy that cropped up occasionally was that whales were like money in the bank; living off the interest was far more rational than dipping into the principal.

Whalers disagreed about the meaning and value of a rational or sustainable system, with some thinking long-term, some thinking short-term, and some just conflicted. For many whalers, sustainability meant that there should be enough whales in the sea to allow them to conduct their business in the ways that they saw fit for years into the future. H. K. Salvesen, a prominent British whaling company owner, thought that international regulations were unnecessary because honest whalers would not strip their industry of its supplies, and the dishonest ones would not abide by the rules anyway. In the eyes of the honest whalers, the main impediment to sustainable use, then, was their unscrupulous competitors. Norwegian industrialist Lars Christensen demonstrated the limits presented by even a reasonable whaler: "We will gladly discuss with all interested parties the possibilities that exist for a rational whaling industry. But we feel that we have a certain right to carry on whaling particularly in the areas which have been discovered and rendered workable through the Norwegian whaling industry." Even as he wrote that, he acknowledged that "no one can dare to prophesy that the Norwegian industry in the Antarctic can last forever."[17] It was not clear what rational negotiating position might arise from the intersection of the recognition of impermanence with the demand for permanence.

It was particularly hard to reconcile the desire for rationality with a visceral sense that whaling defied logic. A director of South Africa's

Union Whaling Company concluded that his company had to be on a sound financial basis because the "business of whaling was very speculative, there being so many factors which had to be taken into account which could not be foreseen and over which no one had control."[18] Gerald Elliott of Salvesen's found that when he entered the family business in 1948 the accounting was "primitive," the budgeting nonexistent, and planning to deal with various prices for oil and fluctuations in catch "hazy." Despite these stunning limitations, in the 1946–47 season the firm earned a profit of £3.6 million, and it added roughly another million pounds annually for a decade, all the while fighting off efforts to conserve the whales by catching fewer of them.[19] Aristotle Onassis called whaling "the biggest dice game in the world," even as his company pocketed $4.2 million in its first season.[20] The need for a gambling mentality probably attracted people who eschewed rational economic decision making.

Even beyond their economic outlooks, all whalers were not alike. Over time, prominent differences arose based on nationality and means of pursuit. Australians specialized in catching humpback whales from stations on the shoreline, while the Soviets generalized in pelagic, or high-seas, whaling of any species unfortunate enough to cross their paths. Cultural issues might make strange bedfellows or unbridgeable divisions. The Japanese were world leaders in high-technology pelagic whaling and preserving whale meat for the national market, but they tried to claim an affinity with Alaskan Inuit who hunted bowhead whales from small boats for local consumption. Class also mattered. Christensen and Salvesen had a different point of view than the thousands of men they employed for a few months of grueling but very rewarding work each year. While one should be careful not to think of whalers as a monolithic group, then, it does seem fair to conclude that they generally were committed to more whaling in the present rather than postponing their take for the future.

They wanted more now to serve another shadowy constituency: consumers. As a group or as individuals, consumers almost never show up in the records. Some bought their oil by the ton (six barrels of 49.12 gallons, or 374 pounds, each) and some by the pound in the margarine tub in the grocery store. The closest they come to being represented in the story was first in the brief moment around 1930 when Unilever, a grand middleman, nearly monopolized the use of whale oil, and then again in the aftermath of the Second World War when there simply was not enough food to go around in Japan and Europe. People consumed their whales most commonly in the form of margarine made from whale oil, but they also ate whale meat fresh or frozen and ingested vitamin A from whale livers. They fed whale meat or meal to their pets, fur-bearing animals, and farm stock. The rest of the oil became a huge range of products, from lipstick to shoe polish. Consumer demand, reflected in the price of oil, fluctuated dramatically, depending on the general health of the economy and availability of competitive alternatives, whether petroleum or peanut oil. Hence consumers, unorganized and generally unaware of whales in their everyday lives, determined whether whalers had good years or bad, stayed in business or sold out to their rivals, or viewed attempts at restrictions with calm or panic. And of course, they determined whether whales lived or died by the thousands.

Thus long before Garrett Hardin popularized the idea of rational economic actors causing the tragedy of the commons, or Arthur McEvoy explored the complexities of the fisherman's problem, the people who benefited from hunting whales demonstrated why the restraint necessary to make whaling sustainable was in thin supply.[21] In 1968, Hardin spelled out why people generally could not share common resources for long. The "rational" economic actors in his fable of pastoralists would always take a little more than their fair share. McEvoy, like many others, critiqued Hardin's model as a little too simple, but he generally accepted that in the most valuable commons, the oceanic fisheries, fishermen faced a problem in sustaining their resource. Even if they knew that too many people were pursuing too few fish, individual fishermen saw no reward in restraining themselves. If they passed on a fish, someone else would surely take it. If competitors for a resource could build up trust and keep out strangers, then they might be able to regulate themselves in a sustainable fashion, but the efforts to keep out the unknown could be quite brutal. Consumers had a short-term interest in keeping the volume of product flowing, so they viewed attempts at cartelization skeptically. While McEvoy was writing about fishing huge schools of tiny sardines, he might just as easily have been writing about efforts to catch small pods of huge whales. Whalers recognized that they were overtaxing their resource, they tried to organize their trustworthy colleagues, and they did what they could to ruin outsiders. And in the end, they decided that they would not leave a whale behind for some other, less scrupulous, whaler. As one Norwegian whaler admitted, "Catching is the same the world over. You must grab what you can before the next man comes."[22] Sir Sidney had good reason to be worried.

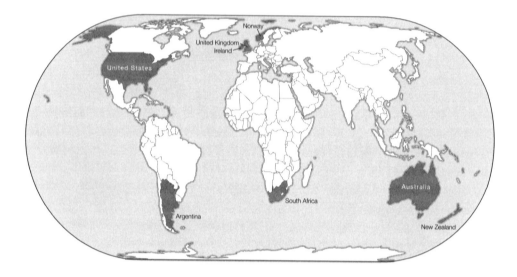

Initial signatories of the 1937 whaling convention.

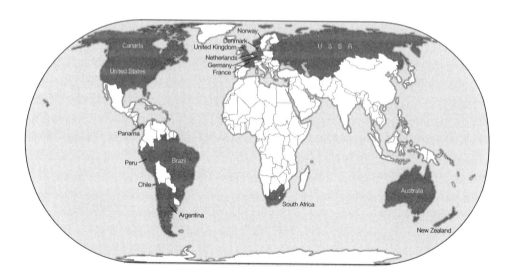

States with delegations at the 1946 whaling convention.

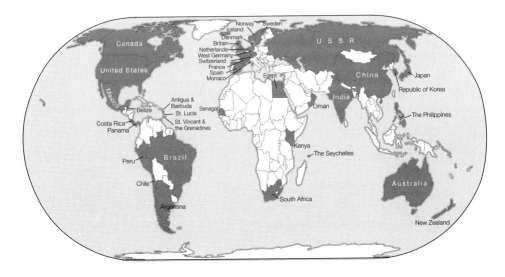

Member states that voted on the International Whaling Commission's 1982 moratorium proposal.

A GLOBAL INDUSTRY AND
GLOBAL CHALLENGES

THE DECISION BY LANDLOCKED SWITZERLAND TO SIGN THE LEAGUE OF
Nations' 1931 Convention for the Regulation of Whaling might seem
merely a humorous oddity, an inexplicable footnote to the history of
diplomacy. Indeed, members of the Swiss Parliament commented during
debate that the prime risk of the convention was the creation of a Swiss
navy, replete with highly paid officers, to protect the Swiss merchant fleet
that was sure to follow from the convention.[1] But the very existence of
the convention and the Swiss signature affixed thereto reveal two related
but ultimately contradictory realities: whaling in the twentieth century
was a global industry of great value, both in terms of its raw material
and the market for its products; and people who paid attention to whaling believed that it was a self-destructive industry that defied regulation
and sometimes even common sense. The League of Nations' attempt to
provide some structure for the industry was simply an early step in what
would turn into a long—and failed—effort to use diplomacy to make
whaling sustainable.

The captains of the whaling industry of the early twentieth century
would have attached a different meaning to the word *sustainable* than
someone might in the early twenty-first century, if they would even have
cared much about the long-term implications behind the modern use of
the word. Whaling was difficult and dangerous work, the oceans were vast
and whales comparatively small, and the markets for whale products were
unpredictable. Under these conditions, a long-term outlook for whaling
might be a few years, or even just the end of the whaling season, when debts

would be settled and crews paid. For most of the early twentieth century, it seemed far more likely that the whaling industry would go extinct before the whales themselves even came close to that fate. People feared commercial extinction, not literal extinction of the whales.

In the decade before Swiss representatives smiled as they approved the whaling convention, the industry got on an unsustainable path very quickly. Technological shifts made it possible to capture large whales, render them, and market their oil. Those developments also made it possible for whalers to operate on the high seas for months at a time, free from oversight and licensing schemes. Whaling companies developed into multinational firms with huge capital expenditures and hence the need to take large numbers of whales; and because most whales were processed into a very basic substance, margarine, the demand was almost insatiable. By the late 1920s, observers were concluding that there needed to be some sort of international control mechanism before whaling burned itself out. Thus the Swiss, consumers of whale products and hosts to the League of Nations, felt compelled to make their small statement on behalf of regulating whaling.

THE RISE OF PELAGIC WHALING

Had whaling remained largely confined to island stations in Antarctic waters in the twentieth century, whale populations in the early twenty-first century might be largely unchanged from a century before. Instead the value of whales rose enough that in the early twentieth century Norwegians in particular applied their genius to devising new ways to process whales at sea. Working with the new harpoons, killer ships, and inflation technology had made it possible to catch blue and fin whales, but it took two critical steps—the invention of the stern slipway and the improvement of methods to generate freshwater—to free whalers from the confines of land stations. One other change, the development of better refining techniques, which allowed for greater use of whale oil, provided the final ingredient in the vast expansion of whaling on the high seas. Such an industry had the power to pursue whales and sell their products anywhere in the world, and, perhaps more important, it could easily transfer its equipment to fishing, shipping, or military activities. Hence whaling became more important and powerful politically, not to mention more destructive ecologically.

Despite the talk about commercial extinction saving the whales before literal extinction set in, these new whaling companies were gaining the ability to hunt until the last whale was taken, after which they would move to another way of making money.

Whalers quickly realized that there was far more money to be made by chasing the blues and fins than waiting for them. The primary obstacles to pelagic, or high-seas, whaling were the size of individual whales and the amount of water necessary to render their fat and meat into oil. It was one thing to drag a whale back to land and carve it up on a cement pad near the water, but to flense a ninety-ton whale on the open seas presented quite a different challenge. Readers of *Moby Dick* may well remember descriptions of the steps involved in stripping the flesh from a large sperm whale in the relatively calm Pacific. It was particularly dangerous work to climb down from the deck onto the whale to commence the process of stripping blubber from the carcass—the whale's body was slippery, the workers carried large knives and sharp hooks, and large predators lurked that might as easily eat a whaler as a whale.[2] With rougher seas and fin and blue whales weighing at least twice as much as sperm whales, the Antarctic whalers faced significantly greater obstacles than the men of the wooden ship era.

Their "triumphant answer" came with the invention of the stern slipway.[3] An obvious solution to the hazards of flensing a whale in the water was to bring it on board, and by the 1920s it had become possible to build a steamship capable of holding a large whale on its deck without capsizing. What was not so obvious was how to get the whale from the rolling ocean to the relative stability of the deck. Lifting a dead weight over the side of the ship was generally tried only once. As early as 1912, a Norwegian whaler, Petter Sørlle, who had caught and processed whales alongside his ice-bound vessel, had designed a model of a ship with a slipway in the stern. Distracted by other things, including the difficulty of pulling a whale over his rudder and propeller, Sørlle did not patent his ideas until 1922, but after that just about every new or converted whaling ship used the slipway to get carcasses on deck. Powerful steam winches and grappling hooks dragged the animal up the inclined surface. The stern slipway kept the whale's weight relatively low and in line with the ship's axis.[4] Even this system was not foolproof. In 1978, much to the cheers of environmentalists, the rogue whaling ship MV *Tonna* capsized when the crew tried to haul a fin whale in via the stern, the winch malfunctioned, and the whale became a dead weight rolling from side to side with the sea.

Once the whale was on deck, flensing became significantly less hazardous and more efficient. Crewmen in spiked shoes clambered over the carcass with long flensing knives that they used to cut the blubber and meat into strips of various sizes, which were then carried to large vats, called cookers. Speed was of the essence, because decomposition and autolysis set in soon after the animal was killed. With the thick layer of blubber keeping in the whale's heat, the carcass could get quite hot, and the meat and blubber could spoil quickly. But the need for speed was countered by the benefits of thoroughness. Roughly as much oil could be extracted from the meat and bones of the average large whale as from its blubber. The director of whaling operations, on land or sea, had to calculate quickly whether it was worth working on a whale that had been stripped of most of its blubber or whether that carcass should be tossed overboard to make way for a new whale.[5]

Rendering—or trying—the whale into oil, water, and by-product was a fairly straightforward process. Crewmen used cranes or muscle to transport the raw material to cookers or boilers, where steam, heat, and pressure broke it down to its basic parts. Oil rose to the top of the liquid mass, and solids fell to the bottom. As technology improved, whalers were able to more easily drain off the oil and get most of the valuable material out of the water.[6] While the oil was the focus in the 1920s, whalers recognized that the by-product, which they called whale meal, was a valuable source of protein that could be used in animal feeds and the like. Given that meal could easily make up 25 percent of the end product of rendering a whale, it could make the difference between profit and deficit for an expedition. Meat for human consumption rarely drew the attention of commercial whalers in Britain or the United States. At both the low and high end, consumers received encouragement to eat whale meat, whether in the form of wartime propaganda posters that emphasized that whale meat was neither fish nor expensive, or in the form of a fancy meal at Delmonico's in New York that offered "whale pot au feu." But Americans, at least, tended to compare whale meat with horse meat, ignoring that it was supposedly a "first-rate food that is palatable and wholesome."[7]

The machinery necessary to render a whale was basically the same on land as on the water, but limited space on board the ship presented a challenge. At the start of the twentieth century, the technology for rendering large animals consisted mostly of big vats that required a lot of energy and water. Big open vats on a slippery, pitching ship were not especially popular with crewmen, so whalers experimented with ways of placing and minimizing vats, lids, and other equipment that maximized deck space, cooking capacity, and safety—it is hard to find a replacement worker three hundred miles south of the Falklands. One observer in the 1950s reported at least four deaths from stripping baleen, but Gerald Elliott of Salvesen's thought that "whalers were remarkably free of accidents."[8] Whalers also worked to create cookers that worked better with bone and meat, and they experimented with ways to try the blubber more quickly. The major breakthroughs in that regard came first in 1911 with the rotary operation of the Hartmann cooker, followed in about 1930 with the invention of the Kvaerner cooker, which was reputed to be especially good at getting oil out of meat.[9]

Having solved the problems of bringing a huge whale on board without sinking their ships and taking it apart in a confined space, whalers faced one last hurdle: getting the enormous amount of freshwater necessary to reduce a piece of megafauna into clear oil, bones, and sticky by-product. As historians J. N. Tønnessen and A. O. Johnsen noted, "On the very first trip it was evident that supplies of fresh water would be the major problem for floating factories."[10] The original floating factories had enough steam to power the engines or run the processing plant, but not both.[11] Even a small whaling vessel could use 80 tons of water a day, and the big ones of the 1950s were designed to produce 600 tons of water per day.[12] Shore stations had usually been located near vigorous streams, but there was no way that a ship could carry enough water for its steam engines and all of the rendering apparatus. The solution was to build large evaporators to squeeze water out of the air, making a factory ship truly independent of land.

All of the technological developments made it easier to catch and process whales but did not address the other end of the problem; the uneven market for whale oil. Having lost out to petroleum as a fuel for lamps, and usually too strong to be palatable as human food, whale oil was dismissed by one author as "an inferior industrial fat."[13] Lars Christensen argued that the rise of pelagic whaling ended whale oil's status as a seasonal commodity, which was critical for getting it into the supply chain for margarine.[14]

Really high-grade whale oil was converted into margarine by 1910, but most whale oil was not suited for that purpose yet. It still was useful in the production of the explosive nitroglycerine, though, so the First World War created a surge in demand that drove prices to more than 100 British pounds per ton. The return to peace and the inevitable postwar recession weakened the industry's position. In 1925, chemists changed the shape of industrial whaling by figuring out a way to refine whale oil that eliminated the strong taste, making it a prime edible fat, ready to be sold to consumers as margarine. American scientist Remington Kellogg later noted that "whale oil moves freely in international commerce. . . . It can be stored after treatment for a period of at least five years without deterioration."[15] Companies like Unilever saw the potential in whale oil and began buying most of the world's supplies to make margarine for Europeans, so that in the late 1920s the whaling industry was booming. Oil was the dominant product from whaling until about 1960, when it fell below meat and meal in importance.

Combined, these advances in technology allowed for a new business strategy for the whaling companies. Rather than investing in fixed plants on the limited number of islands near the southern whaling grounds, they could now invest in building floating factories or, more commonly in the early years, converting cargo vessels for the task. In a way, the twentieth-century floating factories were just updated versions of the wooden whalers of nineteenth-century Nantucket, but they were huge, far more complex, and more specialized. One sailor concluded that the *Southern Reaper* "offended every concept of grace; she violated every law of naval architecture."[16] Where the *Essex* and the *Pequod* went out on their own, the new floating factories took with them small flotillas. Most important were the killer or catcher boats; over the course of the century anywhere from four to fifteen went out with each factory. The factory was frequently accompanied by a tanker or two, which would take on the oil and transport it to the market so that the factory could stay on the whaling grounds. When a wooden whaler's hold and deck were full, it had to go home. With all of these vessels, companies began to speak of whaling expeditions, which seemed only appropriate heading into the wild waters of Antarctica, in the neighborhood of expeditions led by men like Scott, Amundsen, and Shackleton.

Like those expeditions, these lasted for extended periods of time. A typical cruise could take eight months, beginning with the departure from European ports in September. The factory vessel would then head to the vicinity of the Falklands, with a stop or two in the tropics for fresh food and to add a few extra crewmen if need be. Crewmen would be kept busy preparing the ship, doing such things as putting a new layer of wood over the deck or tuning up the rendering plant. The catcher vessels would usually be retrieved from storage somewhere in the Southern Hemisphere, and by November the whaling flotilla would be on the whaling grounds.[17] Operations would continue until the weather deteriorated too much in April, and the factory vessel, accompanied by a tanker usually, would return north sometime in May. For many Norwegians in the Vestfold area, southwest of Oslo, the whaling season was just short enough to allow them a brief farming season in the northern summer. When whaling was good, these men around Tønsberg and Sandefjord could live quite well. In fact Vestfold was the human center of the whaling industry from the early 1900s into the 1950s. Most European harpooners and many crewmen came from there, and their highly paid jobs were very important to the entire Norwegian economy.

The ability to hunt any whale meant that, from a hunting standpoint, the bigger whale was finally the better whale. Gunners referred to blue whales shorter than 68 to 70 feet as "inexperienced youth" because they would come right up to the catcher boats "without exhibiting any kind of fear." Once the whales crossed the 68- to 70-foot threshold, they became shy of the catcher—at least those that had survived being so inquisitive. Given a choice, whalers preferred the largest whales, but no harpooner would turn down a shot at a 68-foot blue whale or a mature fin whale of the same size unless he had specific instructions to do so. But in favoring the largest blue whales, those over 75 feet, whalers were taking adult females disproportionately, which was not sustainable.[18] From a management standpoint, the best long-term strategy would have been to focus on adult males more than on females or immatures, but that is the kind of advice that sounds better in a committee meeting than while pitching and rolling near the pack ice in pursuit of a whale that might be anywhere from 70 to 75 feet in length.

The one limiting factor that technology could not overcome was the weather. The austral summer petered out by late March, not that it ever got too much momentum below the Falklands anyway. When the days got shorter and the ice on deck got too thick to chip away, then it was time to head north. The drawback was that the whales were at their peak then in terms of fat, so there was an incentive to stay as long as possible. Given that the crews got bonuses based on performance, they were probably nearly as ambivalent as the expedition commanders. Conversely, whalers opened the season as soon as the pack ice opened enough to get at the whales, usually around 1 November, but at that time of year the whales really were too thin to be hunted profitably. Data from the early 1950s shows that whales at the end of the season could produce 44 percent more oil than at the start.[19]

The whaling expedition brought with it a hierarchy of command, although at times that command was not militarily linear. Usually, each expedition had a manager who had overall authority vested in him by the whaling company. The floating factory had a captain, who usually had the most practical nautical experience. It is easy to imagine that the business sense of the manager and the nautical sense of the captain did not always mesh and that authority occasionally had to be hammered out on the spot. This relationship might be even more clouded by the presence of a political officer, whether a Soviet commissar or occupation military officials on Japanese whalers right after the Second World War. In addition, each of the catcher boats had its own captain, and these men were usually the lynchpin of the whole operation because they also served as the harpooners. One whaling company owner said that a harpooner had to have "a combination of a steady eye with drive, stamina and leadership."[20] Harpooners were subordinate to the officials on the factory, but in a way they were the hardest to replace and thus the most valuable; they had their own union but were usually paid several times what the average sailor made. The men on the boats, especially the Norwegian and British boats, had their voice. Seamen's unions and engineers' unions played a role from the planning stages to, on occasion, the decision to return home. One wonders what Captain Ahab would have said to a shop steward. Finally, radio meant that the whalers were never completely cut off from direction from home ports, although it appears that companies tended to leave their expeditions alone once they set off.

In many countries, national organizations also played an important role. Companies frequently consulted one another on policy matters, since most of them had common interests in keeping access to the whales as wide as possible. British whaling company owners often met, even as they nominally competed with one another. The Japanese certainly coordinated their positions and lobbied the US occupation authorities or their own government. The Norwegians took the lead by organizing a Norwegian Whaling Association, which had to be one of the most powerful lobbying groups in the country, given the great wealth that whaling brought to the nation. The whaling association also played a critical role in the Hvalrådet, or Whaling Council, which set national policy on such matters as diplomacy, labor laws, and catching regulations. The Hvalrådet also included union leaders and government officials from several ministries. Whatever they negotiated affected what happened on almost every whaling vessel in the Antarctic.[21]

Conditions on board were rough, but the pay and the indefinable lure of the Antarctic kept whalers coming back. The weather provided one obvious set of challenges, but it paled compared to the dangers and unpleasantries of the work itself. A floating factory was an assault on the olfactory. One visitor spelled out her reaction:

> No words can describe the beastly stench wafted across to us—the first sniff nearly bowled me over! I, who have lived for a year among the smells of London slums, ought to have been able to stand anything of that sort—but this was indescribable!
>
> Just imagine a sickening vapour of tepid blood, trickling along the deck in barrelsful, and down the ship's side: entrails, blubber, train-oil, and boiling oil. One can't think of it, one can only smell it![22]

The trickling ooze on deck made for poor footing, and the various cutting implements and winches made it vital to stay on one's feet. To top it off, when the catchers found whales, the work was nonstop and hence exhausting. The pay had to be good to keep men coming back. It did not hurt that the Antarctic had a pull that was hard to describe. One British chemist wrote in 1950 that he could not wait to return to Britain, but he knew that as soon as he was home he would try to find a way to get back south.[23] A British whaling officer in the postwar era wrote about the "call to the South" that gripped men as the whaling season neared, but he was unable to explain why anyone would return to a job that he considered poorly compensated with difficult conditions.[24]

By 1925, new technology had revolutionized the industry, setting up a staggering expansion. The floating factory that was capable of breaking a huge whale down to sacks of protein and barrels of oil became the center of every expedition, accompanied by a small flotilla of killer boats. Although people would continue to tinker with the tools of the trade, looking into such things as electric harpoons or better ways of inflating struck whales so that they would not sink, the whaling vessels of 1975 would look a lot like their counterparts of fifty years earlier. The most important change would be scale, as factory vessels grew from an average of 25,000 tons to more than 33,000, with the largest being the *Soviet Ukraine* at 43,000 tons.

INTERNATIONALIZATION OF THE INDUSTRY

With all of the technological changes came expansion and internationalization of the industry. In 1900 there had been no whaling expeditions operating in the Antarctic seas; by 1930 there were more than forty, flying the flags primarily of Britain and Norway but also New Zealand, France, South Africa, Argentina, and the United States. By the end of the 1930s, Germans, Japanese, and Soviets (in the North Pacific) would all enter the pelagic whaling ranks. By operating on the high seas, these whalers managed to separate themselves from many legal obligations, so the twin forces of technological advances and the expansion of demand combined to make it almost impossible to regulate most of whaling around the world.

The place of the harpooners is most interesting, not only for shedding light on the human arrangements of an expedition, but also for showing the complex international forces at work. Once Svend Foyn invented his exploding harpoon, he did a masterful job of controlling it, not so much by limiting production in other places but rather by taking the lead in training gunners. It might not seem hard to hit a seventy-foot-long, eighty-ton beast, larger by far than the proverbial barn door. But on a raised platform on the prow of a rolling ship chasing a diving, fleeing animal that shows only brief glimpses of the appropriate spot to hit, harpooning actually is quite difficult. With years of practice in inshore waters, Norwegians had become masters of the job, and most foreign companies found hiring Norwegian gunners preferable to training their own. From the beginning of the twentieth century, most whaling companies had Norwegians in important positions. In the middle part of the century, it was common for a factory ship to fly a British flag while its catchers flew the Norwegian colors, reflecting that from the money to the manpower these were Anglo-Norwegian expeditions.

This reliance on Norwegian gunners suggested the inherent tension between nationalism and capitalism in the whaling industry. No doubt, nationalism was a crucial factor, as governments looked on whaling vessels as a means to carry their flags into coveted Antarctic waters—and maybe even to the intimidating continent itself. Many nations had laid claim to pieces of Antarctica, and many officials believed that those claims would be more substantial with a regular presence in the area. It was unclear what riches the continent might hold, but just a few years after the apparent wastelands of Alaska and the Yukon had yielded enough gold to fill Fort Knox, governments desired to stake their claims and sort out the details later.[25]

While the company owners themselves did not seem too worried about ownership of Antarctica, they appear to have had a stronger sense of national identity than most businesspeople today might. Even though it would have been easy for the British and Norwegian whalers to shift their operations to another European country, apparently only two whaling company owners sought a flag of convenience before 1970: H. K. Salvesen briefly based a vessel in Ireland in the 1930s, and Aristotle Onassis registered his in Panama in the 1950s. In the 1930s, one Norwegian company formed a partnership with US businessmen to get access to the US market without paying high tariffs on whale oil, but even those expeditions built around the *Frango* and the *Ulysses* kept their catcher boats registered in Norway. The whalers were businessmen at heart, though, and their dedication to running a profitable company sometimes threatened their national loyalty. This tension was most evident in the second decade of the twentieth century, when the Norwegian and British governments contemplated extending whaling licenses to cover the activities of pelagic whaling. Whalers operating from land stations had to obtain licenses, and, because the number of possible stations was so small, they were willing to accept the regulations that came with such a rare opportunity. But pelagic whalers strongly opposed any licensing scheme that threatened more than rudimentary regulations. They reasoned that they gained little from their government, so therefore they should not yield their rights to free use of the high seas. They were especially hesitant when they could see that their rivals in the industry might not face the same restrictions.

The established pelagic whalers occasionally threatened to find flags of convenience, with important consequences. That is, they warned their governments that heavy-handed rules would force them to shift their operations from their home ports to countries with more relaxed laws. Since most whalers operated from Britain and Norway and most skilled whalers came from those two countries, this was an interesting threat. Registering whaling vessels in other countries would not be especially difficult, although it might create complications for the trained crewmen and the somewhat nationalistic sea captains of the industry. Government officials realized that they had lost the upper hand with the invention of the floating factory. In the late 1920s, two floating factories worked close inshore to New Zealand's Ross Dependency. They had licenses from Wellington to work this territory just off Antarctica and had made money up to 1927, when an unlicensed ship sailed just outside territorial waters and began competing for whales.[26]

The new technology hindered any efforts to curtail whaling. In 1932, the Norwegian minister of commerce, I. Kirkesby-Garstad, called on Parliament to ratify the 1931 Convention for the Regulation of Whaling. Changing technology had created a need for this convention: "The moment we transferred to floating factories, which were independent of countries and executed their business within international waters, a change of these conditions occurred. No single country held the power anymore to regulate this business with regard to the general view one assumed concerning the size of the whale population. Thus, the view emerged very quickly, that entailed in this new whaling method was the danger of immensely over harvesting the whale population."[27] Not only did the new floating factory ships give whalers the chance to work far from land, and thus far from government officials, the whalers now had the chance to change their country of registry if they felt hampered by their government's restrictions. Governments worried about the possibility, with the result that few governments created their own stricter rules or advocated for such in diplomatic settings.

British officials specifically commented that if they created strict laws, it would encourage whalers to transfer flags.[28] The technological advances had made whalers wealthier and more independent. In peacetime they needed almost nothing that a government could offer them. Even if London and Oslo cooperated in requiring licenses or setting rules, the whalers could easily move their operations to the United States, Argentina, Australia, Germany, or any other sovereign nation with less regulation and a desire to get into whaling and Antarctica. Salvesen based the *Salvestria* in Dublin for the 1935–36 season to avoid British regulations, which probably triggered the effort by Norway and Britain to invite Ireland to participate in whaling diplomacy in 1937. Markets for whale oil were international enough that sellers would always find a customer, except in the very deepest part of the Great Depression. Christensen noted that the whalers now had "an entirely new world . . . characterized by a very high degree of technical self-sufficiency. . . . [Pelagic whaling] has also changed the entire condition of the whaling industry with regard to international rights in connexion with the 'free ocean.'"[29]

The new technology raised difficult questions about sovereignty and enforcement. Every ship in the world is supposed to fly a national flag, symbolizing that it operates under the laws of a specific government. If members of the crew violate those laws, they are supposed to answer for their violations, either on board the ship or upon return to the home port. Governments cannot put police officials on every ship, so the tradition arose that the captain and his officers enforce the law. This relationship can be tricky if a ship's officers perceive that the law runs counter to their interests. If the owners of the ship perceive things the same way, then they may begin to lean toward changing flags to find laws that support their interests.[30]

At the same time, since the 1600s a body of international law has developed. At least theoretically, international law should apply to everyone equally, even if it might run counter to national law. In the early part of the pelagic whaling era, most governments accepted the idea that they had sovereignty out to three miles from shore, and beyond that international law would apply. The law mainly served to allow both free taking of marine resources, in a finders-keepers framework, and free movement of navies and merchant ships. This vision of open seas for fisheries had been reinforced in the long-running dispute over the fur seals of the Bering Sea, as arbitrators in 1893 and diplomats in 1911 acknowledged that seals born on American islands became fair game for hunters once they left the three-mile zone.[31] Whales that never touched land would certainly be as free for the taking. Sailors on the high seas were free to do almost anything, embracing traditions known generally as freedom of the seas. In sum, only a thin veneer of law limited what whalers could do in the Antarctic.

In a way, the Antarctic seas themselves contributed to this sense of lawlessness. Not that the laws there were any thinner than they were in the North Sea, but the remoteness and wildness of the Antarctic seas no doubt contributed to the difficulty of enforcing a civilized set of laws. An old sailors' saying goes, "Below 40 degrees no law, below 50 degrees no God." With a whaling vessel away from British or Norwegian ports for as much as eight months, enforcement was in the hands of a ship's officers. If whalers made an illegal catch, who would know? Most whalers were not likely to care. In an environment defined by hardships, where survival was not a given and huge whales were abundant, the finer points of whaling regulations were easily overlooked. As one British whaling company owner put it, whaling was "pursued bleakly beyond the margins of the civilized world."[32]

The floating factories could be brought within the realm of the law if competent inspectors were on board. When thinking of inspectors, it is hard not to imagine a sheriff in a town full of ruffians in the American West, although some scenes seem more like *Blazing Saddles* than *Shane*. Lt. Cdr. John Chrisp, who had worked as an inspector on board the British vessel *Southern Reaper* for three years in the 1950s, acknowledged that he served many masters with diverging interests. If gunners harpooned a few whales just before the season was supposed to start, "well, that was a thing that no inspector could be expected to prove!" If a whale came in just under the legal size limit, "shall an inspector let his tape measure lie with an almost unnoticeable kink" so that it was recorded at a legal size? Apparently the answer on his ship was "yes," because he acknowledged that "good sense and tact" assured that "differences between inspectors and whaling captains are exceedingly rare."[33] The chummy relationship with whalers on his ship did not extend beyond the railing, though. Chrisp called inspectors game wardens, "keeping an eye on the world's greatest and most valuable reserves of food. Poaching and other illegal activities must be stamped out, or else the whale may all too easily suffer the fate of the dodo."[34]

The leaders of the whaling industry were usually willing to have inspectors on board—so long as the authority and salary issues were worked out—if they believed that the rules were enforced fairly. A recurrent complaint was that different nations had different standards of law and inspection. If a nation with lax laws developed a reputation for appointing lazy inspectors, resentment would grow among the whalers who faced strict enforcement. In the early part of the century, this problem was negligible, but as the industry further internationalized and established more rules, it became more prominent. Inspection would be a thorn in the side of whaling diplomacy into the 1970s.

Still, in the 1920s, inspection was a relatively small issue as the industry boomed and few people worried about waste or regulation. By any measure, the catching power of the whaling fleets was growing rapidly, and the number of whales hauled in was keeping pace. As this book's appendix shows, blue whales made up the bulk of the catch, with fin and humpback whales the only other species that really mattered. The whales were so plentiful and the rules so few that the whalers regularly took the best pieces of the whale, rendered them, and tossed the rest overboard. Evidence for this conclusion comes from the yield of oil, which steadily increased as whales became more scarce. The machinery and methods continued to become more efficient, so the lower yields were not just a product of waste, but there can be no doubt that the whalers of the 1920s were reveling in their circumstances.

THE SEARCH FOR ELUSIVE INTERNATIONAL SOLUTIONS

Since before the First World War, some observers had called for international cooperation to regulate whaling, and those murmurs had grown in volume after the war. Still, the constituency supporting regulation was small and weak well into the 1920s, as stronger voices suggested either that international discussions would only complicate things or that restraint simply was unnecessary. The British government had the chance to push for sustainable use of whales, but British leaders consistently concluded that such efforts were bound to fail.

As early as 1911, diplomats and scientists discussing the status of the North Pacific fur seal agreed that other sea creatures would be fruitful subjects of diplomacy. After settling the seal dispute, they went on to recommend a ten-year closed season on right and bowhead whales as well as a ban on floating factories. In October 1911 the trustees of the British Museum (Natural History) requested that the Colonial Office begin to manage whaling from the Falklands and their dependencies, rather than just handing out licenses. At the very least, they could begin to take data on the humpbacks that were caught to see if the animals were related to those that migrated to South Africa. In a lament that would recur, the trustees' letter reminded Lord Harcourt, the secretary of state for the colonies, that whalers had a pattern of overhunting stretching back to the Basques who had depleted right whales four hundred years before.[35]

The trustees were not alone in their concern. On South Georgia, J. Innes Wilson, the stipendiary magistrate (a type of judge), got to know the whalers and understand their jobs. He reported to Harcourt that the whalers had a difficult time separating males from females on the high seas, which is hardly surprising. But he was clearly angry that whalers admitted to hunting calves to take advantage of the females' desire to protect their young. Wilson demanded regulations to halt this despicable practice.[36]

Harcourt was swayed. In 1912, after gathering data on whaling around the world, he decided not to issue new leases in southern waters, and he acknowledged that old licenses might not be renewed every time. Twenty-two licenses for South Georgia existed, and whalers asked the governor for more.[37] The Colonial Office understood the problems involved: the "magnitude of the vested interests" would make restriction difficult, the wastefulness of the new floating factories was offset by their utility in places where no shore station could be built, and the problem was ultimately one that would have to be solved internationally.[38] Whales migrate, so one country can inflict harm on another country's interests, but thin science meant that it was hard to prove who was hurting whom. It was almost impossible to stop poaching in the vast uninhabited spaces, although Harcourt did not describe how one could poach something that was free to anyone on the high seas. Harcourt worried about the unenforceability of law, if for no other reason than the whalers' escape route via flags of convenience. The only trump card that governments held was that whalers had to come to port at some point. Nevertheless, Harcourt thought that an agreement with Norway, the Dominions, and relevant South American states might lead to an end to waste and a limitation on the number of whaling vessels.[39]

Sir Edward Grey, the foreign secretary, was not easily persuaded. True, extinction of "rare and valuable species" was to be opposed, but a system of licensing seemed much more practicable than an international agreement.[40] Even when the German ambassador, Prince Lichnowsky, concerned that whales were headed toward extinction, suggested an international conference, Grey ignored him.[41] From around the dominions came depressing reports about local conditions, such as this Australian conclusion: "In the opinion of the Department of Trade and Customs the modern appliances for the capture of whales are so efficient as to threaten possible extermination."[42] Canadian scientist William Wakeham concluded that whaling on Canada's east coast had maybe one more season before the whales were all chased away or driven to extinction. Finally, in March 1914, the British government convened an interdepartmental committee to study the question, but it failed to act before the First World War killed any chance of international cooperation.[43]

Whaling did not go away as an issue. In 1918, Americans and Canadians formed the International Fisheries Commission to discuss their problems. They agreed that cooperation on whaling was important, but they concluded that whales' migration and the inability of a nation to fix regulations beyond its territorial waters left the impact of such action doubtful. Instead, they agreed that maritime nations should meet after the war to discuss a global convention to prevent extinction and perpetuate the industry. Neither government pursued that lead after the war, when "world conditions . . . have been so unsettled" and "the industry has not been pursued with much vigor."[44]

While the Canadians and Americans proclaimed their principle, they did not know that Great Britain had concluded that whaling was not a fit subject for multilateral diplomacy. The official British line was that bilateral treaties covering specific problems were acceptable, but otherwise the science of whales and whaling was not far enough advanced to support an international convention. In reality, the British saw any conference that could address the issue as the greatest threat to the Anglo-Norse industry. They concluded that simply raising the issue would invite other states to seek a share of the industry, and any agreement that did not include every great maritime power would be "rendered futile" by those powers.[45] Finally, they admitted that any conference on whaling would have to include Argentina, which would endeavor to make an issue out of British control of the Falklands. All told, London concluded that it was best to use platitudes to stall any drive toward international whaling regulations.[46]

So no one acted until 1924, when the League of Nations asked members to designate sticky areas in international law that the league could address. Many states pointed to use of marine resources, especially whales, perhaps because they recognized quickly what the new pelagic expeditions meant for the whale stocks of the Antarctic seas, and by 1925 the league's Economic Committee was examining questions about marine fauna.[47] This investigation led to a visionary proposal from a committee chaired by Jose Leon Suarez, an Argentine professor. Suarez's draft included rotating sanctuaries, closed seasons, and the principle that all nations should be involved. By April 1927, a meeting of whaling experts in Paris was considering a revised draft of Suarez's treaty prepared by French professor Abel Gruvel, who had first proposed regulation of whaling in 1913. Gruvel endorsed a utilitarian idea of sustainability unlike the Suarez draft by saying that "France has thought that all the naturalists of the world should join together and come to an understanding, not to interfere with an interesting industry but to try to regulate the destruction of the animal species in the interest of Science in the first place and in the interest of the world industry in the second place." When Norwegian scientist Johan Hjort raised concern that some whaling states might refuse to sign the agreement, Gruvel concluded that the agreement would depend on "the honesty and good-will of the powers," and his colleagues argued that scientists would lean on their governments to act.[48]

The French draft, the league's interest, New Zealand's complaints about unlicensed whalers in the Ross Sea, and Norwegian willingness to sign a wide-ranging bilateral deal prompted the British government to call a meeting of officials from eleven different government agencies. Representatives from the Foreign Office, Colonial Office, India Office, Admiralty, and Ministry of Agriculture and Fisheries, as well as several other agencies, convened in October 1927 to consider their options. What became clear was that gridlock within the empire was going to be as great a problem as interstate diplomacy. Stanley Kemp, from the Discovery Committee (a group of scientists funded by a tax on whale oil), declared that fin and blue whales were as numerous as ever, and even humpbacks, which were harder to find, might just have been migrating differently. Others agreed, but they concluded that if the price of whale oil rose it would create a spike in the number of unlicensed whalers and hence pressure on the blues and fins. Still, the group as a whole first established that "the object to be kept in view was to safeguard the economic future of the industry, and ultimately to secure that the annual destruction of whales should not exceed the natural annual increase."[49] The most influential nation, Britain, had adopted a lukewarm policy of sustainability for whaling, but it depended on figuring out the natural increase and using it to compel whalers to limit their annual take, neither of which seemed likely.

The conferees spent a great deal of time discussing enforcement of whaling regulations. Newfoundland's recent bill banning floating factories from local ports in nonemergency situations presented a problem for the Board of Trade, which could easily imagine retaliation; the empire would not consider trade sanctions or restrictions as a means of stopping unlicensed whalers. The Admiralty led other British departments in arguing that the threat from flags of convenience made any British-Norwegian deal difficult. With no feasible system of patrol boats, each factory would have to carry a government inspector, but no one had a good system in mind for making that work.

Fearing that a multinational conference might encourage other nations to stake whaling claims, British leaders focused on a scheme to divide the southern oceans into British and Norwegian zones, with each nationality granting licenses to catch whales in specific parts of the zones. Since the British controlled larger portions of the seas, they anticipated guaranteeing licenses to most Norwegian companies, if for no other reason than to prevent them from crossing over to German ports and flags and encouraging German activity in the Antarctic. This wide-ranging discussion had touched on most of the major problems that would undermine whaling diplomacy for the next fifty years—scientific uncertainty, inability to predict the market, the fear of the haves that they might simply line the pockets of the have-nots, and a realization that enforcement would rely on lone inspectors embedded with whaling crews. It is not surprising that the British concluded that a cautious approach was probably best.

Britain's Polar Committee took control of the issue in 1929. Chaired by Sir Sidney Harmer, who had recently retired as the director of the British Museum (Natural History), the committee was an interagency task force designed to formulate a coherent, comprehensive policy for the empire on polar issues. Representatives from the Foreign Office, the Colonial Office, the Admiralty, and various lesser agencies met on a regular basis to address the problems posed by the legal uncertainty and economic potential of both poles, but particularly the southern one. Whaling was not central to the committee's mission, but it inevitably came up because it was so closely tied to political claims in the South Pole region and because the British had tried to maintain some foresight regarding the use of the region's marine mammals.

Under Harmer's prodding, Britain asserted leadership by providing its embassies guidance in an attempt to head off "ill-conceived and embarrassing" proposals, which seemed to be anything coming from the League of Nations.[50] In the sometimes circumlocutious language of diplomacy, one British official assured a Canadian colleague of the propriety of Britain's leadership: "In view of the widespread and, as it would seem, not unjustifiable apprehension that the continued unrestricted killing of whales may so reduce the stock as to bring the whaling industry into danger of destroying itself, the time would appear to have arrived when an endeavour may be made, with some prospect of success, to secure international cooperation in the work of conserving the whale."[51]

The League of Nations committee, in conjunction with the International Council for the Exploration of the Sea, also continued to work on whaling, under the leadership of Norwegian scientist Johan Hjort, who oddly also served as an unofficial agent for whale oil interests on occasion, including at the meeting in Geneva that finalized the treaty meant to conserve whales.[52] In 1929, the year that Norway passed a law to regulate whaling on the high seas, Hjort acknowledged a point that would bedevil whaling experts for decades: "It is difficult to draw a sharp line between the scientific and other sides of the questions." He expressed the central problem of the late 1920s, "a great fear of further expansion within the industry," but he also reported a range of possible solutions that fit Britain's concept of "ill-conceived, if not actually embarrassing," such as a closed season, an international convention, a cap on the number of expeditions that could sail, and a rotating sanctuary. Hjort worried, though, that expansion was happening so fast that science would not be able to answer fundamental questions in time.[53] Hjort found some agreement in London on this point, as one participant of the British committee meetings wrote, "It was felt in other words that merely to proceed with studies designed to arrive at a basis for regulation, while the stock were attacked so intensely and increasingly would be to make their work somewhat artificial."[54] Yet at the same time, an Australian diplomat had concluded in 1928 that "our knowledge of habits, migrations, and everything else connected with whales is totally inadequate." Nor could he find anyone with a clear sense of what restrictions ought to apply or how they might be administered.[55]

While the Norwegians took the lead in regulating whaling through legislation, the British took the lead in scientific exploration. From export duties on oil acquired from the land stations, the British government funded the Discovery Committee. Among other duties, this committee oversaw research on whales, mainly from the *Discovery* research vessel, formerly used by Captain Scott. Beginning in 1925, the *Discovery* worked the southern seas for long stretches, hoping to learn more about whales and pelagic whaling. The British were not alone, as Norwegian scientists had been conducting their own research since 1923, and Johan Hjort was careful to note that Norway's efforts were of "great scientific importance." He proposed that Norwegian whalers place him in charge of an Antarctic research expedition so that scientists could "provide a more concrete basis" for answering questions of stock size and sustainable catch limits. If that was not feasible then the research would have to be done under international auspices.[56] British scientists rarely cooperated with foreigners, and in fact the British and Norwegians had very different ideas about one of the most basic questions: how and where whales migrated.[57]

As late as 1928, the industry bulletin *Fishing News* could still declare whales to be "the least known of existing mammals."[58] It is not surprising that an animal that spends most of its life below water, frequently in far-flung and dangerous places, would elude the focus of most scientists. On the other hand, whales were the most valuable wild animals around, and getting to know them would seem to be a high priority. *Fishing News* reported a key problem: a chasm between scientists and whalers over the impact of whaling. The whalers, it reported, were confident that whaling from the stations in the Falklands dependencies could not possibly affect the whole Antarctic. Many scientists, however, thought that whales might migrate in a circumpolar manner, thus bringing them all past the stations at some point. This specific disagreement reflected the larger problem of perspective: "Every captain has his own idea of what ought to be done to protect the industry, and none knows more about whales than how to catch and reduce them. Scientists know the anatomy of whales, but little of their breeding habits and, except in the case of humpbacks, nothing of their migratory movements."[59]

This assessment of the scientists was not very charitable. A number of scientists made important progress during the 1920s, led especially by Neil A. Mackintosh—a British scientist who produced important work on pack ice and krill as well as whales—and Hjort.[60] They were starting nearly from scratch. Scientific knowledge about whales came from an odd collection of sources: strandings, the occasional sighting by a scientist, and bits and pieces—sometimes literally—gathered by the whalers. Very basic knowledge about life cycles was all that they had, such as rough migration paths and cycles as well as birthing seasons, size ranges, and food sources. They also had some data on such things as the relationship between size and sexual maturity for most species. For instance, by 1928 scientists knew that the baleen whales ate krill by filtering it out of seawater, but the krill and the plankton it fed on were species incognito.[61] Fundamentally, scientists were missing critical information on biology, meteorology, and oceanography that would help them understand whales and their environment, but they were working diligently to gain that information.

Any data that depended on careful study of a series of whales were hard to get. And so one of the long-running desires of whaling scientists was to examine the ovaries and testes of whales on the flensing deck, with the hope of figuring out a way to age animals, match that to data on size and evidence of sexual maturity, and then possibly determine a population structure for a stock of whales—in the 1950s, work on gonads would be accompanied by efforts to collect and dissect waxy earplugs. As historian Graham Burnett has argued, scientists relished their chances to literally dig into the whales on the flensing decks in the hope that they could at least begin to understand the animals better, which he called hip-boot cetology. Whatever its merits, hip-booted science would not help anyone learn much about how to manage a population of whales.[62]

The cutting-edge data gathering put together by the scientists of the *Discovery* expeditions was whale marking. A bit like an ambitious form of banding or ringing migratory birds to follow their migration patterns, whale marking required catching a bunch of whales, recording data about them, and then catching them again years later to compare the two sets of data. After several failed attempts, scientists came up with a solution to the first catching, which was to fire a foot-long aluminum tube from a crossbow or shotgun into a whale. The tube was engraved with a serial number and a return address. As each whale was marked, someone recorded the serial number, date, location, species, and size of the whale. Since the Discovery Committee was not in the business of hunting whales, the scientists would then await the return of their marks from whalers who had caught the whales in question and found the tubes embedded deep in the whales' blubber. Fewer than 10 percent of the tubes were ever returned to the committee, but they helped to unravel more of the mysteries of the whales' life cycles.[63]

Even without powerful scientific tools, members of the Polar Committee and Discovery Committee were growing increasingly pessimistic about whaling. Citing the tripling of the industry's output in a mere four years, in 1930 Harmer began making speeches and writing reports on the impending collapse of pelagic whaling. He noted that the industry had demolished species after species over the decades, so its natural trend was toward destruction.[64] As one colleague put it, "If the stock of whales is to be saved from a depletion disastrous to the industry, measures for their preservation must be taken without delay."[65] But even those who subscribed to that idea had to acknowledge that the scientific basis for such decision making was far too thin, despite the frantic efforts of the previous decade. The Polar Committee assembled a series of recommendations, acknowledging that "they are evidently beset with great difficulties of both an international and practical character, but if the industry is to be saved from collapse these difficulties must be faced." After reviewing the report, one reader wrote across the bottom: "I feel sorry for the pelagic whale."[66]

Meanwhile, the other important effort to gather basic data was underway at the Bureau for International Whaling Statistics in Sandefjord (sometimes translated as International Bureau for Whaling Statistics). By compiling data from the whaling companies, the bureau was succeeding in putting scattered pieces of the industry into one larger picture. That picture was one of a rapidly expanding industry that by the late 1920s was pulling huge numbers of blue whales from the seas (see the appendix). Whalers had caught fewer than 100 blue whales *total* between 1905 and 1908, when humpbacks had been their targets; they had seen their catch balloon into the thousands annually after 1910 with improved technology; and then they witnessed a run-up in the floating-factory era to the unimaginable season of 1930–31, when more than 29,000 blue whales and

10,000 fin whales became tubs of margarine. While people like Harmer, Hjort, and Mackintosh worried that such a catch could not be sustained, the evidence did not always support that conclusion. Even as the catch of blue whales grew from 2,600 in 1920–21, to 4,700 in 1925–26, to 29,000 of 1930–31, the number of floating factories was not going up as quickly, from 8 to 15 to 41. The number of factories had quintupled, but the catch had gone up by more than a factor of ten.

Still, a consensus of sorts was developing that whaling efforts in the late 1920s could not be sustained. Scientists worried about trends that showed that the largest blue whales were disappearing; a handful of conservationists called for more regulation; consumers of whale oil wanted a stable (albeit cheap) supply; governments wanted to extend regulation over that which was unregulated; and even the whalers themselves were open to the idea that unfettered competition might not be in their long-term interest, partly because the price for whale oil had slipped from the low £30s per ton to the upper £20s and then crashed in 1931. The problem would be reconciling all of the different ideas about what constituted a reasonable response. Harmer concluded, "We know from experience how slight is the probability of obtaining the consent of other Governments to any proposal calculated to interfere with the profitable employment of whaling vessels." J. O. Borley of the Foreign Office, while agreeing that "the interested dealings of buyer and catcher should be sufficiently farsighted to lead to a satisfactory conservation of supply," thought that the science was too thin and the political will for a rigorous inspection scheme too lacking to provide adequate protection.[67]

The League of Nations committee thus entered the story in 1928, as it was becoming obvious that whaling was an international industry beyond the control of national governments working alone. In the spirit of the league, an international group held several meetings to discuss the nature of the problem and feasible solutions. Britain and Norway were active as nations interested in protecting their whaling interests but so too were nations like France and Japan, both of which had been whaling close to home for some time and had desires to expand their industries. Because this was a league effort, it also drew attention from nations with no direct stake and from some that were not league members, like the United States.

While Britain and Norway had the most to lose from mismanaging the whaling industry, some of the earliest stirrings for scientifically based conservation came from two states with very small whaling industries, New Zealand and the United States. Britons and Norwegians tended to talk about maintaining the industry's long-term interests, but Americans and New Zealanders were more prone to think about the whales, perhaps because each nation had extensive experience with whaling but neither was dependent on whaling for much of anything any more. In October 1929, one report out of Wellington put maintenance of the world's whale oil stocks on the same level as conservation of the whale fishery, suggesting that New Zealand's interest fell under utilitarian conservationism. In the United States, scientists and conservationists in the newly created Council for the Conservation of Whales, a wholly owned subsidiary of the American Society of Mammalogists, peppered the State Department and president with calls to protect "these wonderfully adapted creatures, the greatest mammals that have ever inhabited the globe."[68] The State Department took their comments reasonably seriously. Both the United States and New Zealand would play critical roles in defining conservation of whales into the twenty-first century.

The Economic Committee of the League of Nations took the lead in building the convention on whaling, with a meeting in Berlin in the late summer of 1930. Among delegates in attendance was Remington Kellogg, a recent addition to the staff of the Smithsonian Museum, who would help chart the course of whaling diplomacy until 1965. In 1930, though, he was a relatively young man with an expertise in fossilized whales, and he was sent to represent the Council for the Conservation of Whales, with the lukewarm blessing of the US government. His position suggested both the State Department's lack of interest in the matter and the state of whale science. Indeed, American officials had to discuss whether it was a problem sending Kellogg so far to work with the suspect League of Nations.[69]

Kellogg would grow into a leadership role that few, including Kellogg himself, would have predicted in 1930. Born in Iowa in 1892, Kellogg came of age at the height of the Progressive era, from which he took his utilitarian approach to resources. During grade school, he collected and mounted bird and mammal specimens, which led him to the study of natural history and eventually a doctorate from Berkeley for analysis of how whales had evolved for life in the sea. In 1920, Kellogg married a fellow Berkeley student, but even his letters to Marguerite from the various conferences reflect his taciturn nature, which was probably a mixed blessing as an amateur diplomat. In the 1920s, he worked with a team of scientists that engaged in vivisection of porpoises, but he was best known in scientific circles for his work on fossils. Under the influence of Alexander Wetmore and John C. Merriam, he worked for several years for the Biological Survey as a mammalogist before landing the job at the Smithsonian in 1928 that put him on the twin paths of being a central figure in whaling diplomacy and eventually director of the US National Museum, paralleling Harmer's path in Britain. Kellogg's one attempt at engaging the public beyond the visitors to the Smithsonian was a 1940 article in *National Geographic*, which presented whales as complex, interesting creatures. Kellogg attended more than twenty international meetings on regulating whaling, but it was not until the later meetings, in the 1960s, that he really spoke forcefully. His written prose was remarkably reserved, but his spoken words were often remarkably profane. At the Smithsonian, he eventually became known as the Abominable No-Man for his salty language, but in 1930 he was simply unknown.[70]

When Kellogg got to Berlin, he found a draft convention that used Norway's 1929 whaling law as a blueprint. Representatives from most of the whaling countries pieced together a conservative convention that would be largely adopted in 1931. They suggested more research to learn whether it was wise to outlaw whaling in tropical and subtropical waters, but otherwise they emphasized that it was possible "to assist the whaling industry by international convention."[71] Two British officials summarized their government's mixed feelings when they commented both that the convention made "no substantial contribution to the solution of the pressing problem of the limitation of whaling" and that they supported its approval "in order to mark the beginning of international regulation of whaling."[72] Americans were slightly more enthusiastic, even if for narrower reasons, as an official in the Commerce Department summarized the extent of US interest: "It is the opinion of the largest consumers of whale oil at the present time in this country, that the species of whales which are the source of the supply of whale oil of commerce, should be protected from indiscriminate slaughter of the type that has been practiced in the past, in order that the future of the whaling industry may be assured."[73] Norway's government was happy enough with the convention that it authorized its diplomats to sign it on the first day it was open for signature.

On 24 September 1931, delegates in Geneva began signing the Convention for the Regulation of Whaling (CRW). Reflecting the lack of knowledge about whales, signatories agreed that they would gather a broad range of biological and technical data about whaling and forward it to the Bureau for International Whaling Statistics. The convention banned the hunting of right and bowhead whales, which were thought to be rare, as well as suckling calves and their mothers for all species of baleen whales. It required signatories to use each whale carcass fully, even as it acknowledged that land stations could do more with a whale than a floating factory could. Aborigines were exempt so long as they eschewed both modern technology and commercial economics, but industrial whalers needed to get a license from their flag states even as they faced no technological constraints. Finally, although signatory nations could exempt their territories or mandates, the convention encompassed both high seas and territorial waters globally. The CRW would not take effect until Norway, Britain, and six other countries ratified it.[74]

The decision to make right whales the wrong whales to hunt certainly seemed like a good idea, but it ended up demonstrating some of the problems of trying to regulate pelagic whaling. In 1936–37, whalers from countries that had signed the 1931 convention took at least fifteen right whales; probably several more killings went unreported, given the prohibition. Of those fifteen, at least four were pregnant. For a species numbering in the few hundreds with a very slow reproduction rate, the loss of four pregnant females was disastrous. It is also hard to imagine how a trained gunner could mistake a slow-moving right whale, with a distinctive V-shaped spout, for anything that might be legally hunted, raising all sorts of questions about quality control aboard ship and the very plausibility of any sort of restrictions on hunters' actions. If they could repeatedly violate this simple rule, then they probably could not be trusted with anything difficult, like size limits or prohibitions on taking nursing females.[75]

At the same time, the CRW left out steps that might well have been taken, some of which had been proposed in the original draft. As early as 1930, the British Polar Committee had gotten behind the idea of defining a sanctuary, focusing particularly on the area from the Ross Sea to Peter I Island—or roughly longitude 180° to 90° west. Its members also agreed that a universal licensing system was necessary to make any sort of international regulations work.[76] Neither of these ideas got anywhere in 1930, in part because the Norwegians resisted the licensing scheme and in part because whalers from the Pacific Rim states saw a sanctuary to their south as harmful to their interests. But beyond those specific objections, the Polar Committee's ideas failed because they were simply too radical and probably unenforceable. One member pointed out that a potential enforcement mechanism, closing imperial ports to whaling vessels, would run afoul of the British Board of Trade's authority and, given the long-range nature of factory vessels, would be ineffective anyway. Another commented that the pressure for whalers to move to US or Argentine flags would be too great if a restrictive convention became Britain's law. A strict global treaty was appealing, but it was also dreaming.[77]

The formal completion of a treaty's text meant nothing unless it was signed and ratified by enough states. Norway moved quickly on both fronts, and Britain signed quickly too. Most of the Dominions followed, and even some of the landlocked European countries, like Switzerland and Czechoslovakia, signed during the six-month window when the convention was left open for signatures. One nation that dragged its feet was the United States, despite letters of support from both the Commerce Department and leading scientists. League of Nation officials urged the United States to sign, both to head off flags-of-convenience transfers and to contribute its "considerable moral effect in inducing other states to sign." The only objection, beyond procrastination, seemed to be the problem of enforcement, as no one seemed to have discussed what the treaty meant in terms of US obligations. Finally, the American minister in Switzerland signed just days before the closing period, and the US government announced that the convention was meant to preserve "whales from indiscriminate and wasteful slaughter."[78]

But even as the convention was coming together, events were outstripping attempts to control them. With constantly shifting ecosystems and market forces, participants soon recognized that it would be almost impossible to use a fixed treaty to control an industry that harvested wild animals. The whaling industry's expansion had collided with the opening ripples of the Great Depression in 1930, so that the huge production of oil in 1930 ran parallel to a collapse in the market. A ton of oil that had sold for as much as £36 in the late 1920s barely fetched £12 by early 1931 on the open market. Several hundred thousand tons of whale oil were left unsold after the 1930–31 season, and the leaders of the whaling industry faced a crisis.[79] Only the strongest companies survived that crisis.

The problem was the huge expansion in production, from seventeen floating factories in 1926–27 to forty-one by 1930–31, even as the number of refining companies was shrinking through mergers. The newly formed Unilever Combine, as the British called it, held the vast majority of the whale oil market at the start of 1931. Before the 1930–31 season, Unilever had unwisely signed a contract to take unlimited Norwegian oil supplies at £25 per ton, which had seemed like a good price for Unilever. Production grew faster than Unilever had expected, and the company took a £5 million bath. Now that it had a massive surplus, for which it had paid dearly, Unilever was content to make the whalers miserable through hard-nosed negotiations, which seemed to hold the only hope for effective control of the industry. One official concluded that "any effective restriction in the production of whale oil and consequently effective preservation of the pelagic whale, who is rapidly being exterminated, depends . . . more on the attitude of the 'Unilever' company, which absorbs 80% of the total production, than on anything else."[80]

The logical course for whalers was to reclaim the upper hand by organizing or consolidating. In fact, both happened, as some whaling companies left the business and the rest used vehicles available to them to cooperate. The problem was that those vehicles did not cross national boundaries, and the British and Norwegian companies found themselves lacking trust in their fellows. The members of the Norwegian Whaling Association took the amazing step of canceling the 1931–32 season as a means to restore their bargaining position. This was obviously a difficult decision, as it meant both that the companies would have to live off their accumulated reserves of previous years and that hundreds of Norwegians would lose good jobs. But, as the association members feared, a few British whalers, led by Christian Salvesen Ltd., of Leith, Scotland, and Unilever's Southern Whaling and Sealing Ltd., sent out five floating factories anyway. The Norwegians concluded that a self-imposed limitation would not be politically feasible for the next season.

Unilever's sudden rise to a position of dominance sparked a fascinating discussion inside the British government about the corporation's motives and the possibilities of the situation in the spring of 1931. Prodded by Sidney Harmer and Henry Maurice, both of whom feared that the whaling industry was headed toward disaster, the Ministry of Agriculture and Fisheries showed surprising sympathy toward Unilever.

Rather than seeing the company as an aggressive monopoly that might single-handedly destroy Anglo-Norse cooperation, Maurice and Harmer suggested that Unilever had been mistreated by the whalers, and it was "quite legitimate for Unilever to make the best of the position now." In squeezing the Norwegians, Unilever presented the best chance to save the whaling industry that Maurice or Harmer could foresee. Maurice called Unilever's directors "shrewd and far-sighted people, and it would be much easier to persuade them to take a long view than to induce a large number of persons, mostly foreigners with divergent interests, to do so."[81] Of course, those far-sighted directors had agreed to the whale oil contracts that had almost destroyed the new company, so Maurice might not have been so shrewd himself.

The next March, Harmer wrote a lengthy letter to D'Arcy Cooper, the chairman of Unilever's board, laying out the opportunity for Unilever to take control of whaling for the better. Harmer opened by noting that he had turned down a position years before with the firm because he did not want "even indirectly" to be associated with the destruction of whale stocks. But now the industry was in a crisis, governments were likely to seek only their own interests, and the recent convention "does little more than protect those kinds of whales which are not being seriously hunted." The one choke point was Unilever's demand for oil, and Harmer concluded: "I think that your Company might be able to give practical assistance to the problem of avoiding the reduction of the number of whales to the point when no whaling could be profitable. I am further of the opinion that, without some such action, your interests will be seriously threatened." The solution was to tell the Norwegians that they could either limit their factories and catchers in conjunction with Unilever or the company would get all of its supply from Britain and Argentina.[82]

Cooper understood his interests. Less than two weeks later, he visited Harmer for dinner. In detailing how the Norwegians had stuck Unilever with the £5 million loss, Cooper signaled that he was happy to turn the tables. Unilever was now sitting on a pile of whale oil, which appeared not to deteriorate, except that it seemed to lose some of its vitamins. For margarine then, Unilever wanted to keep a fresh supply of oil on hand. But Cooper made clear that if there could be some way of determining how many whales could be taken safely, he would support limiting Unilever's purchases to that number.[83]

Any power that Unilever had in March 1932 was likely to be temporary. If the demand for margarine was high enough, some other company would figure out how to refine whale oil. The German chemical industry was skilled enough—and about to embark on an era of nationalism to boot—that the company's near monopoly was not likely to last. Still, the Cooper-Harmer discussions showed that science and industry did not have to be at loggerheads on whaling matters and that industry might see conservation as in its best interest. The problem was that it was not the whaling industry that saw things that way but the margarine industry, and that one did not have many harpoons.

The 1931 Convention for the Regulation of Whaling was a small step toward a conservation regime that might control whaling. The emphasis has to be on the word *small*, because the limits were, indeed, not much compared to the power of the whaling industry. In fact, events had shown that only the global economy, working in conjunction with a largely centralized whaling industry, could put a check on the demand for whales. Had the whaling fleet been spread out among many countries, it is unlikely that even the market forces of the Great Depression would have kept most of the fleet at home.

Whaling had grown remarkably in the fifteen years prior to the 1931 convention, rising from a small-scale industry, selling a marginal product, dependent on government licenses, to a wide-ranging, capital-intensive, high-tech industry selling a very valuable product—margarine. Leaders of the industry were men of great influence in their political and business communities, and they relished their positions. Few governments were likely to sign treaties that seriously undermined these industrialists' positions.

Still, it would be wrong to dismiss the 1931 convention completely. The trustees of the British Museum (Natural History) viewed "the proposed Convention with satisfaction as a beginning in the International action for the regulation of the whaling industry, which they have so long advocated."[84] In response to a complaint from New Zealand that the convention drafts "impose no restriction upon the number of whales that may be taken," a British cabinet officer sighed that, after two years of discussions, "opinion both in foreign countries and in the industry itself is not yet sufficiently advanced to permit general acceptance of more restrictive measures." And so, he concluded, London had settled for "an elemental standard of conduct" as the basis for more effective action.[85] Had the British government pushed harder, though, it would either have undermined its own interests or created a system that the Norwegians would not have accepted. In agreeing to a limited framework, the framers of the 1931 convention began a long tradition of recognizing that the problem was greater than any feasible solution and of settling for minor progress.

2

THE PELAGIC AND THE POLITICAL

IN JUNE 1938, DELEGATES FROM SEVERAL NATIONS MET IN LONDON AT the Shell-Mex House to negotiate an extension to the 1937 Convention on Whaling. After nearly a week of meetings, which had produced some progress and a consensus that the 1937 convention should be strengthened, Don Manuel Malbran, the delegate from Argentina, which desired to govern the Falklands and aspired to join the pelagic whaling states, offered some very undiplomatic words: "I am inclined to believe that each delegation is taking into consideration, above everything else, the interests of their countries. It seems to me then, that the purpose of the protection of whales is looked at only from the point of view of the interests of each country." He then proved his point: "We could not accept any agreement limiting the activities of the existing land stations, nor any commitment which could prevent us from establishing new land stations." The blunt-speaking chair, Henry Maurice, accepted that "you were entitled to lash us," but he also pointed out that all governments work from their own interests.[1]

Malbran's commentary demonstrated indirectly one of the two key problems of efforts to use diplomacy to make whaling sustainable: the interests of the pelagic whaling states and the states with land stations could not be reconciled easily. The nations with land stations, such as Argentina and France, argued that they were just barely hanging on by catching the few whales that came their way. The pelagic whaling states responded that the land stations were especially disruptive of breeding humpbacks and had to face some limitations if the high-seas fleets were going to accept more limitations. Yet the two groups needed each other. The states with land stations had the expertise to launch competing pelagic whaling expeditions and the ability to offer a flag of convenience for whaling companies that might be disaffected if their governments signed restrictive conventions. The high-seas whaling states had the ability to destroy the whale populations so quickly that they could ruin the shore stations unless the industry was regulated. More directly, Malbran exemplified the other, more consequential problem: that different states had irreconcilable differences when it came to using whales. Delegates at the meetings understood that they needed to restrict the catch of whales somehow, and they discussed different strategies, but they always found that any one solution tended to fall more heavily on some shoulders than others. Those with the weariest shoulders were not likely to suffer in silence but rather to jump ship.

In addition, those who were unhappy often pointed to the lack of useful scientific knowledge on which to base decisions. No one knew how large or old the great whales had to be before they could reproduce, for instance, nor were the migration patterns known for some of the stocks for which there was competition between land and pelagic whalers. Without such basic data, no whaling nations were willing to sacrifice in the name of conservation when they could not be sure that their actions would even be promoting conservation. Less than a week after Malbran scolded other governments for being as self-interested as his was, Maurice cut to the chase: "We have discussed all the various means that suggested themselves to us, and we appear to have rejected them all."[2]

The fundamental issue of whaling diplomacy in the 1930s was the expansion of the industry beyond Norway and Britain and the simultaneous attempts of those two nations to control the ramifications of that expansion. For both selfish and conservationist reasons, whalers, bureaucrats, scientists, and diplomats in the two dominant Antarctic whaling nations feared any sort of expansion. They were especially worried about state support for whaling by governments that had explicitly rejected the League of Nations, which offered the only legal framework (the 1931 convention) for regulating the industry. Malbran had been correct: Norway and Britain worked to protect their own interests, as did Japan and Germany, the new pelagic whalers. Those interests did not seem compatible.

These whaling discussions were taking place in a tense atmosphere. By 1937, the Japanese were gearing up for their second assault on China, the Germans had recently reoccupied the Rhineland, and the Italians were busy with their expanding empire in Africa. Each had larger plans that were suspected, if not known, in capitals around the world. All were attempting to revise the settlements created at the end of the First World War, of which the main proponents were the British and French. Those two countries had embarked on a course of appeasement, hoping to work with these revisionist powers rather than risk war by challenging them at every—or even the occasional—turn. But while tension was the rule on the great issues of state, diplomats and bureaucrats at the lower levels still found themselves working together.

Although it may appear odd today, British diplomats and fisheries officials were working hard to call conferences to discuss whaling with their German and Japanese counterparts, right up to September 1939, when war broke out between Britain and Germany. At least in whaling circles, the British and Norwegians tended to find the Germans to be fairly reasonable, but they had great difficulty getting the Japanese to cooperate. After one failed attempt to get the Japanese to attend a conference on whaling, Foreign Office official G. G. Vereker complained, correctly, that "the reasons underlying their attitude are probably just as much political as pelagic."[3] He might well have said the same about the Germans' cooperation.

The Norwegians and British sought to control whaling throughout the 1930s. They first worked diligently, and with some success, to establish annual deals among companies and sometimes governments to limit the amount of oil on the market; then the Norwegian and British governments led the effort for the 1937 Convention on Whaling, and they spearheaded follow-up conferences on whaling in 1938 and 1939. Even though the industry had been unable to create long-term solutions to its problems, each government understood that captains of the whaling industry and captains of ships had to be consulted, so the governments brought along whalers as well as scientists and fisheries officials to their meetings. Modern whaling diplomacy was born at these long conferences, where stakeholders held firm on some issues and compromised on others, as they all worked toward the common goal of striking a balance between hunting and conserving whales for the future—even as they had different ideas about where the balancing point would be found. It looked as if the whaling nations had finally gotten all of the whalers to buy into a system in the summer of 1939, but the war destroyed any chance of testing that system.

QUOTA, UNQUOTA

Setting whaling quotas by nation or company has been a recurring idea for managing the Antarctic fishery. Fixed targets have had a certain appeal, lending themselves both to conservation of various species and to more rational business practices. The difficulty has been how to divide the pie—deciding the number and distribution of the slices not to mention the size of the pie itself. When British and Norwegian whalers attempted to set their own quotas after the 1931 collapse of the market, they found it easy to agree on a quota system in principle but more complex to develop a system that actually reduced the harvest.

The shakeout that resulted from the market collapse concentrated pelagic whaling in a handful of Norwegian and British companies. A few floating factories came from other countries, like South Africa, but they were rare enough to be unimportant in the larger story. Since the majority of whaling companies was still Norwegian, the first step for any private, voluntary international effort would be for the Norwegians to agree on a quota formula; then they could try to sell that to the British.

In June 1932 the members of the Norwegian Whaling Association (NWA) put together a credible Antarctic quota system for themselves and British whalers, with a goal of reducing production to two-thirds of the 1930–31 season. They began with the assumption that one blue whale should yield 110 barrels of oil; then they established a ratio of blue whales to other species, with one blue equal to two fins, three humpbacks, or five sei whales, which would become the basis for the blue whale unit (BWU) for counting the catch after World War II. Each company got a quota, defined in both whales and barrels. If a whaling company was able to exceed the targeted yield of 110 barrels per blue whale, then as a reward for this thorough use of the carcass, the company would be allowed to take 10 percent more barrels of whale oil than its quota. The whalers agreed to commence operations no earlier than October 20 and to cease on April 30. Some had started earlier than that in recent years, but none had stayed on the hunting grounds to the closing date.[4]

Negotiators struggled to find a formula for devising a quota for each company. As many as forty-one floating factories had operated around Antarctica, but only about fifteen were likely to go out under this agreement. Quotas based solely on capacity would reward those companies that had helped trigger the excess supply problem in the first place. Quotas based solely on one or two years' production would reward those companies that defied the NWA's request to cancel the 1931–32 season. Seeking an equation that would satisfy its various constituents, the NWA started with the midpoint between how many barrels each company had produced in 1930–31 and what it could produce at full capacity. It then reduced that number by 38 percent to set a quota for each factory. Not surprisingly, companies sent out only their most modern and efficient factories for the 1932–33 season, in the hopes of getting the 10 percent bonus. A factory ship could be sold but not to an oil buyer—Unilever—and only with a quota affixed to it as part of the terms of sale. To guarantee compliance, each company had to put up a bond or sign an agreement that it would work within the system. The total quota for all companies in the agreement was just over two million barrels.[5]

The Norwegians had created a clever system, but it did not go far enough, a recurrent theme in whaling diplomacy. The most important shortcoming was that this scheme reduced output by less than 15 percent, not the hoped for 33 percent, even though the market was still awash in oil. If every company hit its quota, then the price for oil would probably drop further. Beyond that, the NWA system was, for good reason, only a one-season agreement. If any major company decided that its interests had not been well-served in the first year, it was under no obligation to obey a quota for the next. Inevitably, someone would have reason to complain, in part because some British companies declined to participate. In particular, Unilever kept its full complement of whalers, known as Southern Whaling and Sealing Ltd., active and out of the quota system, as did Salvesen's. That left an opening for a total of five British factories to head south. Finally, with assigned quotas and the efficiency that comes with weeding out the old ships and less-talented crewmen, the whalers hit new marks for efficiency and produced 60,000 more barrels than expected, from 1,600 fewer BWU than expected. This was an excellent result in terms of increased efficiency, but those extra barrels still yielded just £13 per ton for whale oil, or a pound less than it cost the best expeditions to produce oil.[6]

Many thoughtful observers found the quota system admirable despite these flaws. The Norwegian scientist Johan Hjort termed the agreement better than anything that governments could achieve working alone, and the International Council for the Exploration of the Sea passed a resolution praising the quota agreement. J. O. Borley of the British Foreign Office thought that the high number of barrels expected from each blue whale would discourage waste and excess killing, but the system did not go far enough in this regard. What was needed, he thought, was one powerful international organization that could set quotas and enforce them.[7]

For now, the British could not even manage to pass their own whaling legislation, much less engineer a powerful international organization. Having browbeaten several governments to sign the 1931 convention, British diplomats faced embarrassing questions about Britain's steps to ratify it. The Norwegians in particular wanted to know when the 1931 rules would apply equally to British and Norwegian whalers, but all they heard was "steps are being taken." The Norwegians' frustration grew to the point that, in 1934, they threatened to withdraw from the 1931 convention in order to satisfy angry whalers.[8] To be fair, the legislation was complex, dealing with the many pieces of the Commonwealth, from the pelagic whaling companies based in Scotland to the small whaling stations on islands scattered around the globe. That hardly mollified Norwegian whalers, who already complained that British whalers had demanded unfairly large quotas as incentive to join the Norwegian scheme.

In other countries, too, ratification of the convention required legislative action that would lay the foundation for future whaling laws. In the United States, officials kept an eye on Britain's policies. In November 1933, before the United States had formally ratified the convention, diplomats asked their British counterparts about Britain's progress on the treaty. Given that the treaty would not go into effect without Britain's ratification, the United States was surely not alone in waiting for the British to act before moving forward. Not until the British Parliament passed legislation in 1934 did the US government get serious about drafting the necessary legislation, which was an amalgam of federal bird-hunting statutes, treaty articles, and British law.[9] Final passage did not occur until 1936.

In Canberra, Australia, too, officials were trying to make their legislation fit the 1931 convention. Australia had signed the convention, like most of the Dominions of the empire, but had yet to ratify it by 1935. Australia's constitution placed control of inshore marine resources in the hands of the states, which meant that the federal government could not sign away control over them. In 1934, at a constitutional convention, delegates discussed options for dealing with control over these resources, but they failed to find a solution. Finally, in 1936, the government decided that too much was at stake, and it was imperative to have uniform rules throughout the whaling industry, so it ratified the convention with reservations about local authority.[10]

Meanwhile, Norwegian Whaling Association members were analyzing how the quota agreement had worked for the 1932–33 season. To their surprise, the whalers had used the 10 percent bonus for efficiency, so that total production from quota companies was 2,089,000 barrels of whale oil. If Unilever's 360,000 barrels were included, the total was not far below the 1929–30 record. In a sense, the system had worked, because most whalers had abided by their quotas and had been extremely efficient. But satisfaction with results had been low, because compliance had not been 100 percent and production had been too high to drive up the price of oil.

The Norwegians made another attempt, to see if they could drive up prices. If they could recruit the British companies to participate, then they would try the system for one more year, but this time they would expect 115 barrels per blue whale unit, with allowances for 120. With a reduced quota per floating factory, they anticipated bringing in 2,050,000 barrels in 1933–34. This appeared to be a compromise doomed to failure, as it neither addressed Unilever's participation nor reduced production enough to make a substantial difference in price.[11]

At the same time that Norway's whalers were piecing together a quota system that none of them really seemed to like, they were waffling on their threat to pull out of the 1931 convention. In short, they were torn between doing what they knew was in the long-term interest of the industry and protecting their own interests in the present. The symbol of the national desperation that was welling up was the decision by Lars Christensen, one of the most powerful men in the industry, to bail out of the voluntary quota system and make a deal with hated Unilever.[12]

Christensen's predicament was indicative of the shortcomings of a voluntary quota agreement. He had been willing to work within the NWA for the first quota season, and he suffered through the second. By then he had concluded that the system was not fair because the British—mainly Chr. Salvesen Ltd.—had demanded unreasonably high quotas in return for participating for the second year, and some Norwegians formed new companies that received higher quotas than some older, established ones. Norway's share of Antarctic whaling had dropped from nearly two-thirds to less than half in less than five years. The attempt to coordinate sale prices showed little promise, since there were still so few buyers, and Christensen's attempt to get the whalers to lay up their fleets for another year had been voted down. Rather than play Gulliver among the Lilliputians, Christensen chose to play Godzilla teaming up with Mothra. Unilever agreed to buy 660,000 barrels from him, when the previous quota had allowed him only 289,000.

Christensen succeeded only in making himself the target of every angry Norwegian whaler. Recognizing that the country held one key component—trained harpooners—the Storting (Norwegian Parliament) passed a law in 1934 that imposed strict limits on whalers, including forbidding them from working for companies registered in countries that did not honor the 1931 whaling convention, stopping the transfer of whaling vessels to other national flags, and banning whaling south of latitude 50° south, except between December 1 and March 31. Since Great Britain had not yet ratified the 1931 convention, this law would potentially hit British whalers hard, but it was especially a problem for Christensen, who could neither transfer his vessels and crews to another country nor possibly hope to produce 660,000 barrels in the restricted season. To the delight of many of his countrymen, he found himself locked in a court battle with Unilever rather than partnering with the giant company.[13]

The Norwegian legislation might have been more sweeping. Earlier in 1934, Svend Foyn Bruun, a member of the Storting from the whaling district of Vestfold, had proposed an Anglo-Norse agreement on closed seasons and oil production. To prevent defections to other flags, he thought that the governments could pass legislation that would prevent their subjects and citizens from working for third-party whaling operations. The whalers from Vestfold wanted an aggressive policy that included formal concessions or regional licenses as a means to regulate access, as well as whaling company insurance schemes to protect whalers from being laid off by companies that moved elsewhere.[14]

While Bruun was discussing his idea with British diplomats in Oslo, Norwegian diplomats in London proposed the joint closed season to their British counterparts. The British found the ideas interesting but impracticable because of the threat of using flags of convenience, which suggested that they were unwilling to restrict British subjects' rights to work in other countries. They had no better ideas.[15] Britain was finally able to pass its whaling law in 1934, however, enabling the country's ratification of the 1931 convention. The act put the fisheries department of the Ministry of Agriculture and Fisheries in charge of the whaling industry, which had "brought in profits calculated to make our troubled trawler owners green with envy." Fisheries official Henry Maurice continued that "very soon" his colleagues learned that "the convention did not go far enough if the Industry of Whaling was going to be a permanent one." Speaking in 1938, Maurice suggested that protecting the industry via diplomacy had become a high priority soon after the convention's ratification.[16]

In the fluid year of 1934, one more development caught the whaling community by surprise: the Japanese purchase of most of the elements of a Norwegian whaling expedition. Sometime between May 1, when the voluntary quota agreement expired, and June 25, when the new law regarding transfer of vessels took effect, Nippon Hogei Kabushiki Reisha, a Japanese fishing company, purchased the *Antarctic* and five catcher boats for about NKr11,000,000. The company invested another NKr200,000 in repairs and began hiring a small number of Norwegians to sail with the fleet. The Norwegian government was powerless to halt the sale, and it was unwilling to do anything about the sailors.[17]

The Japanese had been catching whales for centuries, but this was an ominous development. Their pelagic whaling had been limited to smaller vessels in the North Pacific, and they had been interested mainly in meat for their domestic market. The catchers—now rechristened with jarring names like the *William Wilson Maru*—were old, but they had up-to-date harpoon guns, and the *Antarctic Maru* was a fairly modern factory ship.[18] By hiring skilled Norwegians to operate their new equipment, the Japanese had made a major leap forward. British and Norwegian whalers tried to see the sunny side of the purchase, figuring that the oil would go to the Japanese market rather than the glutted European market. They also doubted that the Japanese would have the skill to be efficient whalers. At the same time, they feared that this was just the opening step in the creation of a large Japanese industry when blue whales were already in decline. Such was the anxiety that when the *Antarctic Maru* had a poor initial season, catching few whales, generating only thirteen thousand barrels of oil that found no market in Japan, and alienating the Norwegian crewmen so much that they refused to return for the next season, the news elicited no joy in Sandefjord or Leith Harbour.[19]

European whalers understood quickly that increased Japanese whaling was going to complicate, if not prevent, efforts at international cooperation. It was obvious that the Japanese intended to expand their industry, but it was not clear whether they intended to do so with government subsidies, which might harden their government's position in any negotiations. Cooperation with Japanese companies did not seem likely for Norwegian and British companies, and the Japanese government in 1934 was better known for poking the Western governments than working with them. So, with or without government subsidies, the Japanese whaling industry was going to chart its own course, and it was not going to agree to restrictions until it had built up its strength.

The arrival of the Japanese as pelagic whalers forced new thinking in London. J. O. Borley found himself echoing Sir Sidney Harmer's prophesy from 1913: "Experience of other whaling grounds has shown moreover that a decline of stock once begun rapidly increases until total collapse occurs: and in view of the heavy cost of modern whaling expeditions this collapse would occur, perhaps fortunately, at a much earlier stage than with the old whaling. There exists at present a conviction of the need of conservation of the stock of whales, in the interest of whaling, and at the same time a renewed expansion of whaling effort." Writing in 1936 with one eye on the Australian situation and one on the global diplomatic ramifications, Borley suggested following the advice of scientists and conservationists in setting Australian whaling policy, including full use of each animal, given that each one was so very valuable. He added that blue whale units should be used to regulate maximum production quotas.[20]

The Japanese had not signed the 1931 convention, a fact that did not escape the attention of the British and Norwegian governments. Both made formal diplomatic requests to Tokyo that it sign the treaty and set its whaling regulations in conformity with the two European whaling states. In October 1935, the Japanese Foreign Ministry, the Gaimusho, responded as it would on many occasions over the next three years: that such action would be premature because the Japanese whaling industry was young and needed time to catch up. Japanese diplomats also noted that the whaling conventions were complex and needed more study. It was a refrain that Western diplomats would hear right to the outbreak of war.[21]

The Japanese continued to expand their industry despite the rocky first cruise of the *Antarctic Maru*. In one sense, the 1934–35 season succeeded because the Japanese purposely took large crews, with the goal of gaining more experience. With that mission accomplished, the falling out with the Norwegian whalers at the end of the season was not much of a problem. By the start of the 1938–39 season, the Japanese had six floating factories and nearly fifty catcher boats, all operated by Japanese citizens.

The impact of the Japanese on the industry in 1935 was small enough that the Norwegians and British decided to put together one more quota deal, even though they had not had one in 1934–35. In June 1935, the Norwegian cabinet formally set a quota of 1.1 million barrels of whale oil but also took up the question of banning Norwegians from working for foreign-flagged vessels. The British got on board, as the Board of Trade established a similar set of rules for the waters south of latitude 40° south. The question, then, was whether the smaller companies, as well as Salvesen and Unilever, would "play the game," as one official put it, or switch flags to avoid the regulations. Salvesen based his *Salvestria* in Dublin that season, but the rest of Britain's whalers stayed put. The new agreement was "very thorough and elaborate," with heavy fines for violators. The negotiators wanted to restrict the flow of oil onto the market now that it was slowly climbing back from its low of £9 per ton.[22] At that price, a blue whale that generated one hundred barrels of oil, or 16.6 tons, was worth only about £150.

The recurrent willingness of whaling companies to work out new deals reflected not so much their good will—although some of that existed—as their Depression-generated certainty that unregulated whaling would be disastrous. They had seen in the 1920s that the industry could grow too rapidly, and they had no desire to see that happen again. By 1935, it appears that even Unilever's directors understood that any gains they might make by working outside the system would be offset by a collapse of the industry in just a few years. It turned out to be in the oil refiners' interests to keep the catch at a level just above the demand for oil, which meant playing the game with others rather than playing solitaire. Not until 1937 was concern expressed for the whales themselves. Only rarely did conservationists in the 1930s comment that whales were of inherent interest and ought to be preserved for noneconomic reasons. When scientists did marvel at whales, it was usually to observe that the creatures were really big; they might as well have been lamenting the decline of icebergs.

NEGOTIATING A DEAL

Even with the June 1935 quota agreement, the Norwegians were verging on desperation. Their whalers were reporting smaller stocks of great whales in the southern seas, and the Germans had announced plans to use Swedish capital to build their own whaling vessels in Norway. Since Germany was the best market for Norwegian whale oil, this development was worse than the rise of Japanese whaling. One Norwegian official told British diplomat Cecil Dormer that the threatened expansion of whaling was "sheer insanity," and officials on both sides of the North Sea lamented that nothing could be done about German entry into the fray. As another Norwegian put it to Dormer, "If 500 whalers go to Germany, how can we put them all in prison when they return home?"[23] Perhaps most troubling to the Norwegians was that they were slowly losing their grip on an industry that they had long dominated.[24]

Because whale oil prices had risen from £10 to about £20 per ton in just one year, expansion was in the air, and not just from the Germans and Japanese, who were acting on grounds of national policy. Expansion, Australian diplomat Keith Officer reported, meant that "many of the whalers are strongly against any measures of restriction of catch for themselves when whalers of other countries are unrestricted." The 1931 convention and private quota deals had not created a rational safeguard, he reported, and the convention was almost worthless without Japanese and possibly other whalers on board. Yet, at the end of his gloomy letter, Officer concluded that the only reason not to start an Australian expedition would be if an economic analysis recommended against it.[25]

Both Australians and New Zealanders had talked about their need to get into whaling, if for no other reason than to strengthen their claims to the Antarctic. Like Argentines, many in Australia and New Zealand believed that they had something akin to a God-given right to the riches of the deep south, if only they could mobilize their scattered populations and scarce capital to look in that direction. Australian explorer Sir Douglas Mawson groaned, "There is yet no Australian organization for whaling in the Antarctic, yet Japan during the 1934–35 season sent a mother ship and some chasers to the Antarctic."[26] When the Japanese scooped up the *Antarctic*, Australian officials demanded an explanation from London of how it had happened; the Australians' own efforts to procure a factory ship and skilled gunners had been hindered by Norwegian laws. Now they faced the prospect of the Japanese cleaning out the nearly pristine whaling grounds nearby.[27]

The immediate threat of German, Japanese, and other efforts to catch whales, combined with the ongoing operation of companies from South Africa, signaled doom for the private efforts to organize whaling regulations. On one level, the problem was simply the order of magnitude: too many companies operating in too many languages in an age of relatively slow communication. It was just not possible to coordinate all of them. But the greater problem was one that would have existed even if the owners all texted in Esperanto, and that was a clash of interests. The Norwegians were rather obvious in their desire to retain a national hold on the whaling industry, and the British were happy to cooperate with them. Meanwhile, the Germans and Japanese in particular were driving for roles that equaled their perceived national stature, and other businessmen around the world saw an opportunity in the open whaling fields. In short, the old whalers were not about to yield their positions, but the new whalers obviously would not accept the status quo.

The German expansion was in some ways more frightening and in others more reassuring. The scare came from the impending change in the European market for oil. In 1933, the German government had launched a *Drang noch Autarkie*, a "drive to autarky." In other words, German ministers had decided that the nation's economy should be as self-sufficient as possible. One obvious thing to do was to stop importing Norwegian whale oil, since it was free to acquire on the high seas. Since the Germans absorbed about half of the world's whale oil, the decision not to import it would have major ramifications for the industry.[28] So it was not a surprise in May 1935 when investors announced plans for two German whaling companies, although it was a bit disheartening in London when one of the organizers turned out to be its own vice-consul in Tønsberg, Norway, M. Waalman.[29] The chief German negotiator on whaling matters was Helmuth Wohlthat, who held a high-ranking position in the Reich Defense Council, indicating the importance that Germany placed on whale oil. In 1940 *Time* magazine described him as Herman Goering's "right hand."[30] No doubt there were fringe benefits to be had for the Germans, like maritime training and knowledge of the Antarctic that might be useful for any hypothetical wars with Britain, but ultimately, as historians J. N. Tønnessen and A. O. Johnsen conclude, "Norwegian whale oil was assisting Germany's rearmament."[31]

But the *Drang noch Autarkie* was also part of the reassuring elements of German whaling. The Germans were nearly model participants in whaling diplomacy, rather oddly given their use of the diplomatic bludgeon through most of the 1930s. They seem to have concluded that whaling had the potential to be a long-term asset, but only if they joined in conservation schemes, which was not out of line with their general utilitarian approach to forests and other natural resources.[32] They were most definitely not out to strip the oceans of all whales in a drive for foreign currency; the Third Reich needed whales long into the future. We should be careful not to see all of German diplomacy in the 1930s through the lens of World War II. As late as 1938, most Europeans were willing to try cooperating with the Germans, and many Norwegians and British gladly entered business deals with German companies, whether to build ships or provide oil until the German ships could head out to sea.

The established whaling nations had a much less favorable view of the Japanese, and an element of racism entered their thinking even as they understood why the government of Japan refused to join the various conventions. One British official noted that the Norwegians were attempting to win Tokyo's adherence to the 1935–36 quota arrangement, "but it is too much to expect the Japs to submit to that."[33] As another British official commented later, the Japanese businessmen understood that the Europeans were interested in using the treaties to hem them in, so they resisted.[34]

European anxiety went far beyond racial thinking. The extremely low yield from the first expedition of the *Antarctic Maru* hinted at a problem that would come up for the next twenty-five years: waste. The Japanese developed a reputation for producing less oil per whale than anyone else. Their defense, usually, was that they were more interested in meat than the Europeans were, so they did not boil out every last drop of oil. The Europeans were never convinced. They believed that the Japanese were simply stripping off the best parts of the whales and tossing the carcasses overboard, which would have been a violation of the 1931 convention, had the Japanese signed it. Well into the postwar period, the global consensus was that the Japanese ignored conservation practices and, for lack of a better term, cheated.

Even with German and Japanese expansion on the horizon, Norwegian whalers in 1936 tried one last time to create a voluntary quota system.

The whaling companies and government were involved, as usual, but most striking was the role of Norwegian seamen's unions in organizing blockades of British companies that would not cooperate.[35] Into August, they succeeded in altering the plans of British whaling companies that were unwilling to accept Norwegian quota proposals; in doing so, they drew in the British government, which in turn negotiated with the Norwegian government.[36] The unintended consequence was the decision by H. K. Salvesen to hire more Britons, who thought whaling jobs were good, and fewer Norwegians, whom he thought complained too much.[37] The standoff ended up involving Norwegian justice minister Trygve Lie (who would go on to become secretary-general of the United Nations) and the leader of the British Transport Workers' Union, Ernest Bevin (a future foreign secretary). The crisis was resolved when the Norwegian government accepted a British proposal that featured an open season of 8 December 1936 to 7 March 1937, a ban on hunting blue whales and fin whales between latitude 40° south and the equator, limits on catcher boats per floating factory, and inspectors on each factory. It was an impressive list of restrictions, but there would be no quota.[38]

One noteworthy change by 1936 was that most of the negotiations took place on the national level, not between companies. Early in 1936, Johan Hjort and Henry Maurice met with other fisheries officials in London to discuss coordinated proposals to Germany in the face of the "grave danger" of a wave of expansion in response to rising prices for oil.[39] In December, the Norwegian government approached the British with an invitation to a formal diplomatic conference for February or March 1937. British acceptance was not in doubt, so the real subject of discussion was the extent of the guest list. Would it make sense to invite the Germans and Japanese right away, or should there be a preliminary conference that created a common Anglo-Norse position? And if the Germans and Japanese came, would there be obligations to invite other states with smaller whaling interests?[40]

The British took this conference very seriously. An American diplomat reported that British officials "frankly admitted that they are very desirous of preserving the British whaling industry from serious damage through ruthless competition but they are more troubled by the prospect of ultimate extinction of the blue whale unless effective international measures can be taken for its preservation."[41] The British maneuvered the Norwegians into holding the meeting in London by arguing that it would encourage participation by the Dominions—South Africa, Australia, Canada, and New Zealand. In reality, British diplomats wanted the meeting as far as possible from the new Labor government in Oslo, which had recently dismissed Hjort and turned whaling matters over to a committee that, as the appalled Henry Maurice commented, included a mere dentist.[42] While the British acquiesced to Norwegian demands for one multinational meeting, they insisted on a thorough advance exchange of views through the Norwegian legation. Maurice feared that a general meeting that allowed everyone to speak would be "interminable," but one of his colleagues envisioned a real nightmare scenario: "an alliance between Unilevers, the Germans and Japanese to press for a very large permitted production of whale oil."[43] Informal approaches to Berlin indicated the Germans' willingness to attend a conference to discuss regulation of whaling.

On 6 March 1937, the day that Norway agreed to formal invitations for an April conference, bad news came from the east. Ambassador R. H. Clive reported that Japan's minister of fisheries and agriculture had announced to the Diet an ambitious government plan to expand pelagic whaling. Clive predicted that four factories would sail for the south in the fall, with as many as eight planned for 1938–39 and more on the horizon. While the Japanese minister was careful to downplay reports of tension with London and Oslo, Clive reported that the minister said these new whaling vessels would have military uses.[44]

British imperial planners were no doubt worried about any Japanese discussion of preparing for war, but to neutral Norway the threat from eight more factory vessels was almost as dire. A month earlier, in February, Anglo-Norse diplomats had called the Japanese on their whaling practices. Ambassador Clive had presented evidence that Japanese whalers were hunting blue whales with calves, demanding that the government hold its whalers to international standards set out in the 1931 convention. Clive shot the only real arrow in his quiver when he threatened that Britain and Norway would lift all of their regulations on whaling if Japan did not join the club.[45]

Whether or not the Japanese recognized it, this was an empty threat that revealed the fundamental flaw of whaling diplomacy—the stakes were both too high and too low for drastic measures. Lifting regulations on one's own whalers would be an admission of defeat and would not help a nation's whaling industry in the long run. Engaging in a race to the bottom might satisfy a need for spite, but it would not solve any problems. On the opposite side of the ledger, whaling was not so important that it justified a full-fledged trade war or some other means of coercion to get another state to cooperate. If the Germans and Japanese did not draw serious consequences for breaking the Treaty of Versailles or invading Manchuria, then it was unlikely that the British would play hardball over a few blue whale calves.

In this environment, delegates from ten nations convened in London in late May 1937 at the Shell-Mex House, an imposing twelve-story building owned jointly by Royal Dutch Shell and British Petroleum. The Germans had succeeded in delaying the meeting until then by citing their need to collect and analyze data. Henry Maurice considered this a smoke screen that allowed the Germans to generate their own ideas rather than accept whatever Oslo and London proposed, but the delay also facilitated the participation of other countries, including the United States.[46]

In later years the United States would emerge as the leader of whaling diplomacy, but in 1937 it was present largely because of its whaling potential. American tariff laws added just over £17 per ton to the price of imported oil, yet the whaling industry barely existed in the United States.[47] With America's vast potential to generate oil and fat at home, the demand for whale products was very small. If things changed and Americans got the whaling bug again, that would make the German and Japanese efforts a small problem in comparison. So it was imperative to have the United States in the fold of regulated whaling states.

Beyond that practical concern, inviting the United States increased the likelihood that the conference would pay attention to conservation. The United States had a history of promoting conservation of marine resources, with two fisheries treaties with Canada and leadership in a four-party convention to protect fur seals in the North Pacific. American biologists were influential around the world, and there was almost no industry pressure that might undermine their influence at home. The US government had shown interest in whaling matters in the past and had publicly framed them as conservation measures, so it was natural for British and Norwegian officials to want an American at the conference to help pressure the Japanese and Germans to accept restrictions. Even with the United States sliding into an isolationist period, the country carried enough prestige and economic power to make a big difference in a small meeting.

The Japanese refused to attend. The government could have simply declined the invitation but instead it took the unusual step of issuing a semi-official statement in *Domei*, a government-supported photo news-paper aimed at the general public, explaining that no Japanese delegates would attend the London whaling conference, which was simply a front to maintain British and Norwegian dominance of the industry. The Japanese promised to join the regulatory discussions only when they had gained equal footing as a whaling nation.[48] This rather undiplomatic approach frustrated the British, but at least one diplomat acknowledged privately that the plan of the conference was indeed to find a way to halt the expansion of the Japanese whaling industry.[49]

The purpose of the meeting was clear from the British government's welcoming document: "It is desirable to take such measures as may be practicable to prevent the depletion of the stock of whales below the point at which it would cease to be commercially profitable to hunt them."[50] Then, early in the deliberations, Chairman Henry Maurice seemed to turn things around by saying that "when you get companies represented around the table it is just a scramble between them as to who is going to come out of it best."[51] Whether or not the whalers would have a seat, their governments were quick to show that they were prepared to do their scrambling for them. As the German delegate Helmuth Wohlthat bluntly put it, "We have not been able to get that share of whale oil which we wanted to get." Acknowledging that whaling companies would be able to lobby their governments, Maurice commented later that day that "it is not much good to pass a resolution to which we cannot give effect."[52]

In addition to concern about commercial extinction, important delegates raised the specter of actual extinction. On the third day, Norwegian Birger Bergersen, the aforementioned dentist, who would play a central role in whaling policy for the next fifteen years and serve as the first chairman of the International Whaling Commission, started the session with a lament about the "grave sign" that fully grown blue whales were almost impossible to find anymore. About thirty minutes in to his speech, he warned, "A wholly unregulated whaling activity would therefore inevitably lead to an exploitation of the already very decimated stocks, and this would in its turn be fatal for the whaling industry."[53] Maurice added that, without drastic action, blue whales faced extermination.[54]

The challenge would be to translate that general concern about sustainability into proposals that every government could accept. An early point of controversy was setting an open season, which Bergersen called "the first and most important of all the things we have discussed." The British and Norwegians had already settled on 8 December to 7 March, but the Germans held out for 15 March on the theory that it would drive down prices for whale oil, even as they acknowledged that "the catch of whales is too heavy."[55] Delegates finally agreed to an opening of 8 December to 15 March for the 1937–38 season, with a closing date of March 8 for subsequent years. As Maurice put it in 1938, "From the point of view of running the industry on practical lines . . . three months is about as short a period as one could reasonably enforce."[56] The pelagic whaling states compelled countries with land stations to accept restrictions on waste, minimum catch size, and seasons that were similar to those faced by pelagic whalers.

The final draft of the convention represented an advance over the 1931 agreement. It included old language about protecting mothers with calves, requiring complete utilization of the carcass, tying remuneration of gunners to the size of whales rather than the number taken, and mandating the collection of data for scientific purposes. The negotiators set size limits for the four main species of whales hunted—blues, fins, sperms, and humpbacks—and required an inspector for each factory ship. Whalers had to process each whale within thirty-six hours of catching it. Finally, large areas of the sea north of latitude 40° south were closed to pelagic whaling operations. Norway, Britain, and Germany, the three biggest whaling powers, joined the United States, Ireland, Argentina, and the four Commonwealth states (Australia, Canada, New Zealand, and South Africa) in signing the agreement, which would be in force until June 1938. The signatories could extend the agreement before that date, and likewise they could withdraw by notifying Great Britain.[57]

Reaction to the convention was mixed. Bergersen and other Norwegian officials expressed satisfaction, while Norwegian newspapers generally labeled the convention a good start toward effective protection. Anders Jahre and other Norwegian whalers, however, were "particularly severe" in their criticism.[58] Jahre's criticism reflected a general dismay in the industry felt by Britain's H. K. Salvesen, Clifford Carver of the American Whaling Company, South African whalers who came close to getting their government to bail out, and Premier John Willcock of Western Australia (the home of the Australian whaling industry), who accused the prime minister of gaining his support under "false premises."[59] One British diplomat acknowledged what the whalers were saying: "the Japanese are going to benefit from the abstentions of others."[60]

Yet the new treaty was still only a stopgap measure. Without the Japanese on board, the whalers refused to accept a quota, so there were no limits on how many whales could be caught. In addition, attempts to limit the number of catchers per factory ship faltered in the face of German complaints about their need to catch up to their more experienced competitors. Delegates ended by agreeing in principle that signatory states should prevent the transfer of whaling ships to states that were not signatories, even though most did not have the legislation to enforce that proposal. Despite British efforts before the conference to promote a long-term approach, the regulations would apply for only one season unless Norway, Britain, and Germany agreed to extend the agreement.

Signing a convention was just a small part of the equation, though. It then had to be ratified quickly, before whalers made final preparations for their late-summer departures. The terms said that the agreement would go into effect provisionally on 1 July 1937, but governments still had to ratify formally. Whaling vessels left Europe around September, just three months away, and the convention would not take effect until five signatories ratified it. In addition, the Japanese could not accede to the treaty unless it was functioning. Nevertheless, the ratification process dragged on into 1938, with the British Dominions being the slowest to adopt the convention. With Britain, Norway, Germany, and the United States on board, most of the pelagic whalers in the world were operating under the terms of the agreement, but there was fear that some might flee their home ports for flags of convenience. Chile and Panama were especially worrisome as homes for shipowners who had limited allegiance to their homelands, but the immediate problem was Japan.

Throughout the end of 1937 and the beginning of 1938, the four ratifiers attempted to coordinate an approach to Japan that might pressure Tokyo into joining the convention. In retrospect, it is odd to think about the Germans cooperating with Norway and Britain to change Japanese policy, especially because the British and Germans clearly saw whaling in the context of larger global policies. With the memory of the September 1937 Japanese invasion of China in mind, one British diplomat thought that "it might be possible to represent now to the Japanese government that a step so comparatively unimportant in itself might have a useful effect in correcting to some extent the apprehensions concerning their general policy which are now widely held abroad."[61] In part, the British were eager to get Japanese cooperation in order to promote conservation and, in part, to assuage the New Zealanders and Australians, who were fearful that conservation measures would be unraveled by aggressive Japanese whaling.

The Japanese were unyielding. Perhaps they were not impressed by the suggestion that whaling diplomacy would compensate for their invasion of China, which presumably did not need recompense anyway. More likely, they saw no benefit to any regulation of their marine industries by stronger powers with more established whaling fleets. Still, they played the game well, asking the other whaling governments to keep them informed and hinting repeatedly that they might attend future conferences, especially if they received some recognition of their unique position. Their reward was an exhaustive series of diplomatic consultations and maneuvers, none of which panned out before the German invasion of Poland in September 1939 changed the equation radically.

The Japanese strategy, though, reaped other, less desirable rewards. On one level, whaling experts throughout Europe and the United States concluded that the Japanese were irresponsible whalers, a charge that remained firmly in place when the war ended six years later. Even before the Pearl Harbor attack, Remington Kellogg understood that the opportunity would soon come to rewrite Japanese policy, telling Sidney Harmer that

> the Japs have given us a lot of trouble in the North Pacific in peace times as you know. Fur-seals, whales, and fishing-rights in the North Pacific have never been settled amicably during the years of so-called peace. When this job is completed we should be able to settle these matters for some years to come. At the conferences I have never been impressed with any indication of good faith on the part of the Japanese. There were those, however, that thought if we made enough concessions that the Japs would do their part. Let us hope that all of the axis whaling vessels are lost in the present conflict.[62]

Kellogg would get both his wish about the shipping and his desire to settle matters without Japanese input, but he failed to foresee that he would help get the Japanese back into whaling in 1946. Still, after the war the Japanese found themselves at the center of a rancorous debate in the whaling community about their character, and it seems likely that part of their inability to portray themselves as responsible whalers in the twenty-first century has its roots in the late 1930s. To be fair, it should be noted that suspicious whalers cast a wide net, with one diplomat in Oslo reporting that every whaler thought that all the others' inspectors were corrupt. That diplomat concluded that "evidently it will be difficult to awaken a sense of sin in the bosoms of the Norwegians."[63]

The larger lesson, though, was that a whaling convention that did not draw in all whalers was nearly useless. Without Japanese participation, other whalers spent an inordinate amount of time complaining about the unfairness of the rules and speculating about what others might be doing. In August 1937, H. K. Salvesen wrote to Henry Maurice complaining that South Africa had not yet joined the 1937 convention, so the Salvesen company's interests were likely to be hurt. Maurice wrote back tartly that the government was interested in preserving the industry as a whole and would "not be deflected from its purpose by hypothetical considerations of the inequality of the restrictions which may fall upon individual companies." If a reasonable set of regulations could be found for a majority of the industry, then that was good enough.[64] All of the angst was corrosive, and instead of providing some stability the conventions were themselves tenuous instruments that needed annual renewal. The solution that would emerge during the war was to create a permanent commission of the whaling states—actual or potential—and that meant setting standards low enough to entice broad membership.

While diplomats and bureaucrats were able to temporarily resolve many of the problems of the whaling industry, they were confronted almost daily with their inability to deal with other complex problems. The ongoing labor problems of Chr. Salvesen Ltd. were a case in point. H. K. Salvesen determined to have the most efficient whaling operation, which meant laying off some seamen. In the late summer of 1937 he found himself once again dealing with a blockaded factory vessel in Tønsberg, the *Sourabaya*, where the seaman's union was taking retaliatory action.[65] It took several days to negotiate an end to the standoff, which only hardened Salvesen's resolve.

Equally troubling were the odd cases of the *Frango*, property of the American Whaling Company, which was actually owned by Norwegian Lars Christensen, and the *Ulysses*, working for the Western Operating

Company, which was owned by Norwegian Anders Jahre. Both ships, flying the US flag, worked the west coast of Australia in 1937, causing all sorts of international trouble as they caught humpbacks close to shore. The Australian government was, at best, ambivalent about this legal but foreign operation that seemed likely to kill far too many humpbacks in their calving lagoons at Shark Bay. The Norwegian government expressed concern about the wisdom of the *Frango*'s tactics to the US government, which returned the volley by noting that all of the expedition's catcher boats were manned by Norwegians and flew the Norwegian flag. It was rather evident that both the American Whaling Company and the Western Operating Company were legal covers to slip Norwegian whale oil past high US tariff barriers into the waiting arms of companies like Procter and Gamble. What had not been so evident before the expedition was that US Coast Guard inspectors on board the *Ulysses*, Lt. Quentin Walsh, and the *Frango*, Lt. T. R. Midtlyng, would be so diligent. When the crews of the *Frango*'s catcher boats targeted calves to get at lactating females, Midtlyng protested that they were violating the 1931 convention and subsequent US law, took notes, and stood his ground. He reported it all to the Treasury Department, which confiscated about 10 percent of the oil when it arrived in New Orleans in 1938.[66]

The story of the confiscation got wide coverage in whaling circles because of the obvious implications for the world's whalers. At the most basic level, it revealed the near impossibility of regulating the behavior of multinational expeditions, especially when that behavior was merely ill advised rather than obviously illegal. Was it Washington's responsibility to lean on the allegedly American whaling companies or Oslo's responsibility to talk to the captains of the catcher boats, who were actually killing the whales? Beyond that, though, two officers acting independently had shown that an inspection system could work. It is hard to imagine the pressure and ostracism that Lieutenant Midtlyng and Lieutenant Walsh faced, but they did what almost no other inspector ever did: report violations to authorities who cared. It helped that whale oil was less important to the US Treasury Department than the country's conservationist image was, and it probably helped that the *Frango* and *Ulysses* were Norwegian ventures at heart, something the lieutenants likely observed with every meal they ate alone.[67]

GETTING JAPAN ON BOARD (ALMOST)

The short-term nature of the 1937 convention forced diplomats and whalers to convene a year later to discuss a protocol that would extend the treaty's terms and perhaps bring the Japanese and others on board. The irony was that the necessary fifth ratification (from Ireland) did not come until May 1938, when the convention's rules were barely a month from expiration and the Antarctic whaling season was over. In effect, diplomats were already working on replacing the convention before it had gone into effect. The optimists hoped that the signatories could simply agree to extend the convention's rules for another year, but that was not about to happen. Between governments that wanted to see some changes and those that did not have the constitutional authority to accept an extension, there would have to be a new conference in 1938 to set terms for the 1938–39 season.

The 1938 meeting took place in two parts, first in Oslo and then in London, which reflected something of a compromise between the two whaling leaders. The Norwegians and British agreed that the point of the May meeting in Oslo would be to hash out ideas solely among the group that had ratified the 1937 convention; the floor would be turned over to more countries and delegates in June in London. It is hard to say that this format produced better results, but at least it gave the delegates a break between meetings and allowed governments to contemplate specific proposals before the formal convening in June. The format also reflected one of the central challenges of whaling diplomacy: how do the more active members of the whaling community shape the agenda while still allowing a range of input from, and providing a range of satisfaction for, the less active but potentially important members? As Birger Bergersen noted, the goal for the Oslo meeting was that the nations that had the most interest in whaling should work together without creating the impression of a whaling bloc that would overpower and embitter other countries.[68]

Under Bergersen's leadership, the delegates from Argentina (a late ratifier), Germany, Britain, Norway, and the United States first had to decide whether the 1937 convention had been of any use. Helmuth Wohlthat, the lead German delegate, urged all signatories to extend the 1937 convention for at least another year, which received wide support. But the American scientist Remington Kellogg thought the convention a failure, citing the increase in catch in the year after it had been signed. "It seems clear," he said, "that adequate conservation of the world whale stock has not resulted from the London Agreement." No one disagreed with Kellogg, yet all agreed to extend the deal in the hopes of improving it substantially, or at least postponing the day of reckoning. A weak agreement was better than no agreement.[69]

All concurred that whaling was following an unsustainable course, but no one proposed doing anything drastic about it. Three statistics stood out in 1938. First, the number of whales killed each year had continued to increase even with the crash in prices in the early 1930s and the allegedly restrictive agreements of 1931 and 1937. From a low of 9,572 whales in 1931–32, when most whalers had stayed home, the take had risen steadily to more than 46,000 by 1937–38. Equally troubling was the shift in species from the highly sought after blue whales (roughly two-thirds of the 1931–32 catch to less than one-third of the 1937–38 season) to the smaller fin whales, which strongly suggested that blue whale populations were crashing and fin populations were about to follow.[70] Finally, and more subtly, the whalers' data showed that the number of pregnant females taken had nearly doubled since 1932–33 in all three key species, blues, fins, and humpbacks. Kellogg noted that pregnancy rates frequently increase in response to population decreases, so this trend suggested a massive population decline in the largest species.

Near the end of the meeting, Bergersen said what now seems obvious: "The question is not purely an economical one, it is first and foremost, I think, a biological question. You see, we have to think about the next generation. What will they think if we take the last whale? . . . I really think as a biologist that it is a shame, a terrible shame for our generation and for our time, if this wonderful animal, one of the most splendid existing, should disappear."[71] In all of the recorded discussion in the 1930s, this was the only comment that might compare to a modern environmentalist position. One can almost imagine an embarrassed hush falling over the room, with only a few crickets chirping in the corner, before someone cleared his throat and resumed serious discussion.

Yet, Bergersen said what Maurice had suggested in 1937 and certainly others suspected, that the current path of whaling was not just unsustainable but also exterminatory. For nearly a decade, diplomats had been working on regulating the whaling industry on the theory that it was destroying itself, but only rarely had anyone hinted at the specter of extinction for the species themselves. Both the northern right whale and the gray whale that lived off California had been hunted to the brink of extinction in the age of sailing ships, so it should not have been hard to imagine that a more efficient industry might push some species over the brink.

Some US officials were especially frustrated. Not only did Kellogg call the London convention a failure, but he also thought his trips for these meetings were merely "junkets."[72] Only a fear of the conservationist community, which was actually pretty quiet on the issue, sending only a few letters to the State Department, seemed to argue in favor of sticking it out. More important was a sense within the department that the United States had a history of promoting conservation, starting with the 1911 North Pacific Fur Seal Convention and running through the fisheries deals with Canada in the 1920s. To that end, the delegates emphasized conservation even when it harmed the small American whaling industry, which, after all, was mostly Norwegian anyway.

The case of humpback whales highlighted the split between land and pelagic whaling states. The American expeditions off Australia had demonstrated that the humpback population was under assault both in the colder southern waters and in the warmer waters near the equator. The French in Madagascar, New Zealanders, Australians, and South Africans were all picking off other populations of these slow-moving, even slower-reproducing cetaceans. Humpbacks faced nearly constant hunting under the current regime, and it had become clear from the *Discovery* research expeditions that humpbacks were the most endangered species then being hunted. A mark fired into a humpback was three to four times more likely to be recovered than one lodged in a fin or blue whale, which researcher Neil Mackintosh considered to be serious evidence of decline. Even worse, 50 percent of the whales taken off the west coast of Australia were immature, meaning that they had not even had a chance to replace themselves. Mackintosh argued that the biggest problem, beyond simple destruction, was disruption of the calving grounds, which meant that the stock that summered in Australia was perilously close to elimination. Females made up nearly 60 percent of the kill, showing that the current practices were unsustainable.

But the split between the two whaling communities—pelagic and coastal—meant that there would not be an easy solution to the humpback problem. The French, New Zealanders, and Australians were particularly unlikely to accept a ban on inshore humpback hunting, since that was all that they took, but the pelagic whalers would not accept a ban on their taking of humpbacks without a similar limitation on the shore stations. Even a simple act like raising the thirty-five foot minimum length of legal whales would have unequal consequences, because the shore stations had less control over which whales came their way.

A subset of the humpback problem was the land station problem. Various governments defined "land station" differently, with some interpreting it to mean a set of buildings with catcher boats attached, while others thought that a ship moored in one spot in territorial waters for an entire season would count too. Not surprisingly, different nations had different interests, with the French especially interested in using old factory ships in various harbors in their African colonies rather than building permanent land stations in what might have been less-than-desirable spots. The British and Norwegians were concerned that a more flexible definition would mean that whaling vessels would never really retire but instead be moored somewhere for brief periods, able to move around the edges of the whaling grounds as the whales' movements dictated. The whaling nations compromised in the 1937 convention by including in the definition of a land station that it could be "on land, or in the territorial waters adjacent thereto."[73]

Related to the problem of land stations was the problem of sovereignty. The point of the ongoing whaling diplomacy was to circumscribe what pelagic whalers could do on the high seas, since no government could act alone. But land stations were, by definition, under the control of national governments, needing a license in most cases and observing a set of regulations set by a national fisheries bureau. Certainly a convention could regulate land stations as well as pelagic whaling, but that was adding a level of complexity to the negotiations. Kellogg summarized the problem— hunting whales in the tropics was "very injurious to the stock and unprofitable"—but he was hesitant to tell a country what to do in its own waters.[74]

The Oslo meeting succeeded in ventilating differences of opinion and getting new ideas on the table. Henry Maurice suggested a global cap on the number of whales that could be taken, rather than relying on a closed season, which would be known as a global or Antarctic quota, since it would deal only with hunting in the far south. He acknowledged that it would be difficult to administer, especially with the whalers so far from any source of authority, and that it could set off a scramble among countries, but he could see no other way to ensure that only a set number of whales would be killed. Kellogg seconded the idea, noting that whaling companies had managed to have their own quota system in the early 1930s, so even a return to that old system that yielded roughly 2.4 million barrels of whale oil would be better than the current one that yielded nearly 3.2 million barrels and was clearly not viable for the long term. Maurice's idea did not win many adherents—Helmuth Wohlthat said simply, "I do not see how it could work"—but it would reemerge a few years later as the centerpiece of the postwar whaling regulations. Maurice also made clear that whales were just meat and oil: "We are not thinking mainly of avoiding cruelty, the point is to avoid a lot of whales killed and oil wasted. The less whales killed and not used, the better."[75]

Birger Bergersen closed the Oslo meeting as William Morrison, the British minister of agriculture and fisheries, would open the London talks, with a plea for more nations to join the 1937 convention as the first step to better conservation. The biggest impediment to success was the attitude of the Japanese government. Without mentioning the Japanese directly, Morrison welcomed "those whom we missed last year" and offered the hope that they would become "firm and active supporters of our Agreement." He then hammered home the conservationist message, arguing that the only legitimate complaint about the London convention was "the conviction that it does not go far enough." He continued: "We all know that the remaining stock of whales cannot stand up for long against the present rate of exploitation." Because whales were "exhaustible," only conservation measures would save the industry from disappearing "within measurable time." The major goal, then, had to be to recruit new signatories in order to increase its effectiveness, but new amendments "to preserve the economic stability of the industry" would also be on the agenda. He concluded sharply: "None of us can plead ignorance." History, statistics, and scientific investigations all highlighted the need for "rational conservation of the stock." The missing element was cooperation among governments, for if some governments permitted or encouraged uncontrolled exploitation, then others would be unable to restrain their own nationals. "Unless we all rally to the support of measures of conservation," Morrison concluded, "we must be prepared to see whaling decontrolled and whaling enterprises destroyed in every country of the world in which whaling companies exist."[76] Later, Henry Maurice, one of

Morrison's subordinates, compared the speech to chastising the delegates with whips.[77]

Apparently, the delegates were accustomed to being whipped, because their reaction was to spend the rest of the first day in necessary but mundane discussions about committee assignments and meeting times. On the second day, they focused on the issue of French whaling posts around Africa, which, while hardly electrifying, brought the discussions about land stations and humpback whaling into focus. The accession of France and Australia, and possibly South Africa and New Zealand as well, appeared to depend on the resolution of these issues, and yet they were all secondary to pulling Japan's pelagic expeditions into the fold. Maurice, who had been chosen to preside over the conference, was probably hoping to build momentum before tackling the tougher problem of Japanese accession. Still, the energy that Morrison brought to the room seemed to dissipate in a mind-numbing disagreement over whether a factory ship could ever be a land station and, if wording needed to be changed, how various nations would deal with that constitutionally. After two hours of these discussions, Maurice turned to Akira Kodaki, the Japanese delegate who had come over from the embassy in London at the last moment, and asked him to tell the delegates what they most wanted to hear: Japan's attitude toward the London convention.[78]

The signals coming from Japan since 1937 had been confusing. On one hand, Japanese newspapers were reporting that Japanese whalers had been following "Norwegian-style" whaling since 1899 and had just had their greatest season ever in 1936–37. In July 1937, the papers reported that European whalers were frightened by the "brilliant advance" of their Japanese counterparts, and yet just three months earlier a Canadian diplomat had reported that Japan would not attend any meetings until it had caught up with the Western powers.[79] The threat from Japanese whaling was obviously real, though, because Japanese officials were commenting on the military value of whaling vessels even as they were building the *Tonan Maru 3*, the largest commercial ship in Japanese history, and two sister ships. Maurice made clear that governments like Japan had to get involved, even if the cost was a conservation measure: "I am afraid if we try at the moment to introduce limitations we shall have considerable difficulty in getting further adhesions to the Convention."[80] Delegates in London were expecting finally to get an indication from Japan of its real policy.

Kodaki's moment, as it turned out, was a bit anticlimactic. He expressed sympathy with the goals of the conference, asked for patience because he had such short notice and few instructions, and made clear that the Japanese government saw its whalers as so far behind technologically that they could not be expected to abide by the same standards as more established whaling countries. Kodaki was careful to emphasize that his government had planned to send only observers in order to get up to speed on the whaling conventions, but the British government had assured his government of a sympathetic hearing of Japan's special circumstances. To add to his image of ineffectiveness, Kodaki pointedly commented on his ignorance of whaling matters and asked forbearance from his colleagues as he learned the ropes.

Kodaki's immersion into whaling diplomacy only became less acceptable to his colleagues. For the next few days he restricted his comments to a version of "my government will have to consider this matter very carefully." Maurice, who had to prod Kodaki to say even that much, usually offered what appears to be an exasperated "thank you" to this unhelpful response. But on the fourth day, when asked to speak more fully about Japan's position, the Japanese diplomat revealed that his government had four specific reservations about the terms of the 1937 convention, ranging from relatively minor concerns about the North Pacific and home waters to a major demand for a longer open season, longer by six weeks.

One of Japan's points was that it could not accept restrictions for the North Pacific that had not been accepted by the Soviet Union. That situation would create an "unfair disadvantage." Maurice, presumably, could not believe this argument: "I cannot resist saying, and I am sure that Mr. Kodaki will forgive me, that it is equally unfair to the countries which are at present fishing in the Antarctic, that Japan does not adhere to the regulations which are in force in that area. That is a rather brutal observation, I know, but nevertheless perfectly true."[81] Later, when the German, Norwegian, and American delegates were peppering Kodaki with questions, Maurice again intervened. "Acceptance with reservations is not really acceptance," he said. "Governments must be agreeable to the whole agreement or it amounts to no more than a declaration of good will."[82] These exchanges summarized the role of Japan in the 1938 negotiations: a range of demands followed by remarkably sharp responses from the chair and other delegates.

The Japanese government had put itself in a difficult position, a conclusion that might apply at almost any time in its modern whaling history. One Western diplomat in Japan concluded that the Japanese desire for whale products was directly related to the war in China, which was taxing Japanese resources, but Japanese businessmen in the West feared that they might lose more than they could gain due to boycotts because of their whaling policy. At a dinner at the Japanese embassy in London, a high-ranking official from Mitsubishi "was rather more talkative than he realized" in acknowledging that he had spent a fortune cabling the Japanese government and asking for a conciliatory attitude at the 1938 whaling conference. The British Foreign Office called the Japanese position "undesirable and embarrassing," while expressing the opinion that Kodaki wanted to cooperate but needed more direction from Tokyo.[83] When combined with direct pressure from Western embassies in Tokyo, this advice appeared to have the desired effect.[84] On the final day of the meetings, Kodaki was able to promise that Japan would accede to the convention in one year if the delegates agreed to open whaling in the North Pacific, and Japan would also adhere to the common rules in the upcoming season.[85]

Delegates came to very different conclusions about whether whaling diplomacy was making any progress. Kellogg and Maurice sharply debated the effectiveness of the 1937 agreement, which Kellogg dismissed as a failure because "entirely too many whales were taken last year," while Maurice suggested the agreement would have been fine if the Japanese had joined. Kellogg's call for basing decisions on biological grounds prompted Maurice to reply that governments had interests that prevented them from standing on a "biological pedestal."[86] Still, some advances were evident. Thorny matters of interpretation, like the definition of a land station, had been resolved. New conservation ideas, such as a sanctuary in the far southern reaches of the Pacific and a ban on hunting humpbacks for a year, had gained consensus support. The establishment of the sanctuary, which really was a two-year ban on hunting in Antarctic waters between longitudes 70° and 170° west, is particularly noteworthy because the scientists who advocated for it acknowledged that they did not have much data, but they wanted to act before expeditions moved into the area.[87] Although, as one whaler noted, "It was not difficult to get international agreement on a conservation measure which looked important but in fact had no impact on whalers," Mackintosh compared the sanctuary to having money in the bank, echoing the regular call for a rational industry.[88]

Plausible ideas about a global quota, fixed limits on the number of catcher boats per expedition, and the use of electric harpoons all got hearings, setting the stage for future discussions. In fact, Maurice commented without any objection, "We all realize that ultimately if we are going to save the stock of whales we have got to get down to quantitative restriction."[89] There was widespread agreement that conservation of whale stocks was a serious matter that had not been attained and was not on the immediate horizon either. Yet, several countries that had been ambivalent about or hostile to the 1937 convention had agreed to accede to it and the new 1938 protocol. Eight countries complied with or ratified the agreement, and another twelve received invitations to join, so the goal of bringing as many nations on board as possible had only been partially met. Near the end of the meeting, Maurice noted, "If we can get the agreement of Japan, or some more satisfactory proposal, we shall have done pretty good work here."[90]

Yet, with no more than a promise from Japan, the value of the 1938 protocol was up in the air. The central point of the meeting was to find globally acceptable rules, and Japan had come a long way in terms of acknowledging the other nations' positions. The attendees duly signed the protocol, and most ratified it. But the impact on Antarctic whaling was minor. The ban on hunting humpbacks, which made up less than 15 percent of the Antarctic catch, probably transferred some of the burden to other species, but the catch of fin whales dropped by about a quarter in the next season, while the haul of blues stayed steady. Bergersen noted that whalers were not satisfied: "It is difficult for the whalers of the older whaling nations to understand why they should spare the humpback whales for the Japanese expeditions."[91] The sanctuary might have had an impact over the long term, and it is noteworthy that the delegates moved to protect it before anyone used it. But all that would not matter if Japan backed away in a year or chose to use the sanctuary as its own hunting ground. Some observers thought that US officials had pushed to get a special deal for the *Frango*; and the Germans had fought against land stations solely because they had none—just as Don Malbran had predicted.[92]

Kellogg followed his dispute with Maurice by attacking the very basis of the discussions. He wrote to Bergersen in April 1939 that "the general feeling here [in the United States] has been that such conferences are futile, unless they are willing to consider a definite limit on the number of whales that can be killed during the 90 day season, or if that is too complicated, a maximum number of barrels of oil should be set as a quota and when this is reached all whaling should cease." These comments foreshadowed the American position in postwar whaling negotiations, but Kellogg went further still to express his concern for a lack of enforcement. Expeditions with only one inspector tended to bring in all of their illegal whales when the inspector was asleep, "human nature being what it is." Without a drastic change, he concluded, commercial whaling would be over by 1944.[93]

Japan's position on whaling was closely tied to its larger political goal of gaining respect in the world, which involved balancing a combination of muscle flexing and appealing to common interests. A few days after the 1938 conference, the *Japan Advertiser* published a statement from the Foreign Ministry that emphasized that the other nations really wanted Japan to participate. Japan sympathized with the need to protect whales and stabilize oil prices, but its "infantile" industry meant that "the time is not ripe for this country to be controlled equally with other countries." At the same time, the Foreign Ministry implied, the other nations had made several key concessions to Japan's interests.[94] Japan and Germany linked whaling to the possibility of adding territory in Antarctica. The Japanese were following up on an expedition from thirty years before, and the Germans took an expedition to the edge of the continent that used airplanes to drop swastika flags on open lakes and other unclaimed spaces on the continent.

With high hopes, the delegates met once again in August 1939 and quickly were rewarded with Kodaki's report that Japan would accede before the next season started, despite strong opposition from the highly inefficient Japanese whaling companies. In those discussions, delegates agreed to ban hunting of humpbacks for a year and to add a second inspector to the factory ships. The German delegate urged the Japanese government to accept the conventions and protocols because German whalers had complained about the unfairness of the restrictions. Delegates spent time worrying about Chile's moves into whaling and heard Bergersen's lament that "the stock of whales is overtaxed."[95] In a fit of optimism, they agreed to meet again in 1940. With the outbreak of World War II in Europe in September 1939, though, the Japanese announced that they could not accede to the previous agreements, and global whaling diplomacy fell off the agenda for a few years, not to reemerge until 1943. The whaling industry was subsumed into the global war effort, and conservation became merely a way to get the most out of scarce war materiel. In this atmosphere, it was impossible to analyze whether the 1938 protocol would have had any important ramifications or made a practical difference in how whalers did their jobs over the long term. The long pause that the war brought to whaling diplomacy allowed for an important rearrangement of political power among interested states and gave individuals a chance to think about whales and whaling in a new light.

With an unavoidable war just over the horizon, it is hard to call the 1937 or 1938 meetings missed opportunities in whaling conservation. No one outside of Tokyo can be blamed for failing to cut a deal acceptable to Japan; and without Japan's acquiescence, the world's powerful whaling companies and some governments were not about to accept strict conservation rules. In the face of obvious Japanese intransigence, the diplomats, scientists, whalers, and bureaucrats who met in 1937 and 1938 created a set of rules and floated interesting ideas, many of which were infeasible at the time. The framework of conservation proposed in those years would return as reality in 1946 as an American proposal to create a permanent commission with conservation as one of its central foci. But first the Allies had to win the war.

Mrs. Haroy

How people experienced a whale before television and whale watching: a baleen whale (apparently a right whale) on a railroad car, drawing a crowd in the Netherlands, ca. 1913. New Bedford Whaling Museum, Photo 2000.101.20.

Sir Sidney Harmer as depicted by the young Antarctic explorer Denis Gascoigne Lillie, ca. 1913. Copyright reserved; collection National Portrait Gallery, London; D 11155.

Johan Hjort, the Norwegian whale expert, ca. 1930. Hvalfangstmuseet, Sandefjord, Norway.

Whale bones at an abandoned whaling station near Antarctica, King George Island, 2006. Courtesy of Robert Dorsey.

The modern explosive harpoon, ca. 1900. Note the strong rope and the four barbed points just behind the main point. New Bedford Whaling Museum, Photo 2001.100.8121.

Australian whalers harpooning a humpback whale, 1951. The man in the
center is standing on the catwalk that allowed the harpooner to quickly get
from the wheelhouse to the harpoon. New Bedford Whaling Museum, Photo
2000.101.27.40.

The whale catcher *Pol XI* at work in the Antarctic, with ten whales alongside, undated. Hvalfangstmuseet, Sandefjord, Norway.

The floating factory *Thorshammer*, with rendering underway and at least six whales awaiting processing, undated. New Bedford Whaling Museum, Photo 2000.101.29.47.

Chr. Salvesen Ltd. worker on the flensing deck, undated. New Bedford Whaling Museum, Photo 2000.101.25.15.

3

WORLD WAR AND THE WORLD'S WHALES

IN JANUARY 1944, DURING A SPECIAL CONFERENCE IN LONDON TO update the 1937 whaling convention, Henry Maurice, now president of the Zoological Society of London, invited American scientist Remington Kellogg to his office. Perhaps they reminisced about their disagreements in the late 1930s or traded gossip on the fates of Helmuth Wohlthat and Akira Kodaki before they got down to business, as Maurice wanted to impress upon Kellogg the influence of the whaling industry on British policy. H. K. Salvesen, Maurice said, was using the fats and oil crisis to make proposals to enhance his profits. There would never be a time like the present to "introduce more stringent restrictions." Kellogg also met an official, "whose identity I cannot disclose," who allowed him to review letters in his office file that demonstrated that the whalers were particularly influential in the Ministry of Food.[1]

Other British and Norwegian officials also expressed their concern about the way in which the British delegation was using the fats crisis as a means to steamroll conservation principles. One Norwegian even suggested that the British data about a fat shortage in Norway was wrong because there was no shortage, a comment that might have surprised those suffering under Nazi occupation. Birger Bergersen, a leading Norwegian whaling authority, explained to Kellogg what Norwegian whaling circles thought about conservation. Anders Jahre and others were looking for ways to circumvent regulations, Bergersen reported, while Lars Christensen led a group that favored conservation.

These meetings impressed Kellogg so much that he reported them to his contacts in the US State Department, probably the only time that he wrote a memo based on his informal conversations at a whaling meeting.

Most critically, the conversations confirmed what he had been thinking in 1943: that Great Britain could never be the leader in conserving whales because of men like H. K. Salvesen and that Norway was hamstrung by German occupation and a deep split among the whaling company owners. Kellogg, who had dismissed whaling meetings as junkets in 1939, resolved that only the United States could provide the necessary impetus for putting whaling on a sustainable basis; hence, the United States would have to host a conference to create a postwar organization that could manage whaling for the long term, using scientific data and principles.

Kellogg, who would have a long career as an able administrator at the Smithsonian, knew that he could not create such a regime on his own. He first had to convince the State Department that its energy would be well spent on whaling, given all the other crises in the world. In that task he was only partially successful. The more the agency focused on the matter, the less it let Kellogg set policy. More important, he needed foreign governments to agree that US-led conservation was a good idea, and they were torn. Several were not happy to yield leadership to a nation that had no whaling industry and was already taking on so many other new responsibilities. As much as conservation was virtuous, Britain and Norway were facing fat shortages, and their governments were not likely to forgo whales when those whales could feed their people now. The influence of the whaling industry was not about to diminish.

The new US resolve to exert leadership in whale conservation was just one of a few important changes that World War II brought to whaling diplomacy. The outbreak of the war had forced German fleets off the whaling grounds, made the Norwegians cautious about their neutrality, and caused the British to agonize over their commitment to the prewar treaties. Norway's fleets became targets when Germany invaded in 1940. When Japan joined the war, it too was driven off the whaling grounds. The war took its inevitable toll on the floating factories and catcher boats, as well as on skilled whalers, leaving the industry in a precarious position. By the time the war ended in 1945, the only two things that were certain were that a permanent commission would be charged with regulating whaling and that hunger would play a critical role in establishing the regulations.

The efforts to negotiate those details began in 1944 and lasted through the end of 1946. The final compromise, the creation of a new International Whaling Commission, represented a mix of Norwegian, British, and American ideas about the proper shape of a global whaling agency. In the future, particularly the 1970s, the IWC would be known largely for its shortcomings, but in 1946 it represented a novel and innovative attempt to respond to what had seemed an insoluble problem. Fifteen years of whaling diplomacy had not created a sustainable whaling system, partly because nations had been reluctant to risk giving away rights that others retained and partly because of a lack of scientific evidence to direct policy makers. The creators of the IWC believed that whaling could be salvaged if all members would make similar sacrifices, and those sacrifices were based on science.

WAR AND ABROGATION

In the winter of 1939–40, the British government faced a difficult choice: should it withdraw from the whaling conventions in order to maximize fat procurement immediately, or should it remain a defender of the convention structure with an eye toward the postwar world? The debate dragged on for months, as Britons wrestled, on the one hand, with the gloom brought on by a large-scale war and the fear that it might be lengthy and, on the other, the concern about their reputation as responsible leaders. A long war would require not only total mobilization of the resources available to the island nation but also sustained efforts to deny those resources to the Germans. In the end, the British government chose to abide by the treaties with an eye toward the postwar period.

Whalers felt an immediate impact from the British declaration of war on Germany on 3 September 1939. September was normally a month of last-minute preparations and then departure for the whaling grounds, but now it would be a month of scrambling for scarce supplies and worrying about naval warfare. Like many neutral nations, Norway clamped down on the export of militarily valuable materials, many of which were necessary for a whaling expedition. In fact, the list of Norwegian supplies for a floating factory might have been easily confused with those for an artillery unit: 87 pairs of boots, 800 tins of meatballs, 1,000 kilograms of smokeless powder, 3,000 harpoon heads, 4,500 timing fuses and detonators, and 1,400 bottles of beer for the after-action celebration. It took two weeks for the Norwegian Ministry of Fisheries and Agriculture to approve the export of whaling supplies to Britain, which naturally hindered the vessels' departure for the southern seas.[2]

The whaling captains had to think carefully about their departure anyway, as German cruisers and submarines were already at work throughout the Atlantic, waiting for large, slow targets like floating factories. With too few naval vessels available for convoy duty, the whaling vessels would have to make their own way south, zigzagging slowly to the whaling grounds. As of 7 October, no British whalers had left port, while twelve had already left neutral Norway. No British vessel was expected on the grounds before 20 December, nearly two weeks into the usual whaling season. Equally frustrating was that Norway and Japan, the neutrals on the whaling grounds, tended to sell their surplus to German firms, so Britain would not only face its own shortfall but also the prospect of having to win a bidding war with its enemy for the neutrals' oil.[3]

With the delayed start for the British expeditions, British officials began to contemplate the drawbacks of adhering to the 1937 convention, which would prevent them from whaling past 8 March. Instead of three full months of whaling at a time of crisis, British whalers might barely get two full months, leaving the eight expeditions about 190 whaling days—or thirty thousand tons—short.[4] To officials in the Ministry of Food and owners of whaling companies, the obvious answer was to extend the season, allowing each factory an extra day at the end of the season as compensation for each day missed at the beginning because of the war. Edward Clement-Davies, a prominent Liberal Party MP and board member of Unilever, begged the ministry for the extra time, which would result in not only more oil produced but also lower prices, down from roughly £40 to £31 per ton. Clement-Davies was so persistent that his contact in the ministry asked not to meet with him anymore, classifying him as a "bore."[5]

The only impediment was the 1937 convention, so many British leaders concluded that it would have to be amended or abrogated. Even before Clement-Davies called for dumping the convention, Alban Dobson of the fisheries ministry raised the possibility on 1 September, in the mistaken belief that Britain was already at war. Others advocated amending the terms. Few thought that the convention was worth more than the value of whale oil in a time of war. The convention presented two options for legal changes. First, amendments could be negotiated by the member states. One drawback to that approach was that the US Senate was notoriously slow to ratify such protocols, so an amendment was unlikely to be legal by March 1940. A greater challenge was the status of Germany as a member state, since even the most optimistic person held out little hope of German cooperation. As the US State Department pointed out to the British Foreign Office, however, the mere fact of war did not obviate the need to follow diplomatic protocol to the letter, and a few Britons reached the same conclusion.[6]

If amendment was impossible, the other legal option was abrogation. Just about every convention has an article spelling out the steps for withdrawal, and in this case those steps consisted of simple notification to the other signatory powers by 1 January of any particular year, taking effect on 1 July. Whalers advocated an amended form of abrogation, simply denouncing the treaty and announcing new rules as the cleanest, quickest method of withdrawal, but British officials hesitated at something so unilateral. R. Cox, a legal adviser in the Foreign Office, argued "that H.M.G. are in charge of this agreement . . . and . . . if we want to get out of the Agreement we ought—as a long view—to do the thing properly."[7] His colleague J. M. Addis warned that "our moral reputation would be damaged" in the eyes of valued neutrals such as Norway, Japan, and the United States. Was it, he asked, worth 13,000 tons of oil? He reminded his superiors that such a sum of oil would come into a country already awash in oil because Britain had bought the previous season's take from Norway, leaving 240,000 tons—a normal year's supply—in the nation's storage tanks.[8]

The main proponent of extending the season was Sir H. L. French of the Ministry of Food. Diplomatic process mattered far less to him than procurement of fat, and he won the debates on the subject with his incisive comments and warnings to prepare for the worst. It is possible that he used the idea of abrogation as a sort of stalking horse. With officials in the Foreign Office busy arguing about abrogating or amending the agreement, he had effectively assured that there would be some kind of extension of the whaling season. In early December, before the first British vessels reached the whaling grounds, French had argued that whale oil was the "great stand-by against the shortage of fats." The British government needed to do everything it could to increase the supply so as to drive down the price paid by ordinary consumers, while simultaneously keeping oil out of the hands of Germany. He also argued that laying in a big stockpile was necessary in case of a long war, in part because it would free up whaling vessels for convoy duty. Extending the season, he concluded persuasively, was obviously reasonable and a source of harm to no one.[9]

The matter of harm became the core of the Foreign Office's subsequent campaign in favor of simply notifying the neutrals that it was going to extend the season unilaterally. The Foreign Office noted that the Germans generally caught about six thousand whales per season, so if the extra British days yielded anything less than that it would still be a boon to the whale stocks. In addition, the fisheries ministry declared that the humpback whale was off-limits, in line with the decision made by conferees at the 1939 whaling meeting. Not only could the British bill the humpback move as a conservation decision, but also, since the United States had not accepted the humpback limits yet, Britain could hold some high ground when the United States inevitability complained about the extension. It did complain, vigorously for a bit, but then quietly acknowledged that it would not make an issue of the extension as long as Britain was discreet. In the end, the British took only 52 extra whaling days, about 6.5 per factory vessel, and caught only about 600 more whales, for roughly 7,000 tons of oil. As Dobson noted, those were small gains compared to what French had promised; and to make matters worse the Ministry of Food and Ministry of Transport had already decided to commandeer all but two floating factories for convoy use in the 1940–41 season, cutting the whalers loose rather than supporting them. That decision reflected a recurrent theme: that if London supported its whaling companies, then it also looked on them as instruments of the state.[10]

Dobson, who was a long-time fisheries bureaucrat and a future secretary of the IWC, prophetically commented that the extension had produced slim gains in comparison to provoking the displeasure of the United States. He anticipated, correctly, that the United States would remember this controversy in future whaling conferences. The irony was that the lead negotiator for the United States, Remington Kellogg, was probably fundamentally sympathetic with Britain's position, but the extension was a key piece of evidence that British whaling companies were unusually powerful and not at all sympathetic to conservation—a conclusion that would only be reinforced as the war went on.

As the war became desperate in 1940, whaling naturally fell from the discussions with other countries. Occasionally the Japanese would inquire about British plans, but London assumed that any information that went to Tokyo would quickly boomerang to Berlin, so those exchanges were brief.[11] The major move was the sudden German invasion of Norway in April 1940.

A handful of Norwegian factory vessels still at sea made it to the United States, which clandestinely put them to use hunting sperm whales in 1941, but the rest were either destroyed or captured by German raiders like the *Pelikan*, which brought three ships back to France as prizes in 1941.[12] The other major fleets of factory ships, the British and the Japanese, were worn down by convoy duty or sunk by bombs or torpedoes, so that both were useless by the end of the war. Catcher vessels were pressed into service as minesweepers and submarine chasers; while they suffered comparatively few losses (32 of the 240 British and Norwegian catchers had been sunk by the end of 1942), the survivors took a beating and, at the end of the war, required a great deal of effort to convert back to whaling.[13]

The diminution of the fleet led to two indirect consequences. First, other nations thought more seriously about launching whaling expeditions. Australia had long tried to drum up a whaling operation, citing its proximity to whaling grounds that only the Japanese could compete for. New Zealand inquired about splitting an expedition with the Australians. One scientist in New Zealand concluded that sustainable whaling could generate 300,000 tons of oil per year, and New Zealand had a legitimate claim to 50,000 of those tons, which in turn could generate between £2 and £3.5 million per year.[14] Norwegian whalers had shown no interest, in large part because whaling fleets based in Australia would have a problem getting the oil back to European or American markets. With the advent of war, officials in Canberra and even a veterans' organization saw an opportunity in the wartime destruction of vessels to put an Australian stamp on the whaling industry.[15] Likewise, Argentines increased their calls for a widespread presence in the "no man's seas" of Antarctica by starting a pelagic whaling business.[16] These national dreams would play an important role in the deliberations of the established whaling nations as the war came to an end.

Second, whalers adopted a shoot-on-sight mentality for any cetacean unlucky enough to swim within harpoon range. Remington Kellogg reviewed the data from Argentine land stations for 1940–41 and 1941–42 (with Norway occupied, data from factory vessels was apparently hard to come by) and saw red flags everywhere. The data for fin whales showed that the average length dropped from about 68 to 65.4 feet in just one season, and a suspiciously large number had either no size data or came in exactly at the 55-foot minimum. As Kellogg noted, whaling researchers had long deduced that any short whale would be registered as a minimum-size whale to avoid penalties or bad publicity. He also concluded that whatever was happening on these land stations was almost certainly being replicated in the pelagic expeditions because they had the same British and Norwegian financing, which probably determined the policies. "No serious effort is being made to make any selection from those present on the whaling grounds" during the present emergency, Kellogg concluded. He guessed correctly: as one whaler noted, the Norwegians ignored all of the rules in 1940–41.[17]

British, and to a lesser extent Norwegian, actions during the first two years of the war set the stage for Kellogg to assert US leadership in international whaling policy. As late as 1939 he had made clear that the United States would never convene a whaling conference itself, but the steady decimation of the whale stocks had bothered him greatly for years. The wartime devastation of the world's whaling infrastructure opened a window of opportunity, and the destruction of the world order made possible American leadership on a whole range of issues. Kellogg intended to remake the world's whaling industry in the mold of American Progressive reformers, promoting conservation and efficiency by limiting the power of British and Norwegian whaling companies.

COMPETING VISIONS OF THE POSTWAR WHALING INDUSTRY

As the war dragged on, the food shortage, particularly a shortage of fats, was a growing concern. In its obsession to find the fat necessary to feed its people, the British government chose to emphasize increased whaling over increased conservation of whales. The Norwegian government in exile, while focused primarily on regaining its sovereignty, also worried about the severe food shortage that it would inherit when German occupation ended; whaling was an important part of the solution to that problem. Even in the well-fed United States, the global food shortage was a matter of long-range concern as the war wound down. While American officials emphasized the need for conservation of whales, they acknowledged that the demand for fat was a serious political problem in both the Allied and defeated nations, even though they suspected that the British exaggerated the dimensions of the crisis.

Even as the Allies generally agreed that whaling could be part of the solution to the fat crisis, they split over how to prioritize whaling, and that division reflected a larger one about how to deal with the industry in the postwar world. The United States, with Kellogg's prodding, decided that it would have to take the lead if conservation was to have a chance of success. The British were equally determined to retain leadership, perhaps in part because of annoyance about American superiority, real and imagined (in Washington and London). Norwegians tended to see the need for more conservation measures, but they saw whaling as one of the few means of gaining the foreign currency that their country needed to rebuild. And of course there were contradictions in each nation's position, none more important than the developing US insistence that whaling had to be open to anyone, which undermined efforts at limiting hunting even as it fit within the larger pattern of US visions for a postwar order based on expanded trade.

In 1942, when it finally appeared that Britain would survive the war, even if the end was far from clear, British officials began to think about postwar whaling operations. On 6 January, the minister of agriculture and fisheries expressed a desire to begin planning for postwar whaling, a suggestion that struck fisheries bureaucrat Alban Dobson as a bit premature. "At the present moment," he commented, "we have not the slightest idea whether there will be any factory ships left," and the best hope might be to "pinch some" from the Japanese.[18] By August, when the war had turned slightly better for the Allies, he had an exchange with H. K. Salvesen about the international agreements. In response to a lengthy and specific letter from Salvesen on the need to remove restrictions on whaling, Dobson argued, "I am most anxious that whatever it may be found necessary to do by way of suspending any of the existing restrictions on whaling should not be done in a way which would prejudice our position when the time comes to make fresh Agreements for the regulation of Whaling under normal peace-time conditions." Salvesen countered, "I am of the view that immediate production of whale oil on a large scale as soon as possible after the conclusion of hostilities is more important even than the preservation of the stock of whales."[19]

At the end of the summer, the government-funded Discovery Committee and scientist Neil Mackintosh stiffened Dobson's resolve with a strongly worded resolution that international restrictions on whaling had to be put in place during the war, while the industry was weak, or else the slow decline of the whale stocks would recommence after the war. "The present war marks the close of an era of modern whaling," the committee concluded, "for when the industry is resumed after the war it must surely be conducted in different political, economic and technical conditions." Now was the time to restrict the "national and vested interests, which formerly handicapped efforts to conserve the stock." It simply was not possible to keep taking thirty-three thousand whales per year, and "the only real remedy to overhunting is to hunt less." Whale populations had probably not grown during the war, despite the lack of hunting, because mammals did not reproduce as quickly as fish. Prewar efforts at conservation had been arbitrary because scientists did not have enough information to set a "maximum permanent yield," but the war presented an opportunity to set a catch limit below the 1930s figures and stick to it. A stable catch limit over several years would allow scientists to build population models for the hunted species that might allow them to predict how many whales could be taken without causing long-term diminution of the species.[20] In the next few months, at least four floating factories went down under German fire, reminding everyone that the resumption of "normal peace-time conditions" was still far away.[21]

The reference to "maximum permanent yield" is fascinating, echoing the Progressive utilitarian goal of the greatest good for the greatest number for the longest time. The Discovery Committee admitted that it had not produced enough data to determine what the maximum level should be, but it made clear that it was desirable to find that level and make it policy. After the war, maximum sustainable yield (MSY), essentially the same idea, gained prominence as the goal of most fisheries management. The US government, as historian Carmel Finley has demonstrated, adopted MSY as an official diplomatic goal in 1949. She argues that it was a political and economic construct before it was a scientific one, based on the promotion of free access to the seas, and that it created a false sense of security that the oceans could be managed. Scientists and bureaucrats could point to MSY as a target based on science, even if the science was an afterthought.[22] That the idea came out of the Discovery Committee in a sharp critique of the national whaling industry suggests that the evolution of MSY thinking might have been different for whales than fish. Mackintosh, Bergersen, and Kellogg were all on the same page in arguing that whale populations were overtaxed but could be rebuilt and produce more in the long run if industry's hand could be swatted away from the tiller.

By November 1942, the Ministry of Agriculture and Fisheries was trying to figure out how to create policies that would meet the concerns of both Mackintosh and Salvesen. It proposed a three-step program, beginning with meetings of various interested departments, moving next to consultations with the whaling companies, and ending with international discussions. Two mysteries loomed: how much oil would Europe need after the war, and how many ships would be left to pursue whales? Beyond those questions, the ministry would need a plan for reconversion of old whaling vessels and would have to decide if any of the prewar rules needed to be weakened.[23] Reconciling the interests of the various departments would not be easy, though. The Colonial Office tended to side with the Discovery Committee, which operated under its aegis. The Ministry of Food never met a whale that was not delicious, and the Ministry of War Transport took its cue from Salvesen's interest in having newer and better ships under his command. The Ministry of Agriculture and Fisheries regularly saw the tension between those who harvested sea creatures and those who studied them and usually tried to split the difference, while the Foreign Office seemed content largely to act as referee for the agencies while protecting Britain's reputation.

When British policy makers came together on 8 December 1942, they settled in the middle of the road. They agreed first of all that British whalers should get to sea as soon as possible after the war ended and that the Ministry of War Transport should work to expand the British presence on the expeditions that went out from Britain and Norway. If need be, the whalers should get extended time on the hunting grounds, using the 1940 extensions as precedents. Finally, there should be tweaking of rules to allow more efficiency on the grounds. At the same time, though, the conferees agreed that Britain would not opt out of the 1937 convention, and it would endorse the call for a global whaling catch limit as a means to avoid excessive postwar hunting.[24]

The meeting with the whaling leaders took place nine days later. H. K. Salvesen, Rupert Trouton, and E. G. Baines, three of Britain's leading whalers, met with Dobson and his assistants, who began by announcing the results of the interdepartmental meeting. The whalers countered that they needed to denounce the 1937 agreement. Given the demand for fat and the shortage of vessels, whaling would have to operate from October to May whenever the weather would allow it, which the 1937 convention prohibited. Salvesen believed that amendment was unlikely because Argentina would not want to let Britons and Norwegians stay on the whaling grounds that long, if the result would be to drive down oil prices.[25] The whalers had enough support in various ministries to keep up the pressure on their government throughout the war, especially as the dimensions of the food crisis expanded.

Moving to international discussions would be a bit more difficult. Norway's government in exile naturally had to act cautiously in general, but in whaling matters in particular it had a scattered constituency that was frequently at odds during the best of times. The only good thing about the exile, from a whaling standpoint, was that it brought Birger Bergersen, one of Norway's cetacean experts, into regular contact with Neil Mackintosh of the Discovery Committee. Together, they proposed to write to Remington Kellogg for his opinion on the scientific issues that underlay the whaling proposals; Dobson thought better of the idea, insisting that it was up to the US government to seek Kellogg's advice. Dobson was no fan of that government, dolefully commenting at one point that international efforts had to begin soon because "of the delay that invariably occurs in securing the concurrence of the U.S.A."[26]

Circumstances would conspire to keep an international meeting from happening until January 1944, and the British government went into that meeting without a clear policy. Since early in 1943, Salvesen and other members of the Whaler Section of the Ministry of War Transport had been making a concerted effort to play the starvation card, working hard to convince British bureaucrats that whaling was part of the answer to the food problem. In that effort, they got an assist from the UN Relief and Rehabilitation Administration, whose agricultural subcommittee called for expanded postwar whaling. The Whaler Section's campaign was so effective that abrogation of the prewar agreements came up for consideration again in London, and the section found widespread support for its emphasis on fat production.[27]

The American position on whaling, like the British one, was evolving as the war progressed. Two months before the Pearl Harbor attack, Kellogg had connected the war to postwar conservation of whales when he suggested that the imminent war would at least end Japan's rapacious use of the seas. Despite that, no one in the US State Department seemed too concerned about whaling except when the British asked that a blind eye, at least, be turned to their whaling in the early years of the war. When the formal British proposal for a conference arrived in Washington in March 1943, the initial American response was to ask Kellogg what he thought, a remarkable abdication of authority by State Department officials. Later that year, when the meeting had been postponed, one official asked Kellogg whom the department should send to lead the delegation in London. Kellogg demurred, saying only that it had to be someone very competent, with a thorough understanding of policy, or else the United States risked being "seriously embarrassed" by the formidable British and Norwegian delegations.[28] The department agreed and appointed him.

Over the course of 1943, the US government resolved to "assert more leadership with respect to the international whaling situation."[29] Assistant Secretary Breckinridge Long had urged his assistants to take the initiative in international matters where appropriate, and the people thinking about whaling concluded that demands for sperm oil as an industrial lubricant alone made assuming a leadership role worthwhile. At the end of the year, Secretary of State Cordell Hull sent a blunt memo to President Franklin Roosevelt: "There are indications that if the international whaling conferences continue to be held in Europe their success and soundness as to conclusions may be adversely affected by strong economic and political interests."[30] Those words came almost verbatim from Remington Kellogg, who had convinced his admirers in the State Department that men like Salvesen had too much influence over whaling policy when the conferences were held in Europe. The solution was to take the delegations far from the owners and unions who saw whales almost wholly in economic terms. Kellogg acknowledged that the United States had a stake in whaling because of its use of sperm oil, but it appears that he used this "strategic" argument largely as a cover to advance his conservationist agenda.[31]

The meeting was finally called for London in early January 1944, but it had to be postponed a week as Kellogg's plane was fogged in at Bermuda. When he arrived, he was greeted by an impassioned speech by John Maud of the Ministry of Food, who was worried about a possible million-ton shortfall of fat. The decision to let Maud give the opening address, even if he expressed a desire "not to kill the goose that laid the golden eggs," underlined the increasing British focus on whales as food, although canned whale meat was never popular. Americans expressed sympathy for the food crisis but emphasized that there was a difference between a short-term emergency response and allowing whalers to get back to prewar catch levels. The meeting was striking in its odd combination of friendly agreement and deep differences. The rules for the first postwar whaling season were modified without much heated exchange, and there was general agreement that conservation could be achieved while allowing some expanded hunting to address the fat crisis. Delegates agreed to Birger Bergersen's suggestion that there ought to be a quota for Antarctic whaling based on the blue whale unit, which equated one blue whale to two fin whales or two and a half humpback whales. Conferees discussed setting a global cap on Antarctic whaling (sometimes called a global quota or an Antarctic quota) between 15,000 and 20,000 BWU, settling on 16,000.[32] Yet there was an undercurrent of dissatisfaction. As it turned out, the whalers were unhappy with the result of the 1944 meeting. In fact, Salvesen afterward resigned his position as chair of the Whaler Section of the Ministry of War Transport because of the lack of support he got from Dobson, and it was at this meeting that Kellogg was discreetly given access to British officials' files.[33]

Salvesen seemed to declare war on Dobson in 1944. When Dobson was quoted in the newspaper on matters of whaling, there was a good chance that Salvesen would respond with an angry letter. At one point, Salvesen demanded that the *Times* (London) confirm Dobson's assertion that whaling was curtailed by the weather after late March, which Salvesen called "pure nonsense" and evidence that there needed to be at least one qualified expert at the international conferences. Likewise, Salvesen expressed dismay to the editors of the *Guardian* (Manchester) when Dobson was quoted as saying that most harpooners were Norwegian. Neither of these comments was especially egregious on Dobson's part, and Salvesen's responses suggested the depths of his frustration. Nor was it a temporary frustration, as Salvesen attempted to block his colleagues from contributing £10 each to Dobson's retirement present many years later.[34] Dobson got the message, describing Salvesen as "an autocrat," "a very difficult member of society," and a man whose financial interest made it necessary to treat him with reserve and skepticism.[35] It seems as if no one actually liked Salvesen; Kellogg and the other scientists thought that he was short-sighted, and many of his fellow whalers apparently found him to be a difficult competitor. Even the man who replaced him as head of the firm, Gerald Elliott, acknowledged that Salvesen "was only satisfied when he had demonstrated his intellectual superiority and dominated the battlefield."[36] More than any other person, Salvesen was responsible for Kellogg's conclusion that future whaling conferences could not be held in Europe.

The 1944 protocol was stopgap, meant to set rules for just one postwar whaling season, the date of which was unknowable. Norway's government was in no position to agree to anything more, and the United States made clear that it would host the next conference to establish a permanent commission. No one knew when the war would end, and the matter of a few weeks' difference in its ending date could have a large impact on whether any expeditions could catch whales in any particular season—assuming that there would even be any ships left to catch whales, which was looking increasingly unlikely. It was also unknown if any neutral states were making preparations to get whaling underway when peacetime returned.

Most observers assumed that the 1944 protocol would apply just to the 1945–46 season, leaving plenty of time for the organization of a conference by the United States to establish permanent rules starting in 1946–47. A Norwegian expedition based in the United States went south late in 1944, though, before enough ratifications had come in to make the protocol official, and there were also the expeditions off Peru catching sperm whales between 1941 and 1943. The level of confusion caused by these expeditions was indicative of the problems of whaling diplomacy before the creation of the International Whaling Commission. Governments wondered whether the protocol had to be ratified for it to cover the 1944–45 season, and they discussed whether one Norwegian expedition was enough to count as a season.[37]

Some of those questions remained unresolved, as the United States failed to pull together a conference for a permanent solution in the next year, and the war finally ended in Europe in May 1945. All of that set the stage for one last European conference, in November 1945 in London, with the express purpose of establishing temporary rules until the permanent commission could come together. British leaders were dismayed by how slowly things were moving forward, but they agreed to let the United States call the general conference later if the first one would be in London. The food shortage appeared to be getting worse, with British officials complaining about unspecified mismanagement in the United States that had led to less available fat than anticipated.[38] The Ministry of Food was still pushing its claim that it was "absurd" to have some arbitrary conclusion to the whaling season rather than letting nature close the season with bad weather.[39] The new government of Prime Minister Clement Attlee agreed, and in the fall it advocated an extension of the season into late March or April to compensate for the late start that most expeditions would get, knowing that the United States would be displeased.[40]

In October, the British Foreign Office sent out a seven-point agenda for the next month's meeting, with the three key points being extension of the season, setting a quota in terms of blue whale units, and "ventilating" ideas about a permanent commission.[41] The British, Norwegian, and US governments were largely in agreement about what should be done for 1946–47, so the real question was how the long-term issues would be dealt with. In May, the US State Department had pled that it was too busy to plan a conference, but it had the time to prepare several detailed documents by November. The first document spelled out the principles of conservation, emphasizing the idea of "maximum sustainable yield." The license to use a resource did not grant the right to destroy the resource, whose ownership still resided in the hands of the people. The author, Ira Gabrielson of the US Fish and Wildlife Service, then laid out a conservative definition of conservation: "The first fundamental of any sound conservation program is the preservation of an adequate and healthy breeding stock, therefore the basic principles of managing natural resources are analogous to the principles of animal husbandry." He finished with a doomsday scenario that would get widespread coverage in 1948 in books by William Vogt and Fairfield Osborn, that growing population and improved technology would expand the demand on resources, implying that sustainable use would be nearly impossible without drastic measures. Although the document was labeled as a statement on sanctuaries, it was really a warning about using the postwar food crisis as cover for expanding the whaling industry.[42]

The other particularly important statement spelled out by the United States was its idea for a permanent commission, one that could "make recommendations regarding minimum lengths of whales, quotas, lengths of seasons, protected species, sanctuaries, and notification of take." Members would include "the persons best qualified to act in the interests of all countries concerned for the conservation and best utilization of the resource," not just whalers from the major whaling countries. The committee would be driven by scientific expertise in making its recommendations, but in most cases it would be up to the member governments to accept or reject those suggestions. The goal would be to promote effective management and eliminate the need for annual protocols to be approved by the US Senate or other slow-moving governmental bodies, but the committee would not be vested with much real power to act independently. Instead, its reliance on science would be the source of most of its authority, as scientific evidence would presumably persuade recalcitrant members to conserve the resource. In order to broaden membership in this committee, the United States also proposed that member states not export whaling ships or equipment to nonmember states.[43]

The conference hosts, though, had the honor of giving the welcoming address to set the tone for the meeting, and that task fell to A. R. W. Harrison of the Ministry of Food, not someone from the Foreign Office or the Ministry of Agriculture and Fisheries. Harrison's people had their own document, one that showed a shortage of about 2.4 million tons of fat based on prewar global production of about 10.3 million tons.[44] Harrison made clear that his minister kept a close eye on what the British housewife was thinking, and she was thinking that she needed a lot more fat and a little more sugar. He was pleased, then, to hear conferees describe the whale as food, and he called on them to do everything possible to use whales in the subsequent two years: "I think that from our point of view it would be a tragedy if any international machinery were to get in the way of that increased production."[45] For Britain, the war's legacy was hunger almost as much as victory.

The lively discussion that ensued showed that splits were not so much along lines of nationality as along lines of occupation. Bergersen, Mackintosh, and Kellogg were never in open disagreement and sometimes banded together to shoot down ideas from Salvesen and other whalers. Mackintosh was the least vocal of the three, no doubt because of the pressure he felt from his government and possibly the first-hand evidence of a food shortage. But Kellogg and Bergersen effectively fought the conservationist fight, giving in on such issues as the four-month season for ships that arrived late while preserving, against heavy pressure, the opening date of 8 December and the Antarctic quota of sixteen thousand BWU.[46] Kellogg's success seemed not to play as well with Dobson, who found himself siding with Salvesen more than usual. As the conference came to its conclusion, Dobson rose to address the members with "the plainness of the laity." The first thing he targeted was the complexity of getting the rules revised, in part because of Ireland's failure to ratify but more because the US Senate was so cumbersome, which was the opening into a larger attack on the United States, despite saying that he did not want to "put all of the onus on the United States."[47]

Perhaps the Americans looked jowly and well-fed, prompting the grilling that they got. Dobson felt compelled to remind them that Britain was still in crisis, "dealing with war conditions." He accused the US delegation of sticking to the letter of the law when it was obviously not appropriate. He noted that no German or Japanese delegations were present, which a strictly legal position might have required. Yet, with Europe starving, Americans were more interested, he implied, in legal minutia than the big picture. Whalers could not take the full quota under current circumstances, so why were Americans trying to so hard to hold them to unreasonable rules?[48]

Dobson and Kellogg generally got along well, so this plain talking at a diplomatic meeting suggested deep British frustration with the unwillingness of the United States to play an appropriate role. The United States would not call the conference it had promised, it was unsympathetic to the fats crisis, it never moved quickly to solve diplomatic problems, and it had managed to make Salvesen look sympathetic. In the spring of 1946, the British pleaded for international cooperation to extend the whaling season into late March and then into May. To New Zealand, Britain's record at "the forefront in whale conservation measures" proved that the situation must be desperate, which was reason enough to support the request.[49] The petition met with some sympathy in the United States too, until Assistant Secretary of State Dean Acheson finally drew the line, telegraphing that he hoped that Great Britain "will find it in interest of community of nations to defend integrity and established procedure of whale conservation agreements."[50] The Norwegian government also argued that the extension would not generate sufficient gains to offset the damage. The starvation argument would go only so far.

THE UNITED STATES TAKES THE LEAD

Dobson's criticisms did not register in the US State Department, which took its time organizing the long-promised conference to establish a permanent whaling commission. It is unclear what caused the delay, but at least part of the blame could be traced to the department's problem in figuring out how to fit whaling into a larger global strategy. The proposed whaling commission was just one of many organizations on the table as the world moved from war to peace. With the organization of the United Nations and the economic agencies of the Bretton Woods agreements, as well as offshoots like the World Health Organization and Food and Agriculture Organization, the United States did not want the whaling commission to be an outlier but neither was it as important to the United States as other agencies. Even if the whaling commission did not fit under a larger organization, it had to fit into a US vision of what the world should look like. The immediate impact of that decision was that Remington Kellogg would have to accept more oversight from State Department officials than he was used to, which meant that conservation would not be as important.

Dobson was already nagging the US embassy in April 1946 about the lack of progress on the conference. Even Kellogg's gift of three cartons of Hershey bars (perhaps a direct effort to alleviate the fat shortage) was not enough to buy his silence, as he reasserted in July that he needed an agenda if he was going to get the friendly cooperation of the British Ministry of Food and the agriculture specialists in his own department. His exasperation bubbled over: "It seems a little odd that we should be held up by another participating country who are not, in fact, interested in whaling."[51] The US State Department had a person working full-time on drafting the agenda, but it was still a slow process. As US diplomat William Flory noted, the department wanted a full review of all previous agreements with an eye toward crafting one that would supplant them all and clear up the "legal difficulties which have been accumulating year by year."[52] While the State Department was plodding along, the food crisis was pushing the British toward violating the previous conventions. Regarding the few remaining Japanese whaling vessels, the Ministry of Food declared that it was "absolutely essential they operate next season," and the ministry encouraged the Dutch to start whaling too.[53] The Ministry of Food had great influence within the British government, and the Foreign Office was already debating the merits of ignoring the ending date from the 1945 whaling protocol. One official, mixing his metaphors, advised that the "fabric of these International Agreements is rapidly being undermined."[54]

Unknown to Dobson, who had retired in July, US officials were also discussing his role at the conference. The embassy in London recommended that he chair the meeting, but the consensus in Washington was that it was Kellogg's time to lead. The fallback was Bergersen, not Dobson, who was neither the most senior member of his delegation nor totally reliable when it came to controlling the British industry. Whoever got the chair, Flory wanted to be sure that Salvesen would not be there, making a point to the British ambassador that the United States would not bring an industrial adviser so neither should Britain. The British brought Salvesen anyway.[55]

The first formal sign that foreign governments received from Washington came on 2 October 1946, when the State Department sent out "save-the-date" invitations to nineteen nations. No agenda was sent, nor anything particularly useful for the meeting that was to begin in seven weeks, on 20 November. The formal agenda got to Britain on 18 October, but it did not make it to Norway in time for that delegation to see it before the meeting began. The agenda featured few surprises to anyone who had been paying attention, with one New Zealand diplomat calling it "quite unexceptional."[56] The biggest surprise was an omission: there was no proposal to ban the export of whaling materials to nonmember states. This change reflected a major shift in US policy, as Kellogg had to give ground to those officials who were formulating a global postwar strategy of freer trade. They were most concerned with how whaling would fit into the new International Trade Organization, a proposal from the Bretton Woods meeting that was a distant ancestor of today's World Trade Organization. Otherwise, the proposals focused on older ideas about the composition and governance of the permanent commission that nearly everyone agreed had to be created.

The most important element of the proposed commission structure was the objection mechanism. The finished convention would include a schedule of regulations "which are susceptible of change from time to time depending on the conditions of the stocks of whales, of biological and scientific evidence, world requirements for fats and oils, and other factors that may change from time to time."[57] The new commission would have the right to amend the schedule, presumably based on scientific evidence. The draft convention required a two-thirds vote of the members to pass an amendment, but it also allowed any government to file an objection to the amendment within ninety days of formal notice that the amendment had been approved, which would allow that nation's whalers to ignore the amendment. This objection mechanism was controversial from the day it was proposed, but it echoed the kind of thinking that had established a veto for each permanent member of the UN Security Council: a powerful nation should not have to accept being outvoted by weaker nations. Likewise, nations should not be forced to choose between sacrificing their interests or leaving the commission. US diplomats feared that states would be disgruntled and leave the commission, causing its collapse. That, in turn, would strike a blow against the principle of international cooperation.

Norwegian response to the US proposal was mixed. The Norwegian Whaling Council, the Hvalrådet, considered it a mistake to invite countries that had not signed the 1937 convention or even "uttered any wish to participate in the agreement."[58] On other points there was a range of opinion. Some Norwegians wanted to limit the number and power of the whale catchers attached to each expedition, while others thought that such a move would hurt Norwegian interests and would be irrelevant once a global catch limit was imposed. Most agreed that each expedition should carry two inspectors, but the conferees could not agree on whether they should be from the flag nation or from a foreign power. All agreed that the biggest threat was that new whaling nations such as the Netherlands or the United States would demand a national quota as a means of removing the advantage that Norwegians enjoyed based on their expertise.[59]

Some British officials called the US proposal the worst of both worlds, while others thought it was not only an advance but fundamentally what His Majesty's government had proposed earlier. Fisheries officials thought that the lack of national quotas would lead to chaos on the high seas, with ships having to stop whaling suddenly (a prescient comment), but Salvesen believed that national quotas would lead to outrageous requests by countries with no whaling history and that poorly run expeditions would leave whales in the seas. No one seemed to like the objection scheme, with one memo calling it "thoroughly vicious." All agreed that the US idea to put whaling under the Food and Agriculture Organization of the United Nations was premature at best; a far better solution was to have an independent commission in Europe, far away from US efforts to take over whaling diplomacy—which, of course, was one of the American goals.[60]

In the long run, the most important development of this conference might have been what was left out: any attempt to embargo whaling equipment shipments to nonmember states, which had been a US proposal in

1945. When British fisheries official Dobson expressed surprise, one US diplomat reported that it was not appropriate "to include that kind of economic sanction in a strictly conservation measure."[61] Bergersen, of the Norwegian delegation, later expressed his disappointment that the embargo had garnered so little support in 1946 and had lost its American sponsor, since "rational objections were non-existent."[62] This shift made evident that Kellogg had lost control of the US proposals, since he had told Bergersen as recently as April 1946 that only export controls could compel nations to join the whaling commission.[63] The US government was committed to a more open economic world, so Kellogg's desire for conservation had to yield. Instead of using the stick of sanctions to get nations on board, the US had chosen the carrot of the objection system.

What already promised to be an interesting meeting because of Norwegian and British ambivalence started to look even spicier as two controversies erupted in the late summer of 1946. The first was a Dutch-Norwegian feud over Norwegian labor laws, which was really about Norway's position in the whaling industry. There was a consensus among the industry leaders and scientists in Norway that Antarctic whale stocks were in decline; as Bergersen reported to Kellogg, the statistics from the 1945–46 season were depressingly bad, with whales few, lean, and far between. The number of blue whale units caught per day of catcher effort was below one for the first time ever, and the yield of oil per catcher day was down by 30 percent. As Bergersen noted, the data only reinforced how little anyone knew about the workings of that ecosystem.[64] Rather than whales rebuilding their numbers during the wartime whaling holiday, they were probably suffering from a natural fluctuation in population in the Antarctic seas. Whalers assumed that the stocks would have expanded, much as a fish population would.[65]

There was another consensus: that Norway's hard-won place in the industry had been slipping away even before the war and that drastic measures were necessary to stanch the flow. The Norwegian Parliament's solution was to make it illegal for Norwegians to work for whaling expeditions from countries that had not sponsored whaling before the war. While several nations were plotting to begin whaling, the immediate threats came from Sweden and the Netherlands. Neither country could hope to be efficient whalers without trained harpooners, and the vast majority of those in Europe were Norwegian. This was the choke point that Oslo hoped to squeeze. The Swedes soon dropped their whaling plans, but the Dutch were far along, with a bankroll of 15 million florins from the crown prince and encouragement from the British Ministry of Food.[66] Rather than back down, the Dutch made it a very public issue, fighting hard for the principle of free employment. They received support from some Norwegians, who noted that employment in whaling had declined from a peak of 7,000 Norwegians to only 2,000. These were good jobs that had been lost, and all that the government's actions would accomplish would be the hiring of expatriate instead of loyal Norwegians, they charged. One angry whaler even called it a "Nazi-law," a brutal insult in the land of Quisling.[67]

The government in Oslo would not back down, though, even when the Dutch took their complaint to the November 1946 whaling meeting. As historian William Hitchcock has demonstrated, starvation in the western and northern portions of Holland was widespread in the last few months of the war, and no doubt the Dutch recalled the lack of help that came their way. One Dutch delegate explained, "The Netherlands is very scarce on fats and on foreign currency, too, and the Netherlands was forced to enter the whaling business." That delegate also hinted that the Netherlands would not be able to ratify the convention if the country was unable to get the skilled labor it needed to work as efficiently as other members of the convention. Despite Dutch demands, the negotiators decided that this matter could not be resolved at the conference.[68]

Norway benefited from US silence on the issue, and it is possible that there was a quid pro quo relating to a second controversy, the resumption of Japanese whaling. Unbeknownst to almost everyone outside Tokyo, Gen. Douglas MacArthur had authorized Japanese whaling companies to begin refurbishing ships early in 1946. He, like the British, was motivated by a severe food shortage on his island nation—and he did think of it as *his* island nation. He was not, however, particularly forthcoming with his allegedly allied occupiers, and he ignored the muted warnings from Washington that he should cooperate with rather than antagonize them. British diplomats engaged in some entertaining speculation about who was lying when both MacArthur and US State Department officials blamed the other for the order to resume whaling, but it is clear that MacArthur's staff moved on its own. When the Allies learned in August 1946 that the Japanese were moving toward whaling, they reacted with a mix of rage and shock.

MacArthur was not the only American who underestimated the Allied response, which threatened to disrupt larger whaling matters. In December

1946, Secretary of State James Byrnes referred to the dispute as "a seemingly minor matter," which perhaps reflected his general shortcomings as the nation's chief diplomat, but this minor matter held the potential to be the central point of contention at the whaling meeting in November.[69] The Australians and New Zealanders were determined to bring it up, the British were split on the matter, and the State Department wanted no part in having to defend MacArthur. US leaders were not pleased that MacArthur's Supreme Command for the Allied Powers (SCAP) wanted to send a representative to the whaling meeting, which would only stick a thumb in the eyes of the Allies, not to mention suggest that SCAP really did intend to send out Japanese whalers permanently.[70] Bergersen stepped in to tip the balance away from discussing SCAP's whaling interests. While he was probably grateful for the US silence on the Norwegian-Dutch dispute, he at least may have been as concerned that focusing on SCAP's expeditions would prevent reaching the central goal of setting up a permanent whaling commission. He was helped, no doubt, by a mysterious error in the State Department duplicating office, which prevented delegates from seeing documents that had been prepared on the subject.[71]

THE INTERNATIONAL CONVENTION FOR THE REGULATION OF WHALING

When the delegates convened in November 1946, they found themselves creating a new institution that was simultaneously very conservative and somehow radical. The framers of the convention followed in the US Progressive tradition of trying to reconcile the needs of industry with the need to conserve resources by using scientific expertise to frame regulations. The draft convention summarized that Progressive vision of sustainable use in the preamble, which said that "whale stocks in some areas are susceptible of natural increases if whaling is properly regulated and that increases in the size of whale stocks will permit increases in the numbers of whales which may be captured without endangering that natural resource." Even the most enthusiastic Progressives had not tried to create a global commission with as much authority as the new one would have. The codification of the objection clause protected national sovereignty, and yet commission supporters were convinced that they had found a system that would allow for cooperative work.[72]

In sharp contrast to the welcoming addresses in 1944 and 1945 about the need to see whales as swimming blocks of margarine, the 1946 meeting opened with a speech to the delegates and observers from nineteen nations about conservation and cooperation. In his brief remarks on the morning of 20 November, Acting Secretary of State Dean Acheson declared that whales are "the wards of the entire world." In only eight paragraphs, he twice labeled the whales a "common resource" and mentioned their conservation five times. Acheson's main point, though, was to emphasize the need for cooperation in the use of the world's resources. Certainly he wanted to conserve whales for future use, but he reiterated the cooperation theme often enough that it appeared he was mainly interested in fitting whaling into the larger postwar structure of international agencies that the United States was championing. In his first substantive paragraph, he argued that the conference "illustrates increasing cooperation among the nations in the solution of international conservation problems."[73] Conservation was to serve as the means toward achieving cooperation.

Delegates then heard an alternative vision of their task, as Remington Kellogg, the chair of the conference, turned the floor over to Alban Dobson before allowing anyone else to speak; the rest of the morning would be spent on mundane organizational questions. Dobson had come to the meeting in a foul mood, given the delays in pulling together the US proposal and the location. He planned to take a slow boat, he groused, because "we don't want to spend a day longer in Washington than is necessary."[74] In a speech that was about as long as Acheson's, he managed to work in "conservation" only once, instead focusing on how much of Great Britain's cultural treasure had found its way to Washington, whether Shakespeare in the Folger Library or portraits in the Corcoran Gallery. Perhaps unintentionally he was suggesting a metaphor for the transfer of political power as well: so much that had been Britain's patrimony, like global leadership and the world's largest navy, was no longer in London. When he did get to conservation at the end of his remarks, he pledged that Britain's delegation would work so that "the whaling industries of the world may be maintained and an immensely important source of food supply conserved for all time for the benefit of both the producer and the consumer in all parts of the world."[75] The language was admirably far-sighted, but British policy was still focused on hunger.

The only other address to the assembled delegates came several days later from C. Girard Davidson, assistant secretary of the US Interior

Department, who emphasized that science was the key to sustainable use. He delivered a measured but optimistic assessment of previous attempts to conserve resources, and his speech illuminated the motivation of the United States, a nation with no substantial whaling industry, in promoting a convention to regulate whaling. Not surprisingly he first broached the idea that conservation was "an appropriate field for international coopera- tion." But he quickly veered over to Acheson's territory by extolling the "principle that the various nations must get together and work out their problems in cooperation and for their mutual welfare." A matter like whal- ing was important as a practical application of that principle, a contribu- tion "to the vitality and health of international good-will."[76]

To make his point, Davidson described the thirty-year history of coop- eration on conservation in the Western Hemisphere. His first example was the North Pacific Fur Seal Convention of 1911, which came at a "dark period in the history of the resource." Once numerous, the North Pacific fur seal population had dwindled to 130,000 when the convention introduced a program of management by the United States. The 1946 census showed that the population had climbed to an astounding three million. Davidson asked, "Need we feel that we cannot be successful in conserving the whale resource with such an example before us?" Although Davidson posed the question as if the answer were obvious, in fact pelagic whaling raised issues far more complex, politically, economically, and ecologically, than the fur seal crisis. The companies involved in sealing were much smaller, only four nations pursued sealing, and scientists believed that they understood fur seal biology quite well. In contrast, at least eight nations from five conti- nents either were gearing up for whaling or already were deeply committed, and the companies that pursued whales required large amounts of capital and government support.[77] And if anything, cetologists bemoaned how little they knew about whales, which were so hard to study.

Davidson's confidence, then, was probably more appropriate given the centerpiece of his speech: US and Canadian efforts to regulate the halibut fishery off their west coast. In the late part of the nineteenth century hali- but had been incredibly abundant and lucrative, but early in the twentieth century "something was happening to this fishery." Catch per unit of effort (CPUE) data showed that it was taking six times as long to procure the same catch. Bigger and better equipment had masked that fact for years, but scientific data showed the decline "with great accuracy." Because the fishermen came from two countries and the fish wandered between juris-dictions, only an international agreement could save the fishery, and in 1923 Great Britain (for Canada) and the United States produced such a treaty. What was especially noteworthy about the treaty, in Davidson's mind, was that it established a "painstaking study of the halibut" to pro-duce the science necessary to craft regulations, which were in turn the basis of a more substantial treaty in 1930. As of 1945, there had been an increase of ten million pounds per year over the preregulation period. All it would take to save whaling would be an application of science and the spirit of cooperation.

Davidson explained that the United States had learned lessons that were global in their application. "The conservation story," he asserted, "is essentially the same the world over." He then laid out three ways of think-ing about resources in the United States that would have been familiar to anyone working on whales: abundance leads to waste, too much commer-cialization makes it hard for users to cut back in the face of decline, and hesitation to act would prevent a solution until it is was possibly too late. To top it off, the United States had to deal with the problem of states' rights, which mirrored the challenge of getting multiple nations to cooperate. On the negative side of the similarity ledger, scientists were insufficiently knowledgeable about the seas and oceans, and Davidson called on govern-ments around the world to resume oceanic research and engage in "free, complete, and unrestricted dissemination of this knowledge throughout the world." In his conclusion was the crux of the US vision for the Interna-tional Whaling Commission: The commission would be driven by scien-tific excellence in the cause of carefully managing resources that belonged to the world, and in meeting that vision it would contribute to "a more peaceful and happy future for mankind." The war's competing legacies could be seen in this speech and in those from the previous two whaling meetings. A year before, A. R. W. Harrison had focused the delegates' work by giving them the image of a hungry British housewife shopping for margarine; now Acheson and Davidson were saying that the opportunity was peace in their time.

The actual deliberations were not nearly so dramatic. Without comment, the delegates accepted two clauses from US Progressive-era laws: protection of aboriginal hunting rights for subsistence use and authorization for col-lecting whales beyond the quota for scientific purposes. Aboriginal hunting rights would be very controversial in the 1970s, and the Japanese would use scientific permits to get around the commission's ban on commercial hunting in the 1980s. Col. G. R. Powles, head of New Zealand's delegation, commented on the 1946 conference's "noticeable measure of efficiency, harmony, and informality" considering that these were diplomatic proceedings, which he attributed to the number of people who had been working together successfully on whaling matters for more than a decade, as well as the lack of political implications for the work at hand—perhaps he had been unimpressed by Acheson's comments. He also noted that delegates had worked through to agreement on many points that might have been controversial.[78] The biggest surprise of all was the unexpected arrival of a delegation from the Soviet Union, which had requested visas from the US embassy in Moscow the day after the conference began. Because the Soviets had claimed the German floating factory *Wikinger* as reparations, it was evident that they planned to join Antarctic whaling, so it was imperative to get them on board. Delegates made many minor concessions to win Soviet accession to the convention, such as a prolonged season for 1946–47; in turn, US official William Flory noted that the Soviet delegation "contributed materially to the effective operation of the Conference."[79]

The proposal that generated the most debate, the objection scheme, came up late on the Wednesday before Thanksgiving, which the delegates had agreed to treat as a holiday in deference to their American hosts. Dobson submitted the report of his subcommittee, which had the task of turning the US draft convention into a text that all could accept, and he found himself in the awkward position of critiquing his own group.[80] He began by noting that the State Department might have taken "the cue" for the proposal from British comments in favor of such a structure, but he concluded that "the setting up of the Commission has received a considerable setback." The setback was the combination of the two-thirds vote needed to change the schedule of regulations (which spelled out such things as open season, global quota, and rules for processing whales) and the ability of any nation to submit an objection within ninety days of formal notification of the passage of an amendment. Efficiency and "the conservation of whaling" would be hindered, and "we have got a less effective procedure than we had before."

Dobson then imagined a scenario in which a small nation without whaling interests might gum up the works by filing an objection to an approved amendment. Under the terms of the draft convention, other nations would get an additional ninety days to file their own objections. Perhaps the interested countries would follow with their objections, or perhaps they would see that not much was at stake with the unnamed small country and assume that the amendment was in place. If the latter were the case, Dobson feared that a major whaling country would file an objection on the 178th day, exempting itself and leaving all of the others with a different set of rules. Despite Dobson's concerns, his own committee had outvoted him six to three and had amended the proposal so that three-quarters of the convention members would have to agree to an amendment, not the original two-thirds.

Knut Lykke of the Norwegian delegation followed Dobson and argued that the new commission had to have "the power to take binding action for conservation." The three-quarters clause should "safeguard any country against changes which are not thoroughly justified," so the objection clause was unnecessary. As the New Zealander Powles noted later, a commission without an objection mechanism "would be an interesting and perhaps notable step forward in international relations, [but] it was not by any means without precedent." It would fully carry out the goals that countries had in mind when they agreed to establish a whaling commission.[81] New Zealand did not object to the objection system.

With the two most important whaling nations on record in opposition to the objection clause, it was up to those so-called small countries to justify their position. A French delegate commented that the structure allowed "member countries to safeguard their legitimate interests." Likewise, the Dutch emphasized the need to protect "the authority of each Government," which was ironic given its attempt to compel Norway to change its whaling personnel law. Paul Anziani, a French economic specialist, and William Flory, the US author of the convention draft, argued that the objection scheme was central to the very existence of the new commission. Anziani said that, without the objection system, France might face its own crisis: it was ready to invest heavily to equip land stations for catching humpback whales off Africa, a plan that made many whalers and conservationists uneasy. Anziani could imagine the commission deciding to "suppress the activities of land stations," which would leave France with the choice of losing its material investment or withdrawing from the convention. Flory then followed with an acknowledgment that the British proposal "would provide a much more satisfactory and smoother, and, possibly, a more effective administration." But "it raises the exceedingly difficult question of sovereignty—national jurisdiction." The provisions of the American draft were meant "as a protection, as an escape valve," so that a nation would be unlikely to consider withdrawal because of an amendment that hurt its interests. Dobson not only accepted that explanation without a fight, he came back a few days later with a proposal to add another 30-day period for subsequent objections, so that it could take 210 days from the end of a commission meeting to be sure who had accepted the new amendments.[82]

What Flory and Anziani might have added was that the delegates were creating something new, an agency that would curtail governments' freedom of action on the high seas and, therefore, might cause them to sacrifice some economic benefits. Because the model was untested and so many countries were rebuilding from the war, the objection clause was necessary. Without it, the Dutch, French, Soviets, and Americans likely would choose not to join the commission. In fact, the US delegates apparently explained in a committee meeting that the US Senate would never ratify the International Convention for the Regulation of Whaling (ICRW) unless the objection scheme were included.[83] One of the key lessons from the 1930s had been that if any one whaling nation refused to sign a convention, then the others would be hesitant to accept conservationist measures. Beyond the history lesson, it was also true that Soviet, US, and Dutch ratifications were necessary for the ICRW to enter into force.

In retrospect, many critics have seen the failure to reject the objection clause as the great mistake of the 1946 meeting. The objection mechanism allowed countries to unravel progress that had been made in the annual meetings by vetoing amendments months afterward, and the threat of the objection system was quite useful in slowing down both efforts to reduce the global quota in the 1950s and the push for a commercial whaling moratorium in the 1970s. And yet, it seems likely that the British and Norwegian opposition was based on a misreading of the future of the whaling industry. They did not foresee a large-scale expansion by the Soviets and were confident that the Japanese would not be allowed back into whaling on a permanent basis. They foresaw a whaling industry dominated by their two countries, with a Norwegian hammerlock on trained harpooners, keeping other states from getting too involved. Perhaps the Dutch or Argentines would launch an expedition, but no one would be able to challenge the

Anglo-Norse supremacy again. Ten years after the war, Britain and Norway would be desperate to hang on to smaller shares of the whaling pie than they had ever imagined.

Several smaller clashes helped shape the workings of the commission, but none fundamentally altered its goals. The US proposal to place the new commission under the wing of the new UN Food and Agriculture Organization (FAO) landed with a deep thud, despite a lengthy explanation from a US legal adviser that the FAO was interested in both food production and conservation, so whaling would fit right in. Privately, US diplomats worried that Congress was unhappy with supporting all of the new agencies that were sprouting in the postwar world. Both the Norwegian and British delegations, which had had extensive unofficial meetings at the start of the conference as in previous years, strongly opposed being tied down to a UN organization, which might undermine their authority. The Soviets also pointed out that they were not members of the FAO, and that finally killed the idea.[84]

In addition, the delegates broke the formal diplomacy into two pieces. First, they agreed to a new protocol, modeled closely on the protocol of 1945, to govern the 1947–48 season. Second, they negotiated the more complex convention that established the International Whaling Commission to take effect in the 1948–49 season. This move gave signatory nations sufficient time to ratify the ICRW. The final convention needed the ratification of six nations in order to take effect, with Great Britain, Norway, the Soviet Union, the Netherlands, and the United States all required to be part of the six. The parties also agreed to house the new IWC in London (it would move to Cambridge in the 1970s), while appointing Birger Bergersen as the first president and Alban Dobson as the secretary. Dues to fund the commission would be based in part on the number of whales caught, but the fee was kept very low because the Ministry of Agriculture and Fisheries paid for most of the costs of operations.[85]

Setting the open season took some effort. The US proposal was lifted from the 1938 protocol, including a three-month open season from 8 December to 7 March. The rising number of expeditions meant that the catch limit would probably be reached in the 1947–48 season, so the goal was to postpone the season opening date as much as possible. Remington Kellogg cited recent work by Neil Mackintosh showing there were fewer mature blue females in the hunting areas as the season went on.

Mackintosh argued that "blue whales certainly need protection more than fin whales do." Bergersen added that Norwegian whalers agreed that "we have to protect the blue whale as much as possible."[86] The Norwegian and British whalers agreed to accept a later opening date of 15 December, and "all the biologists at the conference were profoundly happy."[87] As compensation, the closing date was moved to 1 April.

Finally, and most important, the convention retained the annual limit of 16,000 blue whale units for Antarctic waters that had been established in 1944. One Soviet delegate pointed out that the catch limit, or quota as it came to be known, should be fixed annually based on scientific evidence, and the Dutch delegate pointedly asked, "Isn't it quite an arbitrary figure?" Kellogg, Bergersen, and Dobson opposed the idea of a fluctuating catch limit, emphasizing the need for continuity so that they could have a "statistical basis on which to determine how many whales there are."[88] In addition, Kellogg reported that the quota of 16,000 BWU was meant to set a limit that was two-thirds of the annual catch in the last seven peacetime seasons, which were widely thought to have been too intensive. This quick defense of the quota number was a little surprising, since Kellogg and Bergersen appeared to agree before the conference that the limit "is probably too high, from a conservation viewpoint, but may appear to be the compromise most acceptable to all parties."[89] Delegates thought that the commission would have to monitor the catch figure closely each year to see if it needed to be changed, but there were probably more who thought that the limit was too low than too high.

The size of the catch limit and the use of the blue whale unit have each garnered a great deal of criticism over the years. In retrospect, it is easy to say that 16,000 BWU was too high, but almost no one suggested a lower number in any of the recorded discussions. British whalers supported a quota between 16,000 and 20,000, and even Kellogg suggested 17,000 as a possible limit in 1943. The two exceptions came from Bergersen, who suggested 15,000–16,000 as a limit in 1943, and the American businessman Clifford Carver, who thought 16,000 was too high in 1946. Since he was no longer in the business, his suggestion did not carry much weight. William Flory believed that 16,000 was too high "from a strictly conservation standpoint" but that there would be pressure to set it at 20,000 because of the fat crisis.[90] In short, the conservationists thought that they got the lowest limit possible. Years later, H. K. Salvesen's lieutenant, Gerald Elliott, declared that the quota had been "a considerable reduction from the last prewar season."[91] Less than a year after the negotiation of the ICRW, whalers pressed to scrap the catch limit for the 1947–48 season, which Ira Gabrielson of US Fish and Wildlife called "so short-sighted that it deserves no consideration."[92]

Likewise, critics have blasted the blue whale unit system. Historian Mark Cioc wrote that the BWU system encouraged whalers to focus on the blue whales first, when the species was already in decline: "All that the BWU system really did was to put a bull's-eye on the largest available species until it was no longer plentiful."[93] Bergersen, however, thought that the BWU system would actually protect blue whales. Two fin whales made one BWU but produced an "equal or even slightly higher amount of oil" than one blue whale.[94] Bergersen might well have failed to comprehend how whalers would calculate their expenditure of effort, but he was thinking about helping blue whales, which no doubt would have had a bull's-eye on their backs anyway, barring some unforeseen change in rules for hunting blues. Henry Maurice also apparently thought that the BWU system was the best way to let the whalers know that they faced a fixed limit.[95] Supporters might also have pointed out that the BWU system encouraged targeting the biggest whales of each species, since a blue whale was one unit whether it weighed 50 tons or 100, and that usually meant that immature whales would have better chances of reaching breeding age. Scientists and fisheries officials from Norway, Britain, and the United States generally thought that the BWU system was the best one available in the 1940s, and it was also one that had been around since the quota agreements of the 1930s.

It is also worth considering how little the scientists knew about the animals they were trying to regulate. In April 1946, Kellogg had reviewed the catch data from the previous season, when whalers were expecting to find fat and rested whales after nearly six years with no hunting. Instead they found that the ice was farther north than usual, the animals were thinner than normal, and the stocks had not grown appreciably. Kellogg lamented that the evidence "shows how little we really know of the factors governing the abundance of krill in Antarctic seas." He continued,

> For my own part, I consider it vital that we have adequate information
> on which to base such decisions as may be agreed upon. Guess work is
> always unsafe and this is particularly true of a natural resource that may

be unduly depleted by unwise exploitation. You [Bergersen] and I at least have always agreed that the perpetuation of this industry should be our first consideration and that the catch should not deplete the annual surplus. We should make an effort to build up the stocks of whales so that we may be assured of an indefinite continuation of whaling operations.[96]

The ICRW had advanced the goal of conservation in several ways. It had established a permanent commission, with an important role for scientists, that would set regulations intended to make whaling sustainable. There was now a permanent global quota for the Antarctic seas. Provisions for a limited open season and full use of the carcass, as well as protections for certain species and lactating mothers, had been retained. Nothing substantial from the agreements of the 1930s had been lost except for the sanctuary idea, which was controversial among scientists anyway.

In his final report on the 1946 meeting, Kellogg wrote simply that the ICRW "is designed to give effective long-range protection to the existing stocks of whales and to provide for the continuing development of those stocks."[97] Privately, though, he was deeply concerned about the power of the whalers, particularly Salvesen, "a far more vigorous exponent of the rights of the whaling industry than the Norwegians." The problem was that "many operators in the whaling industry refuse to believe that whaling has any effect on whaling in the Antarctic." It was particularly troubling to him that "no one wants the industry controlled in such a way that the perpetuation of whale stocks will be assured."[98] Others were equally ambivalent. Just after Christmas in 1946, one American diplomat noted that "no change of major importance was made in the regulations concerning whaling."[99]

British officials were generally pleased. Soon after the meeting, Dobson wrote that "we have achieved all we went to achieve, and the result can therefore be regarded as highly satisfactory." Naturally, he also concluded that the British delegation dominated the conference, especially compared to the French, who "left early after the usual policy of taking all and giving nothing."[100] One Briton hinted at disappointment that national sovereignty had killed British attempts to dump the objection scheme but noted that "we can regard the results as reasonably satisfactory." From the embassy in Washington, a member of the delegation pointed out, "There is, I feel, some value in the argument that it is better for a government to be given an escape from any one feature of the Schedule [of regulations] than to have no alternative than to denounce the whole Agreement." Another regretted that there was no embargo on exporting whaling materials to nonmembers but concluded, "This appears to have been a most successful conference and very satisfactory from the U.K. point of view."[101] From Norway, Bergersen's official report was neutral in tone, but he wrote to Kellogg that "on the whole the results of the last Conference were good."[102]

An Australian economics official thought it was "courting disaster" to combine a fixed catch limit with open competition and national inspectors rather than ones appointed through the IWC. He predicted that cheating would follow soon after the first whaler lost money. Simply put, it was not worth starting a pelagic expedition from Australia under these rules. And yet the Australian delegate concluded that "Australia must subscribe to this general programme of conservation."[103]

As late as 1949, after the first meeting of the commission in London, the whaling situation seemed to be well in hand, even though there were reasons to worry. Bergersen described the first meeting as "very successful. Significant progress was made with regard to protection of the whale population, first and foremost the blue whale." He looked forward to the future with "great expectations."[104] The FAO hinted at high hopes for the commission: "It carries a great responsibility to the world: to supervise the wise use and husbanding of this great natural resource."[105]

But by the next year, the problems that had been smudges on the horizon in 1949 had turned into looming storms. Pondering the new expeditions in the pipeline, Kellogg wrote that "unless some means can be found to bring all operations under the convention the increased exploitation will soon result in serious depletion of Antarctic stocks of whales and eventually the end of whaling operations in that area."[106] The worry of 1950 became alarm in 1951, as the expansion of the whaling fleets and the prospect of widespread cheating caused observers to doubt that whaling could be sustained. Fred Taylor of the US State Department told Norwegian ambassador Wilhelm Morgenstierne that pelagic whaling would be unprofitable by 1957; the ambassador replied that the prediction was optimistic.[107] Whales shortly would be commercially extinct, Morgenstierne concluded. Kellogg reported that the IWC seemed to be functioning well, so that if whalers adhered to the rules "Antarctic whaling may continue for a few years at least"—hardly a ringing endorsement.[108]

Bergersen and Kellogg agreed that the 16,000 BWU quota would have to be reduced, and in fact they now decided that it had been too high to begin with, perhaps regretting their words about holding to a limit for a few years to allow for better understanding of the stocks. Bergersen in particular worried that a combination of factors meant that the kill in the southern seas was really closer to 20,000 BWU.[109] At the same time, the director of the International Union for the Conservation of Nature was expressing his concern that IWC rules were inadequate and that the BWU quota was still too high. He peppered Dobson with questions that demonstrated uneasiness, if not dismay; IWC officials dismissed him as uninformed.[110]

One final cause for the newfound pessimism of the 1950s was concern that the commission would not work as well as had been hoped. At the first IWC meeting, in 1949, there once again had been a lively discussion about the definition of land station. The French had anchored old whaling factories near their colonies at Madagascar and Gabon rather than build new stations on land, but a proposal before the commission would end that practice, which had angered the pelagic whalers since the 1930s. The French wished to engage in hunting humpbacks near their calving grounds, which was legal under the convention but widely regarded as scientifically reckless. The return of oil per whale from tropical stations tended to be far below what could be earned in the far south because the whales themselves were thinner, and inefficient operations meant that the oil from these stations was often a very low grade, because the animals were not processed quickly. The French lost the argument, casting the only vote against the changed definition of a land station. As Paul Anziani had foreshadowed in November 1946, France then filed an objection against the new rule and continued its old practice.[111]

Two years later, at the IWC meeting in Cape Town, South Africa, another amendment led to the use of the objection clause, which this time caused more concern than it had in 1949. The commission had attempted to begin to control the hunting of sperm whales before it became a problem by limiting the season to eight months per year. Frank Anderson of Australia expressed his reservations, and then his government followed up by filing an objection, citing Australia's desire to keep open the option of hunting sperms. Canberra also commented that the new rule would not enhance sperm whale conservation. Bergersen probably spoke for many participants in the commission in expressing his dismay: "Protests of this kind undermine the Commission's possibility of fulfilling its role and lead to the endangerment of the Convention as a whole. It is unnecessary to stress what this would imply for the whaling industry as a whole."[112] Australia had chosen to act against the majority of scientists without even having a tangible interest at stake, which made its decision more troubling than France's.

Two threads of history had come together to create the IWC in 1946. The first was the international concern, stretching back more than 30 years, that whaling on the high seas had to be regulated by treaty. Companies could not regulate themselves, business conglomerations were not possible, and individual states could never hope to control companies that could change addresses. Whale oil was such a fluid commodity that companies that produced it could sell their wares almost anywhere, so a global network was necessary to control the industry. Small steps in the 1930s had created a set of rules, and it seemed plausible to talk about enforceable international regulation, which scientists and bureaucrats wanted before the whaling industry stripped the South Seas.

The other thread, the outbreak of the war, had created chaos and disrupted the normal food supply network. The people of liberated Europe were hungry, and their food security was almost hypothetical when the war ended. The British government began to back away from the whaling agreements when the war was less than a week old, and as things became desperate the British commitment to long-term conservation almost disappeared. Norway, which could easily cover its fat needs from its whaling and domestic production when it was free of occupying armies, was not so swayed by the argument that immediate production of whale oil was better than prudent, long-term planning, and the United States never really accepted the argument's validity.

In 1951, Kellogg expressed his regret at the way those two threads had come together: "It has been my view all along that whaling stocks were badly depleted and that the 16,000 blue whale unit limit was too high. It is indeed unfortunate that stocks of edible fats were so low when we established that limit in 1945. Otherwise we might have obtained agreement on a lower limit."[113] Thus, even as delegates like Bergersen and Kellogg were concerned that a catch limit of 16,000 BWU might be too high, they understood that the creation of the IWC was not just based on biological considerations. They got the best deal they could, the whalers got the best they could, and each hoped that the commission would function reasonably well. There was little historical evidence to suggest whether they had created an organization that might actually work, and the next two decades would reveal its flaws.

4

CHEATERS SOMETIMES PROSPER

IN ONE OF THE MORE FAMOUS COMMENTS ABOUT THE POSTWAR MILI-
tary occupation of Japan, Gen. Douglas MacArthur wrote to his superiors
in Washington just after the Japanese surrender, "Give me bread or give
me bullets."[1] Japan, he observed, was nearly in a state of starvation, and
if he could not win the people over with food he would need to control
them with force. Sustenance and politics were closely intertwined in a
country that had been bombed and blockaded for many months, and occupation officials saw in whale meat and oil one answer to both their food
and political problems. MacArthur was not one to sit around waiting for
anything from a foreign capital like Washington, so he and his staff quickly
turned to the ocean to find the resources the Japanese people needed. They
worked to rebuild the Japanese whaling and fishing fleets and drew up
plans to send those vessels far out to sea in search of food and foreign
exchange. In August 1946, his staff announced that Japanese vessels would
return to the Antarctic seas for the next whaling season. As it turned out,
Japanese whalers returned every year after that and soon came to dominate
the Antarctic whaling industry.

MacArthur's decision might have been minor in the larger scheme of
reconstruction, but it was vitally important in determining the long-term
prospects of the International Whaling Commission's ability to conserve
whales. Japanese whalers brought with them heavy baggage from their
prewar days, when they were inefficient in their use of the whales and
unwilling to join with the Western whaling nations in diplomatic efforts
to regulate the industry. Smithsonian scientist Remington Kellogg concluded that Japan's prewar whaling had been largely undertaken to raise
the foreign exchange necessary to buy petroleum, although they had taken

meat too.[2] Occupation officials worked tirelessly to change the country's practices, but they failed to convince other whalers that the Japanese followed the rules, which in turn piqued long-term resentment among those whalers just as the commission was born. In addition, by allowing the Japanese to get a foot in the door in 1946, rather than cutting them off like the Germans, the Supreme Command for the Allied Powers (SCAP), which served as the occupation government until 1951, set the stage for Japan's long-term expansion, which would hover over whaling deliberations into the twenty-first century. Within a decade of the war's end, the Japanese would be catching more whales than the Norwegians, which marked an important change in the power dynamics in the IWC.

Cheating, both real and perceived, was obviously a problem, undermining faith in the commission and the larger goal of international cooperation. Cheaters corrupted the data that scientists used to draw conclusions about the new whaling convention's schedule of regulations and reduced the ability to tighten regulations. Whalers who flagrantly violated the rules also contributed to the unwillingness of honest members to sacrifice for the common good. British, Norwegian, and Dutch whalers begrudgingly followed the schedule, but they kicked and screamed at any suggestion of more conservation measures because they believed that they would bear the brunt of the restrictions. The old whalers also were convinced that the only way the new expeditions could be profitable was if they were defying the rules. Each new expedition that entered the fray reduced the portion of the Antarctic quota that an existing expedition could hope to get, which further reduced profitability. Consequently, it became harder to reduce the quota even as evidence mounted that the number of whales was declining.

Japanese whalers apparently obeyed the rules about as well as the British and Norwegians did, despite suspicions to the contrary. SCAP expedition commanders and officers in SCAP's Natural Resources Section successfully sold whalers on the idea that they had to follow the rules to win acceptance for their nation in the world community. As the Japanese whaling industry expanded, it appeared wedded to the best practices of whaling circa 1946. Aristotle Onassis, however, with just one wildly illegal expedition, sowed havoc with his open and thorough disdain for the commission's rules. The IWC's inability to punish him or his business partners, and the unwillingness of contracting governments to do much to support the commission, undermined its credibility and revealed the limitations of diplomatic efforts to regulate natural resources. Soviet actions, despite being so well screened that they could not be accurately described until the 1990s, left the other commission members nearly speechless. Because they were unsure exactly how the Soviets were breaking the rules, they could not figure out how to respond, and yet they agreed that the Soviets were more likely to walk away from the commission than respond positively to pressure. Ultimately, they feared that Soviet whalers would operate outside the international structure, as the Japanese had in the 1930s, which would lead to the one thing that Western whalers feared most, a free-for-all in the southern seas.

SCAP GOES WHALING

While this story involves MacArthur, it is much more about the staff officers who created and regulated the Japanese return to pelagic resource extraction. Some were career army officers, but most were civilians who brought Progressive-era ideas of conservation from the United States and used their temporary military authority to try to remake Japanese society. The core of the Progressive conservationist ethos was the idea that resources should not be wasted. Except for a few remarkable species and places, everything should be used, with scientists and technicians using their specialized knowledge to manage resources efficiently. Because whales were so valuable, few Progressives thought that whales should be exempt from hunting. Use was fine, waste was not. The Progressive conservationists in the occupation government's Natural Resources Section reformulated the Japanese attitude toward whaling in a manner that remains largely unchanged many decades later.

In a way, the occupying officers had a remarkable laboratory, a country where an enlightened group of technocrats in military uniform could start almost from scratch. Because of their power, they would not have to worry much about placating interest groups or accepting ancient traditions. The head of the Natural Resources Section, Lt. Col. Hubert Schenck, told a Japanese cabinet minister, "We do not have to bargain with you."[3] The Natural Resources Section could build systems of resource use that would meet citizens' needs but also be managed scientifically for the best long-term returns. Schenck, a professor of geology from Stanford University, suggested that natural resources were the core cause of the war: "The outcome of the Pacific war has given the Allied Powers the opportunity to direct all of their wisdom and good will to mitigate the tragedies of its causes."[4]

In essence, this was a test of utilitarian conservationist reasoning: could technocrats figure out how to maximize yield from a resource without damaging it? The answer was no, of course, because other people used the ocean for a range of reasons, and because no one could possibly understand and manage the complexities of marine ecosystems. But there would never be an opportunity quite like the immediate postwar moment to convert an entire country from wasteful behavior to efficient use. It was the closest thing to tabula rasa that any of the occupiers would ever see.

But the tabula was not quite rasa, and the Americans were not the only ones with chalk. The occupation authorities had to rely on both Japanese good will and their ability to understand their orders. As malleable as the Japanese were, they had their own traditions, including the logical ways to use a whale and the structure of whaling corporations. They may not have been allowed to bargain much, but the Japanese were capable of deflection when it suited their interests. Also, as much as MacArthur acted like an emperor, he was technically part of an international occupation authority, complete with angry allies who could not imagine letting the Japanese back into pelagic activities. Every decision that the American military authorities made faced scrutiny around the world, including in Washington.

By 1951, when Japan regained its sovereignty, its whaling expeditions bore the marks of modernity and efficiency that US military authorities thought were appropriate, and these authorities measured their success in terms of food procured and American tax dollars saved. But the emphasis on meat, rather than whale oil, combined with memories of Japanese behavior in whaling and in war, left most foreigners convinced, inaccurately, that Japanese whalers were wasteful cheaters. At the same time, though, the conversion of Japanese whaling from apparently lawless prewar behavior to highly efficient postwar methods suggested that the proper allocation of science and law could reform even the worst whalers into practitioners of conservationism. Nations that behaved poorly could be reformed if they had wise regulations, carefully enforced.

Life in Japan in the months after the war was grim. About three million Japanese had died during the war, millions more had been wounded, and about fifteen million were homeless or refugees of one kind or another, including perhaps six million overseas. The country to which they hoped to return had been devastated by months of bombing and naval blockade, so that the economy was barely functioning and civilian hardship was indescribable. Anywhere from one-quarter to one-third of the nation's wealth had been destroyed in the war.[5] Japan had long relied on outside sources of food, sometimes buying it and sometimes conquering it. Now lacking the means to buy food or the power to conquer it, Japan was at the mercy of its occupiers. Beyond the physical destruction there was also psychological damage, as the nation whose army had fought so tenaciously in China and across the Pacific had been forced to surrender the home islands. The great empire of 1942 had been reduced to smoldering ashes by 1945.

The Japanese method of restarting their Antarctic whaling operations fits into their general pattern of dealing with the occupation. The Japanese embraced defeat, historian John Dower has shown, accepting their place as the subordinates to the Allied occupiers, especially General MacArthur, who generally treated Japan as his fiefdom. As MacArthur brought his mishmash of Progressive-era reforms, ardent anti-Communism, and outsized ego to the job, the Japanese responded with a mix of openness to new ideas, flattery, and self-interest. It all worked out reasonably well given the potential disaster that military occupations can become, as Japan emerged as a prosperous nation with a stable representative government.

Food rations in Japan fell dangerously low in the first year after the surrender. The situation was oddly similar to Great Britain's, despite the countries' being on the opposite side in the war. Japan was already incapable of feeding itself without massive imports of food. A shortage of young men during the war had hindered agricultural production, which had also been strained by wartime limitations on fuel, transportation, fertilizer, and the like. After the war, repatriated soldiers were straining an already tight food supply. The government would need to restart export businesses to procure the foreign currency necessary to buy food on the global market (which was itself pretty tight), but conversion from military production would take time. In the interim, the only reliable source of food was the United States, which was ambivalent about using taxpayer dollars to feed the country that had attacked Pearl Harbor (even if it was charging some occupation costs to the Japanese government too). MacArthur's orders emphasized that he was to allow Japan any peaceful industry that would help to minimize imports, but he did not have a secure source of food for the Japanese. A year after the surrender, Lieutenant Colonel Schenck concluded: "The one problem which overshadows all others in Japan today is the food problem. It is essentially the same problem that she faced before the war."[6]

Like the British, the Japanese and their American overseers concluded that the sea was an obvious place to acquire tons of protein and fat quickly and cheaply. Even in late 1945, SCAP's Natural Resources Section was allowing the Japanese to catch whales in the country's home waters, both from land stations and small floating factories, to the displeasure of some of the Allies.[7] SCAP had established a zone in the ocean east of Japan where Japanese fishermen could operate freely, and repairing and building boats were high priorities.[8] The Japanese, though, were not supposed to have ships capable of whaling. Such ships would have been immediately seized by the Australians as reparations, a quick way to jump-start their whaling industry and keep the Japanese from coming anywhere close to Australia.

Unbeknownst to the Australians, as early as 11 December 1945, US State Department officials had been considering sending Japanese whalers back to the Antarctic. At a meeting to discuss the best use of eighteen killer boats still in Japanese possession, there was general agreement with US official William Flory's position that the need for fat and oil was dire. The questions were, first, whether anybody besides the Japanese was capable of using their catchers in the near future and, second, whether any oil procured from the boats would go to Japan or to Europe. Despite the late date, Flory thought that some of the catchers might be able to get to the Antarctic whaling grounds during the 1945–46 season, presumably to work with British and Norwegian factories. The attendees finally agreed that it was too late for this season, but it was good to have begun the discussion for the 1946–47 season. They concluded that MacArthur should be wired the text of all existing whaling agreements so that Japan could abide by their rules, which suggested that Japan soon would be back in the ranks of pelagic whaling.[9]

In January 1946, officials from Japan's Ocean Fishing Company met with 1st Lt. Richard Croker of SCAP's Fisheries Division. They were primarily interested in ironing out some of the details of whaling around the Bonin Islands, which had been going on for a few months, but before the meeting ended they surprised Croker with a request for German whaling vessels that appeared to be heading to the United States as reparations, which they wanted to use in the Antarctic seas. The United States would let them have the vessels under no circumstances, Croker responded, and he expressed amazement at their naïveté about Antarctic whaling. In exasperation, he reported, "They were advised to submit a carefully prepared petition as we were tired of discussing vague and incomplete results." Perhaps the Japanese were naïve, but they were closer to reclaiming their position as pelagic whalers than Croker knew.[10] Two months later, the US secretary of agriculture decided that there should be more Japanese whaling. The secretary's representative in Japan, R. L. Harrison, urged MacArthur to resume Japanese Antarctic whaling "in view of the present critical world-wide food shortage." Harrison also mentioned that whale oil could be the source of foreign exchange if Japan produced a surplus, which again implied a long-term endeavor given that Japan was critically short of all sorts of food.[11]

On 16 April 1946, SCAP informed the US government that it was considering resuming Japanese Antarctic whaling. Seeing little controversy in the move, Acting Secretary of State Dean Acheson took a month to write back, requiring only three things: that SCAP keep the department fully informed, that the Japanese understand that there were no guarantees about future whaling, and that given the food shortage SCAP should obtain "reasonably effective production." Not surprisingly, SCAP officials took this message as a green light, although they tended to overlook Acheson's muted warning that British and Norwegian interests would, at the least, expect some sort of pooling of Japanese equipment or production with their own as a way to limit Japanese reentry.[12]

Given the need for food, the lack of concern in Washington, and the reluctance to care what the Allies thought, it is not surprising that SCAP announced a full plan to resume Antarctic whaling on 6 August 1946. The *Hashidate Maru* and the *Nisshin Maru*, both about ten thousand tons, would lead the expeditions, each with six killer boats and a total of seven oil carriers. Japanese whalers were authorized to work an area between longitude 90° east and 170° west, directly south of Australia and New Zealand, but they were not to pass within twelve miles of land en route. As a precaution, SCAP would screen the crews to weed out war criminals, people who might head to the Dutch East Indies to lead a Japanese-inspired revolt, and naval specialists who might use the information gathered for military operations. People who had overseen the 1930s whaling operations that were so widely criticized in the West for being wasteful would be welcomed back, though. The Japanese whalers were to abide by the rules of the whaling conventions and protocols in hunting and processing the two thousand whales they hoped to catch. SCAP's adjutant general, Col. John Cooley, made clear that this authorization did not set a precedent either for future whaling or for the establishment of national fishing zones.[13] But the very fact that SCAP was willing to invest eight hundred tons of scarce food and more than 250,000 barrels of fuel in these expeditions—not to mention the time and energy to refurbish several ships—suggested that occupation authorities expected a large return on the investment.[14]

So it was that no US officials anticipated the angry reaction to MacArthur's announcement, a year after the Hiroshima bombing, that Japan would send these two expeditions to Antarctica for the 1946–47 whaling season.[15] At the very least, officials should have anticipated the charge of duplicity for not revealing that the Japanese had whaling materiel that could have been used as reparations. Or US authorities might have recognized that members of the Far Eastern Commission, which was supposed to serve as a multinational body to oversee the occupation, would wonder why they had not been consulted. Instead, MacArthur and his aides, as they so often did during the occupation, collectively rolled their eyes at those petty foreigners who failed to see the obvious wisdom of their ways. After all, SCAP officials sometimes noted, the United States had borne the brunt of the fighting across the Pacific and the entirety of the occupation for several months. The sneakiness of SCAP's whaling policy was not a one-time error in judgment, though; as late as May 1949, occupation officials were trying to plan whaling expeditions in secret, declining to tell even the US Army and State Department.[16] In Washington, US diplomats regretted the artlessness of the decision, but they did not disagree with it.

The Allies were especially annoyed that they learned about Japanese whaling in the press. In the middle of August 1946, New Zealand's Ministry of External Affairs alerted Australia's diplomats of the news and made clear Wellington's opposition: "Japan's past record is one of failure to accede to the international conventions regarding the taking of whales and of predatory expeditions which threatened the continued existence of the industry and the whale itself."[17] For their part, the Australians leapt in with both feet, demanding explanations and assurances from MacArthur's advisers in Tokyo and US officials in Washington, the latter of whom frequently were as surprised as the Allies were. On 21 August 1946, an

Australian diplomat presented to the US State Department an informal list of complaints that emphasized Australia's strategic interest in Antarctica, including territorial claims. Also on the list were the sanctity of the 1945 whaling protocol, the assignment of Japanese whaling materiel to the Allies, and the belief that it would be nearly impossible to stop Japanese whaling once it had begun.[18] The Australians calculated that the amount of meat the Japanese might procure amounted to only 3.5 ounces per person per day over a five-month period, so the expeditions hardly seemed worth the heartburn.[19] There was a widespread belief among Australians that the Japanese had used fishing, whaling, and other pelagic resource boats as training vessels for their navy and as platforms for spying on Allied harbors. And after the horrible treatment of Australian POWs and the brutal fighting along the Kokoda Track in New Guinea, there was no love lost for the Japanese as a people.

Before the complaints could become more formal, the Commonwealths of the South Pacific were undercut by Britain's unwillingness to close ranks. On 22 August, acknowledging that the Japanese "pre-war whaling record was extremely bad," the British Dominions Office concluded that the need for fats and oils was so critical that it could not support cancellation of the expeditions, especially if all of the oil went onto the world market. The alternative, then, would be to run them as SCAP expeditions, with the highest positions filled by Britons and Norwegians, to ensure that there was no precedent for Japanese whaling and that the Japanese actually followed "modern whaling practice," including all conventions. If that level of authority was impossible, then at the least there would have to be two European inspectors on each factory vessel. In addition, the British and Norwegians would supply the killer boats and crews, an odd proposition given the warning in the same memo that "there would be trouble" if the Japanese expedition encountered a British or Norwegian operation.[20]

The Australians and New Zealanders may have mustered the outrage, but they lacked the power to change SCAP's policy. MacArthur was in no mood to humor them, seeing the problem as simply one of acquiring desperately needed food. He also apparently argued that the Japanese ships were not fit for "six-foot Australians" and other westerners because they were built for smaller Japanese sailors with lower standards of comfort.[21] To assuage them, SCAP reminded the allies that there would be American officers on board the expeditions, and SCAP begrudgingly allowed foreign inspectors on board as well. The Australians and New Zealanders also found no support from London, which looked at Japanese whalers for their contribution to the global food crisis, not their past sins. The Dominions Office instead echoed MacArthur by arguing that it was impossible to get trained crews of Europeans onto the Japanese ships, because Norwegians refused to serve with Japanese, although it is not clear on what that conclusion was based. Still, London was annoyed with MacArthur because the Japanese resumption of whaling and the conversion of vessels signaled that there had been long-term planning without any notice to countries that might be concerned.[22] Of course, that was correct.

Whalers had a generally unfavorable opinion about the possible reentry of Japanese competitors. One British diplomat in Oslo reported that Norwegians assessed Japanese whalers "as unduly cheap managers of their fleet, as ruthless killers, as non-observers of the generally accepted scheme of things, and as being outside the international convention."[23] G. R. Powles, a diplomat from New Zealand at the 1946 conference, reported that Dutch and Norwegian delegates, once they were approached quietly on the subject, made clear their desire to put an end to Japanese pelagic whaling. Yet he also reported that British whaler H. K. Salvesen was not worried about the Japanese but instead about "all these restrictions." His ships had never had an unfavorable encounter with Japanese whalers, and he was confident that they would do a better job of using the catch fully than the "inexperienced" Russians and Dutch. Still, Powles stuck by his position that Japanese whaling should be ended. They might abide by the rules for a short while, but their record was indisputable.[24]

Ambassador George Atcheson, chief of SCAP's poorly named Diplomatic Section, met Allied opposition with scorn. He dismissed the objections as arising "chiefly from Australian and other commercial ambition" and juxtaposed the complaints with the great success of the occupying authorities. The whaling expeditions had come to involve US prestige, he claimed, and reversal of the authorization would be a "clear indication that our predominant role and authority in the Occupation no longer exists and that executive action is not firm but is, rather, subject to derogation upon unjustified foreign representation." Just when the occupation was at its peak in effectiveness and respect, the Allies threatened to upset the cart over a matter of food. Even "the least politically cognizant" Japanese would be shaken in their faith in the government.[25] More broadly, Capt.

William Terry of the Natural Resources Section called the objections "prejudicial and inhumanitarian," reminding his superiors that both the Atlantic Charter and the UN Declaration preserved access to resources for victor and vanquished.[26]

The final shape of the Japanese expeditions came a bit closer to the British proposal. Each expedition was assigned a US Army officer as the highest authority and each flew a specially designed flag to indicate SCAP sovereignty. The expeditions were charged to procure both meat for the home market and oil for the world market, while abiding by the rules established by every whaling convention. Each factory carried a foreign observer, one ship with an Australian and one with a Norwegian, who was allowed access to any part of the operations, and the ships were ordered to stay clear of foreign ports.

What really mattered, though, was the attitude that US officers tried to instill. One officer wrote late in 1946: "It is not our object to solve all the fisheries problems of Japan. But, we should stimulate their thinking and initiative to the end that many pressing and serious problems facing them today will be surmounted by their own efforts."[27] Tension between the need for more food and the desire to rebrand Japanese whaling as a model of modern efficiency took three years to resolve. By the end of the occupation, the Japanese still retained some of the stigma of inefficient, wasteful whaling, but that was at least as much a product of ingrained anti-Japanese feeling as of Japanese behavior. The Japanese were frequently paired with the Soviets as perpetrators of dubious whaling practices in the next few decades, but the Soviets were in a class by themselves, while Japanese infractions were relatively minor.

The rehabilitation had started in July 1946, when Col. Reginald H. Fiedler of SCAP's Natural Resources Section addressed fishermen at Misaki, Kanagawa Prefecture. He encouraged democratization and warned against black-marketeering. He also urged them to use pelagic resources judiciously and to show discretion as they entered new fishing areas and encountered new people: "The propriety with which you conduct yourselves in these contacts will largely determine whether you will be allowed to continue these operations."[28] A few months later, a group from the Natural Resources Section working on radio programs concluded that they should persuade the Japanese to facilitate conservation of whales in Japan's home waters by using the carcass completely and being very selective in which whales were killed.[29] Early the next year, Capt. William Herrington—who, like Capt. William Terry, would have a career in the US State Department working on resource issues—spelled out the requirements for further Japanese rehabilitation: "Research and conservation practices designed to provide for more rational management of fishery and wildlife resources in the interest of sustained and increased yield."[30]

There were moments of discord, however, particularly because the food situation seemed so acute. The day before the planners of the radio program agreed to stress conservation and selective hunting, dignitaries at the departure ceremony for the *Hashidate Maru* had a very different message. It probably was not surprising that the expedition manager and president of the Taiyo Gyogyo Company emphasized the need for food, or that local officials echoed the call, but it was a bit surprising that the keynote speaker, Captain Terry, called on the whalers to bring back as much food and oil as possible. Apparently, no one mentioned conservation or the need to be better neighbors.[31] By the next year, though, the Japanese seemed to have gotten the message. At a meeting to discuss the rules for whaling in October 1947, Iwao Fujita of the Bureau of Fisheries thanked American officials for their assistance and support in the "big job" ahead of them: not only did the Japanese have to utilize the whole carcass, but "we have to do it better than other countries in order to live up to the expectation of General MacArthur."[32]

As SCAP and the Japanese slowly got on message, they emphasized that one of the main rewards of practicing conservation on the high seas was increased respectability abroad. When the *Hashidate Maru* was sent out in November 1947, an American observer reported, "Despite the gaiety of the ceremony and departure activities, there seemed to prevail a sense of responsibility on the part of the Japanese, particularly those directly connected with the expedition, to exert every effort to make this expedition a success through the attainment of high production and efficient operations."[33] The next year Colonel Schenck's farewell message to the whalers noted that if the crews abided by the international rules, then they would "prove again that Japan is worthy of taking her place among the law-abiding nations of the world."[34] In 1949, Schenck hit the trifecta at the farewell for the *Nisshin Maru* when he noted the Japanese commitment to "conserving the great natural resources represented by whales," "improving operating efficiency," and having an "excellent record in conforming to international regulations" in his eight-sentence speech.[35] As the years went on, the farewell addresses from SCAP officials increasingly focused on conservation regulations, suggesting both that food was less pressing and that they felt that the efficient use of resources needed to be emphasized on its own terms.

The shift to emphasizing conservation as a moral good, rather than as a means to win friends abroad, might have been a response to Japan's total failure to win those friends. No doubt some of the concern about being neighborly was directed at Japanese fishermen who would encounter their Chinese and Korean counterparts, but for the whalers it was largely about the Australians and New Zealanders.[36] Australia and New Zealand simply never warmed to the resumption of Japanese whaling, even when they saw whaling as an acceptable activity. The hatred—that is not too strong a word—for Japanese whaling started with Frank Anderson, Australia's fisheries director in the late 1940s, who was a fierce guardian of Australia's right to catch the humpbacks that came up from the south along the country's east and west coasts. It was bad enough that the Norwegians might catch those whales, but to have whalers from the country that so recently had threatened Australia was simply unimaginable.

Anderson's ire was fueled by the certainty that the United States was acting in a "high-handed" manner with its allies. One of his colleagues smuggled out of Japan a copy of SCAP's logbook of correspondence on Antarctic whaling, which revealed that MacArthur's staff had been thinking about Antarctic whaling since April 1946 and had explicitly chosen not to contact the Allies early in the process. In addition, the Japanese had envisioned taking about 6,400 of the 16,000 blue whale unit quota for the 1948–49 season, so they clearly expected to dominate the industry in short order. Even worse, the Japanese would be whaling in waters that were central to Australia's claims to Antarctica. Anderson concluded bitterly that the United States was working to take over Japanese fishing areas in the North Pacific but was placating the Japanese by sending them to Australian whaling grounds.[37] His anger was mild compared to that of one Australian diplomat who suggested that Australia should use military force to expel the Japanese whalers from the waters south of Australia, since Australia was still technically at war with the country that had waged a "war of aggression . . . marked by many of the foulest atrocities in modern history."[38] Cooler heads prevailed, including British prime minister

Clement Attlee, who wrote to his counterparts down under that an open breach with the United States over whaling was not worth it when peace negotiations were looming.[39] New Zealand followed Attlee's lead, leaving the Australians alone in their anger.

The Australian inspector on the *Hashidate Maru* for the 1946–47 season found himself in the middle of a powerful storm. Kenneth Coonan, a retired noncommissioned officer in the Australian Navy, had no experience with or education about whaling, so even an Australian fisheries official called him "an exceptionally poor choice."[40] The US Army officer on board, Lt. David McCracken, was probably even less well prepared than Coonan, and he had the actual authority. Coonan reported just one illegal kill, a sixty-eight-foot blue whale, and on the matter of efficient use of a carcass he noted that the ship had only three boilers and insufficient freshwater supplies, which left it unable to process all of the whales when the flensing deck was busy. On eighteen occasions, the Japanese had dumped bones overboard that should have been processed more thoroughly. McCracken had authorized that violation to make room for the next whale, and to save freshwater, which revealed that the rhetoric about conservation was ahead of the equipment needed to implement it. Dumping bones was something that the prewar Japanese whalers would have done without thinking, but it ran counter to the message of efficiency and maximum use of a scarce resource, and it would not be repeated in future SCAP expeditions. In general, Coonan's report showed that the Japanese wanted meat more than oil and had sent out an ill-equipped ship, but it also suggested that their main sin was inefficiency.[41] In Canberra, Frank Anderson read Coonan's report as damning: "It would appear that the Japanese do not regard the International Whaling Regulations seriously, and that they were supported in their desire to produce salted blubber and meat for food purposes at the expense of oil production."[42]

Coonan ended up having a career as a whaling inspector, working at least into the 1950s on Australian land stations, where he found violations at least as bad as anything he had seen on the SCAP expeditions.[43] His second year as an inspector was back on the *Hashidate Maru* in 1947–48, when he encountered Lt. Col. Waldon Winston, the highest-ranking officer that SCAP sent out on any expedition. Winston was a transportation officer who somehow ended up as the de facto commander of a Japanese flotilla. In an ironic foreshadowing of the 1980s, he decided to take every opportunity to conduct scientific research while whaling. In his most audacious move, he halted all whaling when an 89-foot blue whale was caught because he wanted to be the first to weigh a member of that species. He had the crew cut the whale into pieces, weigh each piece, and then process the animal, calculating that the 136-ton whale generated 40 tons of meat and 133 barrels of oil. In all, he weighed forty-six whales, prompting the Japanese captain to call it a research expedition.[44]

Herman Sundt, the Norwegian inspector, attacked Winston's personality but grudgingly admitted that the expedition had followed the rules. As the *Hashidate Maru* was returning to Japan, Sundt wrote that Winston was a dictator, and he emphasized that the Japanese tolerated him only because they needed the Americans' support. The work was tedious, and Sundt felt as if he were a prisoner on board. Winston knew almost nothing about whaling, ignored American ideas about "liberty," and made strange decisions. He succeeded in showing that the Japanese could be responsible whalers, but only with external supervision. Sundt concluded that US interest in Japanese whaling was purely financial, with the exception of MacArthur's genuine interest in food.[45]

The decision to send Winston seems to have been part of the effort to make Japanese whaling as spotless as possible. With his seniority and his stern approach to the Japanese, he was in a position to dominate an expedition. Coonan had to acknowledge that Winston had succeeded in slowing down the Japanese take to three or four blue whales per week, probably, Coonan thought, to ensure that there would be no errors. It was clear that SCAP wanted to convince the Allies that it ran a tight ship. Winston was fond of quoting from Coonan's 1947 report as a way to indicate that Coonan had been wrong in the past, and then SCAP quoted Coonan in a press release to the Japanese to celebrate the efficiency of Japanese whalers. Coonan had written that "they often cleared up bits of whales as big as a fist to throw into the boilers," and that was all the proof needed that the Japanese were no longer wasteful.[46] To drive home the point, Coonan and Sundt were brought in to see MacArthur upon their return. Coonan assured MacArthur that the second SCAP expedition had been "100 per cent better" than the first, and Sundt suddenly forgot everything negative in his report. The British observer on the *Nisshin Maru* likewise reported that there had been "no question of evading the regulations."[47]

Convincing the Allies to tolerate Japanese whaling would take more than two seasons, though. Before they had seen the reports from 1947 and

1948, the British had concluded that Japanese whaling vessels should be turned over as reparations. The old whaling countries would be able to float sixteen factories for 1947–48, so they could get enough whale oil without Japanese participation. In fact, they would do better than the Japanese, because they had traditionally extracted more oil from each whale. The convention in 1937, the British argued, had been necessary because the Japanese had been pushing whales toward extinction with their wasty ways, but the Japanese had refused to sign the convention. London was pushing back against the new conservation-minded Japanese narrative with its own equally problematic narrative, one that pictured the Japanese as the destroyers of a balanced whaling system.[48]

As one of the last acts of the occupation, the Natural Resources Section compiled a report on whaling in Japan between 1945 and 1951. The author delighted in recounting how much the Japanese had improved under American tutelage. After briefly detailing prewar Japanese whaling and the food crisis that led to the resumption of whaling, the author lauded the success of the 1946–47 expeditions, which led to the decision to send the Japanese fleet out again in future years. By 1951, these expeditions had generated $80 million worth of products. More important, the SCAP expeditions were the height of modernity and efficiency. The prewar Japanese whaling efforts had yielded only 16 tons of products for every blue whale unit, but by 1950–51 they were producing 44 tons per BWU. Europeans allegedly produced, on average, just 25 tons per BWU. Further, SCAP officials had initiated scientific and technological research to improve efficiency and assist in the creation of whaling regulations. Beyond the statistical evidence for a successful rebranding of Japanese whaling, SCAP argued that the whalers' attitude had changed. Under SCAP, infractions were "so low as to constitute in all probability, a world record"; the Japanese government was beginning its own research agenda; and the whaling companies "have displayed a clear understanding of the spirit and aims of international whaling regulations." Finally, the Japanese government had acted on the new attitude by joining the International Whaling Commission in April 1951.[49]

The Japanese ability to get what they wanted within the guidelines set by the occupation authorities became clear in 1950. That winter, officers of Taiyo Gyogyo asked occupation officials to increase the price of whale oil and lower the price of whale meat. The demand for whale meat had "decreased drastically," and the price of oil had been set below international market prices. Captain Terry "questioned seriously the advisability of continuing the expeditions," since they apparently "could not survive in a normal economic situation." S. Suzuki, Taiyo Gyogyo's director, responded by arguing that the food shortage made it necessary to continue, but he emphasized that market prices would produce enough revenue if he could cut costs in labor, management, materiel, insurance, debts, sales, and repairs. Terry understandably was skeptical that Suzuki possessed such power.[50] Perhaps Suzuki was a minor wizard, because he won the right to built two new, larger floating factory vessels in the name of processing whales more efficiently.

The American occupation authorities had instilled in Japan a conservationist ethos right out of the Progressive era, one that argued that resources should be used efficiently for the greatest good and that resource-use decisions should be based on the best scientific and technical advice available. Eventually, the whaling countries accepted Japan into the club as an equal, allowing the 1954 International Whaling Commission meeting to take place in Tokyo. At that meeting, Shigeru Hori, Japan's minister for agriculture and forestry, emphasized in his welcoming address both that his country's whalers had been working in harmony with modern conservation ideas since the seventeenth century and that Japan wanted to extend the principles of cooperation embodied by the IWC to fisheries throughout the oceans. As an observer from New Zealand noted, Hori's speech indicated Japan's "obvious desire to have the rest of the world forget that she has ever been less than scrupulous in conserving marine resources."[51]

CHEATING FOR REAL

In an odd symmetry, the decision to accept Japanese membership in the IWC coincided with the first real challenge to the commission's rules. The culprit was Aristotle Onassis, who sent out his *Olympic Challenger* under the Panamanian flag in the early 1950s. He so successfully muddied his tracks that one Norwegian referred to Onassis's "Greek-Argentine-Panamanian-American expedition."[52] Almost immediately, he was the subject of suspicion and investigation and, eventually, courtesy of Peru, aerial and naval attack. There can be little doubt that Onassis's crew violated several rules that Panama, as a member of the IWC, had accepted. The question for members was how to respond to the violations. The problem persists to this day, with different scofflaws along the way, whether Soviet whalers lying about their catch in the 1950s and 1960s, British investors operating under the Somali flag in the 1970s and taking anything they could, or Japanese whalers in the twenty-first century taking the odd gray whale or other endangered species.

As the Japanese were being welcomed back into pelagic whaling, the Germans faced exclusion. It was punishment, of course, as German whaling vessels became reparations, but it also reflected the division of the country into east and west and the strong presence of Britain in making occupation policy. Anti-Japanese sentiment had been, in part, a product of fear of too many expeditions chasing too few whales. SCAP did not share that fear, because it was focused on Japan's immediate food problem, but the British saw the end of the war as a chance to reassert their domination of the whaling industry with Norway.

Yet, the fear of a resurgent German whaling industry was never far from the surface for nearly ten years after the war. When an Italian company began building a floating factory in Sicily in 1950, Norwegian and British observers quickly smelled a rat. Italians had shown no interest in pelagic whaling before, and they would not be able to hire Norwegian gunners because of Oslo's controversial 1945 crew law. It soon became apparent that the impetus for the vessel came from Walter Rau, one of Germany's leading whaling company owners before the war. In a broad sense, the Italian venture raised the specter of whaling outside the convention, which would threaten the whole industry with a short-lived free-for-all. A slightly better picture involved Italy joining the convention, as the US State Department urged, but then the new expedition, combined with the *Juan Peron*, soon to sail under Argentina's flag, would mean that the whaling fleets of IWC member states would have the capacity to catch 22,000 blue whale units instead of the convention quota of 16,000.[53] An industry with that much excess capacity was headed for some sort of crisis, and the older Norwegian and British floating factories that had been patched back together after the war probably would fail the test first. Perhaps persuaded by such concerns or pressure from IWC members, the Italian government switched its subsidy policy, causing the builders to convert the ship from a whaling vessel to a cruise liner—perhaps the stern slipway could be used as a water slide for tourists.

The quick end to the Italian whaling scheme was the opposite of the long-running attempt by Aristotle Onassis to find glory and profit in the whaling industry, but each was based on a desire to tap the expertise of former German and quisling whalers.[54] Onassis, of course, is famous as a world-class risk taker in the boardroom and the bedroom. He moved from Greece to Argentina as a young man in about 1920 after a bitter family feud. His father bridged the gap by offering him a shipment of tobacco to sell in his adopted land, which he promptly soaked with seawater in order to make an insurance claim. The FBI began building a file on him in 1942 because of allegations from business rivals in the Greek community in Buenos Aires that he was open to fascism, but all the bureau could dredge up on him was that his prime loyalty was to making money in shipping, particularly by registering his ships in Panama. Onassis was a consummate capitalist, always looking for an edge in business deals and open to new angles.[55]

In 1946, he made two fateful decisions that shed light on his operations as a whaler. First, he married a girl nearly thirty years his junior (or perhaps it was twenty-four years, since he was constantly reinventing even basic details about his life, such as his birth date). Fidelity was not really his priority, as he announced to his intended's father that "the rules are that there are no rules"—a comment he echoed when asked about his whaling expeditions a few years later.[56] Also in 1946, he decided to get into the oil tanker business by purchasing seven surplus US vessels under the Surplus Shipping Act. Onassis needed to establish a front company of American investors, United States Petroleum Carriers (USPC), because only US citizens could buy such vessels. Onassis was careful to own less than 50 percent of the stock and more careful to be sure that he controlled enough of the remainder to run the company. These efforts to skirt the law would ultimately put the US federal government on his trail.[57]

In 1949, Onassis teamed up with Clifford Carver, one of the few Americans with whaling experience in the 1930s and a former associate of USPC, to form the Olympic Whaling Company. The evidence suggests that Onassis was using Carver's US citizenship as a means to get US vessels and possibly US registration, which would give him easier access to the US market. He might also have been using Carver for his friendly ties to Norway, hoping that Carver would be able to win a waiver from the 1945 crew law. By 1950 he had dumped Carver and gone off on his own, moving the company headquarters from New York to Montevideo, Uruguay. As early as January 1950, indications were that he was working with a German company to find crewmen and a market for his oil. He had nearly finished converting the US tanker *Herman F. Whiton* to a floating factory in northern Germany, and he was turning old corvettes into catcher boats, all with the financial backing of Metropolitan Life.[58] The factory would be renamed the *Olympic Challenger*, and all of the catchers would have *Olympic* in their names.

Other than the crewmen who were getting lucrative jobs back, no one was happy about this arrangement—and the crewmen would soon find it unappetizing themselves. Birger Bergersen probably spoke for most Norwegians when he came right out and complained about Lars Andersen, Onassis's expedition manager.[59] "Lars the Devil" had signed on with German whalers before the war, and he had openly supported the Nazis during it. He might have been the most qualified man available, but in hiring him Onassis guaranteed that the Norwegians would oppose him implacably. Onassis found Andersen to be "tough, expensive, unpleasant, and an unscrupulous sonofabitch," which only made him seem like a long-lost brother.[60] Beyond Norway, opposition to Onassis was really about the threat to the integrity of the whaling convention. People wondered whether Onassis would register the *Olympic Challenger* in an IWC member country, and indeed his first choice was Honduras, which had not signed. The US State Department diplomatically called on Honduras to join the convention, but the US Fish and Wildlife Service cut to the chase by persuading the Federal Maritime Board to block the transfer of the *Whiton* to Honduran registry. Albert Day, director of fish and wildlife, bluntly wrote that "the operation of even one Antarctic whaling expedition without regard to these regulations would constitute a serious threat to the resource and would serve to defeat the purposes and objectives of the international conservation program to which practically all of the whaling nations of the world have subscribed."[61]

Onassis did not become wealthy by giving up easily, so he turned to plan C and registered the factory in Panama, which had acceded to the convention. The United States, as the depositor (or record keeper) for the convention, listed Panama as an IWC member, but Panama claimed that it had never finished ratification.[62] So the US government could not block the factory vessel transfer, even though Panama was not particularly interested in doing anything related to whaling. There were no qualified inspectors in the country, and Panama's government made no effort to get even unqualified inspectors on board before the *Olympic Challenger* left for its first hunt in the fall of 1950. The Panamanian government compounded the problem by appointing Onassis's lawyer, Roberto Alémán, as Panama's IWC commissioner. As Remington Kellogg noted drily, it "is considered rather inappropriate for any Member Government to be represented at meetings of the Commission only by a representative of the whaling industry."[63]

With so little oversight, it is not surprising that the *Olympic Challenger* became synonymous with corruption. The first violation came with the very first harpoon shot on 6 December 1950, sixteen days before the season began. Onassis's blasé attitude toward whaling became evident when he brought his wife and several of their wealthy friends on board the factory. The men got to try their hands at the harpoon, and the women put up with it all—with his twenty-one-year-old wife relaxing in her crepe nightgowns, which probably left the old salts on board muttering a range of unprintable things into their beards.[64] After a full season of whaling, in which size limits were ignored, the Onassis group was notified that the Antarctic quota had been reached on 9 March 1951. Other vessels turned for home, but the Olympic fleet hid behind an iceberg and kept at it, operating until 26 March. Then it added to its violations by turning its attention to the sperm whaling grounds off Peru, flaunting IWC rules that a floating factory could not work two different whaling grounds in a year. When crew members complained, concerned that Germany would never be allowed to whale again if the cheating was discovered, Andersen and Onassis tried the carrot and the stick, offering extra pay and making threats against "mischief-makers." Onassis sailed out to the *Challenger* to oversee negotiations, which included paying the crew for the days spent off the coast of Peru, which had not been in the original contract. Once the expedition came home, crew members began to make mischief anyway, telling the press in Bremerhaven about the rules violations and the mistreatment of the crew. Those press reports became the first important piece in the collective international file on Onassis the whaler, no part of which painted him favorably.[65]

Once again, in 1951, the *Olympic Challenger* sailed without inspectors on board. Even when the United States pressured Panama to send some along on the resupply ships, the government protested that it was simply too late. Panama was already making its mark as a flag of convenience, generating money by registering ships from other countries, and Onassis had a lot of ships to register. By 1954, one thousand vessels had registered in Panama, pouring $1 million into the treasury each year.[66] Throughout his life, Onassis benefited from a boys-will-be-boys attitude, even earning some measure of respect as a businessman, and in whaling he skated by with only sporadic complaints until 1954. Ron Wall, an outspoken British fisheries secretary, noted that "Panama . . . seems to have no clear-cut policy and is responsible for the whaling fleet owned by the notorious Greek, Mr. Socrates [sic] Onassis, whose care for the rules is also a matter of general doubt."[67] Frank Corner of New Zealand, who normally wrote insightful commentary on commission meetings, was reduced to offering nonsense as analysis, writing that "the Panamanians like most South Americans, are not to be trusted."[68] Simply put, the members of the IWC could not think of a way to punish someone who did not care about the rules.

Unfortunately for Onassis, by 1954 there were two governments ready to enforce their rules, and he was foolishly provoking both of them. Peru had recently joined Chile and Ecuador in claiming an exclusive economic zone over the continental shelf out to two hundred miles from shore. The three states had been driven to this declaration in large part by their desire to tax and regulate US tuna fishermen, finding a precedent in President Harry Truman's 1945 proclamation on conservation and management zones in coastal waters.[69] In the fall of 1954, the government in Lima warned Onassis that it would confiscate his ships if they were found whaling within two hundred miles from the coast, and Onassis poked the government in the eye by replying that his vessels were whaling there already. Peru's military attacked the fleet on 15 November 1954. Warplanes fired shots and naval vessels then tracked down the scattered ships, some more than three hundred miles from the coast. The Olympic Challenger crew had used the time effectively, though, by throwing its logbooks overboard, so there was no record of when, where, or what they had hunted.[70]

The government of Peru found itself with a potential problem. Officials really did not want to use force against every rogue fishing boat that came along, because sooner or later one would be flying the Stars and Stripes. Other maritime states were already worried about the implications of Peru's actions for the law of the sea. The best course was to hammer the Olympic Whaling Company so badly that it would become an example to warn away others while also making it clear that Peru was acting in the best interests of the world. The government framed its indictment in the language of conservation and settled on a fine of $3 million (60 million soles), just about the value of the fleet itself. What it had not counted on was that Olympic Whaling had somehow persuaded Lloyd's of London to insure the expedition less than a month before the confiscation of the vessels. Lloyd's turned to the British government for support in getting the fine reduced, because Lloyd's faced a loss of £2–3 million, depending on the daily fines levied.[71] London and Lima became locked in an exchange over the case, with London oddly forced to defend an expedition that it knew to be predatory. A shrewd operator, Onassis managed to extricate his fleet and get back to whaling for two more years. Finally, in 1956, under indictment for fraud by the US government because of the operations of the USPC, he sold the *Olympic Challenger* and its catchers to a Japanese whaling company for $8.5 million, after having netted more than £5 million as a whaler.[72]

The Olympic Whaling Company created turmoil in the IWC for the six seasons that it operated. The Panamanian-flagged whalers took at least fifteen hundred blue whale units illegally over the 1950–54 period, and they were particularly damned for killing immature whales and whales on the breeding grounds. They were extremely wasteful, too, generating only fifty-four barrels of oil per BWU caught, and their reported catch data were obviously fraudulent.[73] But the IWC had no power to stop the *Olympic Challenger* or to punish Onassis, and the British and Americans could not figure out a way to observe the expedition using military aircraft or naval vessels. Olympic Whaling was such a sore subject that the British whaler H. K. Salvesen was still complaining about its effect in 1962, and for most of the decade the company was the symbol of corruption.[74] Whalers who tried to follow the rules were upset both that Panama's catch counted toward the global quota and that it undermined conservation measures. They argued, predictably, that if Onassis and Lars Andersen could not be stopped, then the only logical response was to loosen the rules for everyone else. This refrain would be the common response to cheating during the whaling years.

CHEATERS EXTRAORDINAIRE

As damaging as Onassis was, he was a piker compared to Aleksei Solyanik and his Soviet whalers. Onassis was blatant about his disregard for the rules, while the Soviets were so effective at laying smoke over their wake that other nations could not determine whether they were reporting too low or too high a catch. In fact, they were doing both. The logical fear was that the Soviets were underreporting their catch, which would undermine conservation by leading to a global catch above the annual quota, but it also became apparent that the Soviets could gain an advantage by overreporting as well. If they inflated their catch statistics it would appear that the global quota had been met, which would trigger a signal from the Bureau for International Whaling Statistics that all expeditions should cease whaling. While the other expeditions headed home, the Soviets could linger until all witnesses were out of the neighborhood and then do whatever they wanted.

The Soviets had caught whales in the North Pacific before the war, and they took advantage of reparations from Germany to launch an Antarctic fleet. The German whaler *Wikinger* had survived the war, more or less, and was towed to the Soviet Union, patched back together, and rechristened the *Slava*. The Soviets took advantage of their power and the unstable political situation to win some concessions, including getting Norwegian gunners on board their catchers and gaining exemptions from some of the rules for the 1946–47 season, since their expedition would be late getting to the hunting grounds.[75] For several years, the prevailing attitude toward Soviet whaling was to allow them to cut corners, out of concern that they could just as happily whale outside the convention as in it.

Given the Cold War, it is not surprising that whalers would be suspicious of Soviet behavior and motivation, and yet governments did a remarkable job of ignoring ideology and focusing on whaling matters when in commission meetings. There were deep ideological splits between Australia and the Soviet Union, for instance, which led to the expulsion of Australian diplomats from Moscow. In 1954, when the Soviet Union offered to host the IWC meeting, officials in Canberra debated whether Australia should or would be allowed to send a delegation. A recently expelled diplomat reported that the conference hotel would be bugged, secret police would follow the delegates, and hotel meals would be "very indigestible."[76] Yet in the IWC, the disagreement between the two countries focused entirely on technique: Australia caught humpbacks from its land stations and demanded steps to preserve them from pelagic whalers, whether Soviet or British. Likewise, the Soviets and Japanese, who took several years to settle their differences after World War II, frequently allied on such issues as the global quota and inspection schemes. H. K. Salvesen urged his fellow whalers to boycott the IWC meeting in Moscow to protest Soviet cheating, drawing a comparison to the 1938 Munich summit that ended with the dismemberment of Czechoslovakia, but no one complied.[77]

Part of the willingness to work with the Soviets was that the alternative could be the end of the IWC. As evidence of Soviet cheating washed in year after year, the recipients of that evidence could not think of a good use for it. If they pressed the Soviets, then they could expect a lecture about Soviet respect for international institutions, the need to protect resources from capitalist exploitation, and the purely innocent reasons for Soviet actions that only appeared to be cheating in the eyes of bourgeois westerners. If the other whalers rejected such platitudes and flimsy excuses, then the Soviets were more likely to walk out in protest than to acknowledge the errors of their ways. Once they were gone, it would be impossible to enforce restrictions for the other pelagic whaling states. As Frank Anderson, the frequently acerbic Australian commissioner, wrote, "Even if they are only giving lip service to it at least we have some knowledge of what they are doing and they are at least making some public effort to observe the articles of the Convention."[78]

Soviet cheating started small and quickly ballooned. In 1946–47, using just one floating factory and Norwegian gunners, the Soviets abided by the rules. Few Norwegians sailed with Soviet expeditions after that, largely because conditions were so bad: the food was poor and insufficient, the crew's efficiency was awful, the ships were always behind schedule, and at least one of the seventy Norwegians died under suspicious circumstances. Soviet desires to expand their fleet were hindered by their inability to get new floating factories built in European shipyards, so it would take a few years before they could have much impact by cheating anyway. Instead, the Soviets focused on learning how to whale from the *Slava*, and by 1950 they were claiming to be better whalers than anyone else. Captain Aleksei Solyanik and three of his gunners were named Heroes of Socialist Labor that year. In the West, no one could be sure what that meant, given that *Slava*'s catch reports were always late and therefore not considered trustworthy. In addition, Soviet data were obviously flawed. For 1954–55 the *Slava* allegedly produced 150,000 barrels of oil, when the average Norwegian expedition, using bigger ships, averaged 80,000.[79]

Soviet behavior was at least as much the cause of the suspicion as was general dislike for the Soviet Union. Other whalers repeatedly observed questionable whaling practices, such as hunting out of season or inappropriate use of whale carcasses as fenders between vessels. The first eyewitness accounts of Soviet cheating had come in December 1950, when the crews from two whale catchers, the *Southern Ranger* and the *Sigfra*, observed Soviet catcher number 10 towing two blue whales ten days before the season opened. Three years later, Salvesen asked his Norwegian counterparts to keep their eyes open for cheating: "As you know it is the current view on the whaling grounds that *Slava* takes considerable numbers of baleen whales before (and probably after) the baleen season. Such whales are now commonly referred to as 'Russian Sperm.'"[80] In 1954, the crew of the South African factory *Abraham Larsen* reported seeing the *Slava*'s catchers at work before the season opened. When confronted with the report, Soviet officials claimed that they were engaging in research. Of course, while the convention permitted research, it also required that the government issue a permit and convey the research plan to the IWC in advance, but the Soviets shrugged that off.

By 1954, enough reports of strange Soviet behavior on the whaling grounds had filtered in that the common assumption was that the Soviets cheated. A British fisheries official reported in 1956 that whalers believed that "the U.S.S.R. could not possibly have been other than guilty of cheating in the Antarctic."[81] Two years later, a US diplomat concluded that "there is little doubt" among British whalers "that Russian whalers take all the whales which come within range of their harpoons, regardless of size or quota."[82] Solyanik himself contributed to the perception. By 1958, it was clear that his data were faked, "and not very well faked at that." When confronted by British whalers with violating IWC rules at boisterous whaling parties, he "freely and smilingly admitted the charge." Everyone cheated, he reportedly said, and he could not be persuaded that inspectors on British and Norwegian vessels did their jobs.[83] In that same year, a writer in a prominent fishing business journal argued that the Soviets were overreporting their catch in order to send the honest whalers home early, which seemed to run counter to the idea that the Soviets caught anything remotely cetacean that passed before them.[84]

The most egregious evidence of Soviet cheating came in 1963, long after everyone had concluded that Soviet data were useless. Using shotguns and crossbows, British scientists had been firing foot-long aluminum tubes into whales since the 1920s, recording the location of the marking, the species marked, and the estimated size and age of the animal. Each mark had a serial number and contact information, so that if a whaler caught the marked animal he could send data on size, age, and location to Britain's Discovery Committee. This system seems to have worked reasonably well, although fewer than 10 percent of the marks were ever returned. As late as 1963, marking was still going on.[85]

So it was difficult to understand the Soviet report on five whale marks found by crews of one of the 1961–62 Antarctic expeditions. The first serial number the Soviets reported had never been used. The next three were listed as coming from species that did not match the Discovery Committee's records. The final number was reported from the correct species, a humpback whale, but the location given for the capture did not match the data that the Soviets submitted to the Bureau for International Whaling Statistics. When asked to explain the audacious discrepancy, Soviet scientists had nothing to offer. A British scientist estimated that identification errors in the marking process occurred less than 1 percent of the time, so he and fellow researcher Neil Mackintosh could conclude only that the data were deliberately falsified.[86]

But why? It made no sense. Perhaps the whalers had found the marks in the boilers long after the whale had been processed and had guessed at the identity of the mark carrier, but that would not explain why their catch data did not match their mark data or how they got an unused serial number. Perhaps it was just sloppiness, but that would not explain why they even bothered to submit the mark data in the first place or how they could be so wrong. There had to have been a certain deliberateness in the decision to send back the data, so that left the equally unlikely possibilities that the Soviets were sending false data as a power play, announcing that they knew what they could get away with, or that some scientist was attempting to show the other whalers how corrupt the data were by sending what was obviously nonsense. The British fisheries secretary concluded that the data showed "rather disturbing results" but determined that no good would come from publicly confronting the Soviets.[87]

If nothing else, the Soviets were audacious. Before the 1964 IWC meeting, M. N. Sukhoruchenko, the Soviet commissioner, told US diplomats that his country would abide by the latest scientific committee report, even though it was probably inaccurate. The data behind the report, he noted, would be flawed because Japan lied about its data and refused to allow observers on its ships. Given that the Soviets were in year nine of their seventeen-year campaign to stop an international inspections system, the insult to the Japanese was stunning. The Soviets had such a large investment in whaling that they naturally wanted a rational approach that preserved the stocks for the future, or so their official line went.[88]

Unbeknownst to the rest of the world, the Soviets were keeping accurate records for their own purposes, which became public in 1994 when Russian scientist A. V. Yablokov published a summary of Soviet cheating in *Nature*, reporting that he and his colleagues had "uncovered an astounding pattern of falsification of official data." The data showed that the Soviets reported more than they caught beginning in 1948–49, the first year that the combined efforts of pelagic whalers came close to the Antarctic quota, or 16,000 blue whale units. Some of the difference was small, just 2 blue whales and 27 fin whales (or 15.5 BWU), but the sperm whale data was completely made up. The next season, the Soviets reported nearly 300 more fin whales than they had actually taken but left out the 511 humpbacks that they had taken out of season. A pattern of widespread fraud had been established, with overreporting of species that it was acceptable to catch masking the catching of protected species. In the twenty seasons between 1947 and 1966, the Soviets inflated their reported blue whale catch by 500, their sperm whale catch by 1,400, their sei catch by 900, and their fin catch by an astounding 6,000. They underreported their humpback catch by an unfathomable 20,000. The official catch numbers for all of the world's pelagic whalers in that period amounted to fewer than 16,000 humpbacks. The pattern continued until Japanese inspectors came on board Soviet vessels for the 1972–73 season. In addition to faking the overall numbers, Soviet reports inaccurately listed ratios of males to females, average sizes, and dates of capture (to cover up hunting before the season opened). Perhaps most egregiously, the official data did not include populations in waters near India (pygmy blue whales), New Zealand (humpbacks), and Siberia (bowheads and Pacific right whales), which were basically wiped out by Soviet whalers operating outside the IWC's prescribed seasons.[89]

The data published in the 1990s were corroborated by a report from a former chief state inspector of whaling, I. F. Golovlev, who had begun his whaling career in 1946 on the *Slava* and had sailed south eighteen times.

He stated bluntly, "It was whaling totally ignoring the Whaling Regulations that I witnessed . . . and participated in." Captain Solyanik made his priorities clear: "a barren desert must remain where the *Slava* has operated. Catch all whales you meet." He then toyed with foreign whalers by reporting a course that took the *Slava* through the ice shelf, musing, "Let the Statistical Bureau puzzle about our work." Golovlev attributed this attitude to Solyanik's certainty that capitalist whalers were doing the same, and the captain even had one of his catchers follow the Dutch factory *Willem Barendsz* for a week, hoping to catch it cheating.[90]

Soviet inspectors were powerless to enforce the rules because their Ministry of Fisheries was more interested in filling production quotas than anything else. The inspectors were paid by the whaling companies, not a government ministry, which might have made them more susceptible to pressure. When one scientist complained about *Slava*'s violations in 1955, he was banned from further work on whaling. Golovlev claimed to have witnessed the *Soviet Ukraine* catch 1,300 endangered and protected southern right whales in one season off Brazil, but he declined to report the infractions. Soviet whaling was, in his words, "extermination," and any killing done within the rules was just "a lucky coincidence." Of the 234,000 whales killed by Soviet whalers between 1948 and 1972, only 140,000 were actually reported, he claimed, and more than 104,000 were caught in violation of IWC rules. On some expeditions, more than 50 percent of the take was illegal. Golovlev also estimated that the Soviets processed only about 30 percent of the weight of each whale carcass, while the Japanese were able to use about 60 percent, so the charge to use the whole whale was widely ignored.

The impact of cheating, real and suspected, was severe. Catch data formed most of the basis for scientific assessments of the stocks, which were necessary for determining changes to the global quota and other parts of the regulation schedule. If the data were suspect, then the conclusions drawn from them were probably wrong and certainly were not going to hold much water with skeptical whalers. Many factors contributed to scientific uncertainty, but none was more damaging than the widely suspected unreliability of the data. In the long run, it became impossible to draw accurate conclusions about populations of whales, even years later, when scientists were trying to understand how many individuals could be taken from any specific stock.

The suspicion that the Soviets, the Japanese, and Aristotle Onassis cheated undermined every argument for tighter conservation efforts, since there was no point to changing the rules if they were unenforceable. A tighter quota or higher size limits would punish only those who followed the rules, while rewarding those who would catch whatever cetacean was unfortunate enough to wander in front of their harpoons. An American diplomat asserted in 1964 that "the problem of lowering quotas is not the critical one at this time, but observers to ensure that existing quotas are not exceeded is vital."[91] H. K. Salvesen nailed the point: "Every restriction upon the expeditions of countries which effectively enforce them helps to increase the catch of the wicked at the expense of that of the restricted expeditions."[92] If the scientists proposed a lower quota, Salvesen would consider it only if Russian actions were taken into consideration, but at the time, of course, no one knew how complex the Soviet data fraud was. Ron Wall concurred, positing a direct link between the suspicion of cheating and the scientists' inability to change the rules.[93] Another British official dramatically claimed that the "bad faith of the U.S.S.R. Government in respect of the operations of SLAVA is the running sore in the body of the International Whaling Commission."[94] In short, the credibility and viability of the IWC were damaged each time someone concluded that the rules were meaningless.

Widespread violations of the regulation schedule suggested that cooperative management of a shared resource was perhaps impossible. "Unless whaling operations are conducted in good faith," Remington Kellogg summarized, "the agreement will break down."[95] Norway's Birger Bergersen decided that if cheating was not halted immediately "the fate of the Whaling Convention will be forever sealed, and the whale population will be extinct in a few years."[96] And US diplomat William Herrington reported that Onassis's "venture has been cited as proof the International Whaling Commission has not been doing an effective job."[97] Proving that cooperation was possible had been one of the key goals of the United States in 1946, and a decade later US leaders began to conclude that the IWC was doing as much harm as good. The State Department acknowledged in February 1956 that the "system has fallen so far short of perfection that a new inspection system has been proposed."[98] At about the same time, lower-level officials in the department began to suggest that the IWC had to be made more efficient to help blunt the progress toward universal adoption of the two-hundred-mile economic exclusion zones advocated by Ecuador and its neighbors.

From the earliest reports that the Soviets were cheating, it was evident that the only solution was to establish an international inspector scheme. The 1946 convention required that each factory ship carry two inspectors, who were almost always from the flag nation and paid by that government. The delegates had been following the model for extracting pelagic resources in Britain, Norway, and the United States, in which private companies were regulated by the national government, even if the companies and government frequently had a cooperative relationship. In this model, industry leaders would help shape the regulatory laws, but government regulators would be free, in theory, to do their jobs once those laws were in place. The convention had not been crafted to deal with either the Soviet or Onassis approach to the seas. One American noted in 1956 that "miscreants" like Onassis had revealed that small countries could be bribed to ignore infractions, so the only option was to capture "the crusading spirit aroused by the Onassis situation" and turn it into an inspection scheme.[99]

Almost every year during the 1950s, delegates at the annual IWC meetings generally agreed that there should be an inspection scheme that placed foreigners on factory ships. In 1955, they also agreed that there would have to be a protocol, a sort of diplomatic appendix to the 1946 convention, that would allow such a scheme. In proposing a formal protocol, Secretary of State John Foster Dulles observed that the only fix for the IWC's failures was "an inspection system that relies on a corps of inspectors or observers whose conscientiousness, probity and objectiveness are above suspicion."[100] Beyond that principle, delegates failed to agree on much at all. It was unclear, for instance, who should pay the inspectors or vouch for their qualifications. To whom would they answer? If one observed an infraction, what would he do about it? The discussions intensified as it became clear that the Soviet cheating was getting worse, but without a protocol the discussions were moot.

The protocol itself was delayed for several reasons. As long as the diplomats were going to address inspections, they might as well take care of other unfinished business, and subjects such as the use of helicopters, pioneered by Onassis to spot and even hunt whales, got added to the mix. As the depository government for the convention, the United States took upon itself the responsibility for drafting the protocol and managing its ratification. It was not, however, above using that position to its advantage. In 1956, when Norway and Panama were headed toward a fiery confrontation over Panama's complicity in Onassis's behavior, the US State Department brokered a deal whereby each toned down its arguments. One inducement offered to the Norwegians was that State Department official William Herrington would do everything he could to get the protocol finalized by the 1957 meeting.[101] Brazil, however, failed to act on the protocol for years, preventing the creation of an inspection system.

In late 1959, the protocol finally was approved, which brought to the fore the ultimate hurdle: Soviet unwillingness to commit to an inspection system. No one was surprised that Soviet actions and words did not match, given the deep suspicion and sporadic evidence of rules violations. If anything, other IWC members marveled at Soviet cooperativeness in the early years of discussions. By chance, 1959 also saw the near collapse of the commission, as Norway, Japan, and the Netherlands withdrew and then engaged in complex discussions about returning. In 1961, the Soviet government withdrew from talks on an observer system because the Dutch would not be present, but the Japanese concluded that the decision was more likely a useful way to cover their cheating.[102] In 1962, when all of the whaling states got back on board, the Soviets finally deployed their own delaying tactics. At the IWC meeting that year, their commissioner, Sukhoruchenko, held off a discussion until he was compelled to give in. He then rejected all of the proposals before him and responded with one that was "particularly vague and complex," according to the Canadian commissioner, G. R. Clark. Clark understood that the Soviets opposed inspectors as a matter of principle, but he still could not understand their willingness to risk the potential value of their whaling industry.[103] If he had known the full extent of their fraud, perhaps he would have understood their stubbornness.

The delays continued, all the while eroding the IWC's ability to gain a clear sense of the harvest and to establish useful restrictions. At the 1964 meeting, Kellogg reported that "the long sought observer scheme" was nearly at hand, but he underestimated the ways in which it could be kept just out of reach.[104] In 1966, Sukhoruchenko, in his new capacity as chairman of the commission, managed to delay progress by failing to appoint anyone to the committee studying the issue. The next year, the Soviets took the offensive by endorsing the neutral inspector scheme and tying it to quotas for land stations, which instantly and cleverly complicated things for several years. Meanwhile, the Dutch, British, and Norwegians were dropping out of pelagic whaling; each time a country left the industry, the Soviets pointed out that the pending deal would have to be renegotiated. They finally gave in in 1972. Oddly, that very year the data the Soviets submitted to the Bureau for International Whaling Statistics matched their actual catch for the first time since 1948.

In its first decade, the IWC faced the recurrent problem that it had no mechanism for dealing with allegations of cheating. Reformed whalers could not prove that they were better behaved, and aggrieved whalers could not get their day in court. In short, the system was simply not fair—some whalers played by a different set of rules than other whalers—and an unfair system has few proponents. The framers of the IWC had thought about ways to curb cheating, but they had recognized that ultimately it was up to member governments to ensure that whalers followed the regulation schedule. Even if whaling states had been willing to join a commission with the power to investigate allegations and punish infractions—and that was unlikely—they probably were not interested in paying the increased dues to make that possible.

To compound the problems of cheating, real or perceived, the Japanese and Soviets were in the midst of expansion programs. By 1949, the Japanese were building new floating factories to replace the two that had headed out in 1946; by the time the postwar occupation ended, they had three fleets heading south. By the end of the 1950s, seven Japanese expeditions worked the Antarctic seas. The Soviets also were planning to expand after the war, but they were constrained by the unwillingness of Western shipbuilding firms to work for them. They finally got their second expedition, headed by the *Soviet Ukraine*, in 1957; soon after, the *Soviet Russia* joined the fray. The Soviets made clear that they intended to keep building; and the fear that they were not bluffing, added to the belief that they were already violating most of the rules, led most of the rest of the world's whalers and scientists to see a grim future for whaling.

Cheaters may have prospered in the short term, but they also destroyed any chance that the IWC would place whaling on a sustainable footing. By not reporting, or misreporting, their catch, cheaters ensured that the IWC's Antarctic quota would be exceeded. More important, the fear of cheating destroyed any chance that there would be a significant reduction in the quota, the need for which was widely accepted by the early 1950s. Even in the 1960s, scientists studying humpback whale populations near Australia and New Zealand suspected that the unexplained population crash was the product of unreported Soviet whaling, but speculation was not sufficient grounds for policy.[105] Reasonably honest whalers concluded that there was nothing to be gained from their own sacrifice, so they let the IWC drift away from efforts to conserve whale stocks and drift into a crisis that almost killed the commission in the late 1950s.

5

MELTING DOWN AND MUDDLING THROUGH

IN 1964, THE INTERNATIONAL WHALING COMMISSION HELD ITS SIX-
teenth annual meeting in the whaling town of Sandefjord, Norway. As the
delegates convened in the newly renovated Park Hotel, owned by one of
the leaders of the Norwegian whaling industry, at least some were aware
of the stark contrast before them. They were in a grand modern building
made possible by the profits from the whaling industry, but the windows
of that building opened on a scene of rusting whaling vessels that faced
conversion to other uses, if not the scrap heap. The Norwegian whaling
industry, which had once dominated Antarctic waters, was now a distant
third behind its Soviet and Japanese rivals, and the great whale populations had been eviscerated.

The course of the meeting hardly brightened anyone's spirits. Scientists and whalers battled over setting the global catch limit in blue whale
units—even though it was no longer legal for IWC members to hunt actual
blue whales in Antarctic waters—but none of the proposals could win support from enough member nations. Tension between scientists and whalers
was so great that the Norwegian who chaired the Scientific Committee,
Johan Ruud, resigned midmeeting to protest his government's support for
the whaling industry. Because of a poorly thought-out rules change from
the previous year, the deadlock over the Antarctic quota left the commission with no quota at all, which was especially problematic when, as one
Norwegian observer pointed out, setting the quota was the central point
of having a commission in the first place.

The dispirited survivors of the Sandefjord meeting had little good to
say about the IWC or its members. "Over time the International Whaling Commission has developed into a poorly suited international tool,"

commented a Norwegian participant, whose government began to consider withdrawing from the commission.[1] "The Commission is powerless to enforce effective measures to protect the whale stocks and the long-term future of the industry," said his counterpart from New Zealand, who also raised the question of whether his government ought to just leave the commission rather than invest money in sending a delegation halfway around the world to witness such failure.[2] A British official wrote dejectedly that "the Commission has shown a lack of heroic virtue."[3] "Personally I am inclined to believe that the future usefulness of the IWC is questionable," added the chief US delegate, Remington Kellogg, who had little to show for his thirty-five years of working to make whaling sustainable.[4]

British biologist J. A. Gulland observed, "It is probably too late to save whaling as a twentieth century industry; certainly it is too late within the framework of the existing convention." His response, perhaps not meant to be taken seriously, was to propose UN ownership of the industry as a last-ditch effort to save the whales and whaling. He envisioned a complete buyout of the remaining whaling companies, followed by minimal whaling to pay off the interest over twenty years or so.[5] His adviser in the now defunct British whaling industry dismissed the possibility, given the "sterile" history of whaling negotiations and the rise in prices for oil and meat that was making the European expeditions profitable even as the stocks declined. Gerald Elliott, H. K. Salvesen's nephew and successor, continued that it "may well be too late in relation to whale stocks."[6] After thirty-five years of whaling diplomacy, things seemed to have gotten worse, not better.

The IWC had reached this nadir for a number of reasons. First on the list was the inherent difficulty of regulating a valuable pelagic resource that was difficult to study and far away from centers of government. Beyond the built-in challenge of whaling, the commission had been hindered by scientists' inability to agree on a firm policy recommendation and the whalers' reluctance to hear bad news about their harvesting. Despite evidence that the Antarctic whale stocks were declining, the commission's restrictions had been a day late and a dollar short time after time. Commission members' unwillingness to change that pattern in 1964, when the evidence of decline was rusting away before their eyes, seemed to signal that the commission had finally failed.

And yet, oddly, that meeting also marked a turning point. After 1964, scientific evidence tended to be taken more seriously, and the whalers tended to find that the burden of proof was on them rather than on the conservationists. Most governments agreed to give scientists the resources to make their work more professional and the political backing necessary to make it influential.

The problems that caused so much angst in 1964 had been around since the beginning of the commission, but they had really bubbled to the surface around 1957. At first there had been enough whales to mute the scientific warnings, but by the middle of the 1950s the data suggested a more serious problem. Aristotle Onassis had been a useful distraction for most of the decade, but once he had gone away in 1956, the commissioners were forced to confront the failings of the allegedly respectable governments. Most important was the struggle to maintain each fleet's economic viability in the face of growing competition for a declining number of whales. In this debate, scientific advice to drastically cut the Antarctic quota was especially unwelcome. When certain governments were not granted the quota they expected, they pursued the best option available, which was to withdraw from the commission. That, in turn, threatened to bring about its demise.

WEAK SCIENCE. WEAK LEADERSHIP. WEAK COMMISSION

Part of what made the IWC unique upon its founding was the attempt to balance the influence of science and industry. The 1946 convention explicitly spelled out the need to develop whaling while using scientific knowledge to expand stocks, which may sound contradictory but in fact reflected hope that the two forces would complement one another. In reality, the whalers had the upper hand more often than not in the crucial early years of the commission, and the scientists were usually frustrated outsiders, trying to reassure themselves that they had at least made progress in delaying the inevitable collapse of hunted whale stocks. The reasons for the scientists' defeats were partially structural, as the convention's objection system and the fear that states might leave the commission and hunt whales on their own made it very hard to make significant changes to the regulation schedule. But at least as important was the problem of scientific uncertainty. Salvesen thought that the population estimates of men like Neil

Mackintosh were, according to one relative, "intellectually dishonest."[7] Ron Wall, the British commissioner for most of the 1950s, put it this way:

> The scientists are not . . . quite unanimous on these matters and are in any event chary of expressing downright opinions on the basis of existing scientific knowledge and the available catch statistics; and this attitude, which is natural enough to scientists working in a field where basic biological knowledge is very incomplete, makes it difficult for the Commissioners of the whaling countries to adopt as strong a line as some of us would like with our whaling industries, who are themselves inclined to take the short view and feel that if they can deploy their existing capital equipment to the maximum during its period of life, the longer-term future can be left to take care of itself.[8]

Wall pinpointed the problems scientists faced, but he also demonstrated that he and other leaders of the commission were part of the problem. They were savvy enough to see the different ways that scientists and whalers operated, and yet they were too spineless to compel their governments to challenge the whaling interests.

For his part, New Zealand scientist W. H. Dawbin had a slightly more balanced perspective. Writing in 1960, he concluded that sufficient evidence had convinced scientists that populations were declining, but this still had to be framed as either a trend or a probability, not a certainty. Even a slender thread of doubt enabled whalers to keep the quota higher than the scientists had recommended. Even when it became obvious that whales were in decline, all scientists could offer was a range for the number of whales that might be taken safely, while industry expected a specific number. Dawbin then elaborated on one cause of the uncertainty: the different approaches among laboratories from around the world, which made it difficult to mesh conclusions.[9] Only in 1961 did the IWC sponsor a meeting of these various scientists to reconcile their methods.

The structural problems were enough that even great leadership and a scientific consensus might not have made a difference. The first problem was the place of scientists in the commission, which established two key subcommittees, the Scientific Committee and the Technical Committee. This innocuous-sounding division meant that the whalers had their own group, the Technical Committee, which could effectively stymie changes proposed by the scientists because its members saw the whaling questions in a different light. On a regular basis in the early years, recommendations from the Scientific Committee would be altered or halted in the Technical Committee. Eventually, the commission recognized that the Technical Committee would have to be folded into the Scientific Committee to get anything done.[10]

Even if an unscathed idea made it out of the committees to the plenary session (and sometimes that meant waiting a year because it had not been on the agenda sent out sixty days before a particular meeting), the IWC voting system made change difficult. Despite the Cold War, the five pelagic countries formed unlikely alliances, so that Japan and the Soviet Union, which did not even have diplomatic relations until 1955, still found themselves able to coordinate policy. When need be, the pelagic whaling states could vote as a bloc and assure that an amendment would lack the support from three-quarters of the members necessary for passage. If any one of the five was likely to break ranks, it was Norway, which prided itself on attempting to husband whales rather than exploit them ruthlessly and could sometimes bring Britain with it. Even then, if only two or three nations voted against an amendment, and it passed, they would surely file an objection, and most other members with a direct interest would object as well, killing the new rule. In practice, all it took was one nation, almost always the Netherlands until 1963, to vote no to kill a rule by triggering the objection landslide. The knowledge that each member had a veto bred caution, so that whalers were unlikely to face a radical proposal.

The other major structural problem was that the commission was run on a shoestring budget. The British agreed to house it within their fisheries ministry and to provide a secretary, Alban Dobson, who had been fisheries secretary for many years. That setup facilitated an IWC membership fee of merely £150 per year, which made the IWC a model of frugality that even a die-hard isolationist in the US Congress could tolerate. It also meant that there was no money for independent research on whales. One research cruise in the South Seas would cost two or three times the IWC's annual budget, and few member states were about to volunteer to charge themselves more. Indeed, it is likely that the British whalers pushed to host the commission partially because they thought that it might grow too powerful if it was on its own in Washington.

Dobson typified the mediocre leadership that hampered the commission in its early years. As secretary, Dobson had little direct power, but his position gave him prestige and the ability to shape the debate subtly. Instead of using that influence, he appeared worn out, even to sympathetic New Zealander Frank Corner, who said that Dobson "was all too obviously past his prime, and the administration of the Commission does no more than stagger along from meeting to meeting."[11] Corner, speaking for a nation with a strong interest in pelagic conservation, was not far off from the opinion of H. K. Salvesen, who had no use for Dobson as a bureaucrat. In fact, very few people had much to say about Dobson one way or the other, except for acknowledging his years of effort, although one Norwegian noted that his three successors as fisheries secretary were all effectively incompetent and hence even worse.[12]

The power, such as it was, lay in the hands of the IWC chairman, who served a three-year term, usually after first serving a term as vice-chairman. The chairman was one of the commissioners, but he was also supposed to be a person with political influence and an understanding of science and industry. The first chair, appropriately, was Birger Bergersen, a jack-of-all-trades. He served as a Norwegian diplomat, a member of the IWC Scientific Committee, chair of the Norwegian Hvalrådet, and a professor of anatomy at a dental school. The second chair was American Remington Kellogg, who probably held the record for length of service to his country on efforts to regulate whaling, thirty-five years. Corner, who generally sympathized with US goals, was frustrated with Kellogg's leadership, which he described as "not very good."[13] Kellogg was an esteemed biologist who, like Bergersen, certainly worked hard to promote conservation, and from his own research experience he had an appreciation for what scientists could not know. But Kellogg had a mixed record as an administrator. His reports were colorless and bureaucratic, often recycling the same language from year to year, in stark contrast with Corner's insightful letters from the meetings. Kellogg's friends remembered him as generally being uncomfortable with people, and his adversaries remembered him as needlessly antagonistic. He was known at the Smithsonian for a roaring temper, which probably explains why apparently only three people from the institution attended his funeral in Washington, DC, even though he had served there for about forty years.[14] He may not have been very effective as a chairman, but there was no doubt that he worked tirelessly to make whaling sustainable.

In contrast, two of Kellogg's four successors were fundamentally negligent. The third chairman, G. J. Lienesch of the Netherlands, used the position to protect his nation's whaling company from the obvious conclusion that too many whalers were chasing too few whales. Corner called his "knowledge of procedure scanty—and impartiality in any matter where Dutch interests are involved doubtful."[15] Lienesch played on scientific uncertainty in a disgraceful manner that still was the subject of discussion nearly sixty years later. The sixth chairman, M. N. Sukhoruchenko of the Soviet Union, used the position to disrupt creation of an observer scheme that would have forced his country to stop the wholesale violation of the regulation schedule.[16]

Finally, the direction of the commission's decisions was in part the product of scientific limitations. Corner noted that "the scientists constantly bewail the fact that very little precise scientific evidence in fact exists. The Schedule . . . is based largely on intelligent guesswork."[17] Because of the limited options for research, cetologists were left with marking data and catch data as the basis for their work. Potentially, this data stream could lead to important insights and conclusions, but its use required sophisticated statistical analysis. No one on the commission was capable of running or paying for such analysis, but by the middle of the 1950s it was obvious that an opportunity was there. Without such a sophisticated analysis, scientists were left with anecdotal evidence of a trend toward smaller whales, which reflected in turn that the populations were in distress. Of course anecdotal evidence could go either way, and some whalers would either report that they were seeing more whales than before or that their knowledge and intuition told them that the whales were still numerous but somehow harder to find in the pack ice.

The Bureau for International Whaling Statistics (BIWS) was producing basic statistical analysis, which should have been enough to show the problem. In 1953, the BIWS was able to chart changes in size of caught whales and changes in the catch per catcher day's work (CDW). Between 1939 and the early 1950s, killer boats nearly doubled in tonnage and more than doubled in horsepower, yet the number of blue whale units per CDW remained just below one. The stasis in the catch number, despite the better catchers, suggested a decline in stocks. More stunning were the raw numbers of blue whales caught, which had declined from 13,848 in 1938–39 to a mere 5,101 in the 1951–52 season. These numbers would finally give the scientists the leverage to propose lowering the Antarctic quota at the 1953 meeting.[18]

While the commission struggled with other issues, such as creation of a sanctuary, ultimately it was the quota decisions that mattered the most and revealed the trouble the scientists faced in putting whaling on a sustainable course. Everyone associated with the commission thought that hunting whales was acceptable, so the core of the disagreement was figuring out the best use of the whalers' capital. Scientists generally wanted to moderate the catch so that whaling could continue far into the future, while the whalers had the shorter-term goal of getting an acceptable return on their investment. The short term almost always prevailed.

LOWERING THE QUOTA

Despite the IWC's many flaws, no government worked very hard to fix the commission before it reached crisis. For all of their complaints, the pelagic whaling states received enough of value from the commission that they did not want to risk setting off a major call for revisions. The rest of the members worried that reform efforts would give the pelagic states an excuse to withdraw and engage in a free-for-all. Most parties agreed that the commission could be made to work better within its current structure. The debate over the Antarctic quota in the late 1950s finally caused the division that developed into a crisis that almost killed the commission.

The Antarctic quota, set at 16,000 blue whale units in 1946, was unchanged in 1953. In his opening remarks as IWC chairman in 1951, Bergersen had said that "every biologist who has examined catch statistics" knew that 16,000 was too high. By the time the IWC appointed Bergersen to lead a subcommittee on the quota at the 1952 meeting, the issue was already a sore point. The hint of a problem had become a full-fledged crisis in the 1952–53 season, when the whalers reported only 14,855 BWU caught, not the full 16,000. J. M. Marchand, the South African director of fisheries, blamed bad weather, but even H. K. Salvesen conceded that whales seemed to be declining and, hence, the quota would have to go down.[19] As a result, and on behalf of the IWC Scientific Committee, at the 1953 meeting Bergersen proposed to lower the quota to 15,000 BWU, to close the seas below South America to catching blue whales, and to postpone the season for blue whales until 15 January.[20]

The Dutch led the opposition to any effort to reduce the quota and in the process earned a reputation for sacrificing objectivity in their effort to keep afloat their whaling company, supported by a generous subsidy. E. J. Slijper proposed that the necessary data justifying a reduction would have to include the size of the stock, the natural mortality rate, and complete information about life history, including life span, number of offspring, and age at sexual maturity. Not only was most of that data unavailable, but changes in the whaling industry also made it impossible to compare prewar and postwar data, he argued. Catchers and factory ships were more efficient, the season no longer included all of November and December, and the whalers were working different waters. The very idea of using CDW data, he claimed, was pointless. Instead, talking specifically of the decline in blue whales caught, the Dutch argued that this reflected the decision by expedition managers to avoid the dangerous pack ice, where it was still possible to find plenty of blue whales. Instead whalers allegedly preferred to hunt the safer open water, which fins preferred. The Dutch acknowledged that blues seemed to be in decline but not so much that the stock could not supply 4,000 animals safely. Assuming another 300 BWU from humpbacks, the demand for fin whales would be 23,400, or less than 8 percent of the Dutch estimate of 300,000 fins in the stock. Slijper cited a Norwegian statistician's similar estimate that 250,000 fins and 100,000 blues were left, suggesting that there was no reason to panic. Or, as the Dutch statement concluded, "At the moment there is no sufficient scientific evidence for the conclusion that it is absolutely necessary to reduce the number of 16,000 Blue Whale Units."[21]

Slijper's argument did not convince anyone who might be considered neutral in the discussions. For instance, the Canadian commissioner, G. R. Clark, concluded that "it was apparent that the Dutch scientists had been given strict instructions to argue against any reduction in the total quota."[22] Frank Corner acidly concluded that Dutch scientists "will not be convinced until every last dead whale has been counted, or until their whaling expedition has been sold."[23] Years later, observers would remember Slijper for his devotion to the Dutch whaling company, not to scientific methods.[24]

While the Dutch were the most forthright in their opposition to lowering the quota, they were joined by most of the pelagic whaling states and even Australia. "Our position here is rather delicate," read an Australian briefing paper. "We should not be placed in a position of supporting a lower total limit, since Australia may then be called upon to reduce the scale of her operations from land stations."[25] W. C. Smith, New Zealand's commissioner, rather bluntly summed up Australia's position: "It is just the same as all the other countries in the Commission; they are all fighting for their own ends."[26] Corner observed that the pelagic whalers, who pretty much dominated the meetings before 1953, found themselves in an unusual position. Their costs were increasing, the price of whale oil was in decline (from £170 per ton in 1950 to £70 by 1955), and competition was "keen."[27] And just at that point, the scientists began to assert themselves by arguing that the quota was too high.

Bergersen's proposal led to a compromise at 15,500 BWU and a late start to the season for blue whales. Even though the vote was unanimous, the whalers clearly had won the day. Kellogg claimed that the members showed "marked concern for the maintenance of stocks of whales" even as he argued that "much more rigorous action was indicated." If that action did not come in the form of trusting scientists, then the United States would have to consider withdrawing from the commission in protest.[28] Neil Mackintosh, chair of the Scientific Committee, told Corner that the ideal arrangement would be a quota of just 10,000 BWU, but without hunting any blue whales for five to ten years. The whalers were happy to accept that position—in 1965. Corner acknowledged, though, that a lower quota would penalize "the relatively honest whalers like the British, Norwegians and Japanese."[29]

The next year, 1954, at the IWC meeting in Tokyo, the quota remained at 15,500 BWU. Delegates agreed to a series of small changes in the rules for hunting blue and humpback whales in certain southern and northern waters. The most important change was delaying the start date for fin hunting to 7 January and blue hunting to 21 January. In terms of the quota, the commission noted only that a drastic reduction in the future was possible, even though the Scientific Committee, over Slijper's dissent, had called for a reduction to 15,000 BWU. The concern about blue whale populations specifically left the Scientific Committee pondering the imminent need to break the global quota into species quotas, with very low limits on the blue whale take.

Kellogg, who was completing his term as IWC chairman, concluded that the amendments "fall short of the minimum protection needed at this time." He blamed the "absence of sufficient scientific data," although he then noted that one key solution was "thorough analysis of the mass of statistical data" available to the Bureau for International Whaling Statistics.[30] Ron Wall, representing a pelagic whaling state, admitted the problem: "Most of the Commissioners probably have an uneasy feeling, as I certainly have myself, that in the Antarctic . . . the annual permitted catch is greater than the stocks will indefinitely bear." He blamed the scientists for not providing "a sufficiently confident and documented" argument for the need for restrictions, but he also expressed hope that the industry itself would begin trimming capacity for economic reasons, which would make it easier to reduce the quota—in effect reversing the order of influence in the commission.[31]

That the IWC followed its meeting in Tokyo in 1954 with one in Moscow in 1955 suggested the new order in whaling diplomacy after the war, as well as the strange alliances that the commission was creating. The delegates met in the new Sovetskaya Hotel, which one Australian described as "wired for sound," meaning that confidential conversation would be impossible. Dining appears to have been risky, as he called the hotel food "unpalatable," with a case of "Moscow tummy" waiting for the incautious.[32] Scientists on yet another special subcommittee wanted a quota of 11,000 BWU, which they knew was politically unacceptable. The Scientific Committee came forward with a cut to 14,500 BWU, only to face formidable opposition. Johan Ruud and Neil Mackintosh made their case strongly, only to be countered by Slijper, "whose docility to his country's whaling interests cast doubt upon his scientific integrity." Corner noted that Panama's attitude was "completely predatory," the Netherlands was interested only in making money as fast as possible, and the British were caught between their eminent scientists and H. K. Salvesen, who "uses any means fair or foul to protect his profits."[33]

The commission accepted a nominal cut of 500 BWU, as well as a further reduction to 14,500 BWU for the 1956–57 season. Because some states had voted against each reduction, the Norwegians and Americans feared that either the Dutch or British would file an objection. Secretary of State John Foster Dulles pressured them not to object, emphasizing that the recommendation for a reduction came from the Scientific Committee; if the IWC was going to be effective, particularly in the eyes of South American states that were organizing their own whaling commission, its members would have to accept scientifically driven conservation measures.[34] While the 1955 reduction held, the Netherlands objected to reduction in the overall BWU quota, hence several other governments, including the United States, followed suit, and the 1956 IWC meeting faced the prospect of reverting back to the 16,000 BWU limit.[35]

As the delegates met at another great capital city, London, in 1956, the quota issue had become the central point of contention. All but the Dutch voted for 14,500 BWU for the 1956–57 season, and even that figure was far above what anyone with basic science education thought acceptable. Corner summed up the situation after the 1956 meeting: "The most important question . . . is whether the Netherlands Government will be so insensitive to the views of all other participating Governments, and so amenable to the pressure from its whaling industry, as to object." An objection would mean that the IWC had reached a "dead-end and failed in its task of achieving a balance between killing and replacement rates of the whale populations," although it should have been evident to a keen observer that the dead-end had been reached around 1953.[36] It was obvious, the Americans concluded, that the argument about scientific evidence was a smokescreen for the deep financial obligations of the Dutch government, which had guaranteed a 6 percent return to shareholders of the Netherlands Whaling Company. Dulles ordered the US embassy in The Hague to pressure the Netherlands not to object to the lower quota, citing the confidential admission of a member of the Dutch delegation that their foreign minister was embarrassed by the lack of merit of the Dutch opposition.[37] It appears that the Dutch Ministry of Agriculture and Fisheries' desire to overturn the reduction was squelched, and the Netherlands accepted the 14,500 BWU quota for 1956–57.

Despite Wall's assertion that it would get easier to trim the quota as the industry recognized whales' decline, in fact it became more difficult. The Dutch could not afford the cuts, because by 1959 they had sunk 32.5 million guilders into subsidizing the *Willem Barendsz*, whose owners were perfectly happy with the arrangement. The Japanese needed more protein, not less, so they were not eager to reduce the quota. British whalers thought that they and the Norwegians would bear the brunt of any reductions, which would simply push them into bankruptcy.[38] The Norwegians had taken action for 1957, organizing a cap on the number of catcher vessels per floating factory, but since the Soviets did not cooperate, and indeed had new factories coming on line, catcher limits were not a long-term solution. Kellogg commented that "reconciling commercial necessity with biological considerations and international conservation efforts to maintain whale stocks is becoming increasingly difficult in view of the mounting economic pressures."[39] Given those pressures, the United States tried a new approach with the Netherlands in 1957, emphasizing that Dutch opposition to the majority of scientific opinion would support "unilateral claims advocated by some countries." With the UN conference on the law of the sea impending, "mere lip service to the scientific side" would reinforce the case made by those advocating "extended exclusive control over offshore fisheries."[40] Surely the Netherlands, as a maritime state, would not wish to reinforce the recent "assaults . . . on the time-honored principles concerning the limits of territorial waters and freedom of the seas."[41]

These American arguments do not seem to have registered with the whaling states, who were, if anything, drifting away from the IWC. As early as December 1956, members of the Norwegian Whaling Association were suggesting that Norway should leave the IWC if Japan and the Soviet Union continued to expand their fleets. Whalers complained that British and Norwegian whalers faced "major handicaps" in competing with government subsidy and outright ownership, and the Norwegians were beginning to think that operating within the IWC rules was completely unproductive. In addition, their government had twice voted to reduce the BWU quota despite the whalers' advice to the contrary. The whalers told the rest of the Hvalrådet, which set national whaling policy, that the situation was "so grave" that the companies would have to keep a "vigilant eye" on the government.[42]

Instead, the Norwegians came up with a new idea: to assign each pelagic whaling nation a portion of the overall quota. If each nation had its own fixed slice, then it could act more rationally than if it was competing for each whale, with the fear that the global quota might be reached before any one expedition caught enough whales to have a profitable season. Rational whaling included catching whales later in the season, when they were fatter, and taking whales more methodically, when possible, so that each whale could be processed fully. The 1946 convention did not allow for individual national quotas, so they would have to be negotiated outside of the commission meetings. In effect, there would be two rounds of discussion about quotas, one inside the commission to determine the global quota and one outside to divvy it up, but it was not clear in what order those discussions would occur or what effect the one might have on the other.

When the Norwegians made their proposal, the other whaling governments and companies reacted cautiously. Only the British openly supported the idea at the 1958 IWC meeting, even though all the pelagic whalers would ultimately see some reason to support it. Not only did they see the possibility of making operations more efficient, but each nation saw an opportunity to protect its self-interest. For the struggling Dutch and British companies, the quota division offered a better chance at profitability, for the Norwegians it offered a means of controlling Soviet and Japanese expansion, and for the Soviets and Japanese it offered a chance to stake claims as the dominant whaling state. These national goals were not necessarily compatible, as negotiators would soon discover.

The Soviets made clear immediately that they would accept 20 percent of the quota as their slice, and in return they would not follow through on their plan to expand to seven expeditions, perhaps because they could see the writing on the wall about the decline in fin whale populations. The other four pelagic whalers were confronted with the choice of granting the Soviets every fifth whale or trying to negotiate with the people who seemed to be breaking every rule and were certainly holding up progress on the observer scheme. Before the pelagic states could work out a choice, in January 1959 Norway and the Netherlands announced that they would withdraw from the IWC. The long-feared free-for-all on the whaling grounds looked imminent.

DEPARTURES AND RETURNS

The decision by two of the European states to leave the IWC and the subsequent departure of Japan and threatened departure of Great Britain were directly tied to the countries' inability to work out a compromise on the quota division. If the quota issue could not be addressed quickly, the IWC would collapse after only a decade of operations, and only self-restraint, never abundant in the whaling industry, might save the industry from destruction. But in the crisis there was also an opportunity to fix some of the problems that had plagued the commission since its inception.

After the 1958 meeting of the IWC failed to significantly change the status quo, Norway decided to take the lead by calling a meeting of the pelagic whaling countries for late November of that year. Norwegian officials were worried because the Soviets were claiming the right, as a world power, to mount between three and six expeditions in the Antarctic—Britain had three, Japan had six, and Norway had nine.[43] The *Slava* was still plying the seas, the huge *Soviet Ukraine* and *Soviet Russia* were about to join her, and two more factory vessels were in planning stages. The Norwegians expressed concern that the Antarctic stock could not take any more exploitation, but the Soviets were not moved. When the Norwegians suggested national quotas, the Soviets balked, arguing that that would open the field to other countries to claim a slice of the pie. The Norwegian delegation returned to Oslo nervous but hoping that the November talks might lead to a cap on Soviet and Norwegian expeditions.

Indeed, the November meeting seemed at first to exceed expectations. The Norwegians proposed that the Soviet catch be allowed to grow from 8 percent of the global quota to 16 percent, while the other pelagic states would gradually absorb reductions of 8 percent. The Soviet delegation explained, in apparently convincing terms, that they were going to take 20 percent in exchange for building just four new floating factories, with the final one replacing the *Slava*. The delegates then agreed that the arrangement would last seven years, starting with the 1959–60 season and covering the time frame of Soviet building plans. The other four states would work to parse the remaining 80 percent of the quota by 1 June 1959. If any other country sent an expedition to Antarctic waters, the deal would be void. A US diplomat in London reported that the meeting was "widely acclaimed as putting an end to cut-throat competition" that threatened to destroy the IWC.[44]

But the reality did not match the reports. The director of the Japanese fisheries agency came to the November meeting with a clear mandate to oppose quotas, so he could only report the 20 percent deal without recommending it, and he and his Dutch counterpart had opposed the others' proposals. For their part, the Dutch demanded 8 percent of the quota as necessary to make a profit, making agreement among the four non-Soviet pelagic whaling states almost impossible. The Japanese emphasized, as they would in opposing environmentalists twenty years later, that they were upholding the true spirit of the 1946 convention. The British whaler H.K. Salvesen had once again recommended letting the IWC die in the summer of 1958, so he was skeptical about any patched-together quota deal. The

Norwegians could see that negotiations over the remaining 80 percent of the IWC quota would be tough, at best. With so much uncertainty, the Dutch and Norwegian governments announced in January 1959 that they would withdraw from the IWC, although each reserved the right to rejoin before the summer if their seemingly mutually exclusive concerns could be reconciled. Less than a month later, Japan exercised its right to announce its departure, calling it a "precautionary measure" while emphasizing that Tokyo had no desire "wantonly to disrupt international cooperation or act selfishly."[45]

In four subsequent meetings, British and Norwegian proposals for dividing the remaining 80 percent failed. When each of the four states presented its demands, the total take reached nearly 90 percent of the quota and, as one US diplomat wrote, "no latter-day miracle of the loaves and fishes was wrought."[46] The Norwegians suggested a complex formula based on an Antarctic quota of 16,000 blue whale units, with national quotas based on what had been caught over the previous five years, but no one else liked that. The Dutch would not budge from claiming 8 percent, which was simply unacceptable to everyone else because the Dutch sent only one of the twenty-two floating factories expected on the whaling grounds in the 1959–60 season. The one-time allies in fighting off the conservation-minded nations were now fighting for their individual lives. Each nation pledged to limit its quota to the demands it had made at the quota negotiations, which meant that the overall catch might reach 17,000 BWU if the Soviets took the full 3,000 they had claimed. That seemed possible, as the *Soviet Ukraine* was being fitted out in Kiel during the talks, expanding Soviet capacity. The new vessels highlighted another problem that had not been addressed—would newer, bigger factories get the same quota as the smaller, less efficient ones?

When a Japanese delegation met with the US officials to discuss the upcoming 1959 IWC meeting, its members found Remington Kellogg and William Herrington in an uncharitable mood. The delegates probably were not helped by their foreign minister's complaint that the twelve nonwhaling countries of the IWC ignored the "rightful demands" of the pelagic states.[47] H. Okuhara, vice-director of fisheries, reported that the Japanese had asked the Dutch and Norwegians to cancel their withdrawals, to no effect. Okuhara saw no hope of an agreement along the lines being discussed and no new proposal on the horizon. Clearly, he wanted the United

States to see Japan as a reasonable state forced into a disagreeable situation. Kellogg and Herrington were unsympathetic. They predicted that "damage to the world at large . . . from the loss of an important resource" would lead to world opinion pressuring the departing states to live by IWC rules, so the advantage of withdrawing from the convention would be slight. Kellogg and Herrington said they would work within the commission to change the rules, with the implication that the departing countries would be compelled to return at some point and accept those new rules. And more important, they argued that the nations that withdrew to protect their own interests would hurt themselves by strengthening the hand of countries that were extending their territorial waters.[48] The 1959 commission meeting was shaping up to be very interesting.

The pelagic whaling states held a meeting among themselves on 18 June 1959, with the full IWC meeting set to convene four days later. The briefing papers in the hands of New Zealand's delegation bluntly stated that the IWC "has reached the crisis which we have been predicting. . . . Unless some satisfactory international regime is established it is inevitable that whales will in effect be exterminated in Southern waters."[49] It quickly became apparent that the pelagic states had not worked out their differences, which meant that the withdrawals would proceed apace. In a desperate effort to save the commission, the Canadian delegate G. R. Clark proposed raising the catch ceiling to 16,000 BWU (after several years of slowly lowering it from 16,000 to 14,500) to allow enough room for each pelagic state to catch what it claimed to need, a move that he said Kellogg endorsed. Only New Zealand immediately opposed the idea.

The divergent reaction of New Zealand and the United States to Clark's proposal showed the complexity of the situation. Each of these countries had long argued that the commission should set the global quota on the basis of the Scientific Committee's conclusions, so each had sent its delegation with instructions to vote for a quota of 14,500 BWU at most. New Zealand's delegate, H. H. Francis, fought hard for the 14,500 BWU limit, even when no one supported him. He told Britain's Ron Wall that he would not give in to the pelagic whalers' blackmail, and he persuaded his government to communicate that position to the other members of the Commonwealth.[50] Canada flip-flopped on the 16,000 BWU limit, forcing Clark to appeal for his government not to undercut him, and Australia also wavered, "judging by the wrath [Frank Anderson, Australia's commissioner] poured on New Zealand" for prompting the review of his position.[51] New Zealand's prime minister refused to budge, arguing that a vote for 16,000 BWU would "deny ourselves any ground of principle on which to stand in the future." He concluded that "our interest remains the preservation, through disciplined catching, of a valuable economic resource."[52]

Whereas New Zealand was pursuing an almost pure conservationist position, the United States found itself thinking about other things. Kellogg played all of his cards, but the dealer had not been kind. Kellogg had come to the meeting wondering "if the Commission [will] survive after the present meeting," and he soon reported to his wife that the whaling industry had "the whip hand."[53] Frank Corner reported that Kellogg was "livid" in response to the proposal for a 16,000 BWU quota, but Kellogg had to consider the fate of the IWC, which he had done so much to create.[54] Even as he was asking Washington for the authority to work with the higher quota, he undercut Clark by publicly indicating support for New Zealand's hard-line stance, hoping to pressure the whalers to compromise.

What the US delegation wanted was the authority to abstain from a vote for a limit of 16,000 BWU, concerned that opposing that proposal would lead to it being voted down with no quota at all as a result. Not only did the Americans fear the effects of a breakdown on the territorial waters question, but they also concluded that "industry operations of countries not obligated by convention will be relatively unrestrained despite pious statements by government to contrary."[55] But while waiting for his instructions, Kellogg pulled out a card he had hidden up his sleeve, the ace of guilt. As elder statesman, he interrupted the discussion at one point with a request to the chair for permission to "reminisce a bit." He reminded the delegates that the IWC had made strides in conserving whales. Had the founders not acted in 1946, Antarctic whale stocks would have been decimated and the industry "finished." They had "managed to avert this catastrophe" because they had maintained some balance between "commercial necessity and scientific and moral considerations." Kellogg probably had not mentioned morality at any previous meeting, but it turned into his main theme. He argued that the balance had always been too far toward commercial concerns, but the 1959 meeting had witnessed a "noticeable deterioration of this less than successful balance." If the balance did not swing toward scientific and moral considerations, then the delegates would have failed in their obligation to "future generations of mankind." "None of us in this room wishes to be responsible for the virtual extermination of whales throughout the world," he said. The emphasis on commercial concerns would lead to the unraveling of the convention and destruction of the whale stocks: "We, as individuals, would have dispersed our posterity's rightful heritage, of which we are the trustees appointed by our Governments."[56]

Kellogg's barrage was insufficient to counter decades of entrenched whaling interests. Simply put, he needed a compromise. William Herrington came through, telegraphing that allowing the higher quota "would do irreparable harm to [the] concept [of] conservation [of] high seas resources," which would prove the point being made by Ecuador and its neighbors. Still, he authorized a compromise: 16,000 BWU for one year, with the appointment of a committee of independent experts to set the quota in the future.[57]

The compromise failed. By linking the 16,000 BWU quota with an independent group of scientists who would assess the health of whale stocks, Canadians and Americans hoped to offer a face-saving option for the three countries that had withdrawn as well as those emphasizing conservation. They knew that the proposal faced hurdles because the IWC did not have the funds to pay for such scientific study, which meant higher dues assessments, particularly for the pelagic whaling states. It also was not clear who would choose the outside evaluators, what data would be available to them, or if the commission would just accept whatever they proposed. The key point was to get the pelagic whaling states to accept the principle. Japan did, announcing on 30 June that it was canceling its withdrawal; Japanese delegates had already told Clark that they regretted the withdrawal, which had hurt Japan's position on other fisheries matters. But Norway and the Netherlands announced on 3 July that they would not return, so Clark withdrew the compromise proposal, and the quota returned, oddly, to 15,000 BWU, which had been set as the permanent maximum quota in 1955.[58]

With three pelagic states in and two out, there was a collective sense of dread. The unregulated free-for-all on the whaling grounds was at hand, and keeping the IWC alive was the only way to prevent it. Technically, the combined catch of Great Britain, the Soviet Union, and Japan could add up to the 15,000 BWU limit, but each of them and Norway and the

Netherlands announced national quotas. Unfortunately for the whales, the national quotas totaled 17,500 BWU, when scientists generally estimated that 10,000 BWU was the most that could be taken without further damage to the stocks. The only consolation was that the fleets were probably capable of taking only 16,500 BWU because the *Soviet Ukraine* would not be ready for the 1959–60 season after all.[59] Each whaling state also pledged to live up to the processing and open season rules. Before the season ended, even H. K. Salvesen concluded that it would be a rough year for whales, in part because the Dutch and Soviets were behaving poorly.[60]

One unforeseen problem was that the Japanese, British, and Norwegian whalers now had to figure out how to divide the quotas their governments had set, because IWC members had never had national quotas before. Britain had set the quota for its whaling companies at 2,500 BWU, even though the industry had pleaded for 2,700 BWU and the average catch of the three previous years had been only 2,013 BWU. Salvesen, owner of the *Southern Harvester* and the *Southern Venturer*, and the Hector Whaling Company, owner of the *Balaena*, struggled to find a compromise even with this inflated figure. Rupert Trouton, chairman of Hector, proposed a simple 2–1 ratio, which Salvesen found completely unacceptable. The latter's ships were more efficient and had caught more whales over recent years, so he should get more per expedition. Trouton argued that Hector could not survive on less than one-third of what the British government had proposed. Eventually, they turned to the Ministry of Agriculture and Fisheries to split the number.[61]

In Norway, whalers approved of a Japanese proposal to retire three older Norwegian factory ships and arrange a joint purchase and retirement of the Dutch *Willem Barendsz*, but Oslo refused to surrender Norway's long-held position as the premier whaling nation. Instead, the Norwegian government sent its delegation to London with a minimum quota demand of 5,000 BWU and instructions to be a follower, not a leader, on any issue other than the observer scheme.

In Japan, three companies tried to come to an accommodation, but the one with the worst record demanded equal treatment. *Shin Suisan Shimbun* (New Fisheries Times), a Japanese trade newspaper, denounced the companies for "muddy competition to get one more whale for their companies," when everyone knew that the Antarctic was an international fishing grounds and the companies had to "be Japanese champions in the international arena." The government imposed individual company quotas that equaled 5,175 BWU, but a national quota of only 5,037 BWU, so each factory could hunt until its quota had been filled or until the national quota had been taken.[62] The idea was to reward companies that were better whalers, but it might have caused whalers to cut corners in their race to fulfill their individual company quotas.

When the 1959–60 season was over, Japan had managed to overshoot its quota, taking 5,200 BWU, while the other pelagic states had failed to meet theirs. The Soviets reported just under 2,800 BWU, the Dutch 1,037 BWU, both of which were reasonably close to their preseason estimates for 3,000 and 1,200 BWU, respectively. The British reported the embarrassing figure of 1,898 BWU, versus their widely criticized quota of 2,500. The Norwegians had a rough year, coming up with just 4,565 BWU when they had laid claim to 5,800. So the season's yield had been just over 15,500 BWU, mostly fins despite almost unrestricted access, which suggested how poor the stocks were.[63]

By 1960, it was apparent that the private whaling companies were barely hanging on, squeezed by declining whale populations and declining prices for whale oil. The Salvesen operations were hemorrhaging money because of a shortage of whales and the IWC's regulation schedule. In the 1958–59 season, Salvesen's two factories and land station on South Georgia had lost a combined £288,000. The next year, operating under the national quota, the *Southern Harvester* was able to generate enough income to move the company into the black by £53,000, and in 1960–61 the company raked in £378,000. And yet Salvesen's estimated that the same ship would lose £170,000 in 1961–62. The company's officials estimated oil prices at £60 per ton and meat meal at £350 per ton, when they would need £74 and £800, respectively, if they got 4.5 percent of the IWC's Antarctic quota.[64]

Salvesen himself, normally full of bluster, admitted in 1960 that "the trend is clearly downward."[65] He had in his hands a chart of BWU caught per catcher day since 1955, which showed that between 0.9 and 1 BWU had been taken per day through 1958–59. Then the number had dropped to below 0.7 BWU.[66] Salvesen thought that changes in hunting patterns and use of the catchers explained most of the diminution, but he was still pessimistic. The breakdown of the IWC had taken its toll on whale stocks, the quota deals had treated Britain unfairly, and the Soviets still cheated. Finally, whale products simply were not that competitive on the market, as vegetable oil was replacing whale oil in making margarine. Of course Salvesen took none of the blame, passing it instead on to his government for tying his hands starting in 1937. He asserted that if his company had been left alone he could have made his own deals with other whalers.[67] He proposed to the Japanese that each country should eliminate a factory vessel and set a global Antarctic quota of 12,000 BWU, but this idea was not seriously pursued. Instead the Hector Whaling Company sold its *Balaena* to a Japanese company in 1960. The next year, Salvesen announced that the *Southern Venturer* and the *Southern Harvester* would go out in 1961–62 for the last time so that his employees would be able to work for one more year before having to find new jobs.[68]

Salvesen's whaling empire had employed 2,147 people at its peak in the 1949–50 season, but by 1961 that number had fallen to 1,199. Since the end of the war, roughly 45 percent of the company's employees had been British subjects, and wages had been very good. The crew of the *Southern Harvester* expedition earned more than £440,000 in 1961–62, and then they had to look for new work. Salvesen was confident that they would find good jobs but not as rewarding as whaling, financially or psychologically. The British government considered offering a subsidy, in line with fishing subsidies, but Salvesen refused to ask for anything, instead rehashing his complaints from 1937. He retired at the end of 1961, lamenting that his work to maintain practical restrictions on whaling had been so undercut by his government that he would be embarrassed to be seen as a member of the British IWC delegation in the future.[69] Lest there be any uncertainty about where he stood, Salvesen fired one last harpoon by signing a letter to the British fisheries secretary, "Yours no longer respectfully."[70]

THE REEMERGENCE OF SCIENCE

During the 1959 meltdown, Remington Kellogg had threatened the withdrawing states, saying that he would work to change the IWC rules in their absence, which implied that he expected them to return. Even though there was nothing like a "Save the Whales" movement in 1960, conservationists on the commission counted on public opinion to persuade the whalers to reenter the fold. Over the next few years, the conservationist commissioners succeeded in drawing the whalers back in and won the IWC's endorsement of a study of whale populations by the "Three Wise

Men," biologists who would turn the commission to more realistic hunting quotas. Some whalers understood the need for the wise men's work, but the fiscal realities of their industry compelled them to hold on for a few more years of ignoring the best scientific advice.

The bleak news of the fleets' inability to come close to their quotas in 1959–60 helped to spur a new round of talks in 1960. In late May, the British put forth an idea from H. K. Salvesen that involved a three-man scientific committee, a return of Norway and the Netherlands to the IWC, immediate negotiations for a quota deal, implementation of an observer scheme, and a delay on hunting blue whales until 14 February to reduce the pressure on that species. About three weeks later, the Americans came calling with a similar proposal, including a special scientific committee, reaccession of the former members, and a quota that would keep everyone on board.[71] The British and Americans were most concerned with pulling Norway back in, because it was unlikely that the Dutch would stand alone. Members of Norway's Hvalrådet, which included owners, sailors, scientists, and government officials, were still arguing about the wisdom of pulling out of the commission, but they agreed that it would be foolish to come back without a quota deal because it would be nearly impossible to withdraw again.[72]

On the other side of the world, officials in Wellington, New Zealand, were reading the same proposals with equal skepticism. They particularly liked the idea of a special committee, and they hoped that one member would be a fellow Kiwi, either K. R. Allen or William Dawbin. But they also wondered why whalers would listen to a new committee when they had so successfully ignored the IWC Scientific Committee's conclusions since 1949. The government was concerned about the costs of sending a scientist to a lengthy meeting in Europe, but Frank Corner argued that the work of the scientists was the only means to save the commission from collapse. Dawbin, more effectively, argued that the cost of sending him to London was the value of two humpback whales, while the IWC's work might save thousands of those animals.[73]

The Norwegian observer at the 1960 meeting spent most of his time fending off pressure from the US and British delegations to rejoin, and he concluded that the Dutch, represented by G. J. Lienesch as an observer, were prepared to give in. After the meeting, at which the major points of the British and American proposals were accepted, Oslo decided to rejoin the IWC in order to lure the Dutch back in and work from within to fix the commission. This decision was most surprising, as the Norwegian Whaling Association had described the requests to rejoin as a "trap" and asserted that the Soviets would "filibuster the negotiations for years to come," which in fact they did.[74] Almost immediately, some members of the Hvalrådet began working to overturn that decision, so observers spent the next fourteen months wondering whether Oslo had any idea of what it wanted from whaling diplomacy, other than a magical return to 1934, when the whales were plentiful and cooperation with the British easier. With no sign of progress on their central concerns, in December 1961 the Norwegians tried to pull the same old rabbit out of the hat, withdrawing again with the promise to rejoin if they got a quota deal by July 1962.[75]

For their part, the Dutch announced that they would not rejoin the IWC until the quota arrangements were finalized. For those governments trying to save the commission, this was hardly reassuring. Within the Dutch government, the Foreign Ministry had been unable to swing the fisheries ministry to a more conciliatory position, despite pressure from foreign governments. The leadership of the Netherlands Whaling Company planned on fighting for the company's share of the whaling quota, and the company was moving into the whale meat business as a means to survive. One company official expressed bitterness that the IWC spent so much time criticizing the Dutch even as commission members admitted that they had to turn a blind eye toward Soviet cheating.[76] In the fall of 1960, the British organized the Commonwealth countries to urge the Dutch to rejoin the IWC, which was the only tool for "placing any restraint upon the continued expansion of the Russian Whaling Fleet." Without that restraint, conservation of whales would fail, with repercussions on "other fields besides whaling." Indeed, if the Netherlands rebuffed these efforts, it would be responsible "for the anarchy that is likely to ensue."[77]

The Dutch remained unrepentant. At a meeting of the five pelagic whaling countries in February 1961, representatives of the Netherlands Whaling Company not only demanded 8 percent of the quota but also returned to taking shots at the Norwegians for their 1945 crew law (which prohibited Norwegian whaling crew members from working for companies from countries that had not been involved in whaling before 1945). The other delegates agreed to offer the Netherlands 6 percent of the quota, with 9 percent going to Britain, 32 percent to Norway, and 33 percent to Japan. The most reasonable member of the Dutch delegation, its spokesman,

J. A. P. Franke, reported privately that the lowest he might be able to go was 6.5 percent, but even 7 percent was unlikely to sit well in The Hague. As these talks progressed over three days, twenty-one Antarctic expeditions were on their way to taking 16,425 BWU, meaning more than 30,000 fin whales. Only with some creative thinking about future seasons did the other whalers come up with a bonus system that would allow the Dutch to achieve close to 7 percent of the quota if their expedition performed well, which the whalers coupled with delaying the open season to 12 December.[78] That was enough to bring the Netherlands back in to the IWC in May 1962.

Like their Dutch counterparts, the Japanese also wrestled with a complex set of constituencies. The decision to come back to the commission for the 1960 meeting was balanced by an ornery streak. The Japanese filed objections to four changes accepted at the IWC's 1960 meeting and were pretty blunt about it. When a delegation of Australians came to Tokyo to discuss dairy and whaling—effectively butter and margarine—they were met by twenty-five Japanese diplomats, fisheries officials, and a host of representatives from the whaling companies. The diplomats were clearly uneasy with their comrades, who among other things berated the Australians for wasting everyone's time by asking for the impossible, the withdrawal of the recently filed objections. The whalers also emphasized, like the Dutch, that the real problem was recurrent Soviet cheating, which they documented orally and in writing. At least the dairy negotiations went well.[79] In the end, the Japanese diplomats won the day, getting their government back into the IWC and accepting the new scientific examination of whale stocks.

The agreement at the 1960 IWC meeting to form a Committee of Three (a.k.a. the Three Wise Men) gave the new committee until the fall of 1961 to report, meaning that the report would be accepted at the 1962 IWC meeting, and then the commission would have two more years to implement the recommendations. In other words, all would be set right in 1964, based on data available in 1961. The IWC actually established a two-tier study group; an ad hoc scientific committee, which consisted of any whaling scientist who wanted to be involved; and the Committee of Three, composed of population biologists who were not necessarily experts on whales, K. Radway Allen of New Zealand, Sidney Holt of Britain, and Douglas Chapman of the United States. Both of these groups existed for only a few years and were separate from the Scientific Committee, which is a permanent fixture of the commission. The hope was that the ad hoc committee would provide the data to the Three Wise Men. Of course, all depended on the pelagic whaling states paying for their work, creating a conflict of interest. In fact, the Committee of Three's first meeting, in Rome in April 1961, ended without any serious progress because they had no funds. They agreed to meet after the IWC meeting in 1962 in Seattle, where Chapman could get access to a powerful enough computer to process all of the data.[80]

The delaying tactics of the whalers paid off for at least one more year, when the delegates at the 1962 IWC meeting failed to make any important changes to the Antarctic quota while the report of the Committee of Three was pending. Remington Kellogg expressed his dismay with the permanent Scientific Committee, which he called "unduly cautious . . . introducing so many qualifying words and phrases into its reports that their force is virtually lost." Even when the evidence was clear that whale stocks were in distress, the committee had let the whalers off the hook. Rather than fight for a reduction and attain no more than "half-measures," Kellogg effectively sighed and accepted the 15,000 BWU quota in 1962. Kellogg had frequently shown remarkable patience with his fellow commissioners, but he had finally lost it. He decided that if the Three Wise Men produced "recommendations for drastic reduction of whaling effort," the IWC must either accept them or "become completely impotent."[81] If the latter happened, the United States would probably have to withdraw.

Kellogg's pessimism boiled over at the end of 1962. J. L. McHugh of the US Fish and Wildlife Service, who had attended his first IWC meeting that year, proposed to Kellogg something that he called "planned over-fishing." Instead of letting the whalers run their course or stopping all whaling in the name of conservation (an admittedly unlikely event), why not tell the whalers that they could keep a high quota for a few years but fix a termination date so that the whales themselves would not be exterminated? The companies could plan for going out of business in a rational way, and the various species would be saved. In the face of this somewhat naïve assessment of what the whaling industry might accept, Kellogg poured out his bitterness about the previous twenty years. His desire for a quota of 12,000 BWU had been defeated by the demand for more fat in 1943; his efforts to get the members of the original Scientific Committee to act on the basis of data and not national interest had frequently been ignored; and his support for setting quotas by species, rather than blue whale units, had not been sufficiently popular in 1946. If anything, industry was less likely to yield to scientists in 1963 when they could convert their floating factories to oil tankers and sell their catcher boats for cost whenever the whales ran out. In other words, the companies had no need for McHugh's plan for the future, because they already had a plan for the end of the industry that served their interests better.[82] What Kellogg could not have known, for instance, was that Salvesen's had saved £13 million since 1946, not counting the money the firm had taken from whaling and invested in fishing materiel.[83]

In fact, each of the countries reacted differently to the events of 1962–63. The Soviets continued to denounce in solemn terms the other nations' lack of commitment to conservation, even as they dragged their feet on the inspection scheme and killed anything with a blowhole. The Japanese continued to buy Western whaling ships and their associated quotas, to expand Japan's whaling capacity. They bought the *Balaena, Southern Harvester, Willem Barendsz,* and a few Norwegian vessels within just a few years. The Dutch and British companies finally gave up the fight in 1963 and got out of whaling. And the Norwegians were slowly moving to the conclusion of their great whaling leader, Anders Jahre, that whaling was "an adventure which we must reluctantly regard as having concluded."[84] By 1967, only one Norwegian expedition, led by the *Kosmos IV,* was still whaling.

The Committee of Three—Douglas Chapman, K. Radway Allen, and Sidney Holt—was a little more successful than the members of the standing Scientific Committee had been in changing the culture of the IWC. They succeeded in planting the idea that whales should be managed by species and that blue and humpback whales should have complete protection, although those bans were not immediately accepted. They returned the commission's focus to the idea of maximum sustainable yield (MSY), a relatively new concept that was endorsed by the International Union for the Conservation of Nature (IUCN) as a target for whale harvesting.[85]

Using the MSY measure required a thorough understanding of the population of a stock: its natural mortality, rate of reproduction, and age of sexual maturity. Proponents of the measure believed that such data would allow them to find the highest number of whales that could be taken without damaging the stock. Managers then could either apply MSY theory to the number of whales on the hunting grounds in 1963, or they could advocate restrictive measures that would allow the stock to grow closer to carrying capacity before allowing harvests to increase. The MSY model was flawed, for pelagic mammals especially, because it could not deal effectively with the natural unpredictability of ecosystems; it tended to treat species in isolation, rather than as parts of an ecosystem; it required accurate data such as population counts that often did not exist; and it may have created a false sense of security about the ability of science to provide guidance. Yet it was an advance because it used the mass of data constructively and thereby increased the weight of scientific conclusions about how many whales might be taken without further diminishing the stocks. Remington Kellogg had suggested that even a basic line graph would strengthen the argument for reducing the catch, and now he was about to get computer models.[86]

But no computer model ever got the better of a Japanese fisheries official. Japanese whalers were already feeling mistreated by Westerners, who hesitated to sell them whaling equipment, and now they rightly saw the Committee of Three as a means to restrict their work. Mr. Kamenaga of the fisheries ministry declared, not surprisingly, the committee's proposed cut from 15,000 BWU to roughly 5,000 BWU to be very drastic. While Japan valued conservation, the recommendation of outside scientists had to be balanced with the economic and social impact in whaling countries. At the 1963 commission meeting in London, the Japanese formed an "unholy alliance" with the Soviets to break up attempts to set a quota for fin whales, although they could not stop the ban on taking blue whales. For once, the scientists seemed united in their opinions, with the Committee of Three's population biologists predicting a catch of 14,000 fin whales from a stock of only 40,000 for the 1963–64 season. But, according to New Zealand's delegate, the pelagic whalers seemed to accept that they could obtain two more years of open slaughter and then deal with the collapse of whale stocks. Not surprisingly, he described the meeting as "tense and bad-tempered" and "more than unusually dispiriting."[87] When the meeting was over, the IWC asked the Committee of Three—now expanded to four with the addition of John Gulland, a British fisheries scientist—to work for another year, but the commission did not provide the committee with financial resources until April 1964.

Despite the delay, the scientists were able to present a powerful report at the 1964 IWC meeting. They noted that their predicted fin catch of 14,000 had been off by 53 whales, an amazing feat that they downplayed by noting that they had overestimated by 10 percent the amount of effort it would take to reach that figure. Their analysis after that was extremely gloomy. Fin whale stocks could hold out for maybe four more years of increased effort before being depleted; and sei whales, which had entered the picture only in the last five years, were probably less numerous than fins. For every year that intense whaling continued, several more years would be required for stocks to rebound in the future. The Committee of Four argued that the best way to maximize return on investment over the long run was to shut down the industry for at least ten years and then resume hunting at the optimum level.

The scientists acknowledged, though, that without knowing the natural replacement rate of fin whales, it was possible that it might take fifty years for the stock to increase to the optimum number. In that case, it might well make sense to allow some hunting. Whenever hunting resumed, they argued, the whalers could catch as many whales with just three or four expeditions as they did in 1963–64, because fin catch per unit of effort (that is, per day of catcher work) had fallen from more than 3 to 0.99 in the last nine years. They did hint, subtly, that the data for catch per unit of effort might be unreliable because "Country A," presumably the Soviet Union, showed far less of a decline than did Countries B and C. The committee members were unable to explain this strange divergence, except to suggest "greater efficiency," but it is easy to read into their report a warning that the data were faulty, since it is likely that they knew about the strange 1963 Soviet report on whale marks. The committee members finished their report with a strong response to Japanese scientists who had argued that the stock of fin whales was between 70,000 and 100,000, suggesting that Japanese studies were simply poorly executed.[88]

One of the most striking elements of this report was the scientists' uncertainty about fin whales' net potential rate of increase, which measures reproduction minus mortality. Estimates for that rate ranged from 0.18, meaning that nearly one in five fin whales would give birth in any given year, to 0.08, meaning that about one in twelve would give birth. At the higher rate, the species might double its population, if free from hunting, within six years. At the lower rate, doubling might take twelve years. While the scientists asserted that 0.12 was the best estimate, the fact that their report allowed for an error factor of 50 percent in either direction suggested why the scientists might occasionally seem unpersuasive to their colleagues on the commission. This difficulty was particularly a problem when one considers that the Committee of Four had unprecedented resources and prestige. If they could not create a persuasive case, then the data simply were inadequate.

With the scientists' report in the works, the United States worked in advance to get the IWC member states to accept it. In May 1964, the State Department sent a briefing to embassies in all member countries detailing what had gone wrong in the commission and giving specific instructions for diplomatic staff in pelagic whaling states. Given the sharp wording of the briefing, embassy staff in the pelagic countries were advised not to pass it on to their host governments but instead to impress upon them that the United States was working with other members to ensure that the Committee of Four would be taken seriously. The State Department's position was that some officials in Tokyo, The Hague, and Oslo were sympathetic to improving conservation measures, and an open show of US support would help them win the day.[89]

Despite this overture, the IWC's 1964 meeting at Sandefjord was a disaster. The four pelagic whalers (now that Britain was out of the industry) formed what a New Zealander called a "somewhat unholy alliance," which was an improvement over the unqualified "unholy alliance" of 1963, in order to fight off the lower quota recommended by the Committee of Four, not to mention the IUCN, the UN Food and Agriculture Organization (FAO), the Fauna Preservation Society, and the World Wildlife Federation. The Netherlands, which had seen its final whaling season, fought to keep the quota high merely to insure a high price for the *Willem Barendsz*, which a Japanese company was about to buy. The year before, in 1963, members had been faced with a choice between 4,000 and 10,000 BWU, and they chose 10,000 BWU rather than risk a spate of objections to the lower limit. So in 1964, Remington Kellogg proposed phasing in a reduction to 2,000 BWU over three years, but the pelagic whaling countries made clear that they would not accept that. Sidney Holt, of the Committee of Four, joined the debate with an impassioned plea for Kellogg's proposal, arguing, "If this Commission, which was created to ensure the proper use of some of those resources of the sea, condones their future misuse, a heavy blow will have been struck against the attempts by the nations of the world to agree on principles and on general measures for the conservation of the high seas fishery resources." The delegate from Iceland, H. G. Andersen, reminded his colleagues of their fundamental utilitarian goal: "The principle should be long-term rational management based on scientific findings for the benefit of all concerned."[90]

The whaling states countered forcefully. Russia's Aleksei Solyanik assured delegates that the scientists were ill-informed and the whalers responsible managers of the resource: "I can tell you here and now, with full responsibility, that we are interested in the conservation of whale stocks even more than those countries who are not participating in the Antarctic pelagic whaling operations." Japan's Iwao Fujita sought sympathy for his plight: "I quite envy the non-pelagic whaling countries who are not engaged in the Antarctic and can discuss this problem clearly in this Commission purely from the point of view of the conservation of natural resources." Japan, he said, could not afford that luxury. Given the deep division, the delegates voted down all motions for quotas, ranging from 2,000 to 8,500 BWU. The commission had failed to set a quota, leaving it to the four pelagic whaling nations to set their own. Their competing interests concerning quotas and the observer scheme, as well as mistrust between the Soviets and Japanese, almost prevented even a private agreement, but in the end they agreed to a quota of 8,000 BWU and cut a separate deal on vessel inspection, which they never finalized. The delegates did agree to ban hunting of humpbacks on the high seas, but they could not agree to end all hunting of blue whales. As bad as some of the previous meetings had been, this one could "scarcely fail to bring the Commission into further disrepute."[91]

In the aftermath of the 1964 meeting, several thoughtful observers pondered dramatic changes. John Gulland, the late addition to the Committee of Four, put forth his proposal for an International Whaling Authority, in effect a commission that would catch whales or issue licenses at a hefty fee. He was realistic enough to know that such an agency was simply not possible, but his goal was to emphasize that the current management scheme was awful. The British Ministry of Agriculture and Fisheries debated the merits of leaving the IWC altogether. Hugh Gardner, the fisheries secretary, opposed leaving on several grounds, including the role that Britain had played in the commission's failure to heed scientific advice in the past, the slim interests that his country still had in Antarctic whaling, and, most important, the chance that someone else would leave first, thus exempting Britain from the charge that it had unraveled the IWC by leaving.[92] The Norwegians, while lamenting the weakness of the commission, found the results to be "satisfactory." They had avoided a quotaless free-for-all by talking their whaling allies down to 8,000 BWU, even if that had required angering the conservationist countries; they had also achieved a deal on the observer scheme that seemed to meet Soviet expectations. W. G. Solberg of Norway's foreign ministry anticipated that his country could mediate between the Soviets and Japanese and work to bring them closer to the majority IWC position, but he also warned that the scientists' predictions of reduced catch might come true, which would force everyone to reconsider their positions.[93] The United States again took the narwhal by the horn by telling the pelagic states that they should attend a special IWC meeting in early 1965, with the understanding that they would accept catch restrictions "that meet conservation requirements as determined by the scientific findings." If they refused, then the United States would talk to its allies in the commission about asking the FAO to call a global meeting on whaling, at which, presumably, the world would get to scold the selfish whaling states.[94]

For the next several years, the IWC made incremental steps toward conserving whales, even as it became clear that the focus was shifting away from Antarctic whaling. The commission finally closed all hunting for blue and humpback whales in 1965 and 1966, respectively. With Norway dropping out of Antarctic whaling in 1967, only the Soviet Union and Japan remained active in the southern seas, but a number of nations maintained small coastal whaling industries. The market for whale oil finally dried up in the middle of the decade. The Japanese expeditions clung to profitability by harvesting meat for people, while the Soviets caught whales in any waters, caring little about IWC prohibitions. Soviet whalers used some meat for mink and fox farms in Siberia, they caught sperm whales for their oil, and they sold other parts of whales as pet food in the West. Interest in the commission waned to the point that membership dropped to only fourteen states, with New Zealand leaving in 1968 and the Netherlands doing the same in 1969. With UN law of the sea negotiations closed for a time and a handful of fisheries treaties in place, the IWC held less value as a symbol of cooperation than ever before. Scientists probably played a greater role than they had before, but that was as much a product of the demise of people like H. K. Salvesen as it was a reflection of a newfound respect for science. The commission was very close to fading away due to indifference, and no one could seriously argue that it promoted sustainable use of whales.

Henry Maurice at the Zoological Society of London, ca. 1944. Courtesy of
Lafayette Photography.

Remington Kellogg addresses the delegates negotiating the International Convention for the Regulation of Whaling, 1946. Smithsonian Institution Archives, Record Unit 7165, Box 10, Folder 4.

The British delegation signs the International Convention for the Regulation of Whaling,1946. Neil Mackintosh is on the far left, Alban Dobson on the far right. Smithsonian Institution Archives, Record Unit 7165, Box 10, Folder 4.

Lt. Col. Hubert Schenck, of the Supreme Command for the Allied Powers'
Natural Resources Section, addresses the crew of the *Nisshin Maru*, 1948. Hubert
Gregory Schenck Papers, Photo Envelope BBB, Hoover Institution Archives.

The launching of the *Nisshin Maru*, 1948. Note the large crowd. Hubert Gregory Schenck Papers, Photo Album mZZ, Hoover Institution Archives.

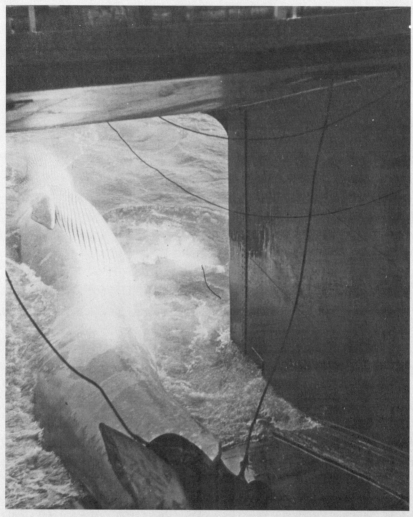

Pulling a whale up the stern slipway of the *Nisshin Maru*, 1948. Hubert Gregory Schenck Papers, Photo Album fM, Hoover Institution Archives.

The *Olympic Challenger* showing the stern slipway, ca. 1950. Hvalfangstmuseet, Sandefjord, Norway.

Ambassador Frank Corner of New Zealand (right) with UN General-Secretary
U Thant (left), 1966. UN Photo Library, 220698.

Maurice Strong, chairman of the UN Conference on the Human Environment
in Stockholm, addresses the "Whale Celebration," with the cameras rolling,
1972. Yutaka Nagata, UN Photo Library, 186101.

Paul Watson kneels on a sperm whale calf killed by Soviet whalers, with the *Phyllis Cormack* in the background, 1975. Rex Weyler/Greenpeace GP01CQU.

Ray Gambell, secretary of the International Whaling Commission (seated on the left), receives petitions from the People's Trust for Endangered Species, 1979. Courtesy of People's Trust for Endangered Species.

A giant inflatable whale and a fitness instructor celebrate Greenpeace's tenth anniversary, 1981. Dan Scott/Vancouver Sun.

Traditional Inuit whaling equipment, early twentieth century. New Bedford
Whaling Museum, Photo 2000.100.200.115.

Whaling on the north coast of Alaska in the early twenty-first century. Copyright Hugh Rose/AccentAlaska.com.

A common way for people to encounter whales today: a humpback whale calf breaches off the coast of New Hampshire, 2012. Courtesy of Len Medlock.

6

SAVE THE WHALES (FOR LATER)

IN JULY 1971, TOM GARRETT OF FRIENDS OF THE EARTH TESTIFIED before a US congressional committee that was investigating a ten-year worldwide ban on commercial whaling. In the midst of statements for and against such a moratorium, Garrett launched a slashing attack on the International Whaling Commission, which had been "exposed as a tragic farce, discredited and impotent." The problem, he continued, was ingrained in the IWC's founding convention, which "contains no expression of ethic, nor definition of moral responsibility." Further, the US commissioner, J. L. McHugh, who happened to be in line to testify too, had had an "entirely negligible" role in commission meetings, and there was little reason to hope for something better. Garrett did not spare the Soviets and Japanese, whom he called "rapacious and intractable," and he concluded that all of the whalers had made a conscious decision years before to exterminate the whales for the largest profit rather than to pursue a "sustainable yield." The problem was global, and the solution was simple: "The bankrupt legal doctrine of *res nullius* [belonging to no one] must be abolished. It must be replaced with a doctrine of *res communis* which takes into account the interconnectedness of all life."[1]

Later that year, Garrett reported that whales "sing with a purity which our ears can only begin to appreciate," which suggested that they should not be hunted at all. At the same time, he seemed to indicate that hunting whales sustainably for food would be tolerable. Lewis Regenstein, of the Committee for Humane Legislation, appeared to be even more conflicted, offering a stirring assessment that the blue whale is closely related to humans, while nevertheless noting that had they been managed better they could provide a valuable source of food for humans.[2] Garrett and

Regenstein conveyed the dominant environmentalist thinking about the commission in the 1970s: the IWC had been dominated by whalers for so long that the only wise course was to shut it down and start over, but whether whaling itself should continue would have to be worked out.

Popular concern about whaling developed almost overnight. In 1970, few people cared about whales, but within two years tens of thousands of people around the world were writing their governments, participating in public protests, and donating money to anti-whaling groups. Their actions sparked pro-whaling movements among people who thought whales should be fair game. The IWC, which had been held in such low regard that Brazil, New Zealand, and the Netherlands had left, had dwindled to just fourteen members. But Brazil and New Zealand rejoined in the mid-1970s, the beginning of a wave of countries that would join (as of 2012 there were eighty-nine member states). Whales became a potent symbol of modern environmentalist concern about how people were damaging the earth. "Save the Whales!" became a rallying cry for environmentalists around the world. Yet for much of the 1970s, reasons for saving the whales were contradictory—whales were both exceptional beings and a wonderful source of protein.

In order to maintain its cohesion, the movement had to address that contradiction. The original protestors had attacked commercial whaling by using scientific evidence that whales were in decline and had unique characteristics; they emphasized the value of whales as commodities as well as the immorality of hunting in general and the cruelty of the harpoon in particular. By 1976, though, whales had become sacred. Perhaps the idea of a sentient source of protein had lost its appeal after the 1973 movie *Soylent Green*.[3] There were no good reasons to hunt whales, and many environmentalists even condemned the subsistence use of peoples who had hunted whales for centuries. Whalers were murderers, and negotiating with them was unacceptable. Whales were basically humans, only perhaps slightly better.[4]

That fervor was, in part, a product of the nature of mass protests. It is difficult enough to convince people that they should care about a whale they will never see in an ocean they will barely experience, but it is nearly impossible to recruit them with a nuanced campaign of ecological analysis. "Save the Whales!" was simply easier if those chanting the slogan did not have to differentiate between blue whales and minke whales, or between

Soviet factory whalers and aboriginal hunters, although some of the protestors were making those distinctions. The movement succeeded in making whales symbols of human rapacity: if we could kill the gentle giant with impunity, then we clearly had to rethink our whole relationship with the planet. Thus people who had never seen a whale or did not know that a whale was a mammal could still be motivated to act on behalf of the planet.

At the time, people were ripe for mass protests—or at least the mass sending of form letters. The anti-whaling movement drew from a triumvirate of forces, which were themselves intertwined: the anti-war, civil rights, and environmental movements of the late 1960s and early 1970s. Beyond the obvious comparisons based on street marches and folk singers, the oddly entertaining groups carrying huge inflatable whales echoed the protestors who tried to levitate the Pentagon in 1970. Members of the Save the Whales movement had learned lessons in mass protest and political organization in the previous decade. In fact, only the Vietnam War generated more protest letters to the White House in the early 1970s than did whaling.[5] More directly, people had been primed to care about the global environment by Earth Day in 1970, the UN Conference on the Human Environment in 1972, and books like Rachel Carson's *Silent Spring* and Paul Ehrlich's *Population Bomb*.[6] If the authorities had failed, then protest was in order. It also seems that governments had grown used to such protests and had learned how to defuse them, so policy sometimes reflected efforts to appease protestors, even at the expense of overruling scientific advice.

Still, one might wonder why whaling, of all of the environmental causes for dismay in the 1970s, emerged as such a powerful symbol. Historian Thomas Dunlap has argued that the growth of ecological understanding of the earth radically changed how Americans thought about wolves and other predators, and such a transformation certainly would apply to whales. He has also noted that environmentalism mimics religious faith, and there can be no doubt that the anti-whaling movement stirred an unusual passion and a fierce intolerance of other views.[7] In large part, whales' size mattered. It was easy to comprehend a sentence like "The blue whale is the largest animal ever." Majestic whales carried weight, but tiny krill did not, even though they made majestic whales possible. Whales also became known as intelligent beings, with some people describing them as sentient. Harpooning seemed especially brutal when one pictured the victim not only feeling pain but also aware that it was dying. Some advocates for whales went beyond anthropomorphizing the animals, claiming that whales were better people than most people. Still, one might ask why this happened in 1972 and not 1962 or earlier.

While the protest culture of the late 1960s was a necessary petri dish, the key development was the recording of whale songs and behavior. Before 1971, the few people who had seen whales in any number or for any length of time were usually hunters or scientists. The rest had to settle for books and, for the truly lucky, fleeting glimpses from the shore or from boats. It is fair to say that most of the whales in books before the 1970s were hard to love. Moby Dick is remembered for being relentless and vicious; Jonah was swallowed by a whale (but apparently filed an objection to being digested). Scientific books focused on biological statements that might incite wonder but were not meant to stir emotion. But with the recordings of whale songs and behaviors, these mysterious beasts were heard on stereo systems in Winnipeg rec rooms and seen on TV in Canberra living rooms. It was easy to romanticize the sounds and assign human emotions to whales. When people saw the slaughter of whales on their TV screens, courtesy of the BBC or PBS, and put that together with the music on the stereo, some decided that whaling was unnecessary and immoral. They were ready to be organized, particularly by new groups like Project Jonah and Greenpeace, some of which offered an anti-whaling campaign as part of a deep critique of industrial society. Ironically, the activists needed the IWC, even as they criticized it as a whalers' club that had betrayed its original conservationist promises.[8]

Finally, the rise and complexity of the Save the Whales movement had an unexpected diplomatic impact. Leaders of IWC member states understood that business as usual was unacceptable to most people who thought about whales in the 1970s. That did not mean that the IWC members all necessarily accepted the idea of a ten-year commercial whaling moratorium. Instead, the whaling states and the conservation states compromised on an Australian proposal known as the New Management Procedure, which was built around the idea from fisheries science of maximum sustainable yield.[9] For a brief moment, just about everyone in the IWC agreed that hard scientific data would guide the commission's decisions. The problem was that the hard data turned out to be pretty flabby.

THE MORALITY OF WHALING

While the rush of sentiment to save the whales was something new under the sun, a hiccup of concern in the 1950s had focused on the brutality of harpooning. Dr. Harry Lillie, a ship's surgeon on one of Salvesen's factory vessels in the 1940s, became a fervent opponent of whaling. Like the whalers with whom he served, he understood the brutality of killing whales with exploding harpoons; unlike them, he determined to tell the world what it took to make margarine. Traveling the world giving lectures and showing short films, he found a small but enthusiastic cohort of followers among humane societies. In his lectures, he compared a harpooned whale pulling against a catcher boat to a draft horse pulling a wagon, screaming in pain as its drover stabbed it until it bled to death. The gruesome image could stay with readers or listeners for years and is used by some anti-whaling groups even today.[10] Lillie was one of the first people to challenge the idea that whales were just a mass of fat and muscle waiting to be reduced to margarine and meat.

Lillie and his supporters hoped to end whaling altogether, but they knew that was unlikely, so they focused on reducing the cruelty of the killing. Lillie worked hard to promote the electric harpoon in the hope that it would kill the whale quickly, thus reducing both the animal's suffering and the time and effort needed to bring the animal into the processing plant. The idea had first gained supporters just before World War II; after the war, Hector Whaling of Great Britain invested hundreds of thousands of pounds researching its effectiveness. It might seem obvious that the combination of a powerful electrical current and spraying water on a pitching, rolling boat would be bad, but the electric harpoon failed because of the difficulty of delivering the current to the whale through a giant, unbreakable extension cord. The current had to be carried through a line that could handle being fired with the harpoon and then stretched violently as the harpoon hit the whale, which would not kill the animal instantly. The risk of electrocuting crew members was relatively small compared to that technical challenge, which was never solved.

Lillie's campaign burned out fairly quickly. He succeeded in getting the UN Conference on the Law of the Sea to consider his ideas in 1958, but he had no real impact on any whaling company or the IWC.[11] If the cruelty of whaling came up for discussion in the 1960s, as it did in W. R. D.

McLaughlin's 1962 memoir of his experience on a whaling ship, it usually was considered the unfortunate price of doing business. On the page after recounting the cruelty of harpooning a whale, McLaughlin wrote that "in spite of what I have said about the death of the whale I found the chase irresistibly exciting."[12] Despite nearly twenty years of efforts to curtail the industry, Lillie was never able to break McLaughlin's way of thinking about whales. Even Remington Kellogg, who offered words of support for Lillie's campaign to reduce suffering, noted that he himself was focusing on reducing waste as a bigger problem.[13]

With Lillie's movement unable to get much traction, the few remaining whalers were left unchallenged in their definition of a whale until the early 1970s. Few of them would have spent any time discussing what a whale was. A whale was simply the source of their livelihoods. It was a package of blubber, meal, meat, and the occasional odd bit that could be commodified if one had skill and tenacity. Those who flensed the whales knew about the smells and textures of a dead animal, and those on catcher vessels knew about the animal's strength and speed. The package did not want to be caught, nor was it neat, but it could be very valuable. Catching whales brought with it some association with their environments, even if few whalers ever thought of their prey as part of an ecosystem. Learning to track whales and hunt them through the ice, McLaughlin wrote, was part of the allure that kept whalers coming back to the tough jobs year after year. In that sense, many whalers were like recreational anglers, enjoying the challenge of catching something that seemed to enjoy disappearing under water and beneath obstacles.[14]

Until 1970, most people who did not catch whales undoubtedly shared the idea that whales were basically fish. Even if they knew whales were mammals, they still gave them the same low level of attention they gave to fish, and bureaucrats almost always considered whaling a fishery. In societies where whale meat was on the menu, like Norway and Japan, the whale was functionally a fish—a wild animal that might need some regulation but was protected by its environment. The goal of government was more often to encourage than to prevent harvesting. In countries where whale was rarely on the menu, whales were mainly a really big curiosity. Few people had been enticed to eat unrationed whale meat during either of the two world wars because canned whale never seemed very palatable. The occasional museum had a whale skeleton or, in the case of the Smithsonian and the British Museum, large plaster or fiberglass models suspended from a ceiling, conveying the enormity of leviathan if not much about the animal's behavior or ecosystem. The new fiberglass blue whale in the 1960s in the Smithsonian was of special interest to Remington Kellogg, who wanted to get it right since it would be the only whale most visitors ever saw. One Smithsonian scientist remembered Kellogg yelling, "'Dr. Hobbs, I wish you would go down to that hall and get those blankity-blank measles off of that whale!' They'd spotted the whale instead of streaked it, and Dr. Kellogg was terribly upset."[15]

In 1969, the eminent marine biologist Victor Scheffer told a tale of a young sperm whale that was a cross between the film *Bambi* and a scientific review article. *The Year of the Whale* won a prize for the year's best natural history book, and it still is a moving read. Yet Scheffer admitted right away that "no man can say that he has probed deeply into the natural history of this whale or any whale. And indeed how could he? . . . The whale biologist does the best he can." He pieces together news stories about sperm whales tangling with a cable three thousand feet down with his own quick specimen work on the skin, ovaries, teeth, and other commercially useless bits that he can get from the flensers, but speculation was still necessary. Scheffer's conclusion included several such telling phrases as "still uncertain," "no one knows," and "moot question."[16] As one of the most renowned marine biologists of his day, Scheffer helped to make whales more accessible for laypeople, but he also conveyed the desire for more knowledge.

Beginning in the late 1960s, new television nature programs helped people around the world see nature differently than they had before. Whales were no longer just static creatures hanging in midair, surrounded by other specimens, but moving aquatic creatures with really interesting behavior. "TV nature program" covers a range of entries, from BBC and PBS specials to Jacques Cousteau's series on oceans and commercial programs like *Mutual of Omaha's Wild Kingdom*, which made Marlon Perkins a household name in the United States as his interchangeable assistants—none of whom seemed to have or need last names—wrestled anacondas and other dangerous animals. What these nature programs had in common was a need to show exotic animals in action; no one wants to watch a wolf sleep all day when the family dog is doing the same thing on the couch. The shows particularly benefited charismatic megafauna, large animals that do interesting things, a category that certainly includes whales. Whatever the scientific merits of the nature shows, they reflected both improved film technology and a growing appetite for information and entertainment based on appreciating wild animals rather than fearing or tasting them. When the BBC carried a special on whales in March 1972, the US embassy received so many requests for information on US conservation laws that it had to request additional information. US Ambassador to Britain Walter Annenberg observed that "programs such as this serve to stimulate the conservationist sentiment that already exists."[17]

The desire to make a film about whales appears to have outstripped the ability to make such a film. In 1969, a researcher for Time-Life wrote the IWC, seeking help in making an educational film that emphasized "ecological aspects" of whaling. She sought film footage and basic information about which nations were active in whaling. The next year, a similar request came from Walt Disney, with the note that populations were declining so fast that available information appeared to be outdated. Neither project seemed to pan out.[18]

The first evidence in the IWC archives of an actual show is dated March 1972, when the secretary of the commission made note of a BBC2 special on dolphins and whales, which reported that whale meat was being used for pet food. One of the commentators was Roger Payne, who had won fame for recording whale noises that quickly became known as songs, particularly those from humpback whales. Not only did he report on the whale songs, but he also critiqued the IWC for its objection system, which made the protection of humpback whales more complex than it needed to be. IWC secretary Reginald Stacey observed that Payne's comment presented the commission with an opportunity to simplify its rules in the face of criticism from the increasing number of people who were "untutored in the Commission's regulations." The US commissioner, J. L. McHugh, responded: "Payne's remarks . . . reflect the naïveté of people with no administrative responsibility so characteristic of most of our 'conservationists' in the United States. Roger can be objective and helpful when he wants to be, as he was as a member of the US delegation to the 1971 IWC meeting, but he also loses his 'cool' at times and gets caught up in the emotional frenzy." In those two sentences, McHugh summarized the divisions among scientists: Payne's sin was to think about whales emotionally rather than rationally.[19]

For the rank and file of the Save the Whales movement, however, Payne was the head of the recruiting office. In 1967, he had used underwater listening technology developed for submarine warfare to record the sounds made by southern right whales, a species that had been nearly wiped out in the nineteenth century and then hammered again by Soviet whalers in the twentieth. His big break came when he began to pick up the haunting voices of humpback whales. Others had been listening to whales since the 1950s, but Payne deserved credit not only for popularizing the noises but also for linking them to behavior that people could understand. Humpbacks were no longer groaning and clicking but singing songs that were probably, as he argued in *Science* in 1971, part of courtship.[20]

In 1970, Capitol Records released an album of whale songs, which quickly entered the popular lexicon. Playing recordings of whale songs became a way to reach out to people, as in the May 1976 concert in Sydney's Royal Botanical Garden where several hundred people heard a plea for a whaling moratorium.[21] In 1978, jazz musician Paul Winter recorded an album called *Common Ground* for A&M Records that featured him playing saxophone accompanied by recordings of wolves, eagles, whales, and African tribesmen (who presumably had superior knowledge about nature). The next year, *National Geographic* inserted a recording of whale songs in one issue with an article on whale songs. In 1986, the popular science-fiction franchise *Star Trek* added a movie in which Captain Kirk and crew come back from a future where there are no whales. Their mission is to bring two humpback whales to the future to communicate with the alien life-form that is destroying earth, because there are no whales to answer the alien's calls.

Of course, no one knows what the whale songs mean to the whales (or space aliens), which gives humans the license to imagine their own interpretations. The *Star Trek* idea that whale songs are so impressive that they are best thought of as interstellar communications was only a little more far-fetched than some scientific theories. It is possible, for instance, that blue whale noises can be heard for thousands of miles, and it is clear that humpbacks are singing in patterns that change subtly over time and are shared by many individuals.[22] Payne offered a dramatic interpretation of whale songs that linked communication and social structure: "I suspect that whales divide up the resources of the sea by fanning out all over the ocean, sharing information about the food sources that the lucky ones stumble across. . . . I believe that whales cooperate in widely scattered societies and that these societies are held together by calls that can carry hundreds of miles. I further believe that these societies exist for the purpose of sharing information on food finds and that they are probably maintained by reciprocal altruism."[23] It is safe to say that human knowledge of whale voices helped create a sense of awe, which combined with knowledge about cetacean brains to support the theory that whales are sentient and probably as smart as people. And if they shared in the way that Payne claimed, then they were certainly more moral than human society too.

Print media also had the ability to alter the debate. In December 1972, *Reader's Digest* printed an excerpt from Farley Mowat's *A Whale for the Killing*, a book about his experience with a fin whale trapped in a cove near Burgeo, Newfoundland in 1967. He described the reaction of average people who had a choice between respecting the trapped whale or tormenting it. Enough chose to torment the whale that he was able to establish what would become one of the central themes of the Save the Whales movement: people are fundamentally pretty ugly, but whales are pure. People could redeem themselves, though, by saving the whales. In Mowat's telling, while people shot at the trapped whale or raced their boats at it to force it aground, fin whales patrolled just outside of the cove trying to support their relative. One guardian whale even surfaced to breathe at the same time as its trapped comrade. People, however, were "like imbecilic children loose in a candy store," stripping the seas of everything and killing out of revenge.[24] Mowat did not lift himself above the rest of humanity, acknowledging a brief spasm of sadness when it looked like the whale had somehow freed herself without his help. When he learned that Moby Joe, as the townspeople called the whale, was still in her pond, he felt a surge of elation, which he admitted was both shameful and contradictory. He felt true despair when he realized that Moby Joe had finally died in the lagoon.

Mowat's wife, Claire, hit upon another theme that would dominate the Save the Whales movement: somehow it was "so much more terrible to shoot a whale" than a rabbit or a groundhog. Neither Mowat elaborated on why it was worse. The combination of the whale's immensity and rarity— how can something so big be so hard to find?—gave the fin whale immediate celebrity status. The Japanese in particular have delighted in asking why it is worse to kill a whale than some other mammal, since people kill millions of mammals each year; but there can be little doubt that in the West Claire Mowat's visceral reaction is widespread.

Finally, *A Whale for the Killing* shone a light on the problem faced by those who wanted to protect whales—was the whale special or useful? Mowat initially thought that the best response to the trapped whale was to emphasize the scientific and commercial value of the creature. A captive whale might be the ticket to prosperity for the little burg of Burgeo, and it might provide science with a chance to understand fin whales better. Mowat rejected that idea, though, deciding that the whale was too special to be left in captivity. Unfortunately, the solution did not win him any friends in town, who split between those who wanted to use the whale for target practice and those who wanted to use it to get a highway built into town. The Save the Whales movement wrestled with the tension between seeing whales as useful and seeing them as special. Mowat chose the special route, and most followed him. But the people of Burgeo, like others who interacted with whales every day, were perfectly happy to see the whale in utilitarian terms.[25]

While Mowat was struggling with whether to free the whale or use it as a tool, he brought in the media, trying to take control of the debate before the various sides had even formed. Knowing that he could not save the whale himself, either by protecting it from gunfire or figuring out a way to get it out of the cove, Mowat tried to make the whale a cause célèbre. He used his agent in Toronto to spread the word, prompting visits from television and newspaper reporters and making his whale international news. The government of Newfoundland named him "keeper of the whale"— and it wanted the whale kept, not freed. Yet, Mowat found that the media could be as problematic as helpful, not keeping to the message that he wanted. One journalist seemed to go out of his way to disturb the whale to get a better picture and then compounded things by writing an article that made the people of Burgeo look as bad as Mowat thought they were but had been wise enough to keep relatively quiet.

Mowat's ambivalence about the media washed over into his thinking about the scientific establishment, another important part of the 1970s whaling debate. He hoped to drum up scientific interest in the trapped whale, and his agent made midnight calls to scientists on the day he learned that the whale was trapped, because he needed their information. He relied on the work of scientists such as Roger Payne to make the case that whales had qualities that humans had never before appreciated. He waited optimistically for Warren Schevill, from Woods Hole, to fight through bad weather to lend his expertise on how to keep the whale alive until it could be led out of its trap. But other scientists earned his disdain because they failed to appreciate the whale's plight, or they were too rigid in their thinking about whales in general. More important, science could provide neither the nearly mystical understanding of Moby Joe that Mowat desired, nor the basic knowledge of whale biology that he desperately needed. If science was going to provide the answers for how many whales ought to be killed, then the answer was likely to be wrong, both in facts and in spirit.

Given the magazine's huge circulation, the excerpt in *Reader's Digest* seemed to generate more commentary than Mowat's book, even though both ended with information on how to lobby for better protection for whales. The Norwegian embassy in Ottawa reported being flooded with criticism, and the IWC received hundreds of letters.[26] The tenor of the letters can be gauged by one that said the IWC needed people "who are really interested in the welfare of the Great Creatures. . . . You can do much more than you have." An IWC employee described that letter as "unusually reasonable."[27] Mowat's book on the whale, five years after the events, succeeded in getting attention and in defining the whale as a Great Creature, even as many people still saw it as great target practice. He had helped make the whale a symbol for a cause.

Among Mowat's many allies among writers, probably none was more prolific than Scott McVay, who peppered the newsstands in the 1960s and 1970s with articles detailing the problems of whaling. He was communicating with the Smithsonian's Remington Kellogg and William Herrington, a marine resources expert in the State Department, in the early 1960s, and his first warning about the plight of the whales appeared in *Scientific American* in 1966. In the 1970s he drew substantial attention as the coauthor for Roger Payne's *Science* article on whale songs, and he followed that with an account of Inuit hunting of bowhead whales before it became controversial. McVay was equally adept at writing lyrical pieces about cetacean intelligence or careful analyses of whaling management. While his films were not as widely distributed, he was able to influence people with them as well, including a documentary on Alaskan bowheads.[28]

Finally, the 1970s brought new opportunities for people to see live whales up close. Whale watching grew dramatically in the 1970s, particularly with companies taking thousands of tourists to see the gray whales off Southern California and Baja California and humpbacks (and sometimes fins and minkes) off New England.[29] Even the *New Yorker* got involved in 1980, with a firsthand account of a whale watch from Cape Cod that emphasized the environmentalist connection, with participants encouraged to sign a petition as they got on the boat.[30] Not many whale-watching companies in existence in the twenty-first century predate the whaling moratorium imposed in 1982, so it is hard to know how many people ever got to see whales and turn that experience into political activism.

Despite the rise of whale watching, most encounters with a live whale occurred at amusement parks. The opening of SeaWorld in San Diego in 1965 sparked the construction of larger oceanariums and aquariums throughout the United States, Canada, and Australia, with the capacity to hold dolphins and orcas. The animals could be trained to perform fascinating stunts, and their tanks became the center of amusement parks that also had rides and other animal displays. It seems likely that visitors to such parks—more than eleven million in 1993 in the United States alone—gained an appreciation for whales and a desire to stop the killing. It is equally likely that anyone who believed that whales were sentient creatures felt revulsion at the idea that an orca born in the wild could be captured, placed in a cement tank, and taught to do tricks. Paul Spong, who had first worked with whales at an aquarium in Vancouver, took the lead in the 1980s in denouncing such enclosures as "death camps." Oceanariums had once served a purpose for environmentalists by raising awareness and concern, but no more. Humans had learned that whales "are real fellow beings on this planet. They're our sentient companions." Given that, Spong concluded, it was time to "leave them alone."[31]

It seems likely, then, that by the end of the 1970s more people thought of whales as tourist attractions than as food. Even those who grew up far from a coast could imagine seeing a whale someday on vacation. Some who saw whales surely remained unmoved, and therefore raw statistics of people on boats cannot tell us much about the power of this facet of ecotourism. We should also be careful not to draw a stark dividing line between whale watchers and whale hunters: in Iceland, a thriving whale-watching business coexists with a small but energetically defended whaling industry. In any case, between tour boats, parks, and vivid popular media, more and more people were being exposed to whales, and they were responding with a plea to save them.

THE MORATORIUM PROPOSAL

The central goal of the whale protection movement was to end commercial whaling while there were still whales left in the sea, either by persuading governments to outlaw whaling (a commercial moratorium) or by getting the whaling commission to set quotas at zero. Side issues, like aboriginal subsistence whaling, would create complications, but outside of a few whaling states and the offices of a few scientists, almost everyone who cared about whales in the 1970s thought that commercial whaling had to end. The central challenge would be to find a way to persuade Japan and the Soviet Union to close their industries rather than leave the IWC.

It appears that the International Union for the Conservation of Nature made the first proposal for a ten-year moratorium on catching blue whales in 1963, and Friends of the Earth first presented a full moratorium to the IWC in 1971, although the organization had no standing to offer a formal proposal.[32] The IWC had banned the hunting of blue and humpback whales in the 1960s, but discussions were ongoing about individual populations or species. The commission was still committed to the blue whale unit system until 1971, even as scientists and bureaucrats questioned its rationale and suggested that it had not been well suited for the heyday of hunting blue whales, much less the lean years.

The Nixon administration was split on the issue. Stuart Blow of the US State Department, which had been among the strongest supporters of the commission, admitted that the IWC "has been, to say the least, an imperfect mechanism for the conservation of whale stocks."[33] But the department was unhappy with unilateral conservation measures undertaken by other parts of the executive branch. In 1970, the Interior Department had listed eight species of whales as endangered globally, which meant that Americans could not trade in those species. The US Navy and the State Department had objected to the decision to include sperm whales, in part because sperm oil was an irreplaceable lubricant. The State Department also noted that some prominent scientists believed that sei and fin whales were in no danger of extinction. Listing the whales, the agency objected, would prevent the US delegation to the IWC meetings from advocating anything but an end to whaling, which could lead to the collapse of the IWC and "a race to harvest the last remaining whales to the point of commercial extinction."[34] The Interior Department prevailed, but the State

Department's ambivalence was probably mirrored by concerns in the Commerce Department, home to J. L. McHugh, the US commissioner. L. W. Andreas of Archer Daniels Midland spoke for many in the business community, telling Senator Warren Magnuson of Washington State, a leader in legislative efforts to regulate fisheries, that the Interior Department's decision was "arbitrary and unjustified" for many of the same reasons that the State Department had listed.[35]

Andreas was joined in his opposition by other governments, who noted that the endangered listings ran counter to US support of liberal trade rules by making it impossible to import products made from those species. Complaints came from Chile, Peru, Ecuador, Japan, and Norway, with the last two specifically citing the General Agreement on Tariffs and Trade (GATT). As the Japanese pointed out, the listings dealt only with foreign countries, so it was still technically legal to hunt whales in the United States, which ran counter to GATT's rules. Both Japan and Norway acknowledged the desire for conservation, but each suggested that it would be better to work through the IWC. The official response was that GATT did allow conservation of vanishing resources and that the US government would be pleased if the IWC "were to take effective action to assure the perpetuation of whale stocks for man's future benefit."[36] The 1971 hearing where Tom Garrett pounced on the IWC tapped into a discussion about changing whaling policy that was already underway but that was not yet driven by much public pressure. Hundreds of letters had come into the executive and legislative branches in Washington, DC, and the people who testified before Congress frequently noted the membership numbers of their respective organizations, but it was nothing like the deluge that would hit later. Scientists, regulators, and diplomats were wrestling with the IWC's shortcomings and trying to compose new policies to address the shift of whaling effort to the North Pacific and the obvious problems of the blue whale unit system. Both houses of Congress had passed resolutions calling for an end to commercial pelagic whaling in 1971, part of a commitment to make the IWC reasonably relevant.

Things came to a head in November 1971 when the White House called for public comments on the upcoming UN Conference on the Human Environment in Stockholm. Whaling was only a small part of the lengthy agenda, not appearing in the transcript of the hearings until page 249. While the Sierra Club and Audubon Society representatives did not include whaling in their testimony, several other groups did, and all condemned the IWC and whaling nations. When one diplomat commented that the IWC had been getting its act together in the 1960s, Lewis Regenstein exclaimed, "What utter and malicious nonsense!" In the wake of the 1971 congressional hearings, the Nixon administration and its chief environmentalist, Russell Train, chair of the Council on Environmental Quality, decided to support an anti-whaling policy.[37]

In February 1972, the State Department notified its diplomats in more than twenty countries that efforts to curb Soviet and Japanese whaling had gotten nowhere. The only solution was to increase pressure by dealing with those two states at the highest level and using the tools of coercion. Ambassadors were to inform their hosts that the United States would push for a moratorium at the UN Stockholm conference if there seemed to be no other way to agree on whaling reductions. The tougher stance came in part because of US congressional resolutions but also because Japanese ambassador Ryohei Murata had admitted privately that the Japanese had not faced enough pressure on whaling to change the opinion of their fisheries officials, even though the Japanese Foreign Ministry had concluded that whaling did not net enough product to compensate for the bad publicity.[38] Replies from US embassies ranged from John Davis Lodge in Buenos Aires demanding something with teeth to stop "the senseless slaughter" to Armin Meyer in Tokyo reporting that the Japanese thought the Americans were "over-dramatizing" the matter. The United States, Meyer warned, would have to tread carefully lest it destroy the last shred of the IWC's credibility and undermine the progress the United States and Japan had made on conservation of crabs, salmon, and groundfish. Meyer tried to persuade the Japanese environment minister to come to the 1972 IWC meeting, in the hope that he might be more sympathetic than the fisheries officials. Meyer had to settle instead for the insight that the moratorium would be impossible for Japan to accept on economic grounds but that Japan might be willing to live with a slow phaseout of the industry, management by species, or a large scientific catch exemption.[39]

From a whaling standpoint, the Stockholm conference is best remembered as site of the first international discussion of a commercial whaling moratorium. The United States introduced a resolution calling on governments to strengthen the IWC by abandoning the objection clause and contributing more money to scientific research. The Japanese interpreted this resolution as a veiled call for a moratorium, because it implied that the lower quotas were not sufficient to produce badly needed conservation. The final vote on a resolution that included the moratorium was 53–0 in favor, with Portugal, South Africa, and Japan abstaining. The resolution was nonbinding, but it was as close as one could get to a statement of global opinion on a moratorium.[40]

It is fair to say that the whaling nations were not totally prepared for what happened at Stockholm, where environmental activists had unusual influence. Before the meeting, US diplomats reported from countries such as Turkey, El Salvador, and Malawi that their host governments had no interest in whaling, so any progress on the moratorium would have to come from consultations during the Stockholm meeting.[41] Outside of the formal meetings, protestors organized demonstrations in support of the moratorium proposal. Maurice Strong, chair of the conference, spoke to the anti-whaling groups in a show of support. With many delegations headed by environment ministers and thousands of members of environmental NGOs on hand, it is perhaps not surprising that environmentalist measures got more support than usual.

Weeks after the Stockholm meeting, at the late-June meeting of the IWC in London, the United States committed to a strongly environmentalist line. Washington had inserted several items on the agenda, including the moratorium, with the hope of restricting whaling. Among the new items were an effort to coerce nonmember states, like Brazil, to bring their whaling operations under the IWC umbrella and a proposal to manage whales by stock rather than blue whale unit or even by species. The depth of the US commitment was evident in the presence of Russell Train, a political appointee with the ear of President Richard Nixon, as the commissioner. His delegation included Roger Payne and other figures acceptable to environmentalists as well as members of past delegations, including J. L. McHugh, whom Train had tried to kick to the curb in 1971 for not being a conservationist.[42] McHugh had seen the writing on the wall in March 1972 when he unhappily passed along a request by Joan McIntyre of Friends of the Earth to be an observer attached to the US delegation at the IWC meeting. He fretted about the prospect of having the IWC work in "a goldfish bowl" but conceded that his government would probably not agree.[43] The British commissioner, Minister of Fisheries E. W. Maude, observed a deep division between the old and new members of the delegation, because

Train and his "acolytes" were not well versed in the workings of the IWC. Maude grimaced at the embarrassment that the US delegation caused its allies and said that its leadership was "vigorous but on occasions bordered on clumsiness." He admitted, however, that "it is clear that the Commission would not have come to so satisfactory a conclusion without this injection of political abrasion."[44]

Given that Britain voted for the moratorium, which failed, it is interesting that Maude called the conclusion satisfactory. The very presence of a cabinet minister leading the delegation was an acknowledgment of the high level of public attention given to this IWC meeting, and the attentive public wanted a moratorium, not the collection of measures that actually passed. In its briefing papers before the meeting, the British government had dismissed a moratorium as "unrealistic" and decided to urge the IWC's Technical Committee to study the proposal carefully as a means of stalling. Instead of supporting the moratorium, the British intended to work with the American delegation to accept a package of realistic conservation measures, meaning reductions in quotas.[45] But when the time came to vote on a moratorium, Britain joined the United States, Mexico, and Sweden in the yes column, which served to placate public opinion at home. In the end, the IWC endorsed several important changes, including a permanent ban on hunting blue and humpback whales and replacing the blue whale unit system with management by species and region, so that the quota for fin whales, for instance, would be divided between Northern and Southern Hemispheres. In each case, the delegates reported that they had set the quotas low enough to allow populations that had been extensively hunted to begin growing again. William Aron, a new member of the Scientific Committee, later reported that a more senior member of the committee had chastised him for advocating a low quota for a particular stock. This person had no complaint about the interpretation of the data, but he did question Aron's "lack of realism." The Scientific Committee had to seek the lowest number that industry could live with, even in the year of Stockholm. Maude reported that in hallway lobbying it was clear that the Japanese were far more difficult to placate than the Soviets, who seemed to think that whaling was no longer economically feasible.[46]

At least Britain voted consistently. Several governments that had not opposed the moratorium at Stockholm found ways to do so later that month in London. Japan, not surprisingly, moved from abstention on the nonbinding resolution approved in Stockholm to opposition when the vote actually counted; the Soviet Union, which had not been represented at Stockholm, was also in opposition. Those two nations opened the way for others to oppose the moratorium, because it seemed likely that both would file objections, making the whole vote moot. Three decisions made during the deliberations still seem surprising. First, Norway reversed course. The yes vote in Stockholm became a no vote in London, to the dismay of many people, including some Norwegians. With the cover provided by the pelagic whaling states, Canada and Australia also decided to abstain rather than support the moratorium, and that was enough to kill it in 1972 and ensure that there would be bitter debates for years to come. As Maude caustically wrote, "The ease with which some countries who voted for the Stockholm resolution managed to evade the moral commitment and accept instead such reductions in catches as the Japanese and Russians were willing to concede was remarkable even to the more objective observer."[47] Of course, Britain had been prepared to do the same.

Norway's vote attracted the attention of environmental NGOs, who were unsure what to make of Oslo's shifting position. The International Society for the Protection of Animals requested clarification, which set off a tiff within Norway's government between the appalled Ministry of the Environment and the only lightly apologetic foreign ministry.[48] The diplomats argued that a vote for a moratorium in the IWC would have been pointless because Japan and the Soviet Union would have objected or, worse, withdrawn from the commission. Diplomats also argued that the Scientific Committee had rejected the moratorium as having no basis in science. Opponents of the moratorium would use these two points as central foils until it finally passed in 1982. After six months of contemplating a response that might reveal information better left unsaid, Norway's foreign ministry decided just to ignore the matter.

Oddly, as the US Congress was discussing the moratorium in 1971, it was also considering the Pelly Amendment to the Fishermen's Protective Act of 1967. The amendment, which passed in December 1971, allowed the secretary of commerce to decide if another country was undermining "the effectiveness of an international fishery conservation program," which was defined broadly enough to cover the 1946 whaling convention. If the secretary found that a country was acting in such a way, he was supposed to notify the president, who then would have the option of banning or reducing that country's exports of seafood to the United States, while keeping in mind the nation's obligations under the General Agreement on Tariffs and Trade.[49]

The Pelly Amendment grew out of Congressman Tom Pelly's desire to support scientists working under the International Convention on Northwest Atlantic Fisheries, who were trying to save Atlantic salmon and not getting much cooperation from some European countries. Pelly's original amendment focused solely on the Atlantic fisheries, but his colleagues suggested broadening it; with that change it passed. Pelly, a Republican from the Seattle area, had an interest in fisheries work, like his better-known colleague from Washington State, Senator Warren Magnuson, but he died in 1973 before many people had begun to link the amendment to whaling. While the Pelly Amendment was not designed specifically with whales in mind, and the US House report in favor of it did not mention whaling at all, it quickly became a favorite tool of anti-whaling forces.[50] If the IWC would not rein in its members, then the US government could. Both Japan and the Soviet Union had huge fishing industries that ventured into US waters in the 1970s, so it appeared to be an easy step to connect their behavior in the IWC to their other economic interests.

The Pelly Amendment gave the US administration some latitude in whether or not to certify a country and impose sanctions, so it became most useful as a threat. The reality was that the United States was reluctant to certify a country because to do so ran counter to the perceived national interest in removing trade barriers. Instead, the Pelly Amendment was more akin to a yellow card in soccer: the zebra-striped commerce secretary would mention Pelly in connection with an offending country as a way to indicate growing displeasure and the threat of a red card. The amendment got its first test in 1974, when Commerce Secretary Frederick B. Dent certified that Japan and the Soviet Union had taken more fin, sperm, and sei whales than IWC quotas permitted. Even though both nations had been well within their rights when they filed objections to the quotas, the United States threatened sanctions. In the 1974–75 whaling season, Japan and the Soviet Union agreed to accept the IWC quotas, so President Gerald Ford announced that he would not impose sanctions.[51] The Pelly Amendment was invoked three more times in 1978 against Peru, Chile, and South Korea for whaling outside the convention framework, but in each case sanctions were not applied because the country in question moved to join the IWC.[52]

The main problem with the Pelly Amendment, beyond the US government's commitment to freer trade, was that the Japanese and Soviets were not behaving badly according to the rules of the IWC. When they disagreed with conservationist sentiment, they used their votes and the objection system to the letter of the law. Perhaps their rhetoric was self-serving or misleading at times, but every government was guilty of that at some point. Successive US administrations were unwilling to start a trade war with governments that were abiding by the rules of a commission that the US government had helped create. Those opposed to whaling soon realized that they needed a more powerful tool.

AFTER STOCKHOLM

In the aftermath of the defeat of the commercial moratorium in 1972, the whaling commission and the protestors went in very different directions, which led to increasing bitterness in the struggle between whalers and their opponents. The IWC adopted an Australian proposal for a new management strategy that emphasized individual stock assessment and quotas, with a goal of rebuilding decimated populations while still allowing some hunting. At the same time, the proponents of saving whales moved toward a strategy of opposing whaling because whales are special, sentient beings, generally dropping arguments about better utilization of resources. In a sense, the IWC was finally able to manage whales effectively, and there is no doubt that public pressure had a role in that shift. Yet the protestors were no longer interested in better management. Managing whales implied that humans had a right to kill them, and the anti-whaling movement had a harder and harder time accepting that.

The transition in the motivating ideology of the environmentalists can be seen by comparing a few key documents, beginning with a spring 1973 letter to the Norwegian government from twelve US organizations, including such heavyweights as the Audubon Society and the Humane Society of the United States.[53] In calling for Norway to back the moratorium, the authors made a wide range of statements to critique whaling. The explosive harpoon was "cruel," they began, recycling an argument going back to the 1940s about the inhumanity of whaling. They then noted that "the future existence of several whale species" and "the delicate balance of life in the world's oceans" were at stake—and all of that was in one sentence.

The authors then shifted from the ecosystem and biodiversity points to rational economic arguments, which left them in a knot of contradiction. They reminded Prime Minister Lars Korvald that the United States had banned the use of whale products without any adverse effects, because whale products were either not really necessities or were easily replaced by something else. But they tacked quickly and argued that whalers had no right to rob future generations "of this irreplaceable resource." The letter concluded with the idea that whales were "fascinating." The document demonstrates both the ways in which members of the Save the Whales movement were determined to try almost anything to stop whaling and the inconsistencies in their logic that would eventually have to be reconciled.

One of the common arguments in the early stages of the movement was the practical one that whales should be saved so that future generations could use them rationally. In a world facing a population bomb, it was foolish to throw away a potentially valuable source of fat and protein because the IWC was unable to corral its whalers. In a sense, it was a very utilitarian argument that any early twentieth-century Progressive, or most of the proponents of a whaling commission in the 1940s, would have supported—humans had an obligation to manage resources for the greater good and that meant consumption over the longest time. That idea had been a key motivating factor in creating the IWC in 1946, although it had been tempered with a commitment to keep the whaling industry strong.

Closely related to the utilitarian argument was one that took into account ecological relationships among species. Protecting whales was, at least in part, about protecting the species around them. Whales were huge and interesting and therefore an easy way to draw attention to a larger crisis. Everyone knew about whales, but the plight of plankton and krill would not rouse most people to the barricades. Russell Train made the connection explicitly in 1971, writing that "like many other species of wildlife, whales represent both a resource of potential economic value and an integral part of the ecosystem in which they live. Therefore, they may be considered to be both of environmental and of commercial or traditional fish and wildlife concern."[54]

Environmentalists around the world replicated the logic of the organizations that were protesting to Korvald. In New Zealand, the first trickle of concern came in 1973 in the form of letters from individuals seeking to get their government back into the IWC and working to end whaling. Some letters were so well reasoned that they were probably more influential than the stacks of missives that would come through the prime minister's mail room in later years. Just after Easter 1974, nineteen-year-old Rowan Taylor wrote to Prime Minister Norman Kirk, "It seems sad that while we celebrated the death and subsequent 'resurrection' of one man 2000 years ago, the deaths of 400 whales goes unnoticed and their resurrections will be as shoe polish."[55] The next year, with Taylor as an organizer, the letters began pouring in, and they demonstrated both a wide range of arguments against whaling and a knowledge of what was happening around the world, especially across the Tasman Sea in Australia. In 1975, Ecology Action and Project Jonah got between 8,000 and 10,000 people to sign a petition calling for the government in Wellington to take a more aggressive stance against whaling. Both the petition's supporting material and a twenty-five-page position paper put together by eight NGOs argued that whaling was comparable to "the ethical wrongs of genocide" and that properly managed whaling could "yield half a million tons of protein per annum."[56] But by 1978, the groups that had been willing to list waste of resources as a key reason to end whaling were now focused on morality. In a newspaper ad that year featuring a peaceful scene of a whale and its calf, New Zealanders read that whales "talk to each other over great distances, play and make love too." The sperm whale that had once overwhelmed Captain Ahab was now "gentle" and "intelligent."[57]

New Zealand's government responded slowly to the mounting pressure. Into 1976, the prime minister's office was still sending letters stating that the IWC was too ineffective to matter and that New Zealand was taking steps on its own. Soon, protestors began to tackle that assertion by arguing that the IWC was becoming more relevant and that it would only be effective if states like New Zealand joined. Then, in the summer of 1976, the government caved in and decided at the last minute to rejoin the commission, taking a strong conservationist line. The decision was so abrupt that the ambassador in Tokyo complained that a bit of advance notice would have saved him some grief with his dismayed host government, and New Zealand's IWC delegate commented that he was completely unprepared to make a coherent case for conservation, which was somewhat embarrassing. While New Zealand later gained a reputation as a country that would emphatically battle Japan over whaling, in 1976 some ministers were not quite convinced of the cause's merits.[58]

Throughout the world, letter-writing campaigns were targeting both the whaling states and the IWC. Environmental organizations placed ads in newspapers listing the addresses for the IWC or for embassies of countries believed to need new whaling policies. They sent out mailers with fiery rhetoric urging action and distributed preprinted postcards to be filled out and sent by the thousands to whomever was insufficiently committed to saving the whales. One of the prized trophies of the Save the Whales forces was a photo of an IWC official receiving boxes of petitions or postcards generated by an anti-whaling organization. The IWC officials did not make policy, so the petitions were better aimed at the member governments.[59]

The defeat of the moratorium proposal in 1972 meant that it was the central issue of the 1973 IWC meeting. Again the United States advocated for the proposal, and again Japan and the USSR made it clear that they would not accept it. Norway, Iceland, and South Africa joined in voting no, and opponents worked to emphasize that they had the scientists on their side. Since the IWC had done away with the blue whale unit system in 1972, it had to set whaling quotas by species and by region north or south of the equator. Despite the defeat of the moratorium in 1973, conservationist forces still had enough muscle to impose lower quotas on most species, especially for fin and sperm whales, which had increasingly moved into the first rank of species taken, especially as whalers had moved more and more into the Pacific Ocean. Rather than walk away from the meeting defeated, the US delegation congratulated itself on having put pressure on the Soviets and Japanese with its skillful diplomacy, particularly by backing away from "unreasonable positions"—like the moratorium.[60]

With the moratorium unlikely to suddenly gain favor with any two of its five opponents, the three-quarters majority needed for passage was not to be found. The few remaining whaling countries understood that they would continue to face tremendous pressure, and the nonwhaling countries were split between those who were unconvinced that a moratorium was necessary and those who realized that a moratorium was not about to be approved. Even if there had been enough countries to support a zero quota, Japan and the Soviet Union could simply file an objection per IWC rules and kill the amendment.

In 1974, the US government sought help from the whaling states to find a way out of the deadlock. US officials told whaling nations that while they still supported a complete moratorium, they would be favorably inclined toward a moratorium on hunting stocks that were below 50 percent of their prehunting populations. Norwegian officials called this a much more sensible proposal, one that might win support from a number of nations. William Aron, now the US commissioner, emphasized that the United States itself could not make such a proposal given the political pressure at home, but perhaps Japan could.[61]

The Australian government turned out to be the one that stepped forward with a proposal that became known as the New Management Procedure (NMP).[62] The rules were complex, but basically the Australians wanted to translate maximum sustainable yield theory from fisheries science to whaling. The obvious problem was that fish reproduced much more quickly than whales, so even if MSY theory was well-tuned for some fisheries (and that in itself was problematic), it would take a lot of work to make it relevant for marine mammals. It became apparent as the years went on that there were not enough data to reliably calculate sustainable yield for whale stocks. MSY theory requires knowledge of stock population size and reproductive rates, as well as a good deal of number crunching. At its core is the idea that people can manage populations in a stock by controlling harvesting. If a stock has never been hunted, then the MSY level might, counterintuitively, be 60 to 70 percent of the normal population, which was itself fluctuating over time, as wild species do. Such a species should step up reproduction in the face of the killing of adults, and humans could skim off the extra new recruits that would not be necessary to maintain a population at 60 to 70 percent of its normal size. Or, if a stock has been overhunted, humans could protect it, keep track of population increase, and then pick the time when it made the most sense to hunt again, harvesting just enough animals to keep the population in balance in perpetuity. MSY theory works best with stable, robust populations, but even in such cases its proponents had a serious problem dealing with natural and sometimes extreme fluctuations in populations.

To help win support from anti-whaling governments, the Australian proposal included setting quotas by stock rather than simply dividing species quotas into northern and southern populations. In addition, they proposed to split whale stocks into three groups based on their health: those that had been so reduced that they had to be protected, known as Protected Stocks; those that were healthy enough to yield some whales, known as Management Stocks; and those that had yet to be exploited, known as Initial Management Stocks. The IWC agreed to set a target of 60 percent of natural stock size as the optimum that would produce the most whales for sustained exploitation. The New Management Procedure raised predictable questions: what is the definition of a stock, and does anyone have enough evidence to actually differentiate and estimate stocks in the seas both now and in the original condition necessary to set MSY? Over time, it became clear that the difficulty of getting current population numbers would be dwarfed by the challenges of determining historical stock sizes, given problems with existing whaling data and the dynamic marine environment, where populations might fluctuate dramatically over time.

The problems with the NMP quickly became obvious. Even as the IWC accepted the NMP in 1974, it ordered the Scientific Committee to meet before the next commission meeting to figure out stock sizes for hunted whales around the world. Stock assessments required the Scientific Committee to analyze data and build estimates, but disagreements on how to measure stocks led to size estimates that were so broad as to be nearly useless. It then fell to the IWC delegates in the plenary sessions to set quotas based on the recommendations of the Scientific Committee. Skillful diplomacy could, therefore, still be more instrumental than science in making key decisions. At the 1975 IWC meeting, for instance, delegates had to set a quota for sperm whale hunting in the North Pacific, despite a huge range of population estimates. Mexico's long-serving commissioner, Andres Rozenthal, won praise from conservationists for saving thousands of whales by skillfully bridging the gaps between the whalers and their opponents and negotiating a relatively low quota for sperm whales.[63]

The NMP was a classic compromise, which meant that it angered people who saw no grounds for compromise. It represented a huge jump forward in terms of real management possibilities, and almost every IWC member voted for it. Yet the consensus around it from 1974 quickly fell apart. Because the NMP did not require a full moratorium, hard-line anti-whaling protestors were bound to be disappointed. In fact, they found whaling states' support of the NMP to be proof that it was just the old system dressed up in a new piece of the regulation schedule. Project Jonah in New Zealand denounced the Australians as "bad guys" and their management scheme as "essentially a sham."[64] The irony was that at the beginning of the decade, the protestors' long-term goal had been sustainable use of whales based on advice of the Scientific Committee; now that the IWC had tried to adopt such a policy, environmentalists found it unacceptable.

The tension over the value of the Scientific Committee's report was evident at the 1974 meeting between Norwegian and US whaling experts. One Norwegian asked why the United States accepted the Scientific Committee's reports, except when it came to the moratorium. The US response was that the moratorium was about more than science. The Norwegian note taker expressed puzzlement by writing "(?)" after that comment, but over the next few years he would see the same attitude in the Oslo government. Norway's Ministry of the Environment tried to explain the rationale of the whaling opponents for nearly a decade before finally giving up in 1984.

What that Norwegian note taker failed to understand in 1974 was that, for a growing number of proponents of the moratorium, the idea that whales were still being managed as if they were mainly valuable as food for people—or worse, pets—was incomprehensible. The reality was that some whale meat was being processed into pet food and, for the fur industry in the northern Soviet Union, pelt food. Leonard Buckley, a critic for the *Times* of London, was moved by the BBC show *Horizon* describing what became of whale meat: "My cat is a vegetarian. Or at least she will be after the programme last night on dolphins and whales. I shall keep her on carrots and rice."[65] It did not really matter how much whale meat was being fed to domesticated animals; it had simply become unacceptable to use such a magnificent animal that way.

GREENPEACE AND THE REJECTION OF SUSTAINABLE USE

Dozens of organizations helped organize those people who rejected using leviathan as pet food or shoe polish. Some were old, established organizations, like the Humane Society of the United States or the International Society for the Protection of Animals; others were new groups formed specifically to combat whaling, like Project Jonah. And then there was Greenpeace, an organization in the loosest sense of the word that began with an antinuclear mission but made its name fighting against whaling. Of all of the new organizations of the 1970s, Greenpeace has been the most successful at branching out into other issues and entering the everyday lexicon as, for better or worse, what many people think of when they hear the term *environmental organization*. Greenpeace was a master of public relations, but it was just one of many groups to oppose whaling.

The groups that mobilized to pressure IWC members to end whaling (there was no consensus about whether the ban should apply to all whaling or just commercial whaling) were nearly uniform in their rejection of the idea of managed, sustainable whaling. Closely related was the widespread belief that whales were sentient beings with human qualities. The logical step from there was to use almost any tactic to stop whaling, from economic boycotts, to stridently worded mass mailings, to physical confrontation, which included the risk of bodily harm. Politically, the anti-whaling movement made it impossible for many governments to condone industrial whaling and a challenge for them to tolerate aboriginal whaling.

Greenpeace began in 1971 in British Columbia operating under the name Don't Make a Wave, a reference to the planned nuclear testing in the Aleutian Islands. Irving Stowe, Robert Hunter, and the rest of the early organizers were concerned more broadly about nuclear weapons, and their first successful campaign targeted French nuclear testing in the central Pacific.[66] Although the antinuclear campaign never fell far from the hearts of Greenpeace founders, by 1975 a new group of leaders had changed the emphasis to combating whaling. Behavioral scientist Paul Spong went on the lecture circuit with the Greenpeace Whale Show, "a totally absorbing blend of eco-politics, startling, moody sounds, and superb visual art."[67] The ground had been plowed already by Joan McIntyre of Project Jonah, with *Mind in the Waters*, a collection of essays and poems that focused readers on the consciousness of cetaceans while raising money for her organization. She critiqued not only the "Christian version of creation" for preaching that creation had ended after six days but also the idea that whales did not have "feelings, imagination, consciousness, and awareness." The contributing authors were concerned about whales, but more importantly they feared "the death of the spirit of the planet."[68] In many ways, the no-nukes movement shared a basic similarity with the Save the Whales movement, in that each offered a radical critique of both faith in science and the excesses of industrialization. In fact, the very concept of a civilization with tens of thousands of nuclear weapons probably helped make the case that people might not actually be as good as whales.

Greenpeace became a household name thanks largely to one incident in the North Pacific in the summer of 1975. The Soviets and Japanese had expanded their take of sperm whales dramatically in the late 1960s as other species became harder to find. Sperm whale meat was barely edible by people in the first place, and studies later in the 1970s showed that it often had high mercury content, but it could still be used as animal food.[69] More important, though, many nations sought sperm whale oil as a high-value industrial lubricant. The Soviets used it in their intercontinental ballistic missiles, and the Americans used it in nuclear submarines (the US Navy objected when the sperm whale showed up on the endangered species list in 1970).[70] Tens of thousands of sperm whales lived in the North Pacific, and the IWC had started regulating the hunt by Soviet and Japanese factory ships only in the 1960s.

Factory-ship whaling relatively close to North American shores was an obvious target for a group that already had taken its protests directly to the open ocean in 1974, having gotten worldwide attention for disrupting nuclear testing in French Polynesia. Greenpeace's twin challenges would be to locate the whalers, even a large whaling flotilla, in the vast Pacific and then to figure out some way to cause trouble for the whalers. Using a mixture of charm and subterfuge, Spong had persuaded Einar Vangstein of the Bureau for International Whaling Statistics to give him data from the Soviet and Japanese sperm whaling fleets from 1973 and 1974, which gave the Greenpeacers a chance to find the Soviet fleet off Mendocino, California, in 1975. The crew of Greenpeace's *Phyllis Cormack* managed to track down the Soviet whaler *Vlastny* and then launched small inflatable boats known as Zodiacs to act as shields for the sperm whales, hoping to deter the harpooners from firing. When the Soviet gunners opened fire anyway, coming perilously close to impaling the activists, they not only killed a few more whales but also made Greenpeace famous. It helped to have a sympathetic cameraman, and the expedition member filming caught the harpoon shot with the last few feet of film and battery juice he had.[71]

The confrontation with the *Vlastny* was incredibly powerful. Word got back to the IWC meeting that was just winding up, making Spong, who was hanging around trying to make some waves, an instant celebrity. Anchorman Walter Cronkite put the footage on television, and a movie producer tried to piece a deal together for a Hollywood drama. Greenpeace generated more positive feedback from that one afternoon, one analyst concluded, than it had in the previous four years combined.[72] The film footage became part of the cultural milieu of the 1970s, on par with recorded whale songs. Americans who might have no use for the antimodernist parts of Greenpeace ideology were nevertheless appalled by the visual depiction of what whaling really meant. A thousand form letters complaining about exploding harpoons could not equal the power of a few seconds of film of a dying sperm whale, on color television, during dinner.

It also helped to have an unsympathetic opponent, and in the 1970s Japan and the Soviet Union fit the bill. Many Japanese products, like cars and televisions, were clearly superior to most other nations'. The flood of inexpensive, quality Japanese manufactured goods left many in the West conflicted—they bought the goods even as they worried that they were undermining domestic industrial jobs. Some latent anti-Japanese feeling from World War II played a role too, especially in Australia and New Zealand, as did accusations that the Japanese had been irresponsible whalers since the 1930s. So there was widespread dislike for Japan, sometimes even among those people with a Sony eight-track playing whale songs in a Datsun boasting a catchy pro-whale bumper sticker. The Soviets were even easier to distrust. Even for those who opposed the US commitment to a nuclear buildup in the name of the Cold War, the sins of the Soviet system were blatant. Joseph Stalin's show trials, the crushing of dissent in Hungary and Czechoslovakia, and revelations about the Gulag system had dispelled notions of a workers' paradise. It was not hard to believe that a Soviet whaler could be so foolish or brutal as to fire a harpoon right over the heads of fellow humans with a camera present. It did not hurt that the Japanese and Soviets appeared to be in collusion. When Greenpeace protester Paul Watson clambered aboard a sperm whale that the Soviets had harpooned, he concluded that it was undersize. The Japanese inspector on board the Soviet ship attested not only that every sperm whale caught that day was legal but that a person standing on a whale in choppy water could not possibly measure it accurately.[73]

One upshot of this first filmed intervention was that it alienated other environmentalist groups. At least a dozen organizations in the greater San Francisco area in 1975 opposed whaling when the *Phyllis Cormack* sailed into the bay after the confrontation. They were not particularly enthusiastic about this rag-tag bunch of hippies who had wandered into town. "I want to see the whales saved," said Joan McIntyre, the founding voice behind Project Jonah, "but not *that* way."[74]

There is some irony in McIntyre's dismay at Greenpeace tactics, since she had built on Spong's work herself. Historian Frank Zelko details how Spong changed over the course of several years from a slightly eccentric but traditional behavioral mammalogist to a proponent of the radical idea that whales have sentience and intellect equal to humans. Along with John Lilly, who was doing pioneering work on dolphins that flowed from contracts with the US Navy, Spong challenged traditional thinking about what whales were capable of intellectually: they were not just sleek cows. Lilly, starting with physiology, and Spong, working with behavior of captive and then wild whales, provided scientific legitimacy to the idea that whales were too good to kill.[75] For her part, McIntyre helped popularize that notion with Mind in the Waters, which emphasized that whales had intelligence and morality.

Less daring opponents of whaling frequently tried to organize boycotts, but grassroots boycotts did not seem to have much impact. It was not easy to hurt the Soviet Union with a boycott of imports, given that no one wanted Soviet goods in the first place—with the exception of vodka or travel on Aeroflot airlines (and boycotting Aeroflot was really a matter of self-preservation anyway). One effort in New York in 1974 to spark a boycott of Soviet goods and gather signatures on a petition also sold bumper stickers, lapel pins, and posters to passers-by, suggesting that the real goal of the boycott was to generate awareness rather than bring down the Soviet economy one whale at a time.[76] In any case, Soviet leaders were unlikely to change policy based on economic pressure from private citizens and NGOs, given everything else they withstood over the course of the Cold War. Norway, likewise, did not export much to Britain, Australia, or the United States at the time, so targeting that country would be difficult; regardless, Norwegian whaling was small potatoes compared to that of Japan and the Soviet Union. So the boycotts usually fell on Japan, with its surging trade surplus with the United States and other Western nations. Given the steady rise of Japanese goods in the automotive and electronics sectors, the boycotts seemed largely ineffective. Was a consumer really going to buy a Ford Pinto instead of a Honda Civic because the Japanese government objected to a sperm whale quota?

Talk of boycotts was most commonly expressed in the protest letters that piled up in foreign ministries, embassies, and the IWC office. In 1977, the IWC finally opened its own office in Cambridge, England, separate from the Ministry of Agriculture and Fisheries, and it became a magnet for mass mailings. The incoming mail reflected a range of ideas and confusion about the IWC's purpose. As early as 1972, the IWC office had received mail from a leper in the Philippines looking for help and from a divorcée in Branson, Missouri, looking for a pen pal. As protest organizations began coordinated letter campaigns with appeal letters attached, inattentive readers sometimes ended up mailing checks to the IWC instead of to the groups that were tormenting it.[77]

IWC staff read the letters with red pen in hand. In one telling response, IWC secretary Ray Gambell scolded Tom Garrett for a form letter from the Whale Protection Fund bearing Garrett's name as the head of its advisory board. Gambell's exasperation with the tens of thousands of form letters was obvious as he laced into Garrett for associating his name and reputation as a deputy IWC commissioner of the United States with a letter based on shoddy work. Gambell was willing to accept that fund-raising letters "overstate your case on the grounds that the end justifies the means," but he insisted that an organization that claims to educate the public should have the "responsibility to ensure that its material has a factually accurate basis." He then laid out three "demonstrably false statements" about whaling in the Whale Protection Fund letter, which led him to conclude that "you are deliberately exploiting public ignorance of the matter." Gambell also acknowledged that the form of delivery was part of the problem, arguing that the preprinted postcard is hardly a "credible demonstration of public opinion."[78] In a newspaper story about anti-whaling protests, an anonymous observer, who might well have been Gambell, sighed, "When you consider how much money, tens of thousands of pounds, has been spent on these mailing campaigns and then consider how the Whale Research Fund [an IWC sponsored agency] needs money urgently, then the stupidity of it all comes home."[79]

IWC staff members' response to such letters demonstrated their attempt to maintain neutrality and a factual stance on complex issues, which no doubt outraged those who could not imagine being neutral on what they saw as a moral matter. When students from a class in El Cerrito, California, wrote to the IWC for the third year in a row, one noted that IWC staff must be sick of getting the letters. Executive Director Martin Harvey assured them: "We are not. . . . What does make us sad is that somehow you are getting hold of a lot of very wrong information so that some of the things you write, through no fault of your own, are just nonsense."[80] Likewise, he told a representative of the television program *Speak Up America*, which had broadcast a show on whaling, that based on the letters received by the IWC "the programme appears to have consisted entirely of inaccurate statements and erroneous information."[81]

Harvey commented to the students about not only questionable assertions ("no one has seen a blue whale in years") but also simplifications of complex questions (that there are substitutes for all whale products), and he compared whaling to a farmer raising sheep or cows, which probably did not endear him to the protestors. He ended with "the real question": whether "whales should be killed at all." In a lengthy letter to a US Army officer, Harvey engaged the debate on cetacean intelligence. He blamed "sensational and emotive publicity" for producing "a fog of unclear thinking and irrational argument" on the question. The evidence for such sentience was "inadequate," and the IWC was participating in a meeting on whale behavior and intelligence to gain a better understanding.[82]

IWC officials also found themselves in the unusual position of being asked to help an NGO, the People's Trust for Endangered Species, jumpstart an anti-whaling effort. In the fall of 1977, the organization contacted the IWC to announce that it was starting a Save the Whales campaign and hoped to raise money for whale research in Britain. Its first document was a fund-raising letter, complete with short paragraphs, dramatic wording ("The Tragic Facts about Whales"), and a tear sheet to send money to the group and a protest note to IWC secretary Gambell. Seventy-four thousand petitions later, Gambell sent the organizers information about research projects in need of funding, such as a sighting cruise out of Freemantle, Western Australia, and analysis of historical whaling records. A few months later, he sent a thank-you note to the organization for its support of three different projects.[83]

The thick stack of protest mail that the IWC preserved into the twenty-first century consists mainly of form letters, with a smattering of original correspondence. Most of the latter mimicked the form fund-raising letters in their language, and they do not suggest the depth of understanding or even accurate information that dominated early protest letters in, for example, New Zealand's national archives. Commission staff responded to just a few, such as the one that the People's Trust for Endangered Species appeal had generated from Jean Dobson, daughter of the IWC's first secretary, Alban Dobson. She noted the familial connection and cited the usual litany of woe that had been inflicted on whales, before ending with the comment: "How people like Mr. Salvesen can line their pockets as a result of such abhorrent cruelty I can't imagine."[84] Given that Chr. Salvesen Ltd. had been out of the whaling business for fourteen years, one can surmise that the animosity between Dobson and Salvesen from the 1940s had worked its way into family legend. Governments also got stacks of protest mail. When Iceland defied international pressure to end the hunting of fin whales, environmental groups turned up the pressure. The embassy in Washington, DC, reported 60,000 pieces of mail in 1980 about whaling, 59,500 of which were form letters.[85]

Other international organizations also took an interest in whales. The 1973 Convention on International Trade in Endangered Species (CITES) required member states to cease trade in species that the convention listed as endangered.[86] Over the course of several years, CITES listed many species of whales as endangered. It was much easier to list a species as ineligible for trade if it had an "endangered" or "vulnerable" label assigned by the International Union for the Conservation of Nature, the quasi-scientific NGO that had been an early proponent of much more stringent conservation steps in the IWC. Of course, not all of these organizations thought alike, as John Gulland of the UN Food and Agriculture Organization demonstrated in 1981 when he called on the IUCN to recognize that some species of whales had recovered enough that they should be in the "out of danger" category. The FAO believed in "rational utilization" of resources, including whales, and such a move would not only fit into the IUCN's World Conservation Strategy but also highlight "a major conservation success." Without such an acknowledgment, it would be nearly impossible to sell the idea of killing more whales to the general public.[87] Needless to say, Gulland had no chance of winning a public-relations battle with groups like Greenpeace and the People's Trust for Endangered Species.

By 1976, the messy logic of the anti-whaling letters of 1972 and 1973, listing several contradictory reasons to end whaling, had largely given way to the idea that whales were too good to hunt. In the *Sydney Morning Herald*, columnist Joseph Glascott criticized Australia for flip-flopping on the moratorium, for which the United States had fought for five years. After quoting the manager of Australia's Cheynes Beach whaling company, who said that his land station produced jobs and export commodities "without harming" the resource, Glascott asked, "Does man consider important the survival of the friendly, intelligent, and gentle whales, who could be closer to him than any other creature? Or does he value the production of pet and animal foods, lipstick, and shoe polish more highly?"[88]

IWC secretary Ray Gambell spoke at a public conference on whaling organized by Project Jonah in Sydney in 1977, just before the IWC had its annual meeting in Canberra. Gambell argued that whales were a resource to be used and found himself playing Daniel in the lion's den or, as he put it, Jonah in the whale. Peter Magrane, who argued that whales were special based on brain size alone, and philosophy professor Peter Singer of Monash University, who would later gain fame for his radical positions on animal rights, responded by comparing whaling to African slavery, enjoyed more favorable receptions.[89]

The evolution toward defining the whale as a really big person in terms of intelligence, morals, and rights had a number of critical implications for the debate on whaling. Most practically, it destroyed the credibility of the New Management Procedure as an acceptable environmentalist policy. The NMP might have worked if given enough time, but there was only a small window during which conservation organizations were willing to consider sustainable hunting based on scientists' insights. After about 1975, the only acceptable policy for the vast majority of environmentalists—and hence for any government that wanted to respond to them—was the commercial moratorium. The move toward a more absolutist definition of whales also sparked a fierce backlash in whaling countries, particularly Japan, where the argument devolved into a nationalist campaign to defend whaling against perceived external racism. And finally, and in unexpected ways, the definition of whales as equal to or better than people sparked a conflict between environmentalists and the Inuit in Alaska and other aboriginal peoples, which threatened to split the Save the Whales movement and the US government and derail the drive for a moratorium.

The International Whaling Commission limped into the 1970s, largely ignored except by policy wonks and whalers. Whaling was limping too, running out of the largest whales and the largest companies and seemingly in a race toward extinction with the whales themselves. The industry was still hauling in tens of thousands of whales each year and finding markets for its products. Even so the very magnificence of whales—their size, their behavior, their mystery—merged with a burgeoning environmental movement that was sorting out when and how it was acceptable to use scarce resources. Around the world, groups sprang up from the grassroots, motivated by television programs, recordings of whales, whale-watching experiences, and the vivid printed word to urge their governments to curb whaling.

The move to suspend commercial whaling gained widespread support among laypeople and forced governments to decide where their whaling policy should come from—a desire to represent the masses, direction from scientists, or the needs of the whaling industry. The commission deadlocked on the moratorium because there were so many different interests involved, but the muscle finally existed to reduce quotas more quickly then ever before. For a brief moment in the middle of the 1970s, the IWC was finally a body that accepted scientific management even when whalers disagreed. And just like that, environmentalists decided that sustainable yield was not, after all, an acceptable whaling policy. They would spend the years from 1976 to 1982 working to get the sustainable yield scheme overturned by selling Tom Garrett's ideas that whales were *res communis*, the property of the world. Rather than try to convince reluctant members of the IWC to change their positions, environmentalists focused on persuading states to join the IWC specifically with the goal of voting for the moratorium.

7

THE END OF COMMERCIAL WHALING

AT THE 1979 MEETING OF THE INTERNATIONAL WHALING COMMISSION, the American folksinger John Denver showed up for the public comment session, produced a guitar, and began singing the subtly titled "I Want to Live." Denver asked: "Have you heard the song the humpback hears five hundred miles away? Telling tales of history of passages and home." The delegates applauded loudly, according to one newspaper report, except for the Japanese, who were understandably dismayed at the idea of a whale that had a home and liked listening to history—it is very hard to eat such an animal. After Denver left the meeting, he stayed on in London for the original purpose of his journey, to record a Christmas album with the Muppets. The newspaper did not record Miss Piggy's position on commercial whaling.[1]

From 1976 to 1982, the IWC meetings were marked by the steady decline of power of the whaling states in the face of persistent and growing efforts to end whaling. The countries that opposed whaling had briefly backed away from a full moratorium, but they came back to it with a renewed energy, and the environmental groups in their nations were increasingly committed, whether through boycotts, vigorous protest campaigns, or even dramatic direct action to save whales from harpoons. The competing factions argued about three particular questions: was it possible to hunt whales sustainably, were whales sentient and hence too special to hunt, and did a nation or collection of them have the right to compel another nation to halt a particular use of a resource?

In the six years after 1976, a growing number of governments, pushed by a transnational environmental movement, staked their positions in the IWC to a three-part conclusion: the lessons of history showed that commercial whaling could never be sustainable, whales probably were sentient or close to it, and oceanic resources were *res communis* and hence a fit subject for international regulation. Japan led a tenacious but ultimately failed rearguard action to prove that the past no longer applied to framing whaling regulations, that whales were no different than any other delicious animal, and that countries had a sovereign right to hunt what they wanted on the high seas. In 1982, Japan and the other whaling states lost the battle over the moratorium in the IWC, but they continued the fight, under enormous pressure, on other fronts. Environmentalists won in part because they skillfully mobilized pressure on governments, in part because they had compelling scientific and historical arguments, and finally because, unlike other environmental causes, saving the whales required very little sacrifice in most countries. The political struggle garnered observers' attention from the North Slope of Alaska to the wharves of Cape Town and eventually to courtrooms in Washington, DC, before the battle was resolved.

BOWHEAD WHALES AND THE VALUE OF SCIENCE

From 1977 to 1980, the US government was wrapped in a controversial struggle to set a policy for aboriginal whaling that forced the IWC commission members, several US agencies, politicians in various countries, and environmentalists to work through their assumptions about what kinds of whaling were sustainable and acceptable. The moratorium was frequently, but not always, framed as a *commercial* moratorium, not a complete ban on hunting whales, as a means to keep an opening for aboriginal whaling. In the 1970s, environmentalists in the United States, and to some extent around the world, began to use aboriginal peoples as environmental totems, just as the whale became a symbol of a planet under assault. In this popular understanding, Native Americans, for instance, were models of sustainable living. It was a bad day for many environmentalists when they were forced to acknowledge that some of the people who were supposed to be leading by example liked to eat the animal that symbolized a planet in peril.[2]

The aboriginal people in the Arctic have been eating bowhead whales for centuries, so it should have been no surprise to the anti-whaling contingent that the Japanese and Norwegians were not the only people who hesitated to condemn whaling. Bowheads are Arctic specialists, with low numbers, slow reproductive rates, and plenty of blubber. They had been a prime target of eighteenth- and nineteenth-century European and American whalers who risked venturing into their Arctic habitat, but there seemed to be so few left that they had not been worth commercial hunting in the twentieth century. The 1946 International Convention for the Regulation of Whaling had listed bowheads as protected from commercial hunting but allowed aboriginal hunting, which in Alaska was regulated very loosely by the US government. In practice, US Progressive-era conservation laws, such as the ones dealing with North Pacific fur seals and migratory birds, had made an exemption for Native American subsistence use. Over the years, the Inuit had embraced some modern technology, so that their harpoons were hand-thrown, ten-foot-long lances with foot-long projectiles on the tip.[3] The technology would be the key point of contention over aboriginal whaling. How much new technology could a culture adopt and still claim a right to traditional use?

Bowhead whales had deep cultural and nutritional value for the Native Alaskans on the North Slope. Poet and anthropologist Tom Lowenstein did fieldwork in an Inuit village, Tikigaq, also known as Point Hope, in the northwest corner of Alaska, during the 1970s and participated in the whale hunt for three seasons, before the controversy erupted. He noted that the local creation story placed a whale as the backbone of the village's peninsula and that the Inuit had been using harpoons and sealskin floats to hunt bowheads for about thirteen centuries. Whaling was both cooperative and hierarchical, and there were also distinct gender roles. Men in the whaling boats had strict behavioral codes, and there were rules for dividing the catch. The whale's flesh was an important source of food at the end of the Arctic winter, and Inuit igloos were partially constructed out of whalebones. Once the meat and other products were distributed, the whale's head was returned to the water "to ensure the whale's soul's reincarnation." The village's oral history was rich with reference to bowheads, with one of the most intriguing stories telling how one Inuit traveled to Siberia and taught people there how to hunt bowheads with slate harpoon points, rather than gray whales with copper points.[4] Lowenstein made no reference to modern technology and only hinted at cultural shifts.

With a growing population along the north coast of Alaska around Barrow, the demand for meat and muktuk, or blubber, from bowheads grew in the 1970s. Hunting may have been necessary to meet rising local demand, but it also danced on the edge of legality. Both anti-whaling campaigner Scott McVay and the *New York Times* reported that muktuk and other products from bowheads were available for sale to other Native Alaskans for $3 per pound, which was not the intent behind the exemptions for aboriginal hunting. There was no indication, however, that anyone hunted bowheads just to make a profit. As it had been for centuries, protein for the Inuit villages was the driving force behind the hunt. The *Times* also publicized the embarrassing fact that bowheads were often struck and lost. Senator James Buckley, a forty-year member of the Audubon Society who was visiting Point Hope, witnessed both the harpooning of a bowhead and its loss when the harpoon broke free after the whale had died. The hunters worked hard to recover the whale, but it was apparent that they had experience with lost whales, which is hardly surprising given that pelagic whalers with more powerful equipment frequently lost carcasses too.[5]

In 1971, however, when the US Congress was debating bills to protect marine mammals, bowheads were barely on the radar. The three members of Alaska's congressional delegation testified to the House Committee on Merchant Marine and Fisheries, but none mentioned bowhead hunting. Each recommended that Alaska Natives be granted an exemption from hunting bans because, as Senator Ted Stevens said, "Alaska Natives have traditionally been good conservationists," but the testimony focused on sealing on the Pribilof Islands.[6] For a few minutes of his testimony, biologist John Burns of the Alaska Game Management Department offered shocking commentary on the bowhead situation. First, he opined that five bowheads were struck for every one landed, a figure that matched what reporters would witness. Then he guessed that the population of bowheads was about 400. Representative John Dingell pointed out that Burns was suggesting that 90 to 150 bowheads were being harpooned every year out of 400, but then Dingell inexplicably said that the population figure was not vital because the species was basically doomed to extinction, and that was the end of the conversation.[7] Whatever one makes of the exchange, it suggests that no one outside of the North Slope of Alaska was taking the bowhead hunt all that seriously in 1971. Surely it mattered whether there were 400 or 4,000 bowheads if 90–150 were being struck (although it is possible that Dingell concluded that Burns was simply in error about the high strike figure). Otherwise, no one over the next few hours of testimony, including several environmentalists, mentioned the bowhead hunt.

The political problem started the next year because of the heightened awareness of whaling of any kind and because a committee set up at the 1972 IWC meeting to review low-intensity whaling activities had asked for more data on aboriginal hunting of bowheads and gray whales. When scientists looked more closely at the bowhead hunting data, they were generally appalled. They estimated that there were about 800 bowheads left, representing less than 10 percent of the prehunting population, and that each year the Inuit landed between 10 and 25 whales, plus a dozen or so struck and lost each year, numbers far off from Burns's estimate. No one knew whether the "struck and lost" survived, but most scientists assumed that they had been mortally wounded. That meant that 2–3 percent of the population was being killed by humans each year, on top of natural mortality, for a species that was not reproducing very quickly. In short, Inuit hunting appeared to be slowly driving the bowhead to extinction. While that data was being digested, in 1976, the US National Marine Fisheries Service reported that 46 bowheads had been harvested and a shocking 35 had been struck and lost; 10 percent of a species clinging to existence had just been killed.[8]

The issue came to a head at the 1977 IWC meeting in Canberra, when the high number of killed and lost whales in 1976 gave the commission's Scientific Committee an opening to set a zero quota for bowhead hunting after a lopsided debate: the vote was 16–0, with the United States abstaining. The Scientific Committee reasoned that the very small bowhead population was at risk of destruction by some environmental fluctuation, so any hunting could be disastrous. An IWC official concluded that the bowhead was the only cetacean species in the world in immediate danger of extinction, and that was because of Inuit hunting, not commercial whaling.[9]

When the bowhead debate became public, the responses were vivid. Environmentalists split, but the loudest voices called for an end to the hunt. The Inuit could eat other, less sacred things, they suggested. Tom Garrett spoke for many environmentalists when he said that "Eskimo culture would appear to be, by the definition supplied by representatives of the Interior Department, anything that Eskimos happen to be doing at the present time."[10] If the Inuit killed 10 percent of the bowhead population per year, in about a decade no bowheads would be left to sustain their culture.

One animated citizen asserted: "I am frankly in favor of the Eskimo disappearing first if it comes to a choice. . . . There are some things far more important than Predator Man."[11] Those who opposed an objection by the United States to the IWC's bowhead hunting ban emphasized, as Christine Stevens of the International Fund for Animal Welfare put it, that "the last five years of effort since the vote for the ten-year moratorium on commercial whaling at Stockholm would be undermined. We would lose the strong moral position we now hold in the Commission, a position painfully built up but which could be wiped out instantaneously." She continued: "A low quota would not interfere with tradition. Indeed, it would be far more traditional than the inflated killing and wounding that went on last year."[12] Likewise, New Zealand officials concluded that the problem was that the bowhead was in danger of extinction and must be protected. The whale was not indispensable food, and a loss rate of 50 percent was intolerable.[13] Perhaps most amazing was that the government of New Zealand had devoted the resources to a detailed analysis of a small whaling operation in remote northern Alaska. It was clearly a hot issue.

The Inuit and their allies protested that they had barely been consulted and that there were, in fact, more bowheads than the scientists claimed. They fought vigorously to protect their cultural traditions. One Native American leader said the decision to halt bowhead hunting was "in essence genocidal."[14] Whaling captains from several villages formed the Alaskan Eskimo Whaling Commission in August 1977 to lobby on their own behalf and launch their own studies.[15] They were continuing a tradition handed down through the generations, they argued: "I am told to take only what I need, this makes the Eskimos good conservationists, and we have known it; we know it today and will remember it tomorrow."[16] As one ally, a doctor and Sierra Club member from Alaska, wrote to President Carter, hunting was critical to the health of the Inuit because local stores generally carried expensive food of low nutritional quality. He saw hypocrisy in much of the criticism directed at those who hunted bowheads: "As concerned people around the world ask the Eskimo to control the hunt so as not to waste life or meat, let them also ask themselves not to waste in their own lifestyles. Let them work to preserve the whale's habitat, not destroy it through pollution of the Arctic waters in obtaining energy sources such as petroleum that is being wasted across this country which has the highest energy use of any country per capita in the world."[17]

Alaska's congressional delegation weighed in on the side of the Inuit, with Republican senator Ted Stevens concluding that the IWC vote was "an unfortunate intrusion upon the human rights of my Alaska Native Eskimo constituents."[18] Democratic senator Mike Gravel called the Inuit the "endangered species" and emphasized that the science used by the IWC must not be very good, because the bowhead population estimates ranged from 600 to 2,500. He also made the interesting assertion that "the Eskimos know better than anyone else the importance of preserving a healthy stock of bowhead whales"—almost exactly what the Japanese were saying about their whalers and, in fact, what many whalers had been saying about themselves for forty years.[19]

The Japanese whalers and government reacted with glee, although they were careful not to express that too publicly. If it was acceptable for the Inuit to claim a cultural need for whaling, then the Japanese were more than happy to emphasize their hundreds of years of eating whale meat and their small coastal communities that depended on whaling for survival. In 1979, representatives of Japanese fishing workers lobbied the Norwegian government to side with Japan in fighting off the moratorium proposals, in part to save the livelihoods of the two hundred thousand people who supposedly depended on the whaling industry. Not only were the protestors harassing whalers with "prejudiced arguments," but they were missing that "the whale is just as important to the Japanese as it is to the Alaskan Eskimo."[20] Even when they were not making somewhat principled arguments, the Japanese understood that the US government was hamstrung by the time and energy it had to put into dealing with the bowhead issue. American credibility on the moratorium was also at stake, although that was already being damaged by the revelations that US tuna fishers wasted more tons of cetaceans (in dolphin form) than the Japanese and Soviets combined.[21]

In Washington, DC, the bowhead issue created a train wreck. The US government had ninety days to decide whether to file an objection to the zero quota for 1978, and as time wound down in September 1977, the Carter administration faced intense lobbying and internal debate among the State, Commerce, and Interior Departments.[22] The federal government was generally obligated through treaties to let Native nations and tribes hunt and fish in their previously controlled territories, although there were not as many targets as before, nor was the technology the same.

More compelling was a general sense that Native peoples had lost so much in previous legal and military battles that they and their cultures deserved to be treated with some leeway. If Western-educated scientists and policy makers once again told them that they should forsake their traditions for modern ways, then it would be a reminder of past injustices that remained fresh in the minds of indigenous peoples and were slowly being grasped by the American public as a whole. Yet the US government had invested considerable energy and political capital in trying to make the IWC work as a science-based institution and in ending commercial whaling. If IWC scientists concluded that the Inuit should not hunt any bowheads because the whales were being driven to extinction, then how could the US government file an objection? As a congressional report put it, "The United States was put in the embarrassing position in 1977 and 1978, of appearing to be very concerned about all whaling except its own."[23] President Carter, who had been a delegate at Stockholm and was viscerally committed to ending commercial whaling, seemed to have made up his mind in late September, when he wrote to his domestic policy chief, Stuart Eizenstat: "Stu, I don't want to approve hunting of bowhead whales."[24]

Accordingly, in October the State Department announced that it would not file an objection to the ban on hunting bowheads; but it had already created a plan to work with the Interior Department to call a special meeting of the IWC to restore a hunting quota based on a scientific survey, which included a secret decision that the United States would object if there were no suitable compromise. The United States got the IWC to call the special meeting for Tokyo in December 1977 to address the conflicts over bowhead and sperm whales. New Zealand's delegation came with instructions that demonstrated the complexity of the bowhead issue and its importance to the fate of the commission. Three paths were open to the New Zealand representatives, depending on how the other delegations were likely to vote: they might vote yes, no, or abstain on a US proposal to set a bowhead quota of 12 killed or 18 struck, whichever came first, for the next year, with the caveat that the US National Marine Fisheries Service and the Alaska Eskimo Whaling Commission would take a real survey to see how many bowheads were left.[25] The meeting got off to a bad start when, in the opinion of a New Zealand delegate, "a statement of welcome to the delegates was delivered unintelligibly by the Vice-Minister for Agriculture. As you will see from the translated text, it lost little in its delivery."

Since the other primary purpose of the meeting was to resolve the dispute over sperm whale quotas in the North Pacific, the two issues became intertwined. Everyone assumed that the United States was simply ignoring the Scientific Committee, and the Japanese made clear that they would follow the American lead in the future.[26] Still, the US delegation came away with a victory, winning approval for their study of bowheads and a limited catch. The US government would not have to file an objection.

The study of bowheads in the spring of 1978 put the population at precisely 2,264 animals, validating the Inuit claim that they knew the Arctic Ocean better than the IWC's Scientific Committee but also confirming that killing 80 whales a year was going to be hard to sustain. In response, the IWC set quotas for 1979 and 1980 of 18 landed or 27 struck and 17 landed or 27 struck, respectively. It did not make sense to lower the landed but not the struck quota, since the commission was mainly worried about lowering the kill level. It would have been more logical to raise the landed quota and lower the struck quota. Michael Donoghue, a Greenpeace member who was included in New Zealand's delegation in 1980, noted that the United States was "totally compromised by this issue," relying on the votes of the whaling bloc to break up environmentalist attempts to set a zero quota. Donoghue complained, "Conservationist countries were placed in the outrageous position of having to vote in favor of a three-year quota on the most highly-endangered whale in the world, to prevent the U.S.A. from conducting an unregulated hunt."[27]

In addition to undermining US leadership on the moratorium issue and splitting the environmentalist community, the bowhead debate focused a magnifying glass on the problems of using science as the basis for making decisions. The Inuit had been hunting otherwise protected bowheads before the IWC was formed, but apparently no one had bothered to study if what they were doing was sustainable. There were so many other problems to worry about that harvesting a handful of largely unstudied animals from what was generally labeled a "commercially extinct" stock had gone unnoticed. Then, suddenly, someone noticed and called on the IWC to set a quota based on science. In line with the New Management Procedure, the only prudent conservationist thing to do was to set the quota at zero, until someone could prove that it should be otherwise. And people did prove that it could be otherwise. When it turned out that there were almost three times as many bowheads as the IWC's Scientific Committee had estimated, it only reinforced the Japanese position that scientists were too cautious and that they lacked sufficient data. Later research showed that even the 1978 estimate had been too small. In 2007, the US government estimated there were more than 10,000 bowheads in the Arctic seas, from western Russia to eastern Canada. Each year, the Inuit take close to 80 bowheads, and the hunt has expanded into Canada and Russia.[28]

On top of that, the rejection of Inuit hunting depended on the environmentalist argument that nothing harvested from whales was irreplaceable. Some environmentalists wanted the US government to provide other sources of meat to the Inuit. By advocating that the Inuit be given a bowhead quota, the US government was implicitly rejecting that practical argument, which probably only confirmed for the moratorium supporters that they had chosen correctly in their shift from pragmatism to a nearly religious definition of the whale. Pragmatism had left them empty-handed again.

PIRATE WHALING AND THE EXPANSION OF THE IWC

While environmentalists struggled to deal with the ramifications of the bowhead issue, they had moral clarity about whaling outside the IWC schedule of regulation, which they described as "pirate whaling." As early as the 1930s, the framers of whaling conventions had warned that they had to get all whaling states to agree to the same set of regulations or those regulations would never be of value. The 1946 convention had protected members' sovereignty so that all whalers would be willing to join. Still, Aristotle Onassis had been effectively whaling outside the IWC in the 1950s, and everyone had understood that the Soviets violated rules as well, with the predicted undermining of the regulations. In the 1970s, these concerns came to the fore again, both because of the activities of ships that seemed completely unconnected to any IWC member and because some nonmember nations started whaling with a clear connection to a member state—in this case, Japan. One solution was to recruit more nations to join the IWC in the hope that a nation's whalers would obey the commission's rules. But since those nations might vote with Japan and Norway, it was also important to get more governments on board for explicitly conservationist ends. Between 1977 and 1982, the IWC grew from 17 to 38 members, with most joining to fight for a moratorium but some joining to protect their interests as whalers.

The problem of whaling outside the IWC was minor until the 1970s. In 1952, Remington Kellogg urged an effort to bring Portugal into the IWC because that country controlled so many whaling sites in Africa, but there is no evidence that either the IWC or the US government took action. In any case Portugal was back on the IWC's radar in 1972. By then, of course, relatively small whaling operations that had seemed marginal to the main issue of catching blue and fin whales in the Antarctic had become much more important. The IWC reached out to any nation that seemed likely to participate in whaling or already had started a small industry. IWC chairman Inge Rindal urged Spain, Portugal, Brazil, Peru, and Chile to bring their whaling operations under IWC rules. Spain turned him down flat, Portugal and Brazil (which had left the commission in 1966) responded favorably, and Chile and Peru expressed concern about squaring both IWC regulations with their national rules and the commission's existence with Chile and Peru's support for two-hundred-mile economic zones. Rindal's mission succeeded in moving only Brazil into the commission at that time, but the process continued. After 1976, invitations went out to Indonesia, China, South Korea, and Somalia among others.[29]

To induce nonmember whaling states to join the commission, the IWC passed a resolution banning the import of whale products from such states, and the next year, in 1977, it banned export of whaling materiel and expertise to nonmember nations. If the carrot of invitations was not working, then the stick of sanctions would have to do. Objections from Japan and Norway scuttled both restrictions, but in 1978 certification under the US Pelly Amendment (which could lead to a ban on importing a country's fishing products) caught the attention of South Korea, Chile, and Peru, all of whom joined the commission shortly thereafter. No sanctions were applied because each state complied with IWC rules.[30]

The Pelly Amendment was useful, but it was also optional, so US environmentalists looked for a tool that could apply more of a stick to nations that appeared to be undermining the IWC's conservation efforts. Republican senator Bob Packwood of Oregon and Democratic senator Warren Magnuson of Washington State came together in 1979 with a proposal to amend the 1976 Fisheries Conservation Act by placing restrictions on access to fisheries inside the two-hundred-mile economic zone around the United States. Packwood had originally wanted a broad amendment dealing with all fisheries, but Representative John Murphy, Democrat from New York, prevailed upon him to focus on the IWC. Supporters of what would become known as the Packwood-Magnuson Amendment argued that various administrations had been taking too long to certify nations under the Pelly Amendment and then had been reluctant to apply sanctions. The solution was to compel sanctions, but that did not mean that certification could be compelled. In fact, the necessity of imposing sanctions probably made it a bit harder to trigger certification.

Packwood and Magnuson tried to solve the decades-old problem of making the punishment fit the crime. They observed that most whaling nations were also active fishing nations with access to the two-hundred-mile economic zone that the US managed off its coasts. For ideological reasons, the United States allowed foreign-flagged fishermen free access to US waters, but in the 1970s it began to assign quotas to those nations in a failed effort to stop overfishing. Under the Packwood-Magnuson Amendment, a country that was certified as undermining the IWC would lose at least 50 percent of the fish catch that had been allocated to it for the current year. If the offending country did not change its policy, then it would lose its entire allocation for subsequent years, until it rectified the problem. The amendment's supporters argued that "any country in its right mind would give in," because the value of US fisheries was so much more than any whale. The only opponent in the brief congressional debate, John Breaux of Louisiana, pointed out that more than 50 percent of US fish exports went to Japan, the obvious target of the sanctions, and it was unlikely that Japan would let American fishermen off the hook.[31] While the law could not compel an administration to certify a country, it did open the way for environmentalists to use the courts to force the issue. The irony was that this amendment was passed during the Carter administration, and President Carter was more committed to a moratorium than any other major US politician, but it became a tool for the Reagan administration, which was reluctant to put limits on trade. After the Packwood-Magnuson Amendment, if the IWC approved a moratorium, whaling states would run the risk of serious economic hardship if they chose to file an objection or leave the commission.

Nonwhaling states also began joining the commission as a means to support the moratorium effort. In 1978 alone, Ghana, Pakistan, Iran, Costa Rica, Kenya, and Mauritius inquired about joining the IWC, even though none of them had a whaling industry. It is likely that none of them had a grassroots Save the Whales movement either, which suggests that their interest in the IWC was more about positive branding. For countries like Kenya and Costa Rica, which benefited from ecotourism, joining the IWC and voting for a moratorium would be a smart way to reinforce their image as destinations for ecotourists. Iran and Pakistan might have been looking to burnish their reputations as modern, responsible countries and reliable political allies of the United States at very low cost—only £4,500 per year, the minimum membership fee.[32] Given that the budget of the entire commission had risen from £7,000 in 1970 to £130,000 in 1978–79, it was evident that membership costs might rise as the years went on. Still, £4,500 bought a lot of goodwill in certain places around the world.[33] A reasonable person might infer, for instance, that the sudden interest of the Seychelles in the work of the IWC in 1979, as well as its government's decision to appoint prominent opponents of whaling like Lyall Watson and Sidney Holt to IWC positions, was as much a product of funding opportunities from environmental organizations as a sudden awakening of concern among that government's constituents.[34]

The Japanese government and whalers did not take the effort to outvote them lying down, putting together a thorough rebuttal of the antiwhaling argument in English, meant for an international audience. Their arguments fell into three categories: a moratorium was not in keeping with the IWC's mission and would result in its collapse; justification of a moratorium was based on sentiment, not science or rationality; and a moratorium would undermine Japanese culture and society, just as it might harm the Inuit and the towns in northern Norway that depended on hunting minkes. The *Japan Times* in 1976 argued that the "IWC's primary function is not to put a virtual halt to commercial whaling but to insure the conservation, development and maximum utilization of whales."[35] Pro-whaling agencies in Norway agreed with these arguments, particularly the idea that the whaling states would withdraw from the commission if they could not catch whales legally within it.

The Japanese Foreign Ministry generally maintained a level-headed approach to combating the idea that all right-thinking countries should band together to end whaling. Before the 1973 IWC meeting, the Japanese government explained that the moratorium "cannot stand objective critical reviews of informed scientists." Because the Japanese ate whale meat, "the conservation of whale stocks is a matter of prime importance."[36] In the summer of 1982, with a vote on the moratorium proposal likely to go against Japan, Foreign Minister Yashio Sakurauchi wrote to his Norwegian counterpart seeking cooperation at the upcoming IWC meeting. He emphasized cooperation based on "common interests as whaling countries" and the need to protect the IWC's management role. Passage of a moratorium would mean that the commission would be unable to fulfill the part of its mandate to develop whaling, which would therefore mean a possible collapse of the institution. Decisions should be made "on a scientific basis rather than be governed by non-scientific factors." Japan's seriousness could be seen in the recent statement by Prime Minister Zenko Suzuki to the Diet about the nation's tradition of eating whale meat.[37] Less publicly, Japan's commitment to maintaining some whaling was evident in the hiring of Richard Frank, a recent US commissioner in the IWC, as a consultant to advise on how to deal with the Pelly and Packwood-Magnuson Amendments.[38]

By contrast, the Japan Whalers' Association and similar organizations preferred the flamethrower instead of the carefully reasoned argument. As early as 1974, Motokichi Morasawa of the Japan Fisheries Association asserted that Save the Whales slogans were "frantically accepted by a section of women and children abroad." He dismissed "sentimentalism" as "logically unacceptable" because "whales should be classified in the same category as fowl, cattle and swine." Finally, he said that replacing the 123,000 tons of whale meat consumed in Japan each year would require 12 percent of the global beef trade at a time when oil shortages appeared likely to cause a spike in prices for imported food.[39] Seven years later, Motonobu Inagaki of the Japan Whalers' Association bluntly added, "The current danger is not to the whales, it is to truth and justice."[40]

For a nation that had learned how to beat US companies at marketing cars and televisions, Japan was remarkably inept at marketing whaling. A Peruvian named Juan del Mar Cordiviola wrote to the IWC in 1979 that Japanese whalers running his country's shore stations not only were going to exterminate the whales in Peru's economic zone but also were pressuring the government to hold off on joining the IWC for two more years. Peru was under pressure from the United States to join the commission and reduce whaling, but Cordiviola thought that the Japanese were also pressuring Peru to join when the time was right to lead a pro-whaling bloc. He did not comment on American motives, but he concluded that "the charming Japanese friends" were interested only in making money quickly.[41] Perhaps because of the clumsiness of Japanese efforts, the nineteen governments that joined the IWC between 1977 and 1981 were almost universally opposed to whaling.

The battle over new members was especially urgent when those states were engaged in whaling. The invitation to Somalia, for instance, was not based on any great desire to hold an IWC meeting in Mogadishu; rather, the Somali flag happened to be fluttering off the bow of the MV *Sierra*, the ship everyone had in mind when they used the term *pirate whaling*. The *Sierra* first showed up in the whaling industry in 1955 as part of the Dutch catcher flotilla. It reappeared in 1969 as the *Run*, and its owners were asking around Britain's Ministry of Agriculture and Fisheries, looking for information on whaling after an unsuccessful stint at sealing near the Falklands. Ray Gambell, before he served as secretary of the IWC, learned from a crew member of the vessel that the sei and sperm whale meat that was coming from the *Run* was going to the Portuguese army fighting rebel forces in Angola, a British pet food company, and Japanese civilians. Over the next couple of years, the *Run* changed homes almost yearly, from South Africa to Angola to Somalia, with enough ties to the Bahamas that the government there was able to fine its owners several thousand dollars. Control passed through a bank in Oslo when its owners defaulted on a loan, and the ship was in the hands of a company based in Liechtenstein by late 1975. By 1976, the ship's crew was transferring meat, labeled "produce of Spain," to a Norwegian vessel heading to Japan.[42] The *Sierra* may not have caught as many whales as Aristotle Onassis's *Olympic Challenger*, but its owners took the gold in the greased pig competition.

By 1975, the *Sierra* had come to the attention of environmental groups, who saw in its actions evidence of the IWC's failures. The International Society for the Protection of Animals called the impunity with which the *Sierra* operated evidence that the IWC could not make the New Management Procedure actually work. As the *Sierra* continued to pick off a whale or two each day, its take was small enough to seem insignificant, yet the number was less important than the frequency with which the whales caught ended up in Japanese kitchens while the ship's owners seemed constantly one step ahead of the law. In 1979, thirteen US senators, led by Warren Magnuson and Bob Packwood, told Japanese prime minister

Masayoshi Ohira that the dealings between Japanese firms and the *Sierra* showed "contempt" for the IWC.[43] Certification under the Pelly and Packwood-Magnuson Amendments seemed in the cards.

But certification took time. Environmental groups had started to look to direct action to protect whales, and no one was more direct than Paul Watson, captain of the *Sea Shepherd*. Watson had been on a Greenpeace Zodiac in the confrontation with the *Vlastny* in 1975, claimed to be an adopted Sioux who was a medic at Wounded Knee in 1973, and possessed a street fighter's mentality. He had broken from Greenpeace for reasons that remain in dispute, but he had not lost his zeal for throwing his body and his boat into the whaling machinery and hoping that it jammed. In 1979, he and his crew encountered the *Sierra* in Portugal as it prepared to sail. Watson did the only thing that seemed logical to him: he rammed the whaler twice in order to sink it—his vessel had a reinforced bow for just such a moment—and then he took off for the Spanish border, hoping to outrun the Portuguese Navy. Watson ended up in a Portuguese jail but managed to work his way out, after which he scuttled the *Sea Shepherd* and fled over land to Spain. He was more than happy to tell his story, in part because the existence of the *Sierra* was vital to generating support for the anti-whaling forces. The ship was the ultimate bad guy for anyone looking to counter Japanese complaints that the Save the Whales movement was ethnocentric, if not racist. The *Sierra* needed extensive repairs. As it was nearing a return to whaling several months later, it was sunk by explosives placed on the hull; no one claimed credit.[44] Its strange end was rivaled only by that of the MV *Tonna*, which had a similar if shorter history as a pirate whaler with no fixed address. The *Tonna* went down in 1978 with the captain on board after it tried to haul in one last fin whale. The seventy-foot animal got stuck when the winch system failed, and a storm caused the carcass to shift, pulling the ship over so far that it took on water and could not be saved.[45]

Almost all of the whaling done outside of the IWC in the 1970s appeared to be aimed at Japan's market, which absorbed the vast majority of meat. Norwegians also ate a fair amount of whale meat, but almost all was procured from the northern reaches of that nation. South Korea and Taiwan, as well as a few South American countries, hosted whaling companies that signed deals with Japanese companies to import whale meat. Some of the agreements were public knowledge, but at least a few were kept quiet.[46] When environmentalists attacked pirate whaling, they understood that they were attacking Japan.

THE MORATORIUM PASSES

After three years of intense efforts to pass a moratorium—or at least gain points with environmentalist constituents by advocating a moratorium even when it was hopeless—the United States dropped the idea in the mid-1970s. Instead, conservation-minded governments generally focused on ways of whittling away at whaling piece by piece, using the New Management Procedure as the means to save vulnerable whale stocks from hunting. But the moratorium idea had not gone away among anti-whaling protestors. They were still working hard to build support for their goal and, most important, they were adding new members to the IWC and switching some of the old ones to full support of a ban. In the charged atmosphere of increasingly adamant environmentalist groups and concerns about widespread nonmember whaling, it was inevitable that the debates would be fiercer than before and that the whaling states would eventually be unable to muster enough votes to stop a moratorium.

At the 1976 and 1977 meetings of the IWC, no one formally proposed discussion of a moratorium, largely to give the NMP time to prove itself. Support for the moratorium was diluted by the bludgeoning of the United States over the bowhead issue but strengthened by ongoing concerns about pirate whalers. More difficult to overcome for the supporters of the moratorium was the disconnect between the generally conservative nature of the diplomats and fisheries officials who represent governments at these sorts of meetings and the countercultural views of the most assertive environmentalists, elements of whom Ray Gambell dismissed as "anarchists" and "rent-a-crowd."[47] The IWC chair, Australian Arthur Bollen, clearly had no respect for their position either, and one observer noted that his "bias against conservationists sometimes shows."[48] J. V. Scott of New Zealand, representing a country with very strong environmental groups, recognized that "the setting of catch quotas can not be reconciled with a belief that the killing of a whale is somehow different from the killing of any other mammal, and thus inherently wrong." He acknowledged that most of New Zealand's environmental groups supported the moratorium, but he concluded that commercial whaling was not "wrong in itself," in part because "the survival of the whale . . . [was] now no longer in doubt." He saw no scientific justification for a general moratorium; more important, he saw no chance that a moratorium imposed by pressure groups from nonwhaling states would have influence on whaling states. If anything, a very public fight over a moratorium was counterproductive while the commission was working so hard to get whaling states like South Korea and Chile on board.[49]

At the 1978 IWC meeting in London, delegates were prepared to discuss the moratorium for the first time since 1974, as the government of Panama had placed the item on the agenda. To the dismay of environmentalists, who smelled a rat in the form of pressure from Japan, Panama withdrew the agenda item, thus preventing discussion of the issue, much less a vote.[50] Between that change of heart and the tangling of American feet with the bowhead issue, as well as a vote to increase the sperm whale quota for the Pacific Ocean, environmentalists seemed to have lost some momentum. The sense of betrayal and frustration among environmentalists bubbled over, and one protester threw red dye, meant to symbolize whale blood, on a member of the Japanese delegation.[51]

Then a new direction in Australian whaling policy helped shift momentum in the commission. The Australian government had long been a proponent of commercial whaling. It had aspired to sponsor pelagic whaling expeditions in the middle of the century, had worked tirelessly to defend its right to take humpback whales from shore stations, and had exercised the second objection in IWC history to protect a theoretical right to catch sperm whales. In the early 1970s, with Arthur Bollen brusquely leading the commission and transplanted New Zealander K. Radway Allen providing leadership in the Scientific Committee, Australia had played a critical role in shaping the New Management Procedure, which in theory was the scheme that would achieve the twin mandates of rebuilding whale stocks while allowing rational exploitation. Australia was a reliable vote against the moratorium, in large part because the idea did not have the support of the Scientific Committee. As historian Thomas Dunlap has shown, Australians worked on and responded to their environment in unique ways, and whaling was no exception.[52]

In 1977, Prime Minister Malcolm Fraser had ordered a review of Australia's whaling policy, in small part because his eleven-year-old daughter was taken with the Save the Whales media blitz; the larger reason was probably that he was standing for reelection in December of that year. Fraser appointed Justice Sydney Frost to lead the committee of inquiry, which heard public comments; studied the small Australian whaling industry at Albany, Western Australia; and investigated the science and ethics behind whaling. Not all Australians were in agreement, of course. Representative Peter Drummond of Forrest, Western Australia, dismissed the move to end hunting as "irrationally protectionist." "The further people were from the realities of the situation," he said, "the more they opposed whaling."[53]

It was becoming increasingly obvious, even in Canberra, that the science behind the Australian-sponsored New Management Procedure was inadequate. Stock estimates were so broad as to be worthless in many cases, in part because of legitimate scientific disagreements and perhaps in part because of a repeat of the Dutch approach from the 1950s, when scientific arguments were based mainly on accounting needs of whaling companies. After a special meeting in late 1977 set high sperm whale quotas, J. V. Scott wrote that it "must give us pause, and inevitably draw some doubt on the accuracy of what we have described as the best scientific advice at present available."[54] Norwegian authorities, for instance, rejected the idea that the take of minke whales in Arctic coastal waters was undermining the population, and it is hard to imagine that Norway's scientists could have been completely unbiased in their work. On top of all of that, the whaling nations could simply object if a quota came down more quickly than they thought was reasonable. Finally, the very idea of maximum sustainable yield was impossible to reconcile with the idea that whales were special; it was one thing to apply it to a fish population and another altogether to apply it to an animal that many people were starting to see as intelligent. Sidney Holt, one of the Three Wise Men in the early 1960s, spoke for many scientists when he commented, "These current studies seem to reveal a substantial optimistic bias in IWC estimates which will eventually be carefully documented." The population models, especially the ones for sperm whales, had problems, he noted, and using the measure of catch per unit of effort was creating inaccurate population estimates.[55]

In that atmosphere, with the scientific consensus behind whaling fraying and the assertion that whales were special becoming more powerful, it was probably inevitable that Australia would swing over to support a moratorium. Project Jonah had won the public-relations battle, raising $50,000 in six months in 1977 and getting one hundred thousand signatures on petitions to shut down the Albany whaling station in Western

Australia. Twenty thousand people had contacted the Department of Primary Industry with similar requests. But all of that pressure failed to make an immediate change, as Prime Minister Fraser announced that the Cheynes Beach company would be licensed for another year of whaling as the review of policy went on. Fraser's cautious approach cost him the support of the Whale and Dolphin Coalition, which gave $50,000 in support of the Labour Party, which in turn supported the moratorium.[56]

Opposition to whaling appeared to be pretty deep in Australia. Project Jonah polls suggested that about two-thirds of Australians favored an end to whaling in late 1977. More than a third of respondents declared themselves to be very interested in the issue, another third described themselves as a little interested, and fewer than 30 percent said that they were not that interested. Late the next year, more than 80 percent in a Project Jonah poll favored banning all whaling within two hundred miles of Australia.[57] Fraser's Liberal Party won the election at the end of 1977, which suggests that few voters viewed whaling as a make-or-break issue. But his promised inquiry might well have softened some people who were on the fence. By the end of 1978, Justice Frost concluded that Australia should ban the import of whale products, cease whaling in Australian waters, and work for an end to all whaling around the world.[58] Australia's new position was a huge morale boost for the environmental movement and a nudge to other members of the Commonwealth. Britain announced in 1979 that it would advocate a moratorium, and New Zealand acknowledged that it would support it as well lest it be "outflanked . . . by its friends." Given the problems encountered by the Scientific Committee, New Zealand commissioner I. G. Stewart wrote that "conservationists may well be correct in their assertion that the only sure way of ensuring the survival of the whales is by a complete prohibition of commercial whaling."[59] Even within the Norwegian government, the Ministry of the Environment had diverged far enough from other agencies that one official commented that Norway's commissioner had to "coordinate very contradictory interests."[60]

At the 1979 IWC meeting, though, with representatives from thirty-four NGOs looking on and John Denver's voice echoing through the hallways, things did not go as environmentalists desired. It took three days for the Scientific Committee to report that it would not take a stand on the moratorium. The delegate from New Zealand gathered that while most committee members favored the moratorium because of their increasing uncertainty about the New Management Procedure, opponents did a good job of arguing that an end to hunting would mean a loss of the data necessary to draw conclusions. Lyall Watson, using his name recognition from his 1973 book, *Supernature*, offered a proposal from the Seychelles for a three-year phaseout of commercial whaling, but he could not get that hundredth monkey to fall in line.[61] Only eleven countries voted for the moratorium, while five opposed and seven abstained. US delegates were busy lobbying privately on bowheads "at every turn of the corridor," which probably deflected their attention from the moratorium. Sei and Bryde's whales were given protection, which meant, in effect, that only minkes and sperms could be hunted, and the quotas would once again be reduced. The message to whalers was clear: commercial whaling would have to be phased out. But the Japanese delegation appeared to be relieved "that things had not turned out worse."[62]

New Zealand's commissioner found the meeting dispiriting. Because his government had come out in favor of a stronger environmentalist line, "conservation groups" had made "outrageous proposals," expecting support from the government that was not forthcoming. The running of the meeting, he concluded, could "only be described as appalling," including many closed-door meetings to resolve deadlocks. One meeting dragged on for an unimaginable twenty-one hours. The long meetings raised suspicion among environmentalists, who published their "daily rag," *ECO*, with leaked reports on voting and commission intrigue.[63] One plenary session broke down when France and Mexico announced that they had misunderstood a resolution and wanted to change their votes several minutes after discussion had resumed, which would have overturned the outcome of a procedural move regarding the moratorium. When the commissioners went into private session they agreed to expunge from the record the previous plenary session minutes and start over. They then agreed to ban all pelagic catching of anything but minkes. The 1979 meeting, which started with scientist K. Radway Allen being denied a cab ride because he worked with the IWC, ended with delegate Kunio Yonezawa once again drenched in fake blood. The whale had become a symbol of an increasingly militant movement.[64]

Just when it appeared that the pro-whaling coalition had beached, the Japanese stepped up their lobbying, as both that country's fisheries ministry and whalers' association visited embassies of member countries, even those strongly opposed to whaling. Before the meeting opened, the whaling states met and agreed on common policy to keep a united front. The US government also engaged in heavy lobbying, issuing an aide-mémoire that pushed a moratorium as the only option, given "incomplete knowledge of whales and whaling."[65] US diplomats argued that the moratorium finally had a fighting chance for passage, and they hinted that the Japanese government's opposition was largely intended to buy credibility with the whaling industry. In Oslo, the struggle for a coherent position among government departments was intense, and it seems likely that similar disagreements existed in Japan, given the threat of sanctions from the United States.

At the IWC meeting in July 1980, the moratorium again failed, with thirteen in favor, a stunning nine opposed, and only two abstaining. Despite environmentalist pressure, the no votes were accumulating faster than the yes votes, yet the whalers seemed to have run out of new countries to add to their ranks (although Norway had abstained on the moratorium twice, so it might end up as a tenth no vote). "Private discussions have been far more intense than we can recall," wrote one diplomat from New Zealand, who was himself probably on edge from having to lug around fifty pages of instructions (it is worth remembering that the instructions to Remington Kellogg when he led the effort to initiate the IWC in 1946 had been less than ten pages long).[66] The 1980 meeting was "bedevilled [sic] from the outset by the existence of two solid groups" that could block any action. Some of the more stringent conservationist nations, like the Seychelles and Oman, were in favor of allowing the deadlock to continue so that the whaling states would have to regulate the industry themselves; but both moderate members of the conservationist side and the Japanese were worried enough about a collapse that together they brokered a compromise on catch limits.[67]

After the 1980 meeting, a surprising turn came from Ottawa, when the Canadian government announced that it was leaving the IWC. In the early years of the commission, Canada had generally sided with conservationist nations, but in the 1970s it had been less than supportive of a moratorium. Canadian officials were protecting their small coastal whaling stations, but they were also not impressed with the justifications for the moratorium. By the end of the decade, Canada was a leading force for negotiating a new convention to cover all cetaceans and scrapping the IWC altogether. A major concern expressed by Canadian officials was that the general acceptance of a two-hundred-mile economic exclusion zone, which was being hammered out in negotiations at the UN Conference on the Law of the Sea, clashed with the IWC's mandate to regulate whaling on the high seas. Canada was concerned that the IWC might step in to regulate the hunt by First Nations people for belugas and narwhals as it had regulated the bowhead hunt. In fact, the Swedes had proposed regulating all small cetaceans, in part because of the huge bycatch of dolphins in the tuna industry.[68] Canada's 1980 departure from the IWC mattered, because it was not a good time to set the precedent that a nation could leave because it was frustrated with the commission's position on hunting whales, which was exactly what the Japanese repeatedly threatened.

Canada's departure was offset by a huge influx of new members. Seven states joined the commission before the 1981 meeting, and two more joined during the meeting itself. By the time of the 1982 meeting, there were thirty-eight members, much to the dismay of the Japanese delegates, who understood that many of the new members were there to vote with the environmentalists. As one annoyed Japanese official put it, the IWC was "stacked with member countries so small you cannot find them on the map."[69] Not long after, administrators of Japanese foreign aid started finding those nations and mailing them checks. Both the Americans and the whaling states based their strategy for the 1982 meeting on the assumption that the moratorium had enough votes, unless there was some unusually effective lobbying. Whaling state representatives met in March to plan their strategy, and they agreed that "there is no legal or biological ground for the moratorium and that every possible means should be applied to thwart it." Included on their long list of tactics was persuading moderate countries to abstain on moratorium votes, amending proposals so that the moratorium would include aboriginal whaling, and having their scientists target the positions of whaling opponents in the Scientific Committee meetings.[70]

Japanese commissioner Kunio Yonezawa then embarked on his lobbying trip across Europe, looking to shore up support for Japanese opposition to the moratorium at the 1982 IWC gathering. His visit with the Swiss commissioner yielded a promise of an abstention along with a wish to see the moratorium fail. His German counterpart made no promises on a vote but did agree that rational utilization of whales was acceptable, and Dutch officials promised to vote for quotas for Japanese whalers. Separately, the

Spanish government expressed "serious reservations of principle" about the moratorium proposal, opting instead for a population-by-population protection scheme. Not surprisingly, Yonezawa also found support in Moscow and at the UN Food and Agriculture Organization headquarters in Rome.[71]

Shortly after Yonezawa's trip, American John Byrne convened a meeting of anti-whaling commissioners in London. The lack of consensus was apparent, especially compared to what the whaling states could muster. Australia argued for the strongest position that did not cause withdrawals from the commission. Sidney Holt, who represented the Seychelles, predicted that the scientific evidence for the moratorium would be irrefutable at the upcoming meeting, but he was willing to support a phasing out instead of an absolute ban. The Netherlands decided to go back to a species-by-species protection, worried that a moratorium might lead to the collapse of the IWC.[72] The pro-whaling states were much better organized, and probably more motivated, than their opponents.

Objections to two amendments from the 1981 IWC meeting had changed the dynamics. First, animal rights groups had lobbied to change the equipment for hunting minke whales. Svend Foyn's explosive harpoon was not used for hunting minkes because it was too powerful for the relatively small animal, contaminating too much of the meat at detonation. Minke whale hunters had instead long used a nonexplosive weapon, the cold harpoon, that killed by laceration and damaging vital organs. In essence it was just a big arrow. Many observers found this harpoon unacceptably inhumane, in part because it took so long to kill an animal. Environmentalists won a vote in 1981 to ban the weapon within twelve months, but Norwegian whalers and officials argued that there was no acceptable alternative way to kill minkes, so Norway filed an objection, the first since 1978. Iceland followed suit, arguing that it was "overwhelmingly dependent on the rational utilization of the marine living resources off its shores."[73] (Norway found a replacement grenade in 1984 that killed the whale more quickly without spoiling the meat.)

The other objection from the 1981 meeting came from Japan, which protested the reduction in the sperm whale quota for the North Pacific, which the Japanese thought was not based on scientific analysis. Environmentalists were dismayed at Norway and felt betrayed that the Japanese had gone back on what appeared to be a gentlemen's agreement worked out in unofficial meetings during the commission session.[74] It became clear before the 1982 meeting that there would be no more attempts to reach across the divide and broker deals.

With so many new IWC members, the moratorium finally, almost anticlimactically, passed in 1982. Right up until the meeting that summer in Brighton, England, Norway and Japan were hinting that a moratorium would prompt either formal objections from them or their outright withdrawal from the commission. Australian officials were not convinced that they had enough votes for passage, predicting a 22–8 vote (with three abstentions), just short of the three-quarters needed. But then Senegal, Belize, and Antigua joined the commission on the eve of the meeting, solely with the goal of voting for a moratorium.

Five states had formally proposed some form of moratorium for the agenda, but the first proposal on the agenda was from the Seychelles, which had moved away from the ten-year moratorium to a permanent zero quota on each stock of whales that would be phased in after the 1986 coastal whaling season. The proposal addressed the concern about the twin mandates in the convention of 1946 by requiring the Scientific Committee to conduct an assessment of every stock of whales by 1990, so that the commission could discuss raising the various quotas after that date.[75] But the new quotas would need a three-quarters vote to change them from zero, a level that would now be permanently in the regulation schedule. If no supermajority could be found for a quota above zero, then no whales could be caught (at least in theory). Sensing that they finally had the votes, supporters of the moratorium were not interested in negotiating with the whaling states. Norway, Japan, Iceland, South Korea, Peru, Brazil, and the Soviet Union all voted no, and Spain commented that it voted yes but thought that aboriginal whaling should have been included in the moratorium. Still, with a vote of 25–7, with five abstentions, the moratorium finally passed, even if technically what passed were quotas set at zero rather than an outright ban. Until the moratorium went into effect in 1986, the commission would set quotas for minke and sperm whales, the only large species not protected by previous measures, using the New Management Procedure, which meant a few last sharp fights on quota matters, but otherwise the issue had been resolved.

It had been ten years since a whaling moratorium had first been raised at the UN Conference on the Human Environment in Stockholm. In the intervening decade, whaling had been whittled down by commercial weakness (with the losses to Japanese companies sometimes reaching ¥4 billion a year), by the power of public opinion and US sanctions, and by whalers' acceptance that they were on the losing end of many debates.[76] In a sense, then, the moratorium was really a ban on hunting the last two species pursued, minkes and sperms, both of which could sustain some hunting without risk of diminution of numbers. But that kind of sustainability was no longer acceptable to the majority of people paying attention to whaling.

SUSTAINING THE MORATORIUM

Given the long history of the IWC, no one really expected passage of a moratorium to be the end of the issue. The commission still had to set quotas for the last few years of hunting sperm and minke whales, and each hunting nation would have reason to press for as large a quota as it could get. The real problem was the objection clause, with a lesser concern being that nations that voted no might choose to withdraw from the IWC and whale on their own. When four of the whaling nations objected, the question then became how the rest of the members, especially the United States, would react.

In the immediate aftermath of the moratorium vote in July 1982, the reaction in the whaling states ranged from resignation to fury. Writing from Brighton as the meeting ended, a Norwegian diplomat complained that there was little willingness to discuss more fundamental questions regarding future whale management and the regulatory authority of the IWC. The Norwegian newspaper *Dagbladet* editorialized that the vote "has set our minds boiling." The editors continued, "What kind of an attack is this against the nation that has longer traditions within this industry than most and for whom whaling is an integral part of the ocean's romantic saga?" Despite the shock, the editors recommended accepting the moratorium: "As a small nation we will seldom gain from an international system where the strongest right is the only right."[77]

Norway finally had to come to grips with the inconsistency of its whaling policy. Since 1972, when it had voted both for and against a moratorium, Norway had been split. Almost every government official concerned had stated that a moratorium had no scientific basis, several had repeated the warning that a moratorium might lead to whaling nations withdrawing from the commission, and as many had taken to warning that a ban on catching minkes would lead to the depopulation of the far northern reaches of the nation. At the same time, the Ministry of the Environment had never been satisfied with the reasons for opposing the moratorium and had managed to get Norway to abstain on the issue on a few occasions. Beyond the environmentalist reasoning, and there were green groups in Norway expressing their anxiety about whaling, the tangible concern was that the United States would decide that an objection by Norway would warrant certification (and thus possible sanctions) under the Pelly and Packwood-Magnuson Amendments; possible boycotts organized by anti-whaling groups were another worry.

A number of factors influence the decision to file an objection to an amendment. Shortly after each commission meeting, the IWC secretariat sends out the list of new amendments. Under IWC rules, contracting governments have ninety days after this formal notification to object. A government considering an objection has enough time for internal and external consultations, but it cannot linger on the question. Officials have to be sure that they are prepared to take the heat from home and abroad, and they need to know who is with them and who against. If they know that another nation will file an objection, they can work together on the timing of their announcements. The commission's rules also grant a second ninety-day period to object if a nation files an objection to an amendment within the first ninety days. Most important, members recognize that they can always rescind an objection later, but they have only one chance to file an objection.

After the moratorium vote in 1982, John Byrne, the US commissioner, made a public statement that IWC members had worked to ease the pain of a moratorium, but he also was quite explicit in spelling out how the United States might apply sanctions.[78] The message was clearly meant to deter nations from filing an objection. In September, sixty-six US senators signed a statement urging the Reagan administration to use diplomacy to head off objections. They warned whaling nations that the United States would not be "faced down" over whaling and would use the Pelly and Packwood-Magnuson Amendments against states that objected or left the commission.[79] Opponents of the moratorium had long argued that its passage might lead to the collapse of the IWC, and now proponents of the moratorium were warning that an objection might have the same result.

The commission may not have had many supporters, but plenty of people at least pretended to care about its health.

On 2 November 1982, the Norwegian government formally filed its objection. Ambassador Rolf Busch expressed regret that "a sharp divide has occurred" in the commission, but he promised to work to minimize it. Still, he insisted that the fault was with the proponents of the moratorium, who had been unwilling to negotiate on the general management of marine resources. They had pushed a moratorium without the support of the Scientific Committee. They ignored both Article V of the convention, which required amendments to take into consideration consumers' interests, scientific advice, and the convention's principle of development and utilization of the resource; and Section 10 of the regulation schedule, which had put the New Management Procedure into effect. In addition, the foreign minister argued that the moratorium differentiated between similar kinds of whaling, a dig at the US defense of aboriginal whaling. Norway's prime minister added, "If whaling and sealing end, the only thing extinct will be the Norwegian fisherman."[80] The next day the Soviets filed their objection, citing the lack of support from the Scientific Committee.[81]

The day after that, the Japanese issued their own objection with a more impassioned critique. They began with the assertion that there was no scientific basis for the moratorium, adding the unlikely point that not a single scientist on the Scientific Committee supported it. The lack of respect for Japanese coastal whaling communities was problematic, especially given the way the IWC had rolled over on the bowhead hunting issue. There were hundreds of thousands of sperms and minkes, but it was somehow less acceptable to hunt them than the few thousand bowheads. Most troubling was the bleak outlook for the future. The Seychelles motion had promised a review by 1990, even though it could be completed by 1985, but "the present situation of the IWC does not warrant optimism that such a review would in fact be pursued seriously leading to a fair and equitable conclusion by the 1985 IWC Annual Meeting." Without a managed catch, there would be no way to gather the necessary data to set a catch limit in the future. Japan had recently invested $2 million per year studying whale populations, and it would all be for naught.[82]

When Peru filed its objection shortly thereafter, it appeared that the whaling nations were traveling as a herd for safety from the Pelly and Packwood predators circling around them.[83] Even before the moratorium had passed, former US commissioner Richard Frank had advised the Japanese that certification under either or both amendments was less likely if multiple countries were involved, although any whaling that went against a moratorium would be more likely to trigger certification than would a simple objection to a quota that might be a matter of scientific disagreement. He cited William Flory's arguments from the 1946 meeting that the objection clause had been written to protect national sovereignty and concluded that Japan ought to be able to exercise a treaty right without facing sanctions. In addition, the Reagan administration was hesitant to use sanctions, given its general commitment to freer trade. The Interior Department under Secretary James Watt was not likely to lead a fight over whaling, and the Commerce Department had moved to the position that an objection would not trigger certification.[84]

The objections filed in November 1982 represented a diplomatic opportunity because the rules would not go into effect until 1986. For the next three years, lobbying was intense, with the anti-whaling cohort trying to overturn the objections and the pro-whaling states trying to head off sanctions and persuade their opponents that their cause was reasonable. The Japanese were clearly going to be the target of the US sanctions, but the Norwegians also faced pressure. In June 1983, Craig Van Note of Monitor, an environmental consortium representing fifteen environmental and animal rights NGOs, demanded certification of Norway "for that nation's flagrant subversion of the international whaling regulations."[85]

Norway responded vigorously, revealing that Norwegians did not really comprehend the basis of opposition to whaling. The Foreign Ministry began a public-relations blitz to explain that Norwegian whaling was not the factory whaling that everyone seemed to hate, missing that opponents were thinking about the whale, not the whaler. The first press release in June 1983 emphasized that coastal whaling had been going on for a thousand years and had long been focused on domestic consumption. It was more like small-scale fishing than commercial whaling. Regulations were tight, control was local, and respect for science was high. A press release the next month emphasized that minke whales were plentiful, not endangered. The ministry reached out to the Alaska Eskimo Whaling Commission for support in its claim that they had similar relationships with nature, and it hired Terry Leitzell, a former director of the US National Marine Fisheries Service, to act as a consultant. Leitzell reported that the US Commerce

Department would not certify a state until it whaled outside of the IWC regulation schedule, so Norway was safe for now. He suggested that the United States might even encourage a small-scale whaling exemption if it was patterned on the bowhead hunt and satisfied Senator Packwood.[86]

In February 1984, the Norwegian government launched an initiative to win international support for its whaling operations. It had always followed the lead of the IWC's Scientific Committee, it explained to member governments, but the growth of the commission had led to more emphasis on politics and less on science. Whatever its merits, the moratorium had been proposed with large commercial whaling operations in mind, not the family whaling in small communities that Norwegians now pursued. Since everyone understood that factory ship whaling was out but aboriginal whaling was still acceptable, Norway proposed to define small-type whaling as more like aboriginal whaling and allow it to continue.[87]

In April 1984, a delegation of six Norwegians came to Washington to meet with US officials and environmentalists. Ten environmental organizations sent representatives, including Audubon, Greenpeace, the Humane Society, and, oddly, Sea-Air Seafoods. Interestingly, the first subject on the agenda was the cold harpoon, and environmentalists were pleased to hear that a new style of harpoon would be required in the upcoming season and that there were possibilities of exporting it to Iceland and Japan. They then got down to the moratorium and Norway's recent proposal, with Craig Van Note of the Monitor consortium emphasizing that the groups would keep working to overturn the objection. Per Tresselt, the head of the Norwegian group, argued that hunting minkes in the far north was more like whaling in Greenland and had little in common with Antarctic factory whaling. He added that the original moratorium proposal from the UN Conference on the Human Environment in Stockholm had not meant to include North Atlantic minkes, which suggested that environmentalists acknowledged that the catch was not a problem. Christine Stevens of the International Fund for Animal Welfare was among those who pointed out that the definition of commercial whaling came from the activities of the whalers, not from a meeting a dozen years before. Patricia Forkan of the Humane Society added the important point that an exemption for Norway might be a "door opener" for other countries.[88]

As the meeting heated up, Tresselt told his American audience that the more argumentative they were, the harder it would be for his government to change course. Oslo could not let single-issue pressure groups dictate administration of certain issues. Van Note and Forkan responded, probably with some vehemence, that the Norwegian objection was a provocation and the boycotts would continue, focusing on sardines and salmon. Forkan won the prize for blunt talk by telling Tresselt that "the train left the station two years ago, and you were not on it." Tresselt disagreed but no doubt took great pleasure in reporting that Norwegian exports to the United States had risen in 1983 by record measure. After a few more comments, "the meeting was then closed, while showing as much friendliness as the parties at this point could muster." The next day, Tresselt told his American hosts that the environmentalists had been less threatening and more reflective than usual.

The meeting with US officials at the Commerce Department started more smoothly, with John Byrne, the US commissioner and head of NOAA, opening the meeting by saying that friendly nations should be able to work out their differences constructively. The group quickly worked through Norway's progress on the new harpoon and its policies for reducing the number of whaling licenses in the north to fifty-five. They briefly touched on the critical problem of estimating stock size, with Tresselt acknowledging that large fluctuations in estimates that had seemed "intuitively" not very likely were probably due to an error in the population model.

They then settled down to the main order of business, the "door opener," as Tresselt echoed Forkan, of a Norwegian exemption. Forces in Brazil, Spain, and Iceland were unhappy with the situation, Tresselt noted, and might well think about pulling out of the commission if a path for small-type whaling was not opened up, although both sides understood that finding a definition that covered Norway's needs without opening the door to factory ship whaling would be difficult. Tresselt no doubt was thinking about the number of drafts of a policy on that subject that had landed on his desk without finding a happy home. Byrne countered that the United States assumed that the moratorium meant that commercial whaling was dead, and he added the surprising aside that even aboriginal whaling would be phased out at some point in time. This was the breaking point for Tresselt, who said that Norway could not accept a plan that included a formal end to whaling. There was, he concluded, "no basis for common diplomatic activities."

The US response to Norway took one more odd turn with the direct insertion of the Cold War into the decision making. As early as December 1982, Norwegian diplomats were using the idea that if Norway did not maintain whaling, the population of its far northern reaches would have to relocate, in which case there would be no barrier to Soviet encroachment along the Soviet-Norwegian border north of Sweden. In December 1983, the US ambassador to Norway, Mark Austad, told an audience in Los Angeles that "well-meaning US environmental groups" were showing that "a little knowledge is dangerous." If whaling were outlawed, not only would whaling jobs disappear but so too would fish (into the whales' guts) and the jobs they supported. No jobs meant no people, and no people "meant an open invitation to the Soviets. No one can tolerate that miserable climate without a job."[89] It was a remarkable statement by an ambassador of a country that was supposed to be considering sanctions against his host. In the meeting with Tresselt and his team four months later, Forkan asked Tresselt directly if NATO defense concerns, which she found unconvincing, played a role in Oslo's policy. Tresselt dodged the question, perhaps because Americans were doing such a good job of keeping it alive themselves. The debate was echoed three years later, when the United States was leaning on Iceland to drop its whaling industry, and Iceland pointed out that it could deny NATO use of its bases.[90]

Of course, the real attention was on Japan, which had both a much larger whaling operation and a greater vulnerability to fishing sanctions. Environmentalists poured on the pressure to sanction Japan, and the Japanese could read the writing on the wall. In the fall of 1984, the Japanese ambassador in Washington, DC, sent a deal back to his government that avoided sanctions by accepting a phasing out of Japanese pelagic whaling. The Japanese would withdraw their objection by 1 April 1985 and the US administration would hold off certification until then. The United States and Japan would cooperate to set quotas for sperm and minke whale hunts until a final phaseout in 1988. After a bitter fight inside the government that finally had to be resolved by Prime Minister Yasuhiro Nakasone, Japan accepted the deal despite rejecting the moratorium, telling governments around the world that it was forced to withdraw its objection by the threat of US sanctions.[91]

Then, to the Japanese government's dismay, in March 1985 environmentalists in the United States won an injunction against the Reagan administration, demanding that it had to certify Japan under the Pack-wood-Magnuson Amendment. Japanese officials called the ruling "aston-ishing" and "embarrassing," but it was upheld on appeal in August.[92] The court case showed the split between conservationist governments and environmentalist groups. Other member states considered the United States to be the leading power within the IWC for protecting whales, but the environmentalist community that compelled that strong stance was clearly dissatisfied. Some governments seemed to agree with the Reagan administration that the US-Japanese agreement was the best way to keep Japan from breaking with the IWC over the moratorium, but environmen-talists saw it as a sellout by a government that they did not trust in any case. One State Department official complained that the United States would be able to solve the whaling problem if Greenpeace and its allies would just get out of the way, which was not going to happen so long as those groups needed the whaling fight to maintain part of their relevance.[93] And no doubt Greenpeace and its supporters thought things would be better if the pragmatists in the State Department were the ones getting out of the way.[94]

Japan did not give in without a fight, in May 1986 launching a defense of an expanded scientific whaling program that would also put meat in the markets. This position was not a surprise; for more than a year, diplomats in Tokyo had reported that the Japanese would turn to research whaling as a means of keeping its long-range whaling fleet going until the hoped-for resumption of whaling in 1990. The Japanese Foreign Ministry emphasized that Japan, like Norway, had long had a small-type whaling culture, but it was mainly interested in promoting its newfound respect for "scientific whaling." It noted that the whaling convention placed no limits on permits for scientific whaling, "a right endowed to the Contracting Governments under Article VIII." Now more than ever there was a need for research, since there was no commercial take on the high seas to generate data.[95] From the environmentalist standpoint, this was a declaration of war, and it certainly took the pressure off of Norway and the Soviet Union, which had dismissed US sanctions as "all purely political," not scientific.[96]

Japanese scientific whaling became the flash point for whaling protests around the world. Environmentalists argued that it violated both Japan's deal with the United States and the moratorium, but the latter was not so clear. The convention did guarantee the right to conduct research, and all a member state had to do was file a report with the commission. This idea had been part of the Progressive-era framework for the convention proposed by the United States in the first place. As long as the Japanese could make even a remotely plausible claim that the catch of a few hundred minke whales was scientifically valid, it would be hard to certify the nation as undermining the efficiency of the IWC. A range of scientists, including Douglas Chapman of the old Committee of Four, Sally Mizroch from NOAA, and Tim Smith from Woods Hole, dismissed the sampling program as useless and having "no scientific justification."[97]

To most environmentalists, continued Japanese whaling was an outrage. There was nothing that could not be learned from sighting cruises, they believed, so killing whales just to learn about them was not scientifically valuable, much less ethical. Philip Hartstein, living in Ichikawa, Chiba Prefecture, captured the feeling when he sarcastically responded to an article in the *Japan Times* that the crane population in eastern Hokkaido had grown to 424 birds. "Surely," he wrote, "this is a population sufficient to support at least some scientific harvesting of the flock to determine the ages, health and hobbies of the cranes. I suggest that at least 300 be harvested to enable a thorough study of the species before it becomes extinct."[98] Those without a sense of humor were a little more strident, and the Japanese responded with increasingly defiant language about race and culture. The nominal end of commercial whaling in 1986 marked a major change in how nations defined a sustainable use of whales, but it did not mark the end of hunting or controversy.

In 1986, seeing a report in the *Observer* that the end of whaling was nigh, scientist Sidney Holt felt compelled to set the record straight, writing that Japan, Iceland, Norway, and South Korea were all about to start "scientific whaling" and the results would be bad. The stocks of minke whales in the North Atlantic were not well studied and, he thought, probably not able to handle the proposed catches: "The IWC was once rightly blamed for presiding over the virtual extinction of the blue and humpback whales. The blame for the same fate of the smallest species—the minke whale—in the North Atlantic will fall squarely on the Governments of Norway and Iceland."[99] Not only was whaling not coming to an end, but the long sad history of outstripping the resource's ability to replenish itself was going to be repeated at least once more. It was not the happy story that so many people had fought for since 1972.

That the dispute in 1986 was mostly about minke whales, which were barely on anyone's radar in 1972, said a great deal about what had happened in the previous four decades. The large whales had suffered population losses but had also gained protection. Instead, the industry was left to pursue small whales for their meat, since oil was no longer available in enough quantity to be marketable. An assessment by New Zealand's government in 1988 concluded that scientific whaling was against the spirit of the IWC rules, but there was no evidence of illegal whaling.[100] Not surprisingly, meat from protected whales started to filter into the Japanese market, with more than half of a small sample in 1994 turning out to be something other than the expected minke whale.[101] Environmentalists had won many battles for species that they deemed endangered, but they were not in a strong position with a species whose numbers were probably quite high. While the stocks of minkes harvested by Iceland and Norway were not well known, the species as a whole certainly included hundreds of thousands of individuals. One of environmentalists' strongest arguments against catching minkes was that doing so provided cover for catching other, less common species.

The outrage that had fueled the anti-whaling protests dwindled with passage of the moratorium. Whales had lost some of their power as talismans, largely because most people seemed to have concluded that they had been saved. Individual whales might face danger from Japanese scientists or aboriginal hunters, and those threats could generate some ethical concerns; but in a world awash in such concerns, it was hard to justify so much attention to whales. Whaling continued, but the various species had been saved from the threat of extinction from hunting.

Epilogue

IN JUNE 2011, ANDREW REVKIN OF THE *NEW YORK TIMES* POSTED AN interview with Paul Watson, leader of the Sea Shepherd Conservation Society, on his environmental interest blog, *Dot Earth*. Watson had maintained a place in the limelight after his 1979 run-in with the *Sierra* by harassing Icelandic whalers in the 1980s, challenging the Makah hunt of gray whales in Washington State in the 1990s, and interfering with Japanese whalers in the twenty-first century, starring in the television series *Whale Wars*, which fit in nicely with the contemporary trend of brash "reality shows." In the interview and on the program, Watson was largely unchanged from the strong-willed young man of the 1970s who had been willing to take great risks to stop whaling. To emphasize his rejection of the formal niceties of international discussion about whales, which had failed to save them, Watson's ships flew a version of the skull and crossbones, long a symbol of pirates. Ironically, at least one sponsor of *Whale Wars* was a company hawking "ocean-fish flavored" cat food.

In his brief interview with Revkin, Watson compared Sea Shepherd with someone walking down the street who intervenes to halt the stomping of a puppy or kitten—or the rape of a woman. He accused Greenpeacers of cowardice for only bearing witness in the face of such affronts. The Japanese, he opined, were breaking the law by violating the International Whaling Commission's Southern Ocean Sanctuary and hunting minke whales, an endangered species, and his response was to maneuver his ships right up to the stern slipways of the whaling vessels to prevent them from bringing whales on board. His crews threw bottles of butyric acid at the Japanese whalers and tried to foul their props with ropes. His clients, Watson asserted, were sharks, turtles, whales, and fish, and his most powerful tool was his knowledge of strategy and media. To those who accused him of ecoterrorism, he bluntly said "arrest me, or shut up."[1] In the "Comments" section of Revkin's blog and almost every story like it in the Western press, it was obvious that arguments against whaling had not changed dramatically since the late 1970s. Watson's comparison of the whalers to rapists and puppy stompers might have been extreme, but it fit logically with the general idea that whales were as good as people. Several commenters called Watson a hero, while others praised his willingness to defend any species, but particularly whales. A few even mentioned a boycott targeting Japan. Some of Revkin's readers took the points further: one submitted poetry about whale mothers crying, and another staked a claim to ownership of whales as a citizen of the earth. Others, not surprisingly, dismissed Watson as a mere showman or as incredibly naïve. The most perceptive comments often came from those who thought that whaling was only a small part of the problem in the oceans.

While such stories could generate flames of passion, the actions of the IWC had generally cooled the ardor of the Save the Whales movement. Environmentalists have won two major victories in the commission since 1986. In 1979, the IWC had accepted a proposal from the Seychelles (or "Seashells," as one Japanese whalers' group mistakenly rendered it) to declare the Indian Ocean a sanctuary for ten years, and in 1988 it voted to make that status permanent. Japan objected. Four years later, the French proposed a Southern Ocean Sanctuary, covering all waters south of latitude 40° south. After two years of intense debate, the IWC approved the sanctuary. Japan objected.[2] In theory, sanctuary status might trump the right to conduct scientific research contained in the 1946 International Convention for the Regulation of Whaling, but there is no way to test that in a court of law, at least not one that the Japanese are likely to accept. Because the objection system still stands, Japan is probably within its legal rights to use the scientific exemption to catch whales, even if it violates the spirit of the rules. Watson's take on the illegality of Japanese whaling does not seem to have much to recommend it, even if the immorality and offensiveness of that hunt might be more easily argued.

The assertion that the Japanese hunt endangered species is also a matter of dispute. There are at least several hundred thousand minke whales in the world's oceans, and there is no evidence that the species as a whole is in decline. The stock that frequents the Ross Sea, where the Japanese have focused their efforts at the start of the twenty-first century, might not be as stable, depending on who is doing the counting. Japanese proposals in 2008 and 2009 to take up to fifty fin whales and fifty humpback whales are certainly in grayer territory. The Japanese claim that the harvesting of a group of fins and humpbacks will allow them to build a population distribution estimate that will in turn allow an estimate of both species' populations. They also argue that the number of almost every whale species in the oceans as a whole is so large, with no commercial hunting, that really no whale is in danger of extinction from hunting (although northern right whales, for instance, might be in danger from other causes, like ship strikes or a massive oil spill).

The moral clarity of Watson and his followers has been matched by that of the Japanese whalers. Japan's government, perhaps shrewdly, has only stepped up its twin rhetorical messages of sustainability and deep cultural roots. Japanese whalers and government agencies have worked to spread the idea that Japan has been hunting whales for centuries without ill effects.[3] The claim certainly has some merit: in 1916 the American conservationist Roy Chapman Andrews commented, after a visit to Nagasaki, that "few people realize the great part which whale meat plays in the life of the ordinary Japanese."[4]

Eighty years later, sustainability was central in the rhetoric Japan directed at friend and foe alike. The Japanese minister of agriculture, forestry, and fisheries, Taichiro Okawara, included the phrase "sustainable use" three times in less than two hundred words in his letter of thanks to the Norwegian government for cooperation at the 1994 IWC meeting. Two years later, the All Japan Seamen's Union made a statement to IWC delegates that also included some form of "sustainable" three times in less than two pages. Not only did the group praise Japanese scientific whaling for its research value, but it also asserted that the IWC "should expel the countries who are acting against the chapter and spirit of ICRW," by which they meant the twin goals of rebuilding whale stocks while strengthening the whaling industry.[5] In 2002, the IWC met in the southern Japanese port city of Shimonoseki, allowing government officials to emphasize that whale hunting was both culturally important and still responsible. Supporters of whaling demonstrated in Tokyo, holding signs saying "Protect and Eat!" More than forty politicians showed up for a dinner featuring whale sashimi and other whale-based dishes. Kiichi Inoue, a member of the Conservative

Party, which was in the governing coalition, noted that "it takes patience to make opponents understand Japan's cultural attachment to whales." And he asserted that Japan is "committed to both whaling and sustaining the resource."[6]

At the whaling commission meetings, that position is finding an increasing number of defenders, because the Japanese have continued to emphasize their wishes to recipients of their foreign aid. Journalist Andrew Darby concluded that the Japanese began to tie foreign aid to whaling in 1979, when the Seychelles won the fight for the Indian Ocean Sanctuary. Japan responded with an overt threat to its foreign aid allocation to the Seychelles.[7] In 1994, six Caribbean nations abstained from voting on the Southern Ocean Sanctuary. In 2000, six Caribbean nations voted with Japan, and against their fellow island nations in the Pacific, and helped defeat a proposal for a South Pacific Whale Sanctuary. The fisheries minister of Dominica resigned to protest Japan's use of foreign aid money, charging that his government's IWC dues and some travel costs were being borne directly by the Japanese government to control his nation's vote.[8] In the summer of 2006, at the fifty-eighth IWC meeting, Japan surprised many observers by actually winning a controversial vote. For thirty-five years, the Japanese had repeatedly lost votes pertaining to the most important issue before the commission: whether to permit commercial whaling. In 2006, the Japanese once again presented a motion acknowledging that, in principle, the IWC should move toward restoring commercial whaling of abundant species, with all eyes on the minke whale. By a 33–32 vote, the motion passed, prompting surprise from people who thought that the whales had been saved years ago.

In reality, the vote was largely a symbol of the effectiveness of Japanese foreign aid to small countries. On occasion, Japanese officials have been unusually frank in acknowledging both that they used their nation's financial resources to help friendly IWC members and that they worked hard to bring like-minded nations into the commission. A number of smaller island nations joined the commission and took positions fundamentally sympathetic to Japan. As an example, from 1993 to 1995 Dominica voted with Japan on 25 of 32 issues, leading an IWC official to note that "one might therefore conclude that there is a certain similarity in voting patterns."[9] More than $100 million in fisheries aid flowed to three Caribbean nations between 1987 and 2001, including nearly $30 million to Dominica alone. In 2010, commissioners from several small nations admitted that their nations' decisions in the IWC were tied directly or indirectly to Japanese foreign aid. One suggested that the Japanese even used prostitutes to reward compliant commissioners. Naturally the Japanese government denied that it used foreign aid that way.[10] Still, at least a few countries might vote for a general statement in favor of whaling in return for an airport or two before they could be persuaded to cast a specific vote to overturn the popular moratorium and offend its powerful patrons.

When the commission is not refighting the moratorium decision, it has spent considerable time on issues other than hunting. The IWC has, like many activists and scientists, recognized that threats to whales come far less from harpoons than from other sources. Slow-moving and slow-reproducing right and bowhead whales face more pressure from the enormous numbers of merchant vessels on the waters today than from harpoons; if the Northwest Passage opens up permanently, the threat to bowheads will rise dramatically. Whale-watching ships have prompted commission discussions about minimizing the harm that whales face from even well-intentioned people. The Pacific Garbage Patch has come to symbolize how humans have treated the oceans in general, and it is worth remembering that it might take only a single Mylar balloon, placidly floating on the waves after blowing away from a birthday party or car dealership, to choke a small whale and kill it. Naval operations and drills produce sonar bursts that appear capable of causing disoriented whales to strand on beaches and die, which whalers understood in the 1950s, even if it has been hotly contested in this century all the way to the US Supreme Court.[11]

The focus on issues other than hunting has been a bone of contention for nations that aspire to catch whales without being ostracized. Even as they benefit from reminders that even whale watchers might not have clean hands, they really want the IWC to get back to its founding mission of using science to promote sensible whaling. The long-running attempt to create a Revised Management Procedure (RMP) to replace the New Management Procedure of 1974 came to a head in 1991, when the Scientific Committee approved an RMP that had been in development for eight years. The RMP has a goal of generating a safe range of harvesting, using a complex algorithm that takes population estimates for whale stocks and puts them into a feedback loop based on sighting cruises and actual hunting. The IWC approved it in 1992. Twenty years later, the RMP still has not been used on any stock, nor is it likely to be used anytime soon, largely because opponents of whaling were able to tie its implementation to rules about the use of whales, with the total package known as the Revised Management Scheme (RMS). In the Norwegian view, the proponents of protecting whales had added "a long and increasing shopping-list of items to be dealt with" before the RMS could be implemented. The governments of Japan, Norway, and Iceland, among others, have been frustrated by this lack of progress, with Iceland leaving the IWC in 1993 for several years.[12]

At the forty-ninth meeting of the IWC, in Monaco, Ireland offered a compromise to break the impasse between the whalers and their opponents. The Irish government had joined the IWC in 1985 as part of the effort to end commercial whaling, and it had hosted a rancorous meeting in 1995, but two years later it expressed concern that the IWC was in danger of breaking up over the inability of the two camps to compromise on anything. It offered a plan to end lethal scientific whaling, regulate whale watching, complete and adopt the RMS, and allow limited coastal whaling for local consumption. Interestingly, Greenpeace Ireland in 1995 had called on the government to focus on pollution, with one leader of the organization arguing that "saving whales means more than just stopping hunting."[13]

The Japanese cautiously raised their eyebrows in interest. The Foreign Ministry told its Norwegian counterpart that Japan would participate in a meeting with "moderate anti-whaling countries," like Ireland and Sweden. The United States could send someone, too, but the Japanese were not prepared to appear to agree to such a compromise until they knew where the United States and others stood.[14] For its part, Norway argued strenuously that the Irish were right about the impending collapse of the commission, even if the compromise was flawed in limiting rights guaranteed by the 1946 convention. At the IWC's fiftieth meeting, in Oman, the Norwegian opening statement noted that a golden anniversary is "normally . . . a time for celebration." Instead, Kaere Bryn, the Norwegian commissioner, launched into a remedial course on how the commission is supposed to work, especially in relation to accepting recommendations of the Scientific Committee. The next year, the Norwegians continued the offensive by pointing out that since 1964 all of the officers of the Scientific Committee had come from Australia, Great Britain, or the United States. Even the committee had become politicized, to the point that it no longer focused on whaling but included the environment more broadly, which was not an appropriate subject.[15] In 1982, the Norwegians had been disappointed by the commercial moratorium, but they seemed to have hoped that the IWC would work through the stock assessments in the 1990s as promised. By the end of the century, the files of the Foreign Ministry resounded with the words "Resolusjon mot Norge"—resolution against Norway. Norway's faith in the rational basis of the commission had dissipated. As the 2006 vote on restoring commercial whaling demonstrated, the Irish proposal touched a nerve, but it had failed to end the deadlock and polarization.

Revelations in 2010 about the full extent of Japan's efforts to control votes in the IWC helped to derail another effort at compromise along the lines of Ireland's 1995 proposal. For more than two years, Australia and the United States had led a group of nations and some environmental groups, including Greenpeace, in crafting a compromise with the three whaling states that would end whaling in Antarctic seas in exchange for allowing limited whaling elsewhere. Proponents argued that the deal would break the deadlock over the moratorium, end the loophole for scientific whaling, and result in a reduction in the number of whales killed each year, from more than 1,500 to fewer than 1,000. Critics countered that the United States was driven into this unethical bargain largely by a desire to maintain its bowhead quota. In the end, negotiations failed before a vote could be taken.

As of 2012, there are eighty-nine members of the commission, perhaps a third of which are sympathetic to the Japanese position. It seems highly unlikely that Japan will be able to muster a three-quarters majority to overturn the moratorium, barring a widespread reordering of environmental thinking around the world. It seems equally unlikely that Japan will stop whaling, given how entrenched the practice is in the fisheries office. Admitting that whaling is no longer needed for scientific or nutritional purposes would entail a major loss of face, even as Japanese officials sometimes acknowledge that the market for whale meat is already more than filled by their scientific research expeditions. Yet even as reports from Japan suggest that the market for whale meat is "tiny," other people have claimed that whalers have engaged in smuggling prime cuts, which could be sold for about $70 per pound.[16]

The long history of efforts to regulate whaling, including the fifteen or so years before the IWC's creation, parallels contemporary environmental politics. The most prominent environmental issue in the early twenty-first century is global climate change. Despite being more problematic than overhunting a few species of animals, human-induced climate change has certain similarities to twentieth-century whaling. Specifically, in each case scientific uncertainty became an important point of contention. In the IWC, there was broad agreement that the great whales were in decline after World War II, but a few holdouts refused to agree that fin whales, in particular, were overtaxed. Their dissent provided cover for governments that wanted to keep the global whaling quotas high, which in turn delayed efforts to make whaling sustainable. If there had been unanimity among scientists on the status of fin whales, whalers and government officials would have had a much harder time justifying quotas higher than the scientists thought prudent.

From the middle of the global warming debate, it is hard to tell how it will turn out. It is obvious so far, though, that the voices of a few skeptics have carried nearly as much weight politically, in the United States and Australia in particular, as the vast majority of climatologists who are convinced that humans are causing the earth to heat up. In the United States, neither the Senate in the 1990s nor the Bush administration early in the twenty-first century was willing to support the Kyoto Protocol, designed to combat human-induced climate change. Even granting that the protocol might have been flawed, US resistance to it was based as much on its principle as on its specific terms. Scientists today who believe that humans are causing climate change by burning fossil fuels might see in men like Neil Mackintosh and Remington Kellogg a troubling parallel to themselves, certain that they understand the problem but unable professionally to say with certainty what the precise dimensions are or what to do about it. Perhaps the one key difference is that no one questioned Kellogg's objectivity or integrity.[17]

Of course, climate change might well threaten whales too. If oceanic currents shift, pack ice gets redistributed, or sources of nutrients change, the place of whales in the world's ecosystems might shift more quickly than they can modify their behavior. While it seems unlikely that any species of whale would be driven to extinction by climate change, it is certainly possible that a species with a small population might be made more vulnerable to other problems, such as ship strikes.

In just a century, whaling has in some ways come almost full circle. Early in the twentieth century, relatively few whales were hunted, and meat was one of the major products of the hunt. Early in the twenty-first century, relatively few whales are hunted, almost exclusively for their meat. Attention to the industry has waned from just a few decades past. The key differences between now and then, of course, are closely related. Now, even a small amount of hunting draws global attention, and one reason for that attention is that there is no great stock of whales waiting to be exploited if only technology would allow it. One scientific study estimated that there were 239,000 blue whales in the Antarctic seas a century ago, and now, after forty years of protection from whaling, there are still only between 1,000 and 3,000.[18] The IWC estimates that there were 400,000 fin whales in Antarctic waters at the turn of the twentieth century, and as of 1979 it estimated that about 20 percent were left. Humpback whales in the southern seas dropped from about 100,000 to fewer than 20,000 (although that figure is in dispute). Each of these species also has small populations north of the equator that were not hit as hard in the twentieth century, so global estimates are at least double the Antarctic waters estimates.[19]

The story of efforts to regulate whaling leaves one grasping for something good in an otherwise gloomy story of decline, or more often looking for someone to blame for missing an opportunity to save the whales. It is hard to see a point where something sufficiently different might have happened, except for the worse. It is fairly easy to imagine an IWC that collapsed in the early 1950s, leaving no organization to slow down whalers. Without an IWC, it seems unlikely that there would have been any legal prohibitions on whaling, whether in the form of catch limits or protection of critically endangered species; it seems unlikely that a new, better IWC would have come along to replace the old one. Indeed, the Marine Mammal Act of 1972 required the United States to propose a new whaling convention that would export US policies, but the US draft expired quietly after several years of international committee meetings proved that there was no consensus on what such a treaty might entail. Disagreements among the various delegations at one session in Lisbon in 1979 were so great that they failed even to get all the way through the draft convention text before the negotiators ran out of time.[20]

On the other end of the imaginary spectrum, it is pleasing to imagine a commission in which the scientists succeed in shaping the rules early and often. When a quota seemed too high, whalers and governments would yield to the best estimates of the scientists. When the data led to uncertainty, people would err on the side of caution. If a global quota in blue whale units was less effective than stock quotas divided up by nations, then governments would authorize the appropriate changes in the regulation schedule. Proposals that were not approved until the 1970s and 1980s would have been received in the 1940s as visionary, not naïve. Unfortunately, such hopes seem to rest on an overly idealistic view of the world. Opponents of those scientists willing to suggest a reduced quota were driven mainly by an assessment of their own economic interests, with a dash of certainty that Aristotle Onassis and the Soviets were cheating flagrantly and therefore making a mockery of the rules. Men like H. K. Salvesen and Anders Jahre understood whales as resources, as did the vast majority of the consumers who liked to have a little margarine on their morning toast or better-fed chickens for their dinners.

Beyond idealism, the very basis of the argument for treating whales as the equal of people is, at best, a model with limited applicability elsewhere. If intelligence is the determinant for a ban on hunting, then by definition the number of species to be saved will be very small. There can be value at the ecosystem level, of course, in saving keystone species, so in the long run a campaign to save whales based on their minds might be the only way to affect changes in human use of the oceans as a whole. But it is more likely that a focus on intelligence means that once average people think the whales have been saved, they can turn their attention to other things.

The 25 February 2012 issue of the *Economist* made the point unintentionally. The Science and Technology section carried an article titled "Whales Are People Too," which described scholars advancing the idea that whales should have rights similar to what are sometimes called "human rights." The researchers argued that whales have language, culture, complex brains, and self-awareness and hence count as persons with moral rights, including the right not to be removed from their environment. Twenty pages earlier, under the title "Lost Property," the International section described how fisheries are "in an even worse state than feared." The litany of woe sounded suspiciously like the problems of whaling in 1950: uncertain science, unworkable quota schemes, poorly thought-out subsidies, and a rising demand for the product that make tougher restrictions difficult. The lone ray of sunshine was that perhaps fewer fisheries had been destroyed than expected.[21]

The ongoing Save the Whales campaign, featuring celebrities such as Pierce Brosnan and Hayden Pantierre, suggests that the threat is far beyond hunting now, focusing on pollution and climate change. Saving the fish or saving the seabirds, which will certainly benefit from cleaning up the oceans for whales, fails to attract any celebrities. Bird and fish populations are suffering because the bar has been set: you must be this charismatic to stir a public movement. The effort to save the whales bears a certain resemblance to the bison preservation movement from earlier in the twentieth century. As author Andrew Isenberg has shown, it saved the bison from extinction, but it did not save the bison ecosystem, so the bison were left as a zoological curiosity.[22]

There is nothing inherently wrong with saving the whales because they are special, but such a policy provides no guidance on how to treat everything else in the ocean. Whales and most other marine vertebrates depend on krill, small crustaceans that convert plant life to animal life. Their abundance is unfathomable, in the hundreds of millions of tons, and their productivity absolutely critical to marine ecosystems. Probably, they do not sing, do not have culture, and cannot tell themselves apart. But they are an excellent source of omega-3 oils, a natural substance thought to prevent cancer, heart disease, and a host of other health problems. When that fact was discovered, the race to harvest them was on. The US government has banned krill harvesting in a wide swath of its Pacific Ocean waters, and the 1981 Antarctic Convention has some regulations applicable to the southern seas. It is even possible to order a "Save the Krill" T-shirt.[23] But if Sir Sidney Harmer were alive today, he would probably be saying the same thing about krill that he said a century ago about whales: history is about to repeat itself.

Appendix: Whaling Data, 1904–1965

YEARS	BLUE WHALE UNITS (BWU)	BLUES	FINS	HUMPBACKS	SEIS	OIL PRICES (IN POUNDS)	FACTORY SHIPS
1904–5	11	4	180	0	14	0
1905–6	51	104	311	113	19	1
1906–7	20	53	240	0	23	2
1907–8	4	4	1281	0	20	5
1908–9	253	270	3087	0	19	6
1909–10	176	432	5084	346	22	7
1910–11	393	680	8294	195	21	14
1911–12	1109	1680	5755	0	20	17
1912–13	2193	4527	3038	43	22	21
1913–14	2334	4196	1559	191	21	17
1914–15	4203	3894	1489	0	23	15
1915–16	4871	5102	1797	0	30	11
1916–17	3820	2208	399	0	54	6
1917–18	2268	1771	131	49	57	6
1918–19	1801	2791	149	8	67	6
1919–20	1874	3213	261	71	88	6
1920–21	2617	5491	260	36	37	8
1921–22	4416	2492	9	103	32	8
1922–23	5683	3677	517	10	31	13
1923–24	3732	3035	233	193	37	13
1924–25	5703	4366	359	1	36	13
1925–26	4697	8916	364	195	32	15
1926–27	6545	5102	189	778	28	17

1927–28		8334	4459	23	883	30	18
1928–29		12734	6689	48	808	28	26
1929–30		17487	11539	852	216	21	38
1930–31	34662	29410	10017	576	145	12	41
1931–32	6689	6488	2871	184	16	13	5
1932–33	20860	18891	5168	159	2	12	17
1933–34	19836	17349	7200	872	0	15	19
1934–35	22605	16500	12500	1965	266	20	23
1935–36	22341	17731	9697	3162	2	20	24
1936–37	22610	14304	14381	4477	490	20	30
1937–38	28820	14923	28009	2079	161	14	31
1938–39	23931	14059	20788	860	23	26	34
1939–40		11480	18694	2	81	30	
1940–41		4943	7831	2675	110	33	
1941–42		59	1189	16	52	38	
1942–43		125	776	0	73	43	
1943–44		339	1158	4	197	44	
1944–45		1042	1666	60	78	45	
1945–46	7367	3604	9184	238	140	57	9
1946–47	15300	9197	14545	26	394	84	15
1947–48	16280	6876	21049	24	621	100	
1948–49	15920	7371	17081	13	16	90	18
1949–50	15929	6132	17876	2105	101	99	
1950–51	16285	6928	17296	1624	361	141	19
1951–52	15875	5101	20312	1532	31	93	
1952–53	14725	3847	20964	941	115	73	16
1953–4	15284	2667	24675	593	249	77	
1954–55	15180	2154	25608	492	145	83	19
1955–56	14779	1611	25102	1425	274	89	
1956–57	14636	1505	25502	673	708	85	20
1957–58	14769	1682	25067	396	2375	73	
1958–59	15324	1187	25687	2393	1394	76	20
1959–60	15421	1228	26271	1332	3219	73	
1960–61	16373	1739	27299	709	4280	67	
1961–62	15228	1116	26364	309	4716	46	21
1962–63	11306	944	18636	270	5482	62	17
1963–64	8448	112	13583	2	8286	82	16
1964–65	6986	20	7308	0	19874	85	15

Sources and notes: "The Antarctic Whaling, 1904/05–1938/39," USNA, RG 43, File "Material in Connection with International Whaling Conf., 1939"; "Total Antarctic Catch," covering 1937–38 to 1947–48, SIA, RU 7165, Box 11, Folder 8; "Antarctic Catch (Pelagic)," SIA, RU 7165, Box 27, Folder 7; "Pelagic Whaling in the Antarctic in the Season 1931/32—1963/64 (Excl. the War Seasons)," SIA, RU 7165, Box 22, Folder 2. Oil prices are in pounds per ton, mark the middle between high and low sale, and come from Tønnessen and Johnsen, *History of Modern Whaling*, table 69. Data from 1904 through 1947–48 includes land stations; data after 1948 is for pelagic vessels only. Data is not adjusted for Soviet cheating; it is not clear if Aristotle Onassis's catch figures were included. Blank cells indicate lack of data.

Notes

1   Untitled excerpt, source unknown, 7 November 1913, presumably transcribed by Remington Kellogg, Smithsonian Institution, Washington, DC, International Whaling Conference and International Whaling Commission, 1930–1968 (Record Unit 7165), Box 8, Folder 1. A brief biography of Harmer can be found in Neil Chalmers, "Harmer, Sir Sidney Francis (1862–1950)," *Oxford Dictionary of National Biography*, online ed. (Oxford: Oxford University Press, 2009), www.oxforddnb.com/view/article/37512 (accessed 5 July 2012).

2   ICW/1938/14, "Protection of Humpback Whales, Submitted by the German Delegation," US National Archives, College Park, MD (hereafter USNA), General Records of the Department of State (hereafter RG 59), File 562.8F3.

3   In *The History of Modern Whaling*, chapters 5 through 7, Daniel Francis provides a quick introduction to whaling in this period, but the literature on this era, sometimes thought of as the romantic era of whaling, is simply enormous. Readers seeking an introduction might look at Edouard A. Stackpole, *Whales and Destiny: The Rivalry between America, France, and Britain for Control of the Southern Whale Fishery, 1785–1825* (Amherst: University of Massachusetts Press, 1972); Alexander Starbuck, *History of the American Whale Fishery* (1878; reprint, Secaucus, NJ: Castle, 1989); and Francis Allyn Olmsted, *Incidents of a Whaling Voyage* (1841; reprint, New York: Bell Publishing, 1969).

4   ICW/1938/18, minutes of the third session, 18 June 1938, p. 10, USNA, RG 59, File 562.8F3.

5   On Foyn's struggles to perfect the grenade harpoon, see the most important book on twentieth-century whaling, J. N. Tønnessen and A. O. Johnsen, *The History of Modern Whaling* (Berkeley: University of California Press, 1982), 25–36. See also Roy Chapman Andrews, *Whale Hunting with Gun and Camera* (New York: D. Appleton, 1916), 12.

6   Tønnessen and Johnsen, *History of Modern Whaling*, 37–39.

7   Andrews, *Whale Hunting with Gun and Camera*, 132–34.

8   Tønnessen and Johnsen, *History of Modern Whaling*, 36.

9   Lars Christensen, *Such Is the Antarctic* (London: Hodder and Stoughton, 1935), 25–26.

10   John Chrisp, *South of Cape Horn: A Story of Antarctic Whaling* (London: Robert Hale, 1958), 36.

11   Christensen, *Such Is the Antarctic*, 16.

12   Johan Hjort, J. Lie, and Johan Ruud, "Norwegian Pelagic Whaling in the Antarctic," *Scientific Results of Marine Biological Research*, no. 3 (1932).

13   Ibid.

14   Tønnessen and Johnsen, *History of Modern Whaling*, 167, 183–84.

15   Andrews, *Whale Hunting with Gun and Camera*, 1, 20–21.

16   G. R. Clark, report on the eleventh annual meeting of the IWC, 7 July 1959, National Archives of Canada, Ottawa (hereafter NAC), Records of the Department of External Affairs (hereafter RG 25), vol. 5508, File 12386-5-40.

17   Christensen, *Such Is the Antarctic*, 215, 17.

18   Union Whaling Company, *Minutes of Proceedings*, 1950, Durban, South Africa, 28 December 1950.

19   Sir Gerald Elliott, *A Whaling Enterprise: Salvesen in the Antarctic* (Wilby, Norwich, UK: Michael Russell, 1998), 110, 114.

20   Peter Evans, *Ari: The Life and Times of Aristotle Onassis* (New York: Summit, 1986), 139.

21   Garrett Hardin, "The Tragedy of the Commons, *Science* 162, no. 3859 (13 December 1968): 1243–48; Arthur F. McEvoy, *The Fisherman's Problem: Ecology and Law in the California Fisheries, 1850–1980* (Cambridge: Cambridge University Press, 1986).

22   Elliott, *A Whaling Enterprise*, 28.

1. A GLOBAL INDUSTRY AND GLOBAL CHALLENGES

1   Winthrop S. Greene, Third Secretary of Legation, Berne, to Secretary Stimson, 20 December 1932, USNA, RG 59, File 562.8F1.

2   Herman Melville, *Moby-Dick; or, The Whale* (1851; reprint, New York: Modern Library, 1992), 435–40.

3   Sir Gerald Elliott, *A Whaling Enterprise: Salvesen in the Antarctic* (Wilby, Norwich, UK: Michael Russell, 1998), 24.

4   J. N. Tønnessen and A. O. Johnsen, *The History of Modern Whaling* (Berkeley: University of California Press, 1982), 197–98, 264–67, 348–51. The authors discuss at length the various technical breakthroughs in cookers, piping, and centrifuges that were also helpful in making floating factories workable.

5   A firsthand account of the working areas of a whaling ship in the late 1940s can be found in Elliott, *A Whaling Enterprise*, 74–79. A discussion of decomposition and autolysis can be found in Tønnessen and Johnsen, *History of*

Modern Whaling, 252–54.

6   Tønnessen and Johnsen, *History of Modern Whaling*, 253–63, discusses the workings of the floating factory.

7   Untitled poster, USNA, Records of the Fish and Wildlife Service (hereafter RG 22), "Photomechanical: Posters and Broadsides Promoting the Consumption of Fish, 1916–1918," Slide 22-FP-13; "Now for Whale Meat and Sharkskin Shoes," *Current Opinion* 64 (May 1918): 364–65.

8   John Chrisp, *South of Cape Horn: A Story of Antarctic Whaling* (London: Robert Hale, 1958), 59; Elliott, *A Whaling Enterprise*, 99.

9   Tønnessen and Johnsen, *History of Modern Whaling*, 257–58.

10   Ibid., 263.

11   Elliott, *A Whaling Enterprise*, 16.

12   Tønnessen and Johnsen, *History of Modern Whaling*, 268; Chrisp, *South of Cape Horn*, 29.

13   Karl Brandt, *Whaling and Whale Oil during and after World War II* (Stanford, CA: Food Research Institute, Stanford University, 1948,) 1.

14   Lars Christensen, *Such Is the Antarctic* (London: Hodder and Stoughton, 1935), 109–10.

15   Herschel Johnson and Remington Kellogg, report of the delegates of the United States to the International Whaling Conference, held in London, 14–28 June 1938, p. 16, USNA, RG 59, File 562.8F3.

16   Chrisp, *South of Cape Horn*, 18.

17   W. R. D. McLaughlin, *Call to the South: A Story of British Whaling in Antarctica* (London: White Lion, 1962), 49–51.

18   "Minimum Size of Blue Whales," undated, in collection of documents on the 1938 meeting of whaling nations, USNA, RG 59, File 562.8F2.

19   Tønnessen and Johnsen, *History of Modern Whaling*, 569.

20   Elliott, *A Whaling Enterprise*, 40.

21   The Hvalrådet's discussions can be found in the Riksarkivet, Oslo, Records of the Ministry of Fisheries (hereafter Fiskeridept.).

22   From the diary of Lillemor Rachlew, quoted in Christensen, *Such Is the Antarctic*, 62–63.

23   Rudi Diamant, letter home, 5 January 1950, University of Edinburgh Library, Special Collections (hereafter UEL), Archives of Messrs. Christian Salvesen Ltd. (hereafter Salvesen Papers), Entry H36, Box B2, "Whaling History." Note that two weeks later Diamant admitted, "I am getting a bit cheesed off with the Antarctic."

24   McLaughlin, *Call to the South* (quotation). See also Chrisp, *South of Cape Horn*, 16, which suggests that the challenge of overcoming the weather was enough to lure "the last of the pioneers" to return for months of "hardship, loneliness, acute discomfort and no little danger."

25   Tønnessen and Johnsen, *History of Modern Whaling*, 178–82, discusses sovereignty, but the concept also appears regularly in the British and Australian

archival material, and no doubt the Argentinians and Germans also had it in mind.

26 Unsigned, "Whaling in Ross Dependency," December 1927, National Archives of Australia, Canberra, ACT (hereafter NAA), Records of the Ministry of External Affairs (hereafter MEA Records), Series A981/4, File WHA 9, "Whaling and Sealing—Regulation International Measures. To 15.4.30."

27 Kirkesby-Garstad, letter, Riksarkivet, Olso, Fiskeridept., Fangstkontoret, Box "Begrensning av hvalfangsten Internasjonal Avtale av 24/9/31," File XIc, "Norsk ratifikajson."

28 E. R. Darnley and H. S. Moss Blundell, memorandum on the regulation of whaling, 22 November 1928, NAA, MEA Records, Series A981/4, File WHA 9, "Whaling and Sealing—Regulation International Measures. To 15.4.30."

29 Christensen, *Such Is the Antarctic*, 116.

30 An interesting discussion of the law of the sea and the origins of the idea of "flags of convenience" can be found in William Langewiesche, *The Outlaw Sea: A World of Freedom, Chaos, and Crime* (New York: North Point, 2004).

31 In the Paris Arbitration of 1893, diplomats agreed to provide a sixty-mile buffer around the Pribilof Islands but rejected the US proposal that seals on the high seas would remain American property, and the buffer applied only to Canadian sealers. In the 1911 conventions, the United States compensated other sealing nations for refraining from catching Pribilof-born seals on the high seas. See Kurkpatrick Dorsey, *The Dawn of Conservation Diplomacy: U.S.-Canadian Wildlife Protection Treaties in the Progressive Era* (Seattle: University of Washington Press, 1998), chapters 4 and 5.

32 Elliott, *A Whaling Enterprise*, 144.

33 Chrisp, *South of Cape Horn*, 48–49.

34 Ibid., 71.

35 Protocol Number 11 of the International Fur Seal Conference, 1911; and L. Fletcher, British Museum of Natural History, to Colonial Office, 27 October 1911, both in NAC, RG 25, vol. 1125, File 787.

36 J. Innes Wilson to Lord Harcourt, 8 April 1912, National Archives of Great Britain, Kew, London (hereafter NAGB), Records of the Foreign Office (hereafter FO), FO 371 412/109, pt. 2, "Correspondence Regarding the Preservation of Whales."

37 Elliott, *A Whaling Enterprise*, 15.

38 H. W. Just, Colonial Office, to Foreign Office, 20 April 1912, NAGB, FO 371 412/108, pt. 1.

39 Ibid.

40 L. Mallett, Foreign Office, to Colonial Office, 2 May 1912, NAGB, FO 371 412/108, pt. 1.

41 Prince Lichnowsky, German embassy, to Foreign Office, 27 January 1913, and reply, 10 March 1913, both in NAGB, FO 881/10446, "Further Correspondence

Respecting the Preservation of Whales."

42 Governor General Denman, Canberra, to Lord Harcourt, 1 February 1913, NAC, RG 25, vol. 1125, File 787.

43 William Wakeham to Fisheries Secretary, 26 July 1913, NAC, Records of the Ministry of Fisheries (hereafter RG 23), vol. 1081, File 721–19–5[1]; Harcourt to the Duke of Connaught, Governor General of Canada, 11 March 1914, NAC, RG 25, vol. 1125, File 787.

44 A. Johnston, Deputy Minister of Fisheries, to Deputy Minister, Department of Trade and Commerce, Ottawa, 30 January 1923, NAC, RG 23, vol. 1081, File 721–19–5[2].

45 Minutes of Interdepartmental Conference on the Question of International Control of Whaling, 12 October 1927, NAC, RG 23, vol. 1081, File 721–19–5[3].

46 John W. Field, "Proposed International Action for the Protection of Whales," 9 January 1926, NAA, MEA Records, Series A981/4, File WHA 9, "Whaling and Sealing—Regulation International Measures. To 15.4.30"; minutes of Interdepartmental Conference on the Question of International Control of Whaling, 12 October 1927, NAC, RG 23, vol. 1081, File 721–19–5[3].

47 Sir Sydney Chapman, undated note, NAA, MEA Records, Series A981/4, File WHA 9, "Whaling and Sealing—Regulation International Measures. To 15.4.30."

48 Minutes of the International Committee for the Protection of the Great Cetaceans, 7 April 1927, NAC, RG 23, File 721–19–5[3]. A thorough discussion of the evolution of Suarez's draft and Gruvel's changes can be found in Anna-Katharina Woebse, Weltnaturschutz: Umweltdiplomatie in Volkerbund und Vereinten Nationen, 1920–50 (Frankfurt: Routledge, 2012), 174–98.

49 Minutes of Interdepartmental Conference on the Question of International Control of Whaling, 12 October 1927, NAC, RG 23, vol. 1081, File 721–19–5[3] (quotation); Johan Hjort to the Royal Department of Commerce, Oslo, 10 May 1927, Riksarkivet, Oslo, Fiskeridept., Fangstkontoret, Box "Begrensning av hvalfangsten Internasjonal Avtale av 24/9/31," File Xc.

50 Dominions Office to Oscar Skelton, Ministry of External Affairs, 24 October 1929, NAC, RG 25, vol. 1543, File 455, pt. 1.

51 Ibid.

52 In 1931, Hjort reported that he would seek markets for whale oil in central Europe while he attended the conference in Geneva. Hjort to M. Walnum, 20 August 1931, Riksarkivet, Oslo, Fiskeridept., Fangstkontoret, Box "Begrensning av hvalfangsten Internasjonal Avtale av 24/9/31," File Xc.

53 Hjort to Royal Commerce Department, Oslo, 21 March 1929, Riksarkivet, Fiskeridept., Fangstkontoret, Box "Begrensning av hvalfangsten Internasjonal Avtale av 24/9/31," File Xa.

54 J. O. Borley, "Notes on the Meetings of the Whaling Committee of the International Council for the Exploration of the Sea," 18 April 1929, NAC, RG 25, vol. 1543, File 455, pt. 1.

55 M. S. Casey, High Commission, London, to Prime Minister S. M. Bruce, 17 October 1928, NAA, MEA Records, Series A981/4, File WHA 9, "Whaling and Sealing—Regulation International Measures. To 15.4.30."

56 Hjort to Royal Commerce Department, 21 March 1929, Riksarkivet, Oslo, Fiskeridept., Fangstkontoret, "Box Begrensning av hvalfangsten Internasjonal Avtale av 24/9/31," File Xa.

57 See, for example, D. Graham Burnett, *The Sounding of the Whale: Science and Cetaceans in the Twentieth Century* (Chicago: University of Chicago Press, 2012), 83–90.

58 *Fishing News*, 7 January 1928, NAC, RG 23, vol. 1081, File 721–19–5[3].

59 Ibid.

60 For information on Mackintosh, see his obituary in *Geographical Journal*, 140, no. 3 (October 1974): 524–25.

61 *Fishing News*, 7 January 1928, NAC, RG 23, vol. 1081, File 721–19–5[3].

62 Burnett, *Sounding of the Whale*, 146–53, 446.

63 See Burnett, *Sounding of the Whale*, 148–72, for the details about the development of the marking program. Ray Gambell reported in 1969 that 14,000 marks had been placed, with only 1,200 having been recovered. Gambell to P. A. Belton, 8 May 1969, International Whaling Commission Archives, Cambridge, England (hereafter IWC), File K 943, "Miscellaneous Correspondence: July 1973–March 1975."

64 S. F. Harmer, "Warning as to the Effect of the Growth of Antarctic Whaling on the Future of the Whaling Industry," 20 August 1930, NAGB, FO 371 14921 W1/50, 10033.

65 Unsigned, "Note as to Measures Designed for the Preservation of the Whaling Industry," September 1930, NAGB, FO 371 14921 W1/50, 10035.

66 Ibid.

67 S. F. Harmer, "Notes on the Protection of Whales," 25 November 1930; and J. O. Borley, "Note on Various Proposals for Regulating Whaling," 31 December 1930, both in NAGB, FO 371 15670 255/50.

68 "Whaling Industry and Ross Dependency: Historical Sequel of Incidents," October 1929, Archives New Zealand, Wellington (hereafter ANZ), Records of the Ministry of External Affairs (hereafter MEA Records), ABHS 950/W 4627, File PM 104/6/9/1, pt. 2, "Whaling: General"; Clinton Abbott, Director, Natural History Museum of San Diego, to Secretary Stimson, 2 March 1932, USNA, RG 59, File 562.8F1 (quotation).

69 A. Brazier Howell, Council for the Conservation of Whales, to J. Reuben Clark, State Department, 5 February 1930, USNA, RG 59, File 562.8E1.

70 See Burnett, *Sounding of the Whale*, 197–244, for a lengthy section on Kellogg's work in the 1920s. See also Kellogg, "Whales, Giants of the Sea," *National Geographic* 77, no. 1 (1940): 35–90. Details on Kellogg's life can be found in the pamphlet by Frank C. Whitmore, *Memorial to Remington Kellogg, 1892–1969* (Boulder, CO: Geological Society of America, 1969).

71 The Berlin draft and the attached "Report to the Economic Committee on the Question of Whaling," April 1930, can be found in NAC, RG 25, vol. 1543, File 455, pt. 1.

72 P. A. Clutterbuck to A. W. Leeper, 27 November 1930; and Leeper's notes, 1 December 1930, both in NAGB, FO 371 14932 W382/50.

73 Robert Phillips, Liaison Officer, Commerce Department, to Wilbur Carr, Assistant Secretary of State, 19 September 1930, USNA, RG 59, File 562.8F1.

74 The most convenient location for finding the full text of the convention is Mark Cioc's *The Game of Conservation: International Treaties to Protect the World's Migratory Animals* (Athens: Ohio University Press, 2009), appendix C. Cioc argues that the 1931 convention missed opportunities to establish sanctuaries and closed seasons because Britain and Norway protected the interests of their industries (128). A copy can also be found in USNA, RG 59, File 562.8F1/25.

75 ICW/1938/33D, "New Article Concerning Killing of Right Whales," USNA, RG 59, File 562.8F3.

76 Unsigned, "Note as to Measures Designed for the Preservation of the Whaling Industry," September 1930, NAGB, FO 371 14921 W1/50, 10035.

77 Minutes of the thirtieth meeting of the Polar Committee, 22 October 1930, NAGB, FO 371 14921 W1/50, 11125.

78 J. Prentiss Gilbert to Stimson, 26 June 1931 (on the league's position and quotation on flags of convenience); Gilbert to Stimson, 8 January 1932 (on signing); and press release, 31 March 1932 (second quotation), all in USNA, RG 59, File 562.8F1.

79 S. F. Harmer, memorandum of interview with Mr. F. D'Arcy Cooper, 17 March 1932, NAGB, Records of the Ministry of Agriculture and Fisheries (hereafter MAF), MAF 41/81 FG 11040A.

80 Minutes of the thirty-first meeting of the Polar Committee, 8 January 1931, NAC, RG 25, vol. 1543, File 455, pt. 1; note from [A. Colby?] on Ambassador Wingfield, Oslo, to Foreign Office, 13 January 1931, NAGB, FO 371 15671 255/50.

81 Fisheries Secretary, note, 13 May 1931, NAGB, MAF 41/80 FG 11040

82 S. F. Harmer to Managing Director, Unilever, 4 March 1932, NAGB, MAF 41/81 FG 11040A.

83 Memorandum of interview with Mr. F. D'Arcy Cooper, 17 March 1932, NAGB, MAF 41/81 FG 11040A.

84 C. Tate Regan to the Colonial Office, 7 December 1931, NAGB, FO 15659 29/50 W14571.

85 Governor General Bledisloe to J. H. Thomas, Dominion Affairs, 22 April 1931 (New Zealand complaint quotation); and Secretary of State for Dominion Affairs to Governor General, Wellington, 31 July 1931 (British cabinet officer quotations), both in ANZ, MEA Records, File PM 104/6/9/1, pt. 2, "Whaling: General."

1   ICW/1938/21, minutes of the fourth session, 17 June 1938, pp. 15–16, USNA, RG 59, File 562.8F3.

2   ICW/1938/39, minutes of the eighth session, 23 June 1938, pp. 4–5, USNA, RG 59, File 562.8F3. For more on Maurice's extensive work on ocean issues as fisheries secretary and president of the International Council for the Exploration of the Sea, see his obituary by Alban Dobson, "Henry Gascoyne Maurice (1874–1950)," *Journal de conseil* 17 (1950): 1–3.

3   G. E. Vereker, note, 13 April 1937, NAGB, FO 371 21078 N97/63, 2002.

4   J. N. Tønnessen and A. O. Johnsen, *The History of Modern Whaling* (Berkeley: University of California Press, 1982), 402–3.

5   Ibid.

6   Tønnessen and Johnsen, *History of Modern Whaling*, 402–4; Moss Blundell, note of a conversation with D'Arcy Cooper, 19 January 1931, NAGB, FO 371 15671 255/50, 1008.

7   Borley, comment on the agreement, 5 July 1932, NAGB, FO 371 16404 627/50, 8104.

8   Ashley Clarke, note, 12 March 1934, attached to Henry Maurice to Undersecretary of State for Foreign Affairs, 8 March 1934, NAGB, FO 371 18494 884/50, 2377; Vogt, Norwegian Legation, to A. W. A. Leeper, 20 March 1934, NAGB, FO 371 18494 884/50, 2764.

9   William Phillips, Acting Secretary of State, to Ambassador Robert Bingham, London, 29 November 1933; and Norbeck to Cordell Hull, 20 August 1935, both in USNA, RG 59, File 562.8F1.

10 J. A. Lyons, Prime Minister, to Premiers of States, 20 June 1934, and "Int'l Convention for the Regulation of Whaling," 16 June 1936, NAA, MEA Records, Series A432, File 1938/693, pt. 1.

11 This paragraph and the previous one come from Vice-Consul A. C. Olsen to Ambassador Wingfield, Oslo, 14 August 1933, NAGB, FO 371 17320 515/50, 9643.

12 This paragraph and the next one come from Wingfield to Simon, 22 May 1934, NAGB, FO 371 18494 884/50, 5185.

13 This paragraph and the previous one come from Cecil Dormer to Sir John Simon, 27 June 1934 and 16 July 1934, NAGB, FO 371 18494 884/50, 6281 and 6848. See also Tønnessen and Johnsen, *History of Modern Whaling*, 407–10.

14 Wingfield to Simon, 16 May 1934, NAGB, FO 371 18494 884/50, 5184.

15 Royal Norwegian Legation, London, to Prime Minister's Office, 1 June 1934, NAGB, FO 371 18494 884/50, 5351.

16 ICW/1938/12, minutes of the first session of the International Whaling Conference, 14 June 1938, USNA, RG 59, File 562.8F3.

17 "Norwegian Journal of Shipping and Commerce," 20 September 1934, NAGB, FO 371 18494 884/50, 8559; H. Waalman to Mr. Paus, 15 November

1934, NAGB, FO 371 18494 884/50, 10107.

18   "Japanese Venture in Antarctic," *Cape Argus*, 11 December 1934, NAGB, FO
      371 19624 246/50, 468.

19   Cecil Dormer, Ambassador, Oslo, to Simon, 14 November 1934, NAGB, FO
      371 18494 884/50 10107; "Japanese Whaling Operations in the Antarctic,"
      unsigned, 24 June 1935, NAGB, FO 371 19625 246/50, 6593.

20   J. O. Borley, "Data Concerning Whaling in Australian and Neighbouring
      Waters," 10 December 1936, NAGB, MAF 41/72 14857, "Whaling, Australian
      Legation."

21   Gaimusho to Royal Norwegian Legation, Tokyo, 31 October 1935, NAGB, FO
      371 19625 246/50, 10730.

22   Dormer to Foreign Office, 24 June 1935 ("play the game"); and A. R. Garran,
      notes, 25 June 1935 ("very thorough and elaborate"), both in NAGB, FO 371
      19625 246/50, 5444.

23   Cecil Dormer, Oslo, to Foreign Office, enclosure, 8 May 1935, NAGB, FO 371
      19624 246/50, 4042.

24   C. L. Paus, Commercial Secretary, Oslo, note on meeting with M. Walnum,
      Norwegian Fisheries Department, 30 July 1935, NAGB, FO 371 19625 246/50,
      6902.

25   Keith Officer, High Commission, London, to External Affairs, 22 May 1936,
      NAA, MEA Records, Series A981/4, File WHA 14, "Whaling and Sealing—
      Convention of 1931."

26   Mawson to Mr. Strahan, Foreign Affairs, 25 September 1936, NAA, MEA
      Records, Series A461/9, File I 345/1/1, pt. 1.

27   Keith Officer to R. A. Wiseman, Dominions Office, 29 October 1934, NAGB,
      FO 371 18495 884/50, 10032.

28   Kellogg to Cuming, 3 April 1937, USNA, RG 59, File 562.8F2.

29   Dormer to Simon, 4 May 1935, NAGB, FO 371 19624 246/50, 4043.

30   On Wohlthat, see "Occupation: Netherlands," *Time* magazine, 3 June 1940.

31   Tønnessen and Johnsen, *History of Modern Whaling*, 411–12.

32   See Franz-Josef Bruggemeier, Mark Cioc, and Thomas Zeller, eds., *How Green
      Were the Nazis? Nature, Environment, and Nation in the Third Reich* (Athens:
      University of Ohio, 2005).

33   Signature illegible, probably A. R. Garran, note, 12 April 1935, NAGB, FO
      371 19624 246/50, 3219.

34   B. A. B. Burrows note, 13 April 1937, NAGB, FO 371 21078 N97/63, 2002.

35   Norsk Sjømannsforbund et al. to Onesimus Andersen, Tønsberg, 20 May
      1936, NAGB, FO 371 20451 W78/50, 6016.

36   *Times* (London), 25 August 1936.

37   Sir Gerald Elliott, *A Whaling Enterprise: Salvesen in the Antarctic* (Wilby, Nor-
      wich, UK: Michael Russell, 1998), 36–37.

38   B. A. B. Burrows, memorandum on the whaling dispute with Norway, 6
      October 1936, NAC, RG 25, vol. 1832, File 248.

39 Hjort and Maurice, memo of conversation, 26 January 1936, NAGB, FO 371 20450 78/50, 779.

40 Note from Royal Norwegian Legation and memo from Laurance Collier, both 8 December 1936, NAGB, FO 371 20453 78/50, 17719.

41 Bingham to Hull, 11 May 1937, USNA, RG 59, File 562.8F2.

42 Collier, note, 13 January 1937, NAGB, FO 371 21078 N97/63, 187. The dentist was Birger Bergersen, who was a professor of anatomy at a dental school. Bergersen was active in whaling diplomacy and usually a voice for conservation into the 1950s, as well as serving as ambassador to Sweden. Maurice was appalled in part because he had long worked with Johan Hjort on the International Council for the Exploration of the Sea (ICES) and at the time was president of that organization. The interactions between Maurice and Hjort can be found in Helen Rozwadowski, *The Sea Knows No Boundaries: A Century of Marine Science under ICES* (Seattle: University of Washington Press, 2002).

43 Maurice to Collier, 9 January 1937, and Burrows, note, 13 January 1937, NAGB, FO 371 21078 N97/63, 187.

44 Ambassador R. H. Clive, Tokyo, to Foreign Office, 6 March 1937, NAGB, FO 371 21078 N97/63, 1262.

45 Clive, *note verbale*, 10 February 1937, NAGB, FO 371 21078 N97/63, 1450.

46 Collier, memo, 6 March 1937, NAGB, FO 371 21078 N97/63 1317.

47 Kellogg to Cuming, 3 April 1937, USNA, RG 59, File 562.8F2.

48 Clive to Foreign Office, 13 April 1937, NAGB, FO 371 21078 N97/63, 2002.

49 Burrows, note for file, 13 April 1937, NAGB, FO 371 21078 N97/63, 2002.

50 ICW/1937/1, memorandum by HM government, 24 May 1937, Smithsonian Institution Archives, Washington, DC (hereafter SIA), International Whaling Conference and International Whaling Commission, 1930–68 (hereafter RU 7195), Box 3, File "London—Int'l Whaling Conference, 1937."

51 ICW/1937/3, minutes of the second plenary session, 25 May 1937, SIA, RU 7165, Box 3, Folder 6.

52 ICW/1937/4, minutes of the second session, afternoon, 25 May 1937, SIA, RU 7165, Box 3, Folder 6.

53 ICW/1937/5, minutes of the third session, 26 May 1937, SIA, RU 7165, Box 3, Folder 6.

54 ICW/1937/6, minutes of the third session, afternoon, 26 May 1937, SIA, RU 7165, Box 3, Folder 6.

55 ICW/1937/9, minutes of the fifth plenary session, afternoon, 1 June 1937, SIA, RU 7165, Box 3, Folder 6.

56 ICW/1938/20, minutes of the third session, afternoon, 16 June 1938, USNA, RG 59, File 562.8F3.

57 The most accessible copy of the treaty is in appendix C of Mark Cioc's *The Game of Conservation: International Treaties to Protect the World's Migratory Animals* (Athens: University of Ohio, 2009).

58 Dormer to Eden, 16 June 1937, NAGB, FO 371 21079 N97/63, 3239.

59 E. K. Scallan, South Africa House, London, to Undersecretary of State for Dominion Office, 6 August 1937, NAGB, FO 371 21079 N97/63, 4068; Carver to Francis Sayre, Assistant Secretary of State, 19 August 1937, USNA, RG 59, File 562.8F2; Willcock to Prime Minister, 9 November 1937, NAA, MEA Records, Series A981/4, File WHA 5, pt. 1, "Whaling and Sealing. Whaling Conference London 1937 & 1938."

60 A. S. Halford note, 30 October 1937, NAGB, FO 371 21080 N/97/63, 5328.

61 Ronald Lindsay, British embassy, Washington, DC, to Cordell Hull, 17 January 1938, USNA, RG 59, File 562.8F2.

62 Kellogg to Harmer, 20 October 1941, SIA, A. Remington Kellogg Papers, 1916–69 (hereafter RU 7170), Box 3, File "Sidney F. Harmer."

63 Jefferson Patterson, Oslo, to Kellogg, 21 September 1938, SIA, RU 7170, Box 7, File "Department of State, Correspondence and Documents, 1930–39."

64 Maurice to Chr. Salvesen and Co., 13 August 1937, UEL, Salvesen Papers, Entry H36, Box B2, "Whaling History", File "Documents Taken to Meeting with Ministry of Transport on 1/11/61 Re: Future of British Whaling."

65 Houston-Bouswall to Foreign Office, 8 September 1937, NAGB, FO 371 21079 N97/63 4537.

66 W. C. Mendenhall, Acting Secretary of Interior, to Attorney General, 17 May 1940, USNA, Records of the Department of Interior, Office of the Secretary, Central Classified Files, 1937–53, 4–28, Bureau of Fisheries, Whaling Operations, Record Group 48. See also Lt. Quentin R. Walsh, *The Whaling Expedition of the Ulysses, 1937–38*, ed. P. J. Capelotti (Tallahassee: Florida State University Press, 2010). Walsh was a hero of the Normandy invasion too, winning a Navy Cross for taking key parts of Cherbourg with a fifty-man force.

67 "U.S. Government Cracks Down on American Whaler for Violating a Treaty with an Undersized Catch," *Life*, 19 December 1938, 11–17.

68 Proceedings of morning session, Preliminary Whaling Conference, Oslo, 19 May 1938, USNA, RG 59, File 562.8F3.

69 Ibid.

70 Antarctic whaling, 1904/5–1938/39, material in connection with International Whaling Conference, 1939, USNA, RG 59, File 562.8F3.

71 Proceedings of morning session, Preliminary Whaling Conference, Oslo, 19 May 1938, USNA, RG 59, File 562.8F3.

72 Kellogg to Hubert Schenck, 24 March 1939, SIA, RU 7170, Box 7, File "Sap-Sc."

73 Article 19, International Agreement for the Regulation of Whaling, 1937, found in Cioc, *Game of Conservation*, 195.

74 Proceedings of morning session, Preliminary Whaling Conference, Oslo, 19 May 1938, USNA, RG 59, File 562.8F3.

75 Ibid.

76 ICW/1938/11, speech of the Minister of Agriculture and Fisheries, William Morrison, 14 June 1938, USNA, RG 59, File 562.8F3.

77 ICW/1938/29, minutes of the fifth session, 20 June 1938, p. 3, USNA, RG 59, File 562.8F3.

78 ICW/1938/13, minutes of the second session, 15 June 1938, p. 10, USNA, RG 59, File 562.8F3.

79 *Japan Times*, 20 June 1937, NAC, RG 25 ("Norwegian-style"); unnamed newspaper quoted by D'Arcy Mercer, Canadian Embassy in Tokyo, to Ottawa, 13 July 1937 ("Brilliant advance"); illegible, Canadian chargé d'affaires in Tokyo, to Ottawa, 13 April 1937 (Japanese unwillingness to negotiate), all in NAC, RG 25, vol. 1834, File 294.

80 ICW/1938/18, minutes of the third session, 18 June 1938, p. 10, USNA, RG 59, File 562.8F3.

81 ICW/1938/21, minutes of the fourth session, 17 June 1938, pp. 13–14, USNA, RG 59, File 562.8F3.

82 ICW/1938/29, minutes of the fifth session, 20 June 1938, pp. 21–22, USNA, RG 59, File 562.8F3.

83 Foreign Office to Ambassador Craigie, 21 June 1938, NAGB, FO 371 22273 124/63, 2941.

84 A. R. Ovens, Consul in Kobe, to Ambassador Craigie, 22 September 1938, NAGB, FO 371 22274 N124/63, 5309; Thomson to Collier, 13 August 1938, NAGB, FO 371 22274 N124/63, 4060; Craigie to Kensuke Horinouchi, Vice-Minister for Foreign Affairs, 23 June 1938, NAGB, FO 371 22273 124/63, 3757.

85 ICW/1938/39, minutes of the eighth session, 23 June 1938, pp. 4–5, USNA, RG 59, File 562.8F3.

86 ICW/1938/29, minutes of the fifth session, pp. 7, 9, USNA, RG 59, File 562.8F3.

87 ICW/1938/23, report of the Sanctuary Committee, USNA, RG 59, File 562.8F3.

88 Elliott, *A Whaling Enterprise*, 42; proceedings of morning session, Preliminary Whaling Conference, Oslo, 19 May 1938, USNA, RG 59, File 562.8F3.

89 ICW/1938/25, minutes of the fourth session, afternoon, 17 June 1938, p. 14, USNA, RG 59, File 562.8F3.

90 ICW/1938/25, minutes of the fourth session, afternoon, 17 June 1938, p. 6, USNA, RG 59, File 562.8F3.

91 Bergersen to Kellogg, 21 January 1939, Riksarkivet, Oslo, Fiskeridept., Fangstkontoret, Series Db, Box "Hvalrådet Diverse," File "Remington Kellogg."

92 Harriman to Hull, 11 July 1938; and Patterson to Hull, 23 July 1938, both in USNA, RG 59, File 562.8F3.

93 Kellogg to Bergersen, 1 April 1939, Riksarkivet, Oslo, Fiskeridept., Fangstkontoret, Series Db, Box "Hvalrådet Diverse," File "Remington Kellogg."

94 "Conditions Added to Whaling Pact," *Japan Advertiser*, 28 June 1938, clipping in NAC, RG 25, G-1, vol. 1823, File 112, pt. 1.

95 Minutes of International Whaling Conference, second session, 17 August 1939, NAC, RG 25, vol. 1823, File 112, pt. 1.

1   This paragraph and the next two are drawn from Remington Kellogg, undated memorandum attached to an 8 February 1944 embassy dispatch from London, USNA, RG 59, File 562.8F4. The unnamed British official might have been Neil Mackintosh, but a number of British officials knew Kellogg from previous years. Kellogg attended at least twenty international whaling meetings without, apparently, leaving any other official record of his undoubtedly numerous unofficial conversations.

2   Rupert Troutbeck to Clement-Davies, 8 September 1939, attached list "'Southern Princess,' Stores from Norway," 1939, NAGB, FO 371 23661 N337/63, 4240.

3   Dobson, memo, 7 October 1939; and Humphreys to Clement-Davies, 10 October 1939, both in NAGB, FO 371 23661 N337/63, 5140 and 5205.

4   French to Collier, 5 December 1939, NAGB, FO 371 23661 N337/63, 7053.

5   Clement-Davies to J. M. Troubeck, 20 September 1939; and Troutbeck to Collier, 29 September, 1939, both in NAGB, FO 371 23661 N337/63, 4635 and 4586.

6   Dobson to Collier, 1 September 1939, NAGB, FO 371 23661 N337/63, 4088.

7   R. Cox, note, 14 September 1939, NAGB, FO 371 23661 N337/63, 4224.

8   J. M. Addis, note, 24 November 1939, NAGB, FO 371 23661 N337/63, 6473.

9   French to Collier, 5 December 1939, NAGB, FO 371 23661 N337/63, 7053.

10 R. H. Dorman Smith to R. S. Morrison, 28 February 1940, and Dobson to Collier, 21 March 1940, NAGB, FO 371 24186 N3/63.

11 E. O. Coote, note, 23 October 1940, NAGB, FO 371 24816 N3/63, 6215.

12 Sir Gerald Elliott, *A Whaling Enterprise: Salvesen in the Antarctic* (Wilby, Norwich, UK: Michael Russell, 1998), 46.

13 H. L. H. Hill, Ministry of Food, to Dobson, 22 April 1943 and A. M. Lowe, note, 26 November 1942, NAGB, MAF 41/1332 FGB 1576.

14 "Some Notes Relating to Antarctic from Dept. of Scientific and Industrial Research," 10 December 1946, ANZ, MEA Records, ABHS 950/W4627, File 104/6/9/1, pt. 6, "Whaling: General."

15 E. V. Raymont, the Returned Sailors', Soldiers' and Airmen's Imperial League of Australia, to Prime Minister Curtain, 3 December 1943, NAA, MEA Records, Series A 461/9, File I 345/1/1, pt. 1, "Fisheries—Whaling Agreement."

16 Demetrio Brazol, "The Whaling Industry," *La Prensa* (Buenos Aires), 10 March 1941, USNA, RG 59, File 562.8F3.

17 Kellogg to Charles Barnes, 30 September 1942, USNA, RG 59, File 562.8F4; Salvesen to Dobson 22 August 1942, NAGB, MAF 41/1332 FGB 1576.

18 J. A. Sutherland-Harris to Dobson, 6 January 1942; and Dobson's reply, 9 January 1942, both in NAGB, MAF 41/1332 FGB 1576.

19 Salvesen to Dobson, 17 August 1942, NAGB, FO 371 32810 N3772, 5657; Dobson to Salvesen, 20 August 1942, and Salvesen's reply, 22 August 1942, both in NAGB, MAF 41/1332 FGB 1576.

20 Discovery Committee, "A Note on the Condition of the Southern Stocks of Whales and the Prospects after the War," undated, NAGB, FO 371 24816 N3/63, 6102.

21 A chart showing all of the losses of floating factories due to combat can be found in J. N. Tønnessen and A. O. Johnsen, *The History of Modern Whaling* (Berkeley: University of California Press, 1982), 743–44.

22 Carmel Finley, *All the Fish in the Sea: Maximum Sustainable Yield and the Failure of Fisheries Management* (Chicago: University of Chicago Press, 2011), 1–6 in particular.

23 "Post-War Whaling Operations," 2 November 1942, NAGB, MAF 41/1332 FGB 1576.

24 "Conference on Post-War Whaling," 8 December 1942, NAGB, FO 371 32810 N3772, 6276.

25 "Post-War Whaling Arrangements," undated, describes a 17 December 1942 meeting, NAGB, MAF 41/1332 FGB 1576.

26 Dobson to E. O. Coote, 25 February 1943; Collier to Foreign Office, 16 March 1943; and Dobson to W. G. Weston, 8 February 1943, all in NAGB, MAF 41/1332 FGB 1576 (quotation).

27 Baines to Dobson, 2 October 1943, NAGB, MAF 41/1333 FGB 2407; Baines to Salvesen, 14 January 1944, UEL, Salvesen Papers, Entry H 36, "Chamber of Shipping, Whaler Section," Fiche 3325.

28 Bevans and Kellogg, memo of conversation, 30 November 1943, USNA, RG 59, File 562.8F3.

29 Sturgeon to Mathews, 1 December 1943, USNA, RG 59, File 562.8F3.

30 Hull to Roosevelt, 9 December 1943, USNA, RG 59, File 562.8F3.

31 Kellogg to Sturgeon, 20 November 1943, USNA, RG 59, File 562.8F4.

32 Minutes of the second meeting, 13 January 1944, NAC, RG 25, vol. 3263, File 6120--40.

33 Salvesen to Col. J. J. Llewellin, 10 April 1944, UEL, Salvesen Papers, Fiche 3326.

34 Salvesen to the editor, *Times* (London), 30 March 1944, and Salvesen to the editor, *Guardian* (Manchester), 31 March 1944, both in UEL, Salvesen Papers, Fiche 3326; Salvesen to partners, 30 June 1958, UEL, Salvesen Papers, Fiche 3347, "Notes on Whaling Regulations and Quotas."

35 Dobson, notes, 3 June 1944, NAGB, MAF 41/1333 FGB 2407.

36 Elliott, *A Whaling Enterprise*, 56.

37 Ambassador Winant to State Department, 20 January 1945, USNA, RG 59, File 562.8F3.

38 British Food Mission, Washington, DC, to Ministry of Food, 7 March 1945, NAGB, MAF 41/1333 FGB 2407.

39 Llewellin to Rob Hudson, 12 March 1945, NAGB, MAF 41/1333 FGB 2407.

40 Lowe to Humphreys, 28 June 1945, NAGB, MAF 41/1334 FGB 3616.

41 Frederic Hudd, Acting High Commissioner, London, to Ministry of External

Affairs, 18 October 1945, NAC, RG 25, vol. 3263, File 6120-40.

42   Gabrielson, "Sanctuaries as a Conservation Measure," 21 November 1945, NAC, RG 23, vol. 1084, File 721-19-5[15], "Legislation, U.S. and Canada, Protection of Whales."

43   "Establishment of Permanent Commission," US no. 5, 21 November 1945, NAC, RG 23, vol. 1084, File 721-19-5[15], "Legislation, U.S. and Canada, Protection of Whales."

44   "World Oils and Fats Position," IWC Paper no. 5, 20 November 1945, NAC, RG 23, vol. 1084, File 721-19-5[15], "Legislation, U.S. and Canada, Protection of Whales."

45   IWC Paper no. 6, opening session, 20 November 1945, NAC, RG 23, vol. 1084, File 721-19-5[15], "Legislation, U.S. and Canada, Protection of Whales."

46   IWC Paper no. 7, afternoon session, 20 November 1945, NAC, RG 23, vol. 1084, File 721-19-5[15], "Legislation, U.S. and Canada, Protection of Whales."

47   Chairman's remarks at morning session, 23 November 1945, SIA, RU 7165, Box 8, Folder 1. Had Dobson been fair, he would have acknowledged that the Senate had been very quick to give consent to the 1937 convention.

48   Ibid.

49   W. C. Smith, Secretary of Marine, to Head, Prime Minister's Department, 13 March 1946, ANZ, MEA Records, ABHS 950, W4627, File PM 104/6/9/1, pt. 3B, "Whaling: General."

50   Acheson to US embassy, London, 29 March 1946, USNA, RG 59, "File 562.8 London."

51   Dobson to Crowe, 2 July 1946, NAGB, FO 371 58274 UR 159/851, 5871.

52   Flory to John M. Allison, 18 June 1946, USNA, RG 59, "File 562.8 Washington."

53   Ministry of Food to Food Mission, Washington, DC, 27 March 1946, NAGB, FO 371 58272 UR159/851, 1857; Collier to Ernest Bevin, NAGB, FO 371 58274 UR 159/851, 2361.

54   Sir Donald Vandepeer to Sir Frank Tribe, 14 March 1946, NAGB, FO 371 58272 UR 159/851, 1991.

55   Flory to Allison, 3 September 1946, USNA, RG 59, "File 562.8 London."

56   T. P. Davin, Secretary, External Affairs, to Secretary of Marine, 15 November 1946, ANZ, MEA Records, AAEG 950/646a, File PM 106/4/9/1, pt. 4.

57   IWC/20, minutes of the third session, 21 November 1946, p. 15, US National Archives, College Park, MD, Records of International Conferences, Commissions, and Expositions, United States (hereafter RG 43), Records of the 1946 International Whaling Conference, Entry 246, "Working Papers."

58   Bergersen, for the Hvalrådet, to the Commerce Department, Oslo, 13 September, 1946, Riksarkivet, Oslo, Fiskeridept., Fangstkontoret, Box 4, "Hvalrådets, Karter og meldinger, 1945–47," File 1946.

59   Hvalrådet minutes, 2 November 1946, Item 147, Riksarkivet, Oslo, Fiskeridept., Fangstkontoret, Box 4, "Hvalrådets, Karter og meldinger, 1945–47," File 1946.

60 Brief for minister, International Whaling Conference, undated, NAGB, MAF 41/1335 FGB 3646.

61 IWC/44, minutes of the ninth session, 27 November 1946, p. 5, USNA, RG 43, Entry 246.

62 Bergersen, report from the International Whaling Conference in Washington, DC, 20 November–2 December 1946, Riksarkivet, Oslo, Fiskeridept., Fangstkontoret, Box 3, File V-A-4.

63 Kellogg to Bergersen, 8 April 1946, Riksarkivet, Oslo, Fiskeridept., Fangstkontoret, Series Db, Box "Hvalrådet Diverse," File "Remington Kellogg."

64 The data come from a chart "Pelagic Whaling in the Antarctic," SIA, RU 7165, Box 22, Folder 2. See also Bergersen to Kellogg, 28 March 1946, USNA, RG 43, Entry 241, File "General."

65 Elliott, A Whaling Enterprise, 42.

66 Bergersen to Kellogg, 28 March 1946, USNA, RG 43, Entry 241, File "General."

67 Collier to Bevin, 10 January 1946, NAGB, FO 371 58271 UR 159/851, 405.

68 IWC/58, minutes of the thirteenth session, 30 November 1946, pp. 3–7, RG 43, Entry 246. See also William Hitchcock, The Bitter Road to Freedom: A New History of the Liberation of Europe (New York: Free Press, 2008).

69 James Byrnes to SCAP, 26 December 1946, USNA, Records of the Supreme Command of the Allied Powers (hereafter RG 331), Natural Resources Section, Fisheries Division, General Subject File, File 442.2, "1946–7 Japanese Antarctic Whaling Operations."

70 Unsigned, Department of State to US Political Adviser, 26 December 1946, USNA, RG 331, File 442, "Whaling, vol. 1."

71 Bergersen to Kellogg, 14 April 1947, USNA, RG 59, File 894.628; Col. G. R. Powles to Secretary for External Affairs, 10 December 1946, ANZ, MEA Records, ABHS 950, W4627, File 104/6/9/1, pt. 6, "Whaling: General."

72 The US proposal can be found at IWC/3, "United States Proposals for a Whaling Convention," 29 October 1946 (quotation is from p. 2), USNA, RG 43, Entry 246.

73 IWC/11, minutes of the opening Session, 20 November 1946, pp. 1–2, USNA, RG 43, Entry 246.

74 Dobson, note, 16 September 1946, NAGB, MAF 41/1335 FGB 3646.

75 Ibid., 2–3; Corrigendum, USNA, RG 43, Entry 246.

76 IWC/42, address by the Honorable C. Girard Davidson, 26 November 1946, USNA, RG 43, Entry 246. Davidson's quotations in the following paragraphs are from this source.

77 An account of fur seal diplomacy can be found in Kurkpatrick Dorsey, The Dawn of Conservation Diplomacy: U.S.-Canadian Wildlife Protection Treaties in the Progressive Era (Seattle: University of Washington Press, 1998), chapters 4–5.

78 Powles to Secretary of External Affairs, Wellington, 9 December 1946, ANZ, MEA Records, AAEG 950/647a, File PM 104/6/9/1, pt. 5, File "Whaling: General."

79 Memo, Flory to W. C. Armstrong, Soviet Participation in Whaling Conference, 6 December 1946, USNA, RG 43, Entry 243, File "USSR."

80 Unless otherwise noted, quotations in the next paragraph are from IWC/47, minutes of the tenth session, 27 November 1946, USNA, RG 43, Entry 246.

81 Powles to Secretary of External Affairs, Wellington, 9 December 1946, ANZ, MEA Records, AAEG 950/647a, File PM 104/6/9/1, pt. 5, File "Whaling: General."

82 IWC/56, minutes of the twelfth session, 29 November 1946, p. 8, USNA, RG 43, Entry 246.

83 Powles to Secretary of External Affairs, Wellington, 9 December 1946, ANZ, MEA Records, AAEG 950/647a, File PM 140/6/9/1, pt. 5, File "Whaling General 1946."

84 IWC/14, minutes of the second session, 20 November 1946, pp. 18–20, USNA, RG 43, Entry 246.

85 The text of the ICRW is easily found at the IWC's Web site, http://iwc.int/convention.

86 IWC/22, minutes of the fourth session, 21 November 1946, pp. 3–6, USNA, RG 43, Entry 246.

87 Bergersen, report from the International Whaling Conference in Washington, DC, 20 November–2 December 1946, 15 January 1947, Riksarkivet, Oslo, Fiskeridept., Fangstkontoret, Box 3, File V-A-4.

88 IWC/32, minutes of the seventh session, 25 November 1946, pp. 29–30, USNA, RG 43, Entry 246.

89 IWC/22, minutes of the fourth session, 22 November 1946, p. 7, USNA, RG 43, Entry 246. And see, for instance, Bergersen to Kellogg, 28 October 1946, SIA, RU 7165, Box 9, Folder 2.

90 State Department to Kellogg, 21 December 1943, and A. J. Drexel Biddle Jr., to Hull, 17 August 1943, USNA, RG 59, File 562.8F4; Carver to Flory, 17 October 1946, and Flory's reply, 30 October 1946, USNA, RG 59, File 894.628.

91 Elliott, *A Whaling Enterprise*, 51.

92 Gabrielson to George Marshall, 10 October 1947, USNA, RG 59, File 562.8 Washington.

93 Mark Cioc, *The Game of Conservation: International Treaties to Protect the World's Migratory Animals* (Athens: Ohio University Press, 2009), 132.

94 A. J. Drexel Biddle Jr. to Hull, 17 August 1943, USNA, RG 59, File 562.8F4. Biddle was stationed in London and reported on a meeting with Bergersen.

95 Kellogg to Bergersen, 8 April 1946, Riksarkivet, Oslo, Fiskeridept., Fangstkontoret, Series Db, Box "Hvalrådet Diverse," File "Remington Kellogg." Kellogg reported his conversation with Maurice to Bergersen.

96 Ibid.

97 Kellogg et al. to the Secretary of State, undated, report of the delegation of the United States to the International Whaling Conference, USNA, RG 43, Entry 242, File 1946, "Meeting I."

98   Kellogg to J. E. Hamilton, 16 December 1946, SIA, RU 7165, Box 9, Folder 2.

99   Unsigned, Department of State to US political adviser, 26 December 1946, USNA, RG 331, File 442, "Whaling, vol. 1."

100 Dobson, report by the British delegation, 20 December 1946, NAGB, MAF 41/1335 FGB 3646.

101 J. Hasler, note, 20 December 1946, and C. T. Crowe, note, 26 December 1946, NAGB, FO 371 58583 UR 159/87, 10106; A. F. Geolot to Crowe, 7 December 1946, NAGB, FO 371 58583 UR 159/87, 10423.

102 Bergersen to Kellogg, 14 April 1947, USNA, RG 59, File 894.628. Bergersen's report from the International Whaling Conference in Washington, DC, can be found in Riksarkivet, Oslo, Fiskeridept., Fangstkontoret, Box 3, File V-A-4.

103 H. Thomson, Acting Secretary of Commerce and Agriculture, to Cunningham, 28 November 1946; and Frank Anderson, "Ratification of Whaling Convention," 22 September 1947, both in NAA, MEA Records, Series A605, File M15/4/5 "International Convention for the Regulation of Whaling."

104 Bergersen, report on the first meeting of the IWC, 23 June 1949, Riksarkivet, Oslo, Fiskeridept., Fangstkontoret, Box 22, File V-F-2-c.

105 "The International Whaling Commission," FAO Fisheries Bulletin 3, no. 2 (March/April 1950): 31–32, IWC, File H 910, "FAO Correspondence, 1949–74."

106 Kellogg to Bergersen, 27 November 1950, SIA, RU 7165, Box 11, File 5.

107 Wilhelm Morgenstierne to Birger Bergersen, 15 June 1951, Riksarkivet, Oslo, Fiskeridept., Fangstkontoret, Box 24, 1950–53, File V-F-4-b.

108 Kellogg to Col. Hubert Schenck, 20 June 1952, SIA, Records of the Director, US National Museum (A. Remington Kellogg) (hereafter RU 88), Box 6, Folder "Scattergood to Scully."

109 Report, 22 August 1951, Riksarkivet, Oslo, Fiskeridept., Box "Hvalrådets Karter og meldinger, 1948–51," Melding 7.

110 Van Tienhoven, President, Niederlandsche Commissie voor Internationale Natuurbescherming, to President of IWC, 3 July 1951, and Mackintosh to Dobson, 7 June 1952, IWC, File H 913 "IUCN Correspondence."

111 Dobson circular, 12 September 1949, USNA, RG 59, File 562.8 IWC (this file also contains the full transcripts of the 1949 meeting, including French concerns).

112 Bergersen, meetings in London, 21–24 November 1951, Riksarkivet, Oslo, Fiskeridept., Fangstkontoret, Box 24, File V-F-5-b.

113 Kellogg to Bergersen, 16 February 1951, SIA, RU 7165, Box 11, File 5.

4. CHEATERS SOMETIMES PROSPER

1   Quoted in Walter LaFeber, The Clash: U.S.-Japanese Relations throughout History (New York: Norton, 1997), 260.

2   Meeting in Mr. Sturgeon's office, 20 November 1943, USNA, RG 43, Entry 242, File "1944 Protocol."

3   Harry N. Scheiber, *Inter-Allied Conflict and Ocean Law, 1945–53: The Occupation Command's Revival of Japanese Whaling and Marine Fisheries* (Taipei: Academia Sinica, 2001), 70.

4   Schenck, "Natural Resources Problems in Japan," undated, presented in London in late 1948 or 1949, USNA, RG 331, Box 8866, File "Correspondence."

5   John W. Dower, *Embracing Defeat: Japan in the Wake of World War II* (New York: Norton, 1999), 45–51.

6   Schenck, memo for record, 17 September 1947, USNA, RG 331, Box 8866, File "Fisheries: Check Notes, etc., 1947–48." See also Dower, *Embracing Defeat*, 90–103, 115, for the gruesome details of Japanese hunger in the aftermath of the war and a brief discussion of Japanese financial support for the occupation army.

7   J. T. Smith to Thompson, Controller of Fisheries, 13 August 1946; and "Japanese Fishing Areas," 6 July 1946, both in NAA, MEA Records, Series A1067, File P46/10/10/3/1, pt. 1, "Japan—Whaling in Antarctica."

8   See Scheiber, *Inter-Allied Conflict*, 59, for a map of the fishing areas open to the Japanese. On 1945 whaling, see SCAPIN 233 H. W. Allen, Col AGD, 3 November 1945, USNA, RG 331, Box 8870, File "1948–49, Antarctic Whaling, Fisheries Division."

9   "Whaling, Rough Notes on Meeting," 11 December 1945, USNA, RG 43, Entry 243, File "Japan, 1938–1945."

10   Croker, memo, 29 January 1946, USNA, RG 331, Box 8980, File 442, "Whaling vol. 1."

11   Humphries, memo for file, 11 April 1946, USNA, RG 331, Box 8980, File 442, "Whaling vol. 1."

12   Schenck to Chief of Staff, Department of War, 16 April 1946, and Acheson to SCAP, 16 May 1946, RG 331, File 442.2, "1946–7 Japanese Antarctic Whaling Operations."

13   "Japanese Whaling Operations in the Antarctic," 6 August 1946, ANZ, MEA Records, ABHS 950, Acc W4627, EA 1 W2619, File 268/5/15, "Japan: Economic Affairs, Whaling and Fishing Industries."

14   Schenck, memo for file, 13 August 1946, USNA, RG 331, File 442.2, "1946–7 Japanese Antarctic Whaling Operations."

15   "Whaling," USNA, RG 331, Box 8873, File "Fisheries Program in Japan, 1945–51."

16   Capt. William Terry, note for record, "From: SCAP, to Secretary of Army NH-Fi," undated [May 1949], USNA, RG 331, Box 8875, File "1949–50 Antarctic Whaling."

17   External Affairs, Wellington, to External Affairs, Canberra, 15 August 1946, NAA, MEA Records, Series A4534, File 46/2/5, "Asia Japan—Whaling."

18   Embassy, Washington, DC, to External Affairs, Canberra, 22 August 1946, NAA, MEA Records, Series A1067, File 46/38/2, "Whaling Industry in Australia."

19   External Affairs, Canberra, to External Affairs, Wellington, 27 August 1946, NAA, MEA Records, Series A4534, File 46/2/5, "Asia Japan—Whaling."

20   Dominions Office to Australia, repeat to New Zealand, 22 August 1946, NAC, RG 23, vol. 1084, File 721–19–5[16], "Legislation."

21   Australian embassy, Washington, DC, to Ministry of External Affairs, Canberra, 25 June 1947, NAA, MEA Records, Series A1067, File P46/10/10/3/1, pt. 2.

22   Dominions Office to Prime Minister of New Zealand, 25 September 1946, NAA, MEA Records, Series A4534, File 46/2/5, "Asia Japan—Whaling"; Clayton, State Department, to SCAP, 11 September 1946, USNA, RG 331, Box 8980, File 442.2, "1946–7 Japanese Antarctic Whaling Operations."

23   John C. Aird, HM Consul, Oslo, to Commercial Secretary, 30 June 1947, NAGB, FO 371 62880 UE 1500/71, 6147.

24   G. R. Powles, memorandum for Secretary of External Affairs, Wellington, "Japanese Whaling," 9 December 1946, ANZ, MEA Records, AAEG 950, File PM 104/6/9/1, pt. 5, "Whaling—General 1946."

25   Atcheson to War Department, 13 September 1946, USNA, RG 331, File 442.2, "1946–7 Japanese Antarctic Whaling Operations."

26   Terry, memo, 31 March 1949, USNA, RG 331, Box 8980, File 442.5, "Whaling—Antarctic."

27   Maj. John Janssen Jr., memo for record, 30 December 1946, USNA, RG 331, Natural Resources Section, Fisheries Division, General Subject File, 1945–51, File "Fisheries: Check Notes, Memoranda, and Allied Papers Pertaining to Fisheries, 1945–46."

28   Address by Colonel Fiedler (given by Capt. John Kask), 7 July 1946, USNA, RG 331, Natural Resources Section, Fisheries Division, General Subject File, 1945–51, File "Fisheries: Check Notes, Memoranda, and Allied Papers Pertaining to Fisheries, 1945–46."

29   Radio programs on fisheries subjects, 13 November 1946, USNA, RG 331, File "Fisheries: Check Notes, Memoranda, and Allied Papers Pertaining to Fisheries, 1945–46."

30   Herrington, memo for record, 14 March 1947, USNA, RG 331, Natural Resources Section, Fisheries Division, General Subject File, 1945–51, File "Fisheries: Check Notes, Memoranda, and Allied Papers Pertaining to Fisheries, 1946–47."

31   Lt. A. F. Berol, memo for record, 27 November 1946, USNA, RG 331, File "Fisheries: Check Notes, Memoranda, and Allied Papers Pertaining to Fisheries, 1945–46."

32   Schenck, memo for record, 30 October 1947, USNA, RG 331, Box 8876, File "Whaling Data."

33   Wm. C. Neville, Fisheries Division, memo for record, 12 November 1947, USNA, RG 331, File "Fisheries: Check Notes, Memoranda, and Allied Papers Pertaining to Fisheries, 1946–47."

34 "Address by Lt Col Schenck at the Ceremonies Celebrating the Sailing of Japanese Antarctic Whaling Fleets, 12 and 13 November 1948," USNA, RG 331, Box 8870, File "1948–49 Antarctic Whaling."

35 Memo for record, "Departure of Nisshin Maru No. 1 for Antarctic, 1 November 1949," 3 November 1949, USNA, RG 331, Box 8875, File "1949–50 Antarctic Whaling."

36 For SCAP's and Washington's policies toward rebuilding Japan's fishing industry, see Scheiber, *Inter-Allied Conflict*; and Carmel Finley, *All the Fish in the Sea: Maximum Sustainable Yield and the Failure of Fisheries Management* (Chicago: University of Chicago Press, 2011).

37 Anderson to Mr. Critchley, undated [October 1946], NAA, MEA Records, Series A1067/1, File P46/10/10/3/1, pt. 1.

38 Forsyth, draft telegram for Watt, Acting Secretary, External Affairs, undated, NAA, MEA Records, Series A1067/1, File P46/10/10/3/1, pt. 1.

39 Attlee to the Prime Minister, 1 August 1947, ANZ, MEA Records, ABHS 950/ W4627, File 104/6/9/1, pt. 6, "Whaling: General."

40 Unsigned memo for Arnott, 5 November 1946, NAA, MEA Records, Series A1067, File P46/10/10/3/1, pt. 1, "Japan—Whaling in Antarctica."

41 Coonan to Schenck, 3 April 1947, NAA, MEA Records, Series A1067, File P46/10/10/3/1, pt. 1, "Japan—Whaling in Antarctica"; SCAP, Diplomatic Section, to Australian Mission, 3 June 1947, NAA, MEA Records, Series A1067/1, File P46/10/10/3/1, pt. 2. Coonan's report can be found in NAA, MEA Records, Series A4534/1, File 46/2/5.

42 Anderson to Secretary, External Affairs, 15 April 1947, NAA, MEA Records, Series A4534, File 46/2/5, "Asia Japan—Whaling." The American officer on board, Lt. David McCracken, wrote a book, *Four Months aboard a Jap Whaler* (New York: National Travel Club, 1948), that generally painted the Japanese in a positive light.

43 Coonan to Director of Commonwealth Fisheries Office, 16 August 1950, NAA, MEA Records, Series AA19820/28 272/515, pt. 2, "Australian Whaling Commission (dept of C&A)."

44 Coonan, undated report, spring 1948, and press release, Far East Command, 16 April 1948, NAA, MEA Records, A1838/283 479/3/4/1, pt. 5.

45 Herman Sundt, "The Conditions on Board," 25 March 1948, Riksarkivet, Oslo, Fiskeridept., Fangstkontoret, Box 58, File XII-16, "Japan."

46 Radio Tokyo, 8 April 1948, NAA, MEA Records, Series A1838/283, File 479/3/4/1, pt. 5.

47 Schenck, memo for record, 9 April 1948 and 17 April 1948, USNA, RG 331, File 442.3, "1947–48," vol. 2.

48 Dunn to D. F. MacDermott, 15 May 1947, NAGB, FO 371 63768 FE 1382/23, 6700.

49 "Whaling," USNA, RG 331, Box 8873, File "Fisheries Programs in Japan, 1945–51."

50 Terry, "Memorandum for: Head, Processing and Production Branch," 21 February 1950, USNA, RG 331, Box 8878, File "Miscellaneous—Whaling 1950."

51 R. M. Miller, report on the sixth meeting of the International Whaling Commission, 3 August 1954, ANZ, MEA Records, EA W2619, File PM 104/6/9/1, pt. 13, "Whaling: General."

52 Wilhelm Morgenstierne to Birger Bergersen, 5 June 1951, Riksarkivet, Oslo, Fiskeridept., Hvalrådets, Box 24, File V-F-4-b.

53 Bergersen to Kellogg, 7 September 1950, SIA, RU 7165, Box 11, Folder 5; Dobson to Acheson, 30 April 1951, and Ambassador Frank Siscoe, Rome, to Acheson, 30 July 1951, both in USNA, RG 59, File 398.246. For financial reasons, the *Peron* never was used as a whaler. J. N. Tønnessen and A. O. Johnsen, *The History of Modern Whaling* (Berkeley: University of California Press, 1982), 538–40.

54 Details can be found in Tønnessen and Johnsen, *History of Modern Whaling*, 534–38, 552–60, as well as in IWC, File A 541, "Olympic Challenger 1956 Papers."

55 The FBI file on Onassis (BUFILE: 100–125834) can be found at http://vault. fbi.gov/Aristotle Onassis (accessed 15 June 2012).

56 Peter Evans, *Ari: The Life and Times of Aristotle Onassis* (New York: Summit, 1986), 101, 112.

57 Ibid., 113–15.

58 Taylor, "Draft Instructions for Kellogg," 12 June 1950, USNA, RG 59, File 398.246. Evans, in *Life and Times of Aristotle Onassis*, 111–13, reported that Onassis got into whaling as a way of skirting occupation rules about the use of German shipyards.

59 Birger Bergersen to Remington Kellogg, 3 May 1952, SIA, RU 7165, Box 11, File 5.

60 Quoted in Evans, *Life and Times of Aristotle Onassis*, 112.

61 State Department to US embassy, Tegucigalpa, 13 December 1951, USNA, RG 59, File 398.246; Day to G. H. Helmbold, Federal Maritime Board, 29 May 1950, SIA, RU 7165, Box 23, Folder 1.

62 Dobson to Bergersen, 8 November 1948, USNA, RG 59, File 398.246.

63 Kellogg to Secretary of State, 19 September 1951, USNA, RG 59, File 398.246.

64 Evans, *Life and Times of Aristotle Onassis*, 113.

65 *Nordsee Zeitung*, Bremerhaven, 14 June 1951, translation in USNA, RG 59, File 398.246; Sir Peter Scarlett, Oslo, to Harry Hohler, Foreign Office, 19 September 1955, NAGB, FO 371 115384 G6/46.

66 Clough, Panama City, to Foreign Office, 24 November 1954, NAGB, FO 371 110654 G6/74.

67 R. G. R. Wall, report on the sixth annual meeting of the International Whaling Commission, 25 August 1954, FO 371 110654 G6, 32. Socrates was Onassis's middle name, but it seems more as if Wall confused philosophers than chose to use Onassis's middle name.

68 Corner, International Whaling Commission, seventh annual meeting, undated report, ANZ, MEA Records, EA 1, File 104/6/9/1, pt. 14, "Whaling: General, 1955–56."

69 For some background on the Truman Doctrine and the tuna fishing issues, see Finley, *All the Fish in the Sea*, 48, 122–24, 134–35; and Scheiber, *Inter-Allied Conflict*, 9–13, 30–34.

70 S. E. Tomkins, Secretary, Salvage Association of London (Lloyd's), to Undersecretary of State of Foreign Office, 18 November 1954, NAGB, FO 371 110656 G6, 62; Indictment, 26 November 1954, NAGB, FO 371 110657 G6/105.

71 Montagu Pollack, Lima, to Foreign Office, 15 December 1954, NAGB, FO 371 110657 G6/106; Indictment, 26 November 1954, NAGB, FO 371 110657 G6/105.

72 The discussion about Onassis with Peru can be found in NAGB, FO 371 110656 G6. See also "Cargo of Whaler to Be Confiscated," *New York Times*, 27 March 1956; and Evans, *Life and Times of Aristotle Onassis*, 122, 141.

73 Tønnessen and Johnsen, *History of Modern Whaling*, 556–59.

74 Salvesen to Fisheries Secretary Gardner, 16 November 1962, NAGB, MAF 209/2128 FGB 20535. This lengthy document is Salvesen's brief history of the whaling industry.

75 Tønnessen and Johnsen, *History of Modern Whaling*, 515, 523.

76 B. C. Hill to G. R. B. Patterson, 14 June 1955, NAA, MEA Records, Series A1838/1, File 704/8/1.

77 Smith, note for file, 28 April 1955, NAGB, MAF 209/1436 FGB 13423.

78 Anderson, memorandum for the Secretary of External Affairs, 29 March 1955, NAA, MEA Records, Series A1838/1, File 704/8/1.

79 Frank Corner, report on the meeting of the International Whaling Commission, 7 July 1955, ANZ, MEA Records, EA 1, File 104/6/9/1, pt. 14, "Whaling: General, 1955–56."

80 Salvesen to Melsom, Chairman of Hvalfangstselskapers Forbund, Sandefjord, 1 May 1953, NAGB, MAF 209/1436 FGB 13423. Because it was legal to hunt sperm whales outside of the baleen whale season, Soviet officials sometimes claimed that whales caught before the season opened were actually sperm whales and hence legal.

81 J. N. Wood, Ministry of Transport, to Mr. Savage, MAF, 5 June 1956, NAGB, MAF 209/994 FGB 10179.

82 Emil Kekich, Commercial Attaché, London, to State Department, 24 November 1958, USNA, RG 59, File 398.246.

83 Corner, "International Whaling Commission: Tenth Annual Meeting," 12 July 1958, ANZ, MEA Records, AAEG 950/649b, File PM 104/6/9/1, pt. 19, "Whaling: General."

84 *Fishing News*, 21 November 1958, reported in Emil Kekich, US embassy, London, to State Department, 24 November 1958, USNA, RG 59, File 398.246.

85 On early efforts at marking and insights on use of the data in the 1960s, see

D. Graham Burnett, *The Sounding of the Whale: Science and Cetaceans in the Twentieth Century* (Chicago: University of Chicago Press, 2012), 153–71, 476, 487.

86 "Whale Marks Recovered by U.S.S.R. Expeditions, Antarctic Whaling Season, 1961/62," undated, NAGB, MAF 209/1790 FGB 17432A.

87 Hugh Gardner, note for file, 25 June 1963, NAGB, MAF 209/1790 FGB 17432A.

88 Richard Funkhouser, US embassy, Moscow, to State Department, 24 March 1964, USNA, RG 59, Central Foreign Policy Files, "INCO Whales—USSR."

89 A. V. Yablokov, ed., *Soviet Antarctic Whaling Data, 1947–72* (Moscow: Center for Russian Environmental Policy, 1995), 43–44, 153–54.

90 This and the next paragraph are drawn from I. V. Golovlev, "The Echo of 'Mystery of Whales,'" in Yablokov, *Soviet Antarctic Whaling Data*, 11–20.

91 Richard Funkhouser, US embassy, Moscow, to State Department, 24 March 1964, USNA, RG 59, Central Foreign Policy Files, "INCO Whales—USSR."

92 Salvesen to Melsom, 1 May 1953, NAGB, MAF 209/1436 FGB 13423.

93 Wall, note, 20 February 1957, NAGB, MAF 209/1652 FGB 15139.

94 H. E. Gorick to Wall, 6 June 1958, NAGB, MAF 209/1670 FGB 15458

95 Kellogg to Bergersen, 30 January 1952, SIA, RU 7165, Box 11, File 5.

96 Bergersen to Morgenstierne, 23 May 1951, Riksarkivet, Oslo, Fiskeridept., Hvalrådets, Box 24, File V-F-4-b.

97 Herrington to Mr. Sowash, 26 April 1956, USNA, RG 59, File 398.246.

98 John Foster Dulles to US embassy, London, 6 February 1956, USNA, RG 59, File 398.246.

99 Wilcox to Kellogg, 28 June 1956, USNA, RG 59, File 398.246.

100 Dulles to Eisenhower, 6 February 1957, USNA, RG 59, File 398.246

101 Herrington, memo to Ambassador Dreier, 24 August 1954, USNA, RG 59, File 398.246.

102 Chancery, Tokyo, to Foreign Office, 18 August 1961, NAGB, FO 371 158624 G63/33.

103 Clark, report of the fourteenth meeting of the IWC, 2 August 1962, NAC, RG 25, Series G-2, vol. 5508, File 12386–5–40.

104 Kellogg, report of the US commissioner to the sixteenth meeting of the IWC, 15 August 1964, USNA, RG 59, File "INCO—Whales and Whaling, Organizations and Conferences, 1/1/64."

105 See editor's note in A. A. Berzin, "The Truth about Soviet Whaling," *Marine Fisheries Review* 70, no. 2 (March 2009): 20.

5. MELTING DOWN AND MUDDLING THROUGH

1 W. G. Solberg, "The International Whaling Commission's 16th Annual Meeting in Sandefjord," 30 June 1964, Riksarkivet, Oslo, Fiskeridept., Box "Hvalrådet karter og melding, 1963–67," Bilag til Kart III Melding 3, 1964.

2 G. L. O'Halloran, report of the New Zealand delegation to the sixteenth annual

meeting of the International Whaling Commission, 8 July 1964, ANZ, MEA Records, AAEG 950/650a, File PM 104/6/9/1, pt. 20, "Whaling—General."

3   Unsigned memo, "International Whaling Commission—Possibility of United Kingdom Withdrawal," July 1964, NAGB, MAF 209/2354 FGB 22242.

4   Kellogg to Hugh Gardner, 13 August 1964, SIA, RU 7165, Box 27, Folder 3.

5   J. A. Gulland, "International Whaling Commission: 16th Meeting, Sandefjord, Norway," 2 July 1964, NAGB, MAF 209/2354 FGB 22242.

6   Gerald Elliott to Gulland, 26 August 1964, UEL, Salvesen Papers, Entry H36, File "HKS Whaling Incorporating IWC Correspondence," Fiche 3355.

7   Sir Gerald Elliott, A Whaling Enterprise: Salvesen in the Antarctic (Wilby, Norwich, UK: Michael Russell, 1998), 94.

8   R. G. R. Wall, report on the sixth annual meeting of the International Whaling Commission, 25 August 1954, NAGB, FO 371 110654 G6.

9   Dawbin to the Secretary, Marine Department, 2 June 1960 and 10 November 1960, ANZ, MEA Records, AAEG 950/657a, File PM 104/6/9/5, pt. 1, "IWC Meetings of Scientific Committees, 1958–62."

10 D. Graham Burnett, The Sounding of the Whale: Science and Cetaceans in the Twentieth Century (Chicago: University of Chicago Press, 2012), 365–70, discusses the separation of the Technical and Scientific Committees from one another.

11 Corner, "International Whaling Commission: Eighth Annual Meeting," undated report, ANZ, MEA Records, EA 1, File PM 104/6/9/1, pt. 15, "Whaling—General, 1956."

12 Bergersen to Erik Moe, 4 August 1954, Riksarkivet, Oslo, Fiskeridept., Fangstkontoret, Box 25, File V-F-7.

13 Corner, "International Whaling Commission: Eighth Annual Meeting," undated report, ANZ, MEA Records, EA 1, File PM 104/6/9/1 pt. 15, "Whaling—General, 1956."

14 Interview with Watson Perrygo, August–December 1978, SIA, Record Unit 9516, and interview with Herbert Friedmann, April 1975, SIA, Record Unit 9506, Oral History Project.

15 Corner, "International Whaling Commission: Eighth Annual Meeting," undated report, ANZ, MEA Records, EA 1, File PM 104/6/9/1, pt. 15, "Whaling—General, 1956."

16 See chapter 4 for a lengthy discussion of Soviet whaling fraud.

17 Corner, "International Whaling Commission: Fifth Annual Meeting," 8 July 1953, ANZ, MEA Records, AAEG 950/649a, File PM 104/6/9/1, pt. 12, "Whaling—General, 1952–53."

18 Birger Bergersen, International Whaling Commission, "Scientific Subcommittees' Report (Fifth Meeting. Document II)," and appendix, 12 March 1953, USNA, RG 59, File 398.246.

19 J. M. Marchand to the Secretary, IWC, 23 April 1953, included in "Fifth Meeting, Document X," USNA, RG 59, File 562.8F4; John F. Stone,

"International Whaling Commission—July, 1951, Notes," SIA, RU 7165, Box 23, Folder 3.

20 Bergersen, "The Condition of the Antarctic Whale Stocks," 12 March 1953, USNA, RG 43, File "International Whaling Commission, 1953."

21 International Whaling Commission, "Memorandum of the Dutch Delegation on the Reduction of the 16,000 Blue Whale Units," May 1953, USNA, RG 59, File 398.246.

22 G. R. Clark, memorandum, 9 February 1959, NAC, RG 25, vol. 7755, File 12386.5.40, pt. 13.

23 Corner, "International Whaling Commission: Tenth Annual Meeting," 12 July 1958, ANZ, MEA Records, AAEG 950/649b, File PM 104/6/9/1, pt. 19, "Whaling—General."

24 See, for instance, two papers by Norwegian economist Tore Schweder, "Distortion of Uncertainty in Science: Antarctic Fin Whales in the 1950s," *Journal of International Wildlife Law and Policy* 3, no. 1 (2000): 73–92, and "Protecting Whales by Distorting Uncertainty: Non-precautionary Management?" *Fisheries Research* 52 (2001): 217–25.

25 Unsigned, "Australian Brief, Fifth Meeting—International Whaling Commission," undated, NAA, MEA Records, Series A1838/1, File 1514/3, pt. 2.

26 W. C. Smith to Secretary of External Affairs, 17 September 1953, ANZ, MEA Records, AAEG 950/649a, File PM 104/6/9/1, pt. 12, "Whaling—General, 1952–53."

27 Corner to the Secretary of External Affairs, 8 July 1953, ANZ, MEA Records, AAEG 950/649a, File PM 104/6/9/1, pt. 12, "Whaling—General, 1952–53."

28 Kellogg, report of the US commissioner on the fifth annual meeting of the IWC, 24 July 1953, USNA, RG 59, File 398.246.

29 Corner to the Secretary of External Affairs, 8 July 1953, ANZ, MEA Records, AAEG 950/649a, File PM 104/6/9/1, pt. 12, "Whaling—General, 1952–53."

30 Kellogg, report of the US delegate to the sixth annual meeting of the IWC, July 1954, USNA, RG 59, File 398.246.

31 Wall, report on the sixth annual meeting of the IWC, 25 August 1954, NAGB, FO 371 110654 G6.

32 B. C. Hill to G. R. B. Patterson, 14 June 1955, NAA, MEA Records, Series A1838/1, File 704/8/1.

33 Corner, "International Whaling Commission: Seventh Annual Meeting," undated, ANZ, MEA Records, EA 1 104/6/9/1, pt. 14, "Whaling—General, 1955–56."

34 Dulles to US embassy, London, 1 September 1955, USNA, RG 59, File 398.246.

35 Francis Wilcox, State Department, to IWC Secretary, 25 January 1956, USNA, RG 59, File 398.246.

36 Corner, "International Whaling Commission: Eighth Annual Meeting," undated, ANZ, MEA Records, EA 1, File PM 104/6/9/1, pt. 15, "Whaling—General, 1956."

37 John Foster Dulles to the American embassy, The Hague, 10 August 1956, USNA, RG 59, File 398.246.

38 G. R. Clark, memorandum, 9 February 1959, NAC, RG 25, vol. 7755, File 12386-5-40, pt. 13.

39 Kellogg, report of the US commissioner on the ninth annual meeting of the International Whaling Commission, 29 July 1957, USNA, RG 59, File 398.246.

40 Christian Herter, Acting Secretary, to the American embassy, The Hague, 16 August 1957, USNA, RG 59, File 398.246.

41 Aide-mémoire, American embassy, The Hague, 27 August 1957, USNA, RG 59, File 398.246.

42 Frithjof Bettum, "The Conditions for Whaling at Year's End," January 1957, enclosure to Map I, Riksarkivet, Oslo, Fiskeridept., Fangstkontoret, Box "Hvalrådets, Karter og meldinger, 1957–60," Melding 1, Referat s. 1–2, Bilag til Kart I s.1–3.

43 Arne Fliflet, US embassy, Oslo, to State Department, 19 November 1958, USNA, RG 59, File 398.246.

44 Edward N. Cooper, First Secretary of embassy, London, to State Department, 4 December 1958, USNA, RG 59, File 398.246. A copy of the tentative agreement from the November 1958 meeting can be found in NAC, RG 25, vol. 7755, File 12386-5-40, pt. 13.

45 Mr. Fujiyama, "The Minutes of Proceedings of 18 February at Foreign Affairs Committee of the House of Councilors," hand-dated "2.4.59," ANZ, MEA Records, AAEG 950/651a, File PM 104/6/9/2, pt. 1, "Economic Affairs, commodities, whaling and International Whaling Commission—general."

46 Ben Thibodeaux, Economic Minister, US embassy, Tokyo, to State Department, 29 May 1959, USNA, RG 59, File 398.246.

47 Statement by Foreign Minister Fujiyama, 18 February 1959, NAGB, FO 371 141640 G63.

48 "Japanese Views on International Whaling Agreements," 10 June 1959, USNA, RG 59, File 398.246.

49 International Whaling Commission, eleventh annual meeting, "Agenda Item 8: Notices of Withdrawal," 9 June 1959, ANZ, MEA Records, AAEG 950/651a, File PM 104/6/9/2, pt. 1, "Economic Affairs, Commodities, Whaling and International Whaling Commission—General."

50 H. H. Francis, report on the eleventh meeting of the International Whaling Commission, ANZ, MEA Records, AAEG 950/651a, File PM 104/6/9/2, pt. 1, "Economic Affairs, Commodities, Whaling and International Whaling Commission—General."

51 Clark to Prime Minister, 30 June 1959, NAC, RG 25, vol. 5508, File 12386-5-40.

52 Minister of External Affairs to High Commission, London, 25 June 1959, ANZ, MEA Records, AAEG 950/651a, File PM 104/6/9/2, pt. 1, "Economic Affairs, Commodities, Whaling and International Whaling Commission—General."

53 Kellogg to Capt. R. R. Waesche, 11 May 1959, SIA, RU 7165, Box 25, Folder 3; Kellogg to Marguerite Kellogg, 28 June 1959, SIA, Remington Kellogg Papers, ca. 1903–69 (hereafter RU 7434), Box 4.

54 Corner to Ministry of Foreign Affairs, 24 June 1959, ANZ, MEA Records, AAEG 950/651a, File PM 104/6/9/2, pt. 1, "Economic Affairs, Commodities, Whaling and International Whaling Commission—General."

55 Whitney, US embassy, London, to Secretary Herter, 26 June 1959, USNA, RG 59, File 398.246.

56 Untitled excerpt from the transcript of the 1959 IWC meeting, SIA, RU 7165, Box 23, Folder 5.

57 Herrington to Kellogg, 25 June 1959, SIA, RU 7165, Box 25, Folder 4.

58 Clark, condensed report, to Prime Minister, 3 July 1959, NAC, RG 25, vol. 5508, File 12386-5-40.

59 Arne Flifet, US embassy, Oslo, to Herter, 9 October 59, USNA, RG 59, File 398.246.

60 Salvesen report on the 1958–59 season, 5 February 1960, UEL, Salvesen Papers, Fiche 3330.

61 Wall, note, 3 September 1959, and surrounding documents in that file, NAGB, MAF 209/1802 FGB 17525.

62 *Shin Suisan Shimbun Weekly*, 12 October 1959, Riksarkivet, Fiskeridept., Box "Hvalrådets Karter og Meldinger, 1957–60," File "1960 Hvalrådets møter Melding nr. 1," møtet 11 January 1960; Chancery, Tokyo, to Foreign Office, 27 October 1959, NAGB, FO 371 141644 G63.

63 Hvalrådet, Report, 4 May 1960, Riksarkivet, Oslo, Fiskeridept., Fangstkontoret, Box "Hvalrådet, Karter og Meldinger, 1957–60," Melding 4, Referat s. 1–3.

64 "Results for Seasons 1958–59, 1959–60, and 1960–61" and "'Break Even' Prices," UEL, Salvesen Papers, File "Documents Taken to Meeting with Ministry of Transport on 1/11/61 Re: Future of British Whaling."

65 Salvesen to Fisheries Secretary Engholm, 8 June 1960, UEL, Salvesen Papers, File "Documents Taken to Meeting with Ministry of Transport on 1/11/61 Re: Future of British Whaling."

66 "Graph Showing Fall in Average Catch of Blue Whale Units per Catcher Day between 1955/6 and 1960/61—World Fleet," undated, UEL, Salvesen Papers, File "Documents Taken to Meeting with Ministry of Transport on 1/11/61 Re: Future of British Whaling."

67 Salvesen to H. E. Gorick, General Council of British Shipping, 6 November 1962, UEL, Salvesen Papers, File "Documents Taken to Meeting with Ministry of Transport on 1/11/61 Re: Future of British Whaling."

68 Salvesen to Fujita of Japanese Whaling Association, draft telegram, UEL, Salvesen Papers, Fiche 3350, "HKS Whaling Incorporating IWC Correspondence"; "10/26/61 Whaling Industry," notes from Chr. Salvesen & Co. Ltd., UEL, Salvesen Papers, File "Documents Taken to Meeting with Ministry of Transport on 1/11/61 Re: Future of British Whaling."

69   General Council of British Shipping, Whaling Industry, meeting with
     Ministry of Transport, 1 November 1961, notes for Chairman (W. Errington
     Keville), UEL, Salvesen Papers, File "Documents Taken to Meeting with
     Ministry of Transport on 1/11/61 Re: Future of British Whaling" (this file
     also has the data about employment and profits); Salvesen to Gorick, 6 June
     1961, UEL, Salvesen Papers, Fiche 3353. The Salvesen company lived on as a
     firm with many manifestations, including fishing and frozen foods. Note too
     that, by 1962, the Norwegian fleets employed only 2,400 men, down from a
     peak of 4,500. *Norwegian Press Bulletin*, 13 August 1962, NAGB, FO 371 165132
     G63.

70   Elliott, *A Whaling Enterprise*, 161.

71   Herter to US Embassies, The Hague and Oslo, 6 June 1960, USNA, RG 59,
     File 398.246.

72   Hvalrådet, report, 4 June 1960, Riksarkivet, Oslo, Fiskeridept., Fangstkon-
     toret, Box "Hvalrådets, Karter og Meldinger, 1957–60," Melding 6, s. 1–4.

73   Corner to the Prime Minister, 7 April 1961; and Dawbin to the Secretary,
     Marine Department, 2 June 1960 and 10 November 1960, both in ANZ, MEA
     Records, AAEG 950/657a, File PM 104/6/9/5, pt. 1, "IWC Meetings of Scien-
     tific Committees, 1958–62."

74   Erik Ribu, London, to Foreign Ministry, Oslo, 28 June 1960; and Norwe-
     gian Whaling Association to Ministry of Industry, 1 July 1960, both in Rik-
     sarkivet, Oslo, Fiskeridept., Fangstkontoret, Box "Hvalrådets, Karter og
     Meldinger, 1957–60," Melding 8, Kart I og Bilag til Kart I.

75   Ambassador Paul Koht to Secretary Rusk, 29 December 1961, USNA, RG 59,
     File 398.246.

76   Sandy M. Pringle, US embassy, The Hague, to State Department, 14 October
     1960, USNA, RG 59, File 398.246.

77   Secretary of State for Commonwealth Relations to Ottawa, 28 September
     1960, NAC, RG 25, vol. 5508, File 12386-5-40.

78   G. R. Clark, "Report Re: Conference of Representatives of Antarctic Whal-
     ing Countries, London, February 21–23, 1961," 1 March 1961; and Clark,
     "Report of the Fourteenth Annual Meeting of the IWC," 2 August 1962,
     both in NAC, RG 25, vol. 5508, File 12386-5-40.

79   Moroney to Senger, 2 December 1960, NAA, MEA Records, Series A1838/1,
     File 704/8/1, pt. 7.

80   Dawbin to the Secretary of the Marine, 1 June 1961, ANZ, MEA Records,
     AAEG 950/657a, File PM 104/6/9/5, pt. 1. An excellent, detailed discussion of
     the relationships between the ad hoc scientific committee and the Commit-
     tee of Three, and among their members, can be found in Burnett, *Sounding
     of the Whale*, 466–97.

81   Kellogg, report of the US commissioner to the fourteenth annual meeting of
     the International Whaling Commission, London, 20 July 1962, USNA, RG
     59, File 398.246.

82   McHugh to Kellogg, 10 December 1962, and Kellogg's reply, 20 December 1962, SIA RU 7165, Box 27, Folder 1. There does not appear to be anything in the records about Kellogg holding those positions in 1943 or 1946.

83   Elliott, *A Whaling Enterprise*, 119.

84   Jahre is quoted in J. L. W. Hobbs to Morison Johnston, 12 March 1963, NAGB, FO 371 170891 G63. Details on the sales of the floating factories can be found in J. N. Tønnessen and A. O. Johnsen, *The History of Modern Whaling* (Berkeley: University of California Press, 1982), 603–8.

85   The IUCN resolution from its meeting in September 1963 in Nairobi can be found in ANZ, MEA Records, AAEG 950/650a, File PM 104/6/9/1, pt. 20, "Whaling—General."

86   Carmel Finley argues that MSY was a political theory before it was a scientific concept, which was its central limiting factor. Finley, *All the Fish in the Sea: Maximum Sustainable Yield and the Failure of Fisheries Management* (Chicago: University of Chicago Press, 2011). See also Kellogg, report of the US commissioner to the fourteenth annual meeting of the International Whaling Commission, London, 20 July 1962, USNA, RG 59, File 398.246.

87   High Commission, London, to Wellington, 1 July 1963, ANZ, MEA Records, AAEG 950/649b, File PM 104/6/9/1, pt. 19, "Whaling—General."

88   IWC 16/10, "Report of the Committee of Four," June 1964, SIA, RU 7165, Box 21, Folder 6.

89   Rusk to Buenos Aires et al., 13 May 1964, USNA, RG 59, "INCO—Whales 3."

90   The quotations in this paragraph and the next come from IWC 16/15, "Plenary Minutes, Third Plenary Session, 26 June 1964," SIA, RU 7165, Box 22, Folder 1.

91   G. L. O'Halloran, report of the New Zealand delegation to the sixteenth meeting of the International Whaling Commission, 8 July 1964, ANZ, MEA Records, AAEG 950/650a, File PM 104/6/9/1, pt. 20, "Whaling—General"; Kellogg, report of the US commissioner, 1964, USNA, RG 59, File "INCO—Whales 3."

92   Gardner, memo, 25 July 1964, NAGB, MAF 209/2354 FGB 22242.

93   W. G. Solberg, "The International Whaling Commission's 16th Annual Meeting in Sandefjord," 30 June 1964, Riksarkivet, Oslo, Fiskeridept., Box "Hvalrådet Karter og Melding, 1963–67," Bilag til Kart III Melding 3, 1964.

94   Rusk to embassies in Buenos Aires et al., 18 September 1964, USNA, RG 59, File "INCO—Whales 3."

6. SAVE THE WHALES (FOR LATER)

1   US Congress, 92nd Cong., 1st Sess., hearing before the House Foreign Affairs Subcommittee on International Groups and Organizations (26 July 1971), statement of Tom Garrett, Wildlife Consultant for Friends of the Earth, pp. 25–27.

2   Transcript of proceedings, meeting of the Secretary of State's Advisory Committee on the 1972 UN Conference on the Human Environment, Washington, DC, 22 November 1971, USNA, RG 59, Lot 73D344, Bureau of Oceans and International and Scientific Affairs.

3   *Soylent Green* was a dystopian science fiction film in which the protagonist, played by Charlton Heston, discovers that the government's solution for a food crisis on an overcrowded planet is to harvest human corpses and pass them off as plankton wafers, of all things.

4   For an in-depth analysis of the language of the anti-whaling movement, from a political-science perspective, see Charlotte Epstein, *The Power of Words in International Relations: Birth of an Anti-Whaling Discourse* (Cambridge, MA: MIT Press, 2008).

5   Reginald Norby, note, whaling meeting with Dr. Aron and Mrs. Fox, 6 May 1974, Kongelige Utenriksdepartementet, Oslo (Royal Norwegian Foreign Ministry) (hereafter NFM), File 51/2/4, Folder 79.

6   Rachel Carson, *Silent Spring* (New York: Houghton-Mifflin, 1962); Paul Ehrlich, *The Population Bomb* (New York: Ballantine, 1970).

7   Thomas Dunlap, *Saving America's Wildlife: Ecology and American Mind, 1850–1990* (Princeton, NJ: Princeton University Press, 1991); Thomas Dunlap, *Faith in Nature: Environmentalism as Religious Quest* (Seattle: University of Washington Press, 2004).

8   Frank Zelko, "From Blubber and Baleen to Buddha of the Deep: The Rise of the Metaphysical Whale," *Society and Animals* 20 (2012): 91–108, emphasizes the connection between video recording of the animals and countercultural thinking. D. Graham Burnett, *The Sounding of the Whale: Science and Cetaceans in the Twentieth Century* (Chicago: University of Chicago Press, 2012), focuses on the work of scientists such as John Lilly in defining the whale as intelligent and worthy of protection.

9   Gregory Donovan, "The International Whaling Commission and the Revised Management Procedure," in *Additional Essays on Whales and Man*, ed. E. Hallenstvedt and G. Blichfeldt, 4–10 (Lofoten, Norway: High North Alliance, 1995), www.highnorth.no/library/Management_Regimes/IWC/th-in-wh.htm (accessed 16 July 2011).

10   A Google search in July 2011 for "Harry Lillie" showed at least three Web sites highlighting Lillie's horse/whale comparison.

11   J. N. Tønnessen and A. O. Johnsen, *The History of Modern Whaling* (Berkeley: University of California Press, 1982), 702–5.

12   W. R. D. McLaughlin, *Call to the South: A Story of British Whaling in Antarctica* (London: White Lion, 1962), 18–19.

13   A sampling of Lillie's correspondence with Remington Kellogg can be found in SIA, RU 88, Box 4, Folder "Licht to Lynch."

14   McLaughlin, *Call to the South*, 15–16, 38.

15   Horton J. Hobbs Jr., Senior Scientist, interview, 14 May 1976, SIA, RU 9509,

Oral History Project. On building the blue whale model, see SIA, RU 88, Box 2, Folder "Fraser, Francis C."

16   Victor B. Scheffer, *The Year of the Whale* (New York: Scribner's, 1969), 4–7.

17   Annenberg to State Department, 9 March 1972, USNA, RG 59, File "INCO— Whales 1/1/70." A brief discussion of the first whales on TV, including Flipper the dolphin, is in Andrew Darby, *Harpoon: Into the Heart of Whaling* (Cambridge, MA: Da Capo, 2008), 98–99. For an analysis of nature on TV, see Jennifer Price, *Flight Maps: Adventures with Nature in Modern America* (New York: Basic Books, 1999), chapter 5.

18   Mary Batten, Chief Researcher, Time-Life Films, to IWC, 9 April 1969; and Trudy Knapp, Walt Disney Pictures, to IWC, 18 February 1970, both in IWC, File K 943, "Miscellaneous Correspondence: July 1973–March 1975."

19   Stacey to McHugh, 10 March 1972; and McHugh's reply, 20 March 1972, both in IWC, File K 943 "Miscellaneous Correspondence: July 1973–March 1975."

20   Roger Payne and Scott McVay, "Songs of Humpback Whales," *Science* 173, no. 3997 (13 August 1971): 585–97.

21   *Sydney Morning Herald*, 24 May 1976, 3.

22   Richard Connor and Dawn Micklethwaite Peterson, *The Lives of Whales and Dolphins* (New York: Henry Holt, 1994). Chapter 4 gives a concise account of communication by whales and dolphins.

23   Roger Payne, *Among Whales* (New York: Delta, 1995), 36.

24   Farley Mowat, *A Whale for the Killing* (New York: Little, Brown, 1972), 67, 96, 111.

25   Historian Richard White has examined the complex relationship between working in nature and utilizing nature in "'Are You an Environmentalist or Do You Work for a Living?' Work and Nature," in *Uncommon Ground: Rethinking the Human Place in Nature*, ed. William Cronon (New York: Norton, 1995), 171–85.

26   Jan Nyheim, Chargé d'Affaires, a. i., Ottawa, to Foreign Ministry, 21 November 1972, NFM, File 51/2/4, Folder 76.

27   Norma Boyd, Oxford, OH, to IWC Chairman Rindal, undated, IWC, File K 943, "Miscellaneous Correspondence: July 1973–March 1975."

28   McVay to Kellogg, 20 July 1962, SIA, RU 88, Box 4, Folder "Macbeth to Macy"; Herrington to McVay, 1 June 1965, SIA, RU 7165, Box 22, Folder 3a; Payne and McVay, "Songs of Humpback Whales"; Scott McVay, "Last of the Great Whales," *Scientific American* 215 (August 1966): 13–21; Scott McVay, "Stalking the Arctic Whale," *American Scientist* 61, no. 1 (January 1973): 24–37; Scott McVay, "Reflections on the Management of Whaling," in *The Whale Problem: A Status Report*, ed. Warren Schevill (Cambridge, MA: Harvard University Press, 1974), 369–82; Scott McVay, "One Strand in the Rope of Concern," in *Mind in the Waters: A Book to Celebrate the Consciousness of Whales and Dolphins*, ed. Joan McIntyre (New York: Scribner's, 1974), 225–29.

29   A congressional report in 1976 claimed that hundreds of thousands of people

had seen gray whales in Southern California. US Congress, 94th Cong., 2nd Sess., "Saving the Gray and Bowhead Whales," Committee on Merchant Marine and Fisheries, House Rpt. 94-1574 (16 September 1976).

30 "Watching Whales," *New Yorker*, 30 June 1980, 29–30.

31 Paul Spong, "Non-Consumptive Abuse of Cetaceans," paper given at the Whale Alive conference, Boston, MA, 6–12 June 1983, NFM, File 51/2/4, Folder 99. The 1999 movie *Free Willy* captured the nature of the dilemma by featuring a young boy who helped an orca escape from an aquarium to rejoin its pod. Despite the obvious message of the movie, the SeaWorld chain continues to thrive, posting record attendance. An interesting analysis of SeaWorld's marketing is Susan G. Davis, "'Touch the Magic,'" in *Uncommon Ground: Rethinking the Human Place in Nature*, ed. William Cronon (New York: Norton, 1996), 204–17.

32 Eighth General Assembly of the IUCN, 24 September 1963, IWC, File H 913, "IUCN Correspondence"; IWC 1972, "Consideration of a Global Moratorium on Whaling," agenda item 8, June 1972, NAGB, MAF 209/3052.

33 US Congress, 92nd Cong., 1st Sess., hearing before the House Foreign Affairs Subcommittee on International Groups and Organizations (26 July 1971), statement of Stuart Blow, Acting Coordinator of Ocean Affairs, Department of State, p. 9.

34 There was vigorous debate at the time whether sperm oil could be replaced with synthetics or oil from the jojoba plant, and it is no longer in use. Secretary Rogers to Secretary Hickel, 28 August 1970, USNA, RG 59, File "INCO—Whales 1/1/70."

35 L. W. Andreas, Archer Daniels Midland, to Senator Magnuson, 21 July 1970, USNA, RG 59, File "INCO—Whales 1/1/70."

36 J. D. Lodge, Buenos Aires, to State Department, 14 September 1970; aide-mémoire from the embassy of Japan, 30 November 1970, and from the embassy of Norway, 1 December 1970; and US reply, 8 February 1971 (quotation), all in USNA, RG 59, File "INCO—Whales 1/1/70."

37 Transcript of proceedings, meeting of the Secretary of State's Advisory Committee on the 1972 UN Conference on the Human Environment, Washington, DC, 22 November 1971, USNA, RG 59, Lot 73D344, Bureau of Oceans and International and Scientific Affairs. For more on Russell Train and Richard Nixon, see J. Brooks Flippen, "Richard Nixon, Russell Train, and the Birth of Modern American Environmental Diplomacy," *Diplomatic History* 32, no. 4 (2008): 613–38.

38 Jack Perry and Ryohei Murata, memo of conversation, 14 February 1972, and State Department to embassies in Moscow and Tokyo, 24 February 1972, USNA, RG 59, File "INCO—Whales and Whaling 1/1/70."

39 Lodge to State Department, 2 March 1972; and Meyer to State Department, 8 March 1972, both in USNA, RG 59, File "INCO—Whales and Whaling 1/1/70."

40 Russell Train, report of the US delegation to the UNCHE, 20 June 1972, USNA, RG 59, File "INCO—Whales 6/1/72."

41 See USNA, RG 59, File "INCO—Whales 6/1/72."

42 Train to Secretary Rogers, 4 November 1971, USNA, RG 59, File "INCO—Whales 1/1/71."

43 McHugh to Stacey, 8 March 1972, IWC, File H 910, "FAO—Correspondence, 1949–74."

44 E. W. Maude, International Whaling Commission meeting, 10 July 1972, NAGB, MAF 209/3057.

45 IWC 1972, "Consideration of a Global Whaling Moratorium," agenda item 8, June 1972, NAGB, MAF 209/3057.

46 William Aron, "The International Whaling Commission: A Case of Malignant Neglect," paper presented in Corvallis, OR, July 2000, posted on www.planetoceanalliance.org/forum (accessed 10 August 2011); E. W. Maude, International Whaling Commission meeting, 10 July 1972, NAGB, MAF 209/3057.

47 E. W. Maude, International Whaling Commission meeting, 10 July 1972, NAGB, MAF 209/3057.

48 [Clive Deon?], ISPA, to Mr. Trygve Bratteli, 6 July 1972, NFM, File 51/2/4, Folder 76.

49 The text of the amendment can be found in US Congress, 92nd Cong., 1st Sess., Public Law 92-219, Pelly Amendment to Fishermen's Protective Act of 1967, 85 State 786.

50 On Pelly's goals, see Jon Conrad and Trond Bjørndal, "On the Resumption of Commercial Whaling: The Case of the Minke Whale in the Northwest Atlantic," *Arctic* 46, no. 2 (June 1993): 169; US Congress, 92d Cong., 1st Sess., "Enhance the Effectiveness of International Fisheries Conservation Programs," House Rpt. 92-468 (16 August 1971).

51 "Fishermen's Protective Act, Amendments," 31 March 1978; H. Rpt. 1029, 95th Congress, 2d Session, Serial set vol. 13201-3, Session vol. 1-3, 9.

52 Juanita Kreps, Commerce Secretary, to President Carter, 14 December 1978, Carter Presidential Library, Atlanta, Jimmy Carter Papers (hereafter Carter Papers), Staff Office—CEA (Council of Economic Advisers), Box 42, File "Hutcheson, Rick 12/78 [2]."

53 This paragraph and the next are drawn from John Clark et al., to the Right Honorable Lars Korvald, 21 May 1973, NFM, File 51/2/4, Folder 77.

54 Train to Secretary Rogers, 7 June 1971, USNA, RG 59, File "INCO—Whales 1/1/71."

55 Rowan Taylor to Prime Minister Kirk, 18 April 1974, ANZ, MEA Records, ABHS 950 W4627, File 104/6/9/6, pt. 1, "Correspondence from the Public, 6/73–6/75."

56 "Submission to the Government of New Zealand on the Subject of Whale Conservation," undated, ANZ, MEA Records, AAEG 950/650b, File PM

104/6/9/1, pt. 21, "Whaling: General."

57 Undated clipping, found with material from July 1978, ANZ, MEA Records, ABHS 950 W4627, File 104/6/9/1, pt. 23, "Whaling: General."

58 For an example of the reasoning against New Zealand rejoining the IWC, see Treasury memo on IWC, 27 May 1976, ANZ, MEA Records, ABHS 950 W4627, File 104/6/9/2, pt. 6, "Whaling: International Whaling Conventions."

59 See, for instance, the photo of IWC secretary Ray Gambell receiving a stack of petitions from People's Trust for Endangered Species, IWC, File H 928, "Ray Gambell and PTES."

60 Report of the US delegation to the twenty-fifth meeting of the International Whaling Commission, 25–29 June 1973, USNA, RG 59, File "INCO—Whales and Whaling 1/1/70."

61 Reginald Norby, note, whaling meeting with Aron and Mrs. Fox, 6 May 1974, NFM, File 51/2/4, Folder 79.

62 Donovan, "International Whaling Commission and the Revised Management Procedure."

63 D. B. G. McLean, High Commission, London, to the Ministry of External Affairs, 18 July 1975, ANZ, MEA Records, ABHS 950 W4627, File 104/6/9/3, pt. 2, "International Whaling Commission—General."

64 Project Jonah, newsletter no. 3, February 1975, ANZ, MEA Records, AAEG 950 650B, PM 104/6/9/1, pt. 21, "Whaling General, 1966–75."

65 Leonard Buckley's review of Horizon, Times (London), 7 March 1972, RG 59, File "INCO—Whales 1/1/70."

66 For a balanced and very entertaining history of Greenpeace, see Frank Zelko, Make It a Green Peace! The Rise of Countercultural Environmentalism (New York: Oxford University Press, 2013).

67 "Greenpeace to Sail Again . . . but for Whales," Ottawa Journal, 6 March 1975, NFM, File 51/2/4, Folder 80.

68 Joan McIntyre, ed., Mind in the Waters: A Book to Celebrate the Consciousness of Whales and Dolphins (New York: Scribner's), 8–9, 237–38.

69 Holt to Cordiviola, May 1979, IWC, File A 2, "Convention: Adherence of Non-Member Countries."

70 Wayne Andreas to Warren Magnuson, 21 July 1970, and Donald McKernan to John S. Gottschalk, 28 August 1970, USNA, RG 59, File "INCO—Whales 1/1/70."

71 Zelko, Make It a Green Peace, 215–26.

72 Ibid., 354–58.

73 Shozo Kumashiro to Stacey, 19 May 1976, IWC, File A 502, "Allegations (Greenpeace)."

74 Quoted in Zelko, Make It a Green Peace, 227.

75 For a lengthy discussion of Lilly's work, with a sprinkling of Spong too, see Burnett, Sounding of the Whale, chapter 6.

76 "Boycott," Talk of the Town, New Yorker, 11 March 1974, 27.

77 See various letters in IWC, File K 943, "Miscellaneous Correspondence: July 1973–March 1975." On misdirected donations, see *Cambridge Evening News*, 1 September 1978, IWC, File K 945, "Press Clippings."

78 Gambell to Garrett, 13 November 1979, IWC, File H1008, "Whale Protection Fund" (no reply was in the file).

79 *Cambridge Evening News*, 1 September 1978, in IWC, File K 945, "Press Clippings." The Whale Research Fund was run by the IWC and provided money for scientific work on whales.

80 Harvey to Mr. Bianchi's class, El Cerrito, 26 March 1980, IWC, File K 970, "Protest Letters—IWC."

81 Harvey to Ms. Kathleen Dodge, 16 September 1980, IWC, File K 970, "Protest Letters—IWC."

82 Harvey to 2nd Lt. Mark B. Wroth, 20 March 1980, IWC, File K 970, "Protest Letters—IWC."

83 Jennifer Moseley, Director, People's Trust for Endangered Species, to Gambell, 2 October 1977; Gambell to Burman, 9 November 1977; and Gambell to Moseley, 13 September 1978, all in IWC, File H 928, "People's Trust for Endangered Species."

84 Jean Dobson to Gambell, 7 October 1977, IWC, File H 928, "People's Trust for Endangered Species."

85 Finn Bergersen, Fisheries Attaché, Washington, DC, to Oslo, 26 June 1980, NFM, File 51/2/4, Folder 87.

86 The CITES Web site, www.cites.org, has the convention and list of species. Just about every nation has joined CITES.

87 John Gulland to Lee Talbot, 30 March 1981, IWC, File H 1331, "IUCN."

88 Joseph Glascott, "Blasting the Whales to Extinction," *Sydney Morning Herald*, 22 May 1976.

89 *Sydney Morning Herald*, 6 June 1977, 3.

7. THE END OF COMMERCIAL WHALING

1 *Express*, 10 July 1979, IWC, File K 945, "Press Clippings." Denver's song was the title track from his 1977 album and can be found on www.allaboutmusic.com (accessed 6 August 2012). As recently as 2001, IWC staff were using kitchen equipment donated by Denver.

2 One of the most interesting examples of this clash came with the effort by the Makah in Washington State to hunt gray whales in the 1990s, recounted in Robert Sullivan, *A Whale Hunt* (New York: Scribner's, 2000). Shepard Krech has written the most important analysis of American Indians as role models, including the problems of this association; see his *Ecological Indian: Myth and History* (New York: Norton, 1999).

3 "Alaska Whale Killed as Buckley Watches," *New York Times*, 26 May 1974.

4 Tom Lowenstein, *Arctic Land: Sacred Whale; The Inuit Hunt and Its Ritual*

(New York: Harvill Press, 1994), ix–xi, xxi–xxvi, 25–27.

5   Scott McVay, "Stalking the Arctic Whale," *American Scientist* 61, no. 1 (January 1973): 24–37; "Alaska Whale Killed as Buckley Watches," *New York Times*, 26 May 1974; "Buckley Explains His Trip to Alaska," *New York* Times, 3 June 1974.

6   US Congress, 92nd Cong., 1st Sess., "Marine Mammals," hearings before the Subcommittee on Fisheries and Wildlife Conservation of the Committee on Merchant Marine and Fisheries, House of Representatives (9, 13, 17, 23 September 1971), 326.

7   Ibid., 458.

8   US Congress, 95th Cong., 2nd Sess., "Report on the Activities of the Merchant Marine and Fisheries Committee," House Rpt. 1834 (2 January 1979), 225.

9   Ray Gambell to N. A. Anderson Jr., 5 September 1977, IWC, File A 350, "Bowhead Whales"; Martin Harvey to Jean Dobson, 12 October, 1977, IWC, File H 928, "People's Trust for Endangered Species."

10   Tom Garrett to Richard Frank, NOAA, 1 December 1977, IWC, File A 350, "Bowhead Whales."

11   Mrs. J. R. Stallings to Secretary Juanita Krebs, 9 May 1978, IWC, File A 350, "Bowhead Whales."

12   Stevens to Stuart Eizenstat, 18 August 1977, Carter Papers, White House Central Files, Natural Resources, Box NR-3, File NR 2 1/20/77–12/31/77.

13   Martin Cawthorn to J. V. Scott, minute sheet, 22 November 1977, ANZ, MEA Records, ABHS 950, Acc W4627, File 104/6/9/4, pt. 7, "International Whaling Commission: Meetings."

14   Dell Steve, Chairman, Intertribal Council of Nevada, to President Carter, 21 November 1977, IWC, File A 350, "Bowhead Whales."

15   Alaska Eskimo Whaling Commission, www.alaska-aewc.com/aboutus.asp (accessed 16 July 2011).

16   Roger Silook to IWC commissioners et al., 26 June 1978, IWC, File A 350, "Bowhead Whales."

17   J. Michael Holloway, "Subsistence in Rural Alaska," position paper, 11 October 1977, Carter Papers, Staff Offices: Cabinet Secretary and Intergovernmental Affairs, Box 133, File "Alaska Native Americans (Eskimos), 1977–81."

18   Senator Ted Stevens to Jimmy Carter, 28 September 1977, Carter Papers, White House Central Files, Natural Resources, Box NR-2, File NR 2 1/20/77–1/20/81, File NR 2 5/16/77–7/31/77.

19   Senator Mike Gravel to Jimmy Carter, 17 October 1977, Carter Papers, White House Central Files, Natural Resources, Box NR-2, File NR 2 1/20/77–1/20/81, File NR 2 5/16/77–7/31/77.

20   Koji Murakami, National Association for the Protection of Japanese Fisheries, to Ambassador Bjørn Blakstad, Tokyo, 25 June 1979, NFM, File 51/2/4, Folder 84.

21 J. N. Tønnessen and A. O. Johnsen, *The History of Modern Whaling* (Berkeley: University of California Press, 1982), 676–77.

22 J. V. Scott, "International Whaling Commission: Bowhead Whales," 29 November 1977, ANZ, MEA Records, ABHS 950, Acc W4627, File 104/6/9/4, pt. 7, "International Whaling Commission: Meetings."

23 US Congress, 96th Cong., 2nd Sess., "Report of the Activities of the Merchant Marine and Fisheries Committee," House Rpt. 1563 (2 January 1981), 196.

24 Carter to Eizenstat, 29 September 1977, Carter Papers, Staff Offices, Office of Staff Secretary, Handwriting File, Box 52, File 9/29/77.

25 "IWC 30th Annual Meeting: Bowheads," 29 June 1978, ANZ, MEA Records, ABHS W 4627, File 104/6/9/4, pt.10, "International Whaling Commission: Meetings."

26 R. M. Miller, "Whaling IWC Special Meeting in Tokyo," 20 December 1977, ANZ, MEA Records, ABHS 950 W 4627, File 104/6/9/4, pt. 8, "International Whaling Commission: Meetings."

27 Michael Donoghue, untitled memo, 27 August 1980, ANZ, ABHS 950 W 4627, File 104/6/9/4, pt. 16, "International Whaling Commission: Meetings."

28 NOAA Alaska Fisheries Science Center, National Marine Mammal Laboratory, "Bowhead Whales in Alaska" (2007), www.afsc.noaa.gov/nmml/bowhead_iwc.php (accessed 16 July 2011).

29 Rindal, report by chairman of the IWC, 12 December 1972, IWC, File A 3, "Convention: Adherence of Non-Member Countries." Letters of invitation are in this file and File A 2.

30 Juanita Kreps to Carter, 14 December 1978, Carter Papers, Staff Office—CEA (Council of Economic Advisers), Box 42, File "Hutcheson, Rick, 12/78 [2]."

31 US Congress, 96th Cong., 1st Sess., *Congressional Record*, 1 August 1979, vol. 125, pt. 17, 21742–43, and 2 August 1979, vol. 125, pt. 17, 22082–84. The law is Public Law 96-61, 93 Stat. 402.

32 The various letters of inquiry and replies are in IWC, File A 2, "Convention: Adherence of Non-Member Countries."

33 Budget figures are from K. R. Allen, "Development of Control of Whaling," in Government of Australia, *Whales and Whaling*, vol. 1, *Report of the Independent Inquiry*, conducted by the Honorable Sir Sydney Frost (1978), 43.

34 An anonymous but well-informed position on Seychelles IWC history can be found in letters to the editor, "Whaling: Has Seychelles Been Paid for Her Silence?," *Seychelles Weekly*, 23 June 2006, www.seychellesweekly.com/Contents_6-23-06/page7.html (accessed 25 July 2011).

35 *Japan Times*, 25 June 1976, in NFM, File 51/2/4, Folder 80.

36 "View of the Government of Japan on the Total Prohibition of Commercial Whaling," presented to the Norwegian Foreign Ministry, 12 June 1973, NFM, File 51/2/4, Folder 77.

37 Sakurauchi to Foreign Minister, 3 July 1982, NFM, File 51/2/4, Folder 95.

38 The report, filed in October 1981, is in NFM, File 51/2/4, Folder 92.

39 Motokichi Morisawa, "International Opinion on Whaling and Japan's Position: Historic Background of Japanese Whaling," *Keidanren Review*, no. 31 (November 1974), in NFM, File 51/2/4, Folder 80.

40 Inagaki to Prime Minister Mr. [sic] Gro Bruntland, 24 June 1981, NFM, File 51/2/4, Folder 91.

41 Juan M. del Mar Cordiviola to IWC, 31 March 1979, IWC, File A 2, "Convention: Adherence of Non-Member Countries."

42 L. E. Taylor, memo, 28 April 1970; Nick Carter, ISPA, to Secretary Stacey, 5 November 1975; and David Willers to Secretary, 23 June 1979, all in IWC, File A 542, "Reports on Whaling by 'The Sierra.'"

43 International Society for the Protection of Animals, October 1975; and Warren Magnuson et al. to Prime Minister Masayoshi Ohira, 1 May 1979, both in IWC, File A 542, "Reports on Whaling by 'The Sierra.'"

44 Paul Watson, *Ocean Warrior: My Battle to End the Illegal Slaughter on the High Seas* (Toronto: Key Porter, 1994), 1–31.

45 Ibid., 16.

46 Craig Van Note, "Outlaw Whaling Operations around the World," November 1978, p. 2, IWC, File H 929, "Conservation Groups General."

47 *Cambridge Evening News*, 1 September 1978, in IWC, File K 945, "Press Clippings."

48 D. G. B. McLean, report on the twenty-eighth meeting of the International Whaling Commission, 16 July 1976, ANZ, MEA Records, ABHS 950 W 4627, File 104/9/6/4, pt. 5, "International Whaling Commission: Meetings."

49 Tim Groser, signing for J. V. Scott, report on the twenty-ninth meeting of the International Whaling Commission, August 1977, ANZ, MEA Records, ABHS 950 W 4627, File 104/6/9/4, pt. 6, "International Whaling Commission: Meetings."

50 Ministry of External Affairs to High Commission, London, 24 November 1978, ANZ, MEA Records, ABHS 950 W 4627, File 104/6/9/4, pt. 11, "International Whaling Commission: Meetings." Andrew Darby, *Harpoon Into the Heart of Whaling* (Cambridge, MA: Da Capo, 2008), 125, says that Japan threatened to dump a sugar deal with Panama.

51 Ryu Kiyomiya and Yuzo Yamato, Whaling Problem Discussion Committee, circular to IWC and contracting governments, August 1978, IWC, File A 502, "Infractions—Allegations (Greenpeace)."

52 Thomas Dunlap, *Nature and the English Diaspora: Environment and History in the United States, Canada, Australia, and New Zealand* (New York: Cambridge University Press, 1999).

53 *Sydney Morning Herald*, 10 November 1977, 1. Frost's report was published as Government of Australia, *Whales and Whaling*, vol. 1, *Report of the Independent Inquiry*. Drummond's quotation is from Government of Australia, Parliamentary Debate, House of Representatives, 31st Parliament, 1st Sess., 3rd Period, vol. HR 113 (4 April 1979), 1518.

54   Scott to Minister of Foreign Affairs, 10 January 1978, ANZ, MEA Records, ABHS 950 W 4627, File 104/6/9/4, pt. 9, "International Whaling Commission: Meetings."

55   Holt to Dr. Margaret Klinowska, 28 March 1978, IWC, File H 927, "CITES."

56   *Sydney Morning Herald*, 31 October 1977, 3.

57   *Sydney Morning Herald*, 6 December 1977, 3, and 30 September 1978, 5.

58   Government of Australia, *Whales and Whaling*, vol. 1, 55–61.

59   I. G. Stewart to the Ministry of External Affairs, 16 May 1979, ANZ, MEA Records, ABHS 950 W 4627, File 104/6/9/4, pt. 14, "International Whaling Commission: Meetings."

60   Mona Elisabeth Broether, note for Assistant Secretary Boegh, 13 March 1980, NFM, File 51/2/4, Folder 86.

61   Lyall Watson was a best-selling author of quasi-scientific books who apparently parleyed his connection to a wealthy Iranian with a villa in his adopted Seychelles into a place on the nation's first delegation to the IWC. Later, in 1979, he would publish *Lifetide*, which is probably best known for Watson's report of shared behavior among monkeys in Japan, including an implication that when a critical mass of monkeys adopted a behavior, the behavior could be transferred to other monkeys that were physically separated from the first group.

62   Brian Lynch, report of the New Zealand delegation to the thirty-first annual meeting of the IWC, July 1979, ANZ, MEA Records, ABHS 950 W 4627, File 104/6/9/4, pt. 14, "International Whaling Commission: Meetings."

63   R. C. Gurd, report on the thirty-first annual meeting of the IWC, 27 July 1979, ANZ, MEA Records, ABHS 950 W 4627, File 104/6/9/4, pt. 14, "International Whaling Commission: Meetings."

64   Brian Lynch, report of the New Zealand Delegation to the thirty-first annual meeting of the IWC, July 1979, ANZ, MEA Records, ABHS 950 W 4627, File 104/6/9/4, pt. 14, "International Whaling Commission: Meetings."

65   Aide-mémoire from the US Embassy, Wellington, 9 July 1980, ANZ, MEA Records, ABHS 950 W4627, File 104/6/9/4, pt. 15, "International Whaling Commission: Meetings."

66   Unsigned, High Commission, London, to Wellington, 21 July 1980, ANZ, MEA Records, ABHS 950 W 4627, File 104/6/9/4, pt. 15, "International Whaling Commission: Meetings."

67   Unsigned, report from IWC meeting, 30 July 1980, ANZ, MEA Records, ABHS 950 W4627, File 104/6/9/4, pt. 15, "International Whaling Commission: Meetings."

68   Ibid.

69   Ambassador Craig, Tokyo, to Ministry of External Affairs, Wellington, 7 June 1984, ANZ, MEA Records, ABHS 950 W 4627, File 104/6/9/4, pt. 19, "International Whaling Commission: Meetings."

70   Untitled memo (3 pages, in English), 16 April 1982, NFM, File 51/2/4, Folder 94.

71 K. Yonezawa, "Confidential Summary Record, etc.," undated, June 1982, NFM, File 51/2/4, Folder 95A.

72 "IWC: Meeting of Likeminded Countries," 15 June 1982, ANZ, MEA Records, ABHS 950, PM 104/6/9/3, pt. 9, "International Whaling Commission: General."

73 Ministry of Foreign Affairs, Iceland, to IWC, 4 November 1981, NFM, File 51/2/4, Folder 93.

74 Lyall Watson to Per Tresselt, 26 October 1981, NFM, File 51/2/4, Folder 92.

75 Canberra to Wellington, 16 March 1982, ANZ, MEA Records, ABHS 950 W 4627, File 104/6/9/4, pt. 17, "International Whaling Commission: Meetings"; I. L. G. Stewart to Wellington, 27 July 1982, and "Notes to Provisional Agenda," June 1982, both in ANZ, File 104/6/9/4, pt. 18, "International Whaling Commission: Meetings."

76 The loss of ¥4 billion comes from Magnuson, Packwood, et al. to Masayoshi Ohira, Prime Minister, 1 May 1979, IWC, File A 542, "Reports on Whaling by 'The Sierra.'"

77 Dagbladet, 27 July 1982, clipping in NFM, File 51/2/4, Folder 95.

78 John W. Byrne, statement after vote, 27 July 1982, NFM, File 51/2/4, Folder 95.

79 Norwegian embassy, Washington, DC, to Oslo, 17 September 1982, NFM, File 51/2/4, Folder 96.

80 Ambassador Rolf Busch to Gambell, 2 November 1982, IWC, File A 102, "Schedule Amendments—1982"; Ambassador Mark Austad, "Political Hardball in the Arctic," address to the Los Angeles World Affairs Council, 9 December 1983, summarized in B. Stangholm, Consul General, Los Angeles, to Oslo, 19 December 1983, NFM, File 51/2/4, Folder 101.

81 I. Nikonorov to Gambell, 3 November 1982, IWC, File A 102, "Schedule Amendments—1982."

82 Unsigned, from embassy of Japan in London, to Gambell, 4 November 1984, IWC, File A 102, "Schedule Amendments—1982."

83 Peru withdrew its objection in 1983 after getting a threat of sanctions and a promise of a quota.

84 Richard Frank, memo on Pelly Amendment, undated, NFM, File 51/2/4, Folder 92.

85 Craig Van Note, Monitor, to Ted Kronmiller, 22 June 1983, NFM, File 51/2/4, Folder 99.

86 "Norway Information: Norwegian Small-Type Whaling," June 1983; Lynn Sutcliffe to Per Tresselt, 30 August 1983; and Leitzell memo, 21 August 1983, all in NFM, File 51/2/4, Folder 100. For a scathing critique of the idea that Norway or Japan might be able to compare their whaling to the Inuit, see Harry Scheiber, "Historical Memory, Cultural Claims, and Environmental Ethics in the Jurisprudence of Whaling Regulation," Ocean and Coastal Management 38 (1998): 5–40.

87   Briefing for distribution to foreign governments by ambassadors, 17 February 1984, NFM, File 51/2/4, Folder 101.

88   This paragraph and the next three are drawn from "Minutes: Meetings Regarding Whaling Matters," Washington, DC, 9–10 April 1984, NFM, File 51/2/4, Folder 102.

89   Ambassador Mark Austad, "Political Hardball in the Arctic," address to the Los Angeles World Affairs Council, 9 December 1983, summarized in B. Stangholm, Consul General, Los Angeles, to Oslo, 19 December 1983, NFM, File 51/2/4, Folder 101.

90   Terry Leitzell to Finn Bergersen, 29 May 1987, NFM, File 51/2/4, Folder 109.

91   Embassy in Tokyo to External Affairs, Wellington, 18 April 1985, ANZ, ABHS 950 W 4627, File 104/6/9/3, pt. 11, "International Whaling Commission: General"; untitled press release, 25 June 1985, NFM, File 51/2/4, Folder 104.

92   Embassy in Tokyo to Wellington, 8 March 1985, ANZ, MEA Records, ABHS 950 W 4627, File 104/6/9/4, pt. 20, "International Whaling Commission: Meetings"; Monroe Leigh, "American Cetacean Society v. Baldrige [sic], 768 F.2D 426, U.S. Court of Appeals, D.C. Cir., August 6, 1985," *American Journal of International Law* 80, no. 2 (April 1986): 352–54. Press coverage includes "Court Rules U.S. Sanctions Required against Japan for Hunting Whales," *Washington Post*, 6 March 1985, A15, and "Federal Court Upholds Cut in Japanese Fishing: Disregard for World Whaling Ban Cited," *New York Times*, 7 August 1985, A6.

93   Embassy in Washington, DC, to Wellington, 27 March 1985; and Stewart to Wellington, 21 July 1985, both in ANZ, MEA Records, ABHS 950 W 4627, File 104/6/9/4, pt. 20, "International Whaling Commission: Meetings."

94   Susan-Jane Owen, Greenpeace, to Cecile Hillyer, with attached briefing, 31 May 1985, ANZ, MEA Records, ABHS 950 W 4627, File 104/6/9/3, pt. 11, "International Whaling Commission: General."

95   "Small-Type Whaling in Japan's Coastal Seas" and "Comment on Working Group on Special Permits for Scientific Research" (quotation), both May 1986, sent from the Japanese government to Oslo, NFM, File 51/2/4, Folder 107.

96   Alexander Vladimirov, *TASS*, 10 April 1985, NFM, File 51/2/4, Folder 104.

97   Sally Mizroch to Ray Gambell, 6 November 1987; Tim Smith and Tom Polacheck to Gambell, 9 November 1987; and Chapman to Gambell, undated, all in NFM, File 51/2/4, Folder 109.

98   Philip Hartstein, letter to the editor, *Japan Times*, 29 January 1988, in ANZ, MEA Records, ABHS 950 W 4627, File 104/6/9/3, pt. 14, "International Whaling Commission—General."

99   Sidney Holt, letter to the editor, *Observer*, 13 July 1986, in IWC, File K 1300, "Press Coverage."

100   Draft intelligence report, 11 May 1988, ANZ, MEA Records, PM 104/6/9/3, pt. 14, "International Whaling Commission—General."

101 "DNA Tests Find Meat of Endangered Whales for Sale in Japan," *New York Times*, 13 September, 1994, C-4.

EPILOGUE

1 Andrew Revkin, *Dot Earth*, 4 June 2011, http://dotearth.blogs. nytimes.com/2011/06/04/whale-wars-leader-arrest-me-or-shut-up/?scp=1&sq=revkinwatson&st=cse (accessed 1 August 2011). In 2012, the German government did in fact arrest Watson on an outstanding warrant from Costa Rica for interfering with fishermen.

2 Andrew Darby, *Harpoon: Into the Heart of Whaling* (Cambridge, MA: Da Capo, 2008), 125–27, 169–70.

3 See, for instance, Arne Kalland and Brian Moeran, *Japanese Whaling: End of an Era?* (London: Curzon, 1992), a study by a pair of anthropologists with backing from the Japan Whaling Association and the Institute for Cetacean Research, among others, that was at least sympathetic to pro-whaling arguments.

4 Roy Chapman Andrews, *Whale Hunting with Gun and Camera* (New York: D. Appleton, 1916).

5 Okawara to Foreign Minister Bjorn Tore Godal, 15 July 1994, NFM, File 523.48-1, Folder 94; statement by All Japan Seamen's Union to the forty-eighth annual meeting of the IWC, NFM, File 523.48, Folder 96.

6 "Japan Begins Pro-whaling Offensive," *Cincinnati Post*, 10 May 2002.

7 Darby, *Harpoon*, 124.

8 *New York Times*, 27 May 1994, A2; *Christian Science Monitor*, 10 July 2000, 8.

9 Ray Gambell to Gill Sampson, 16 February 1996, IWC, File K 1661, "Requests for Information (Non-Standard Replies) Continuation."

10 Jun Morikawa, *Whaling in Japan: Power, Politics, and Diplomacy* (New York: Columbia University Press, 2009), 100; "Flights, Girls and Cash Buy Japan Whaling Votes," *Sunday Times* (London), 13 June 2010.

11 On whale watching, see the results of a 2010 workshop in Puerto Madryn, Argentina, at the IWC Web site, http://iwcoffice.org/meetings/whalewatching10.htm (accessed 7 August 2011). Information on the Pacific Garbage Patch, which is allegedly the size of Texas, is detailed at the advocacy Web site www.greatgarbagepatch.com/ (accessed 7 August 2011). The account of a whale killed by a Mylar balloon is in Edward Laws, *Aquatic Pollution: An Introductory Text* (New York: John Wiley & Sons, 2000), 602, http://books. google.com (accessed 7 August 2011). On whales and sonar, see "Navy Settles Lawsuit over Whales and Its Use of Sonar," *New York Times*, 29 December 2008, www.nytimes.com/2008/12/29/us/29sonar.html?scp=18&sq=whales_sonar&st=cse (accessed 7 August 2011); and Sir Gerald Elliott, *A Whaling Enterprise: Salvesen in the Antarctic* (Wilby, Norwich, UK: Michael Russell, 1998), 104.

12   "Opening Statement," Norwegian delegation to the forty-ninth meeting of the IWC, 20 October 1997, NFM, File 523.48, Folder 96.

13   "Opening Statement," Irish Delegation to the forty-ninth meeting of the IWC, 20 October 1997; and "Greenpeace Says Pollution Biggest Threat to Whales, *Irish Times*, 29 May 1995, both in NFM, File 523.48, Folder 96.

14   Chikira Yokozawa, Japanese embassy, Oslo, to Foreign Ministry, 22 December 1998, NFM, File 523.48, Folder 99.

15   "Opening Statement on the Past, Present and Future of the IWC," Norwegian delegation to the fiftieth meeting of the IWC, Oman, 16 May 1998, NFM, File 523.48, Folder 98; "Opening Statement," Norwegian delegation to the fifty-first meeting of the IWC, Grenada, 24 May 1999, NFM, File 523.48, Folder 99.

16   "Flexibility Needed on Whaling Issue," *Japan Times*, 8 July 2010; "Whaler Turns Whistleblower to Reveal Research Crews' Prime Cut of Japanese Black Market," *Guardian* (Manchester), 15 June 2010.

17   An interesting book that puts the history of cetology squarely in parallel with the global climate change discussions is Michael Heazle, *Scientific Uncertainty and the Politics of Whaling* (Seattle: University of Washington Press, 2006).

18   Trevor Branch, Koji Matsuoka, and Tomio Miyashita, "Evidence for Increases in Antarctic Blue Whales Based on Bayesian Modeling," *Marine Mammal Science* 20, no. 4 (October 2004): 726–54.

19   Simona L. Perry, Douglas P. DeMaster, and Gregory K. Silber, "The Great Whales: History and Status of Six Species Listed as Endangered under the U.S. Endangered Species Act of 1973," special issue, *Marine Fisheries Review* 61, no. 1 (1999), http://spo.nwr.noaa.gov/mfr611/mfr611.htm (accessed 7 August 2011).

20   Ray Gambell to Erik Suy, 3 June 1981, IWC, File A 16, pt. 5.

21   "Lost Property" and "Whales Are People Too," *Economist* 402, no. 8773 (25 February 2012): 71–72, 92–93.

22   Andrew Isenberg, *The Destruction of the Bison* (Cambridge: Cambridge University Press, 1999).

23   UN Food and Agriculture Organization, Fisheries and Aquaculture Department, "*Euphausia superba*," Species Fact Sheets, www.fao.org/fishery/species/3393/en (accessed 7 August 2012); "Teams Track a Food Supply at the End of the World," *New York Times*, 12 March 2012. For tee-shirts, see Zazzle, www.zazzle.com. For the convention, see Commission for the Conservation of Antarctic Marine Living Resources, www.ccamlr.org.

Bibliography

ARCHIVAL COLLECTIONS

Archives New Zealand, Wellington (ANZ)
    Records of the Ministry of External Affairs
Carter Presidential Library, Atlanta
    Jimmy Carter Papers
Hoover Institution Archives, Palo Alto, CA
International Whaling Commission Archives, Cambridge, England (IWC)
Kongelige Utenriksdepartementet, Oslo (Royal Norwegian Foreign Ministry)
    (NFM)
National Archives of Australia, Canberra (NAA)
    Records of the Ministry of External Affairs
National Archives of Canada, Ottawa (NAC)
    Records of the Department of External Affairs (Record Group 25)
    Records of the Ministry of Fisheries (Record Group 23)
National Archives of Great Britain, Kew, London (NAGB)
    Records of the Foreign Office
    Records of the Ministry of Agriculture and Fisheries
Riksarkivet, Oslo
    Records of the Fisheries Ministry (Fiskeridept.)
Smithsonian Institution Archives, Washington, DC (SIA)
    International Whaling Conference and International Whaling Commis-
    sion, 1930–68 (Record Unit 7165)
    A. Remington Kellogg Papers, 1916–69 (Record Unit 7170)
    Remington Kellogg Papers, ca. 1903–69 (Record Unit 7434)
    Oral History Project (various record units)
    Records of the Director, US National Museum (A. Remington Kellogg)
    (Record Unit 88)
University of Edinburgh Library, Special Collections (UEL)
    Archives of Messrs. Christian Salvesen Ltd.

US National Archives, College Park, MD (USNA)
> General Records of the Department of State (Record Group 59)
> Records of International Conferences, Commissions, and Expositions (Record Group 43)
> Records of the Department of Interior, Office of the Secretary (Record Group 48)
> Records of the Fish and Wildlife Service (Record Group 22)
> Records of the Supreme Command of the Allied Powers (Record Group 331)

NEWSPAPERS AND MAGAZINES

Cambridge Evening News
Cape Argus
Christian Science Monitor
Cincinnati Post
Current Opinion
Dagbladet
Economist
Express
FAO Fisheries Bulletin
Fishing News
Guardian (Manchester)
Japan Advertiser
Japan Times
Keidanren Review
La Prensa (Buenos Aires)
Life
Los Angeles Times
New York Times
New Yorker
Norwegian Journal of Shipping and Commerce
Observer
Ottawa Journal
Shin Suisan Shimbun Weekly
Sydney Morning Herald
Time
Times (London)
Washington Post

WEB SITES

Alaskan Eskimo Whaling Commission, www.alaska-aewc.com/aboutus.asp
Commission for the Conservation of Antarctic Marine Living Resources, www.
    ccamlr.org
Convention on International Trade in Endangered Species of Wild Fauna and
    Flora, www.cites.org
Dot Earth, http://dotearth.blogs.nytimes.com
The Great Garbage Patch, www.greatgarbagepatch.com
High North Alliance, www.highnorth.no
International Whaling Commission, http://iwcoffice.org

GOVERNMENT DOCUMENTS

Government of Australia. *Whales and Whaling*. Vol. 1, *Report of the Independent
    Inquiry*. Conducted by the Honorable Sir Sydney Frost. 1978.
———. Parliamentary Debate. House of Representatives, 31st Parliament, 1st
    Session, 3rd Period, vol. HR 113. 4 April 1979.
US Congress. 92nd Congress, 1st Session. Public Law 92-219, Pelly Amendment
    to Fishermen's Protective Act of 1967. 85 Stat. 786. 1971.
———. 92nd Congress, 1st Session. "Ten-Year Moratorium on Whaling."
    Hearing before the House Foreign Affairs Subcommittee on International
    Groups and Organizations. 26 July 1971.
———. 92nd Congress, 1st Session. "Enhance the Effectiveness of International
    Fisheries Conservation Programs." House Report 92-468. 16 August 1971.
———. 92nd Congress, 1st Session. "Marine Mammals." Hearings before the
    Subcommittee on Fisheries and Wildlife Conservation of the Committee
    on Merchant Marine and Fisheries, House of Representatives. 9, 13, 17, 23
    September 1971.
———. 94th Congress, 2nd Session. "Saving the Gray and Bowhead Whales."
    Committee on Merchant Marine and Fisheries, House Report 94-1574. 16
    September 1976.
———. 95th Congress, 2nd Session. "Fishermen's Protective Act, Amend-
    ments." House Report 1029. 31 March 1978.
———. 95th Congress, 2nd Session. "Report on the Activities of the Merchant
    Marine and Fisheries Committee." House Report 1834. 2 January 1979.
———. 96th Congress, 1st Session. *Congressional Record*, vol. 125, pt. 17. 1–2
    August 1979.
———. 96th Congress, 1st Session. Public Law 96-61, 93 Stat. 402. 1–2 August
    1979.
———. 96th Congress, 2nd Session. "Report of the Activities of the Merchant
    Marine and Fisheries Committee." House Report 1563. 2 January 1981.

Andrews, Roy Chapman. *Whale Hunting with Gun and Camera*. New York: D. Appleton, 1916.

Anon. Obituary of N. A. Mackintosh. *Geographical Journal* 140 (October 1974): 524–25.

Berzin, A. A. "The Truth about Soviet Whaling." *Marine Fisheries Review* 70, no. 2 (March 2009): 4–59.

Branch, Trevor, Koji Matsuoka, and Tomio Miyashita. "Evidence for Increases in Antarctic Blue Whales Based on Bayesian Modeling." *Marine Mammal Science* 20, no. 4 (2004): 726–54.

Brandt, Karl. *Whaling and Whale Oil during and after World War II*. Stanford, CA: Food Research Institute, Stanford University, 1948.

Bruggemeier, Franz-Josef, Mark Cioc, and Thomas Zeller, eds. *How Green Were the Nazis? Nature, Environment, and Nation in the Third Reich*. Athens: Ohio University Press, 2005.

Burnett, D. Graham. *The Sounding of the Whale: Science and Cetaceans in the Twentieth Century*. Chicago: University of Chicago Press, 2012.

Carson, Rachel, *Silent Spring*. New York: Houghton-Mifflin, 1962.

Chalmers, Neil. "Harmer, Sir Sidney Francis (1862–1950)." In *Oxford Dictionary of National Biography*, online ed. Oxford: Oxford University Press, 2009. www.oxforddnb.com/view/article/37512 (accessed 5 July 2012).

Chrisp, John. *South of Cape Horn: A Story of Antarctic Whaling*. London: Robert Hale, 1958.

Christensen, Lars. *Such Is the Antarctic*. London: Hodder and Stoughton, 1935.

Cioc, Mark. *The Game of Conservation: International Treaties to Protect the World's Migratory Animals*. Athens: Ohio University Press, 2009.

Connor, Richard, and Dawn Micklethwaite Peterson. *The Lives of Whales and Dolphins*. New York: Henry Holt, 1994.

Conrad, Jon, and Trond Bjørndal. "On the Resumption of Commercial Whaling: The Case of the Minke Whale in the Northwest Atlantic." *Arctic* 46, no. 2 (June 1993): 164–71.

Darby, Andrew. *Harpoon: Into the Heart of Whaling*. Cambridge, MA: Da Capo, 2008.

Davis, Susan G. "'Touch the Magic.'" In *Uncommon Ground: Rethinking the Human Place in Nature*, ed. William Cronon, 204–17. New York: Norton, 1996.

Dobson, Alban. "Henry Gascoyne Maurice (1874–1950)." *Journal de conseil* (now *ICES Journal of Marine Science*) 17 (1950): 1–3.

Donovan, Gregory. "The International Whaling Commission and the Revised Management Procedure." In *Additional Essays on Whales and Man*, ed. E. Hallenstvedt and G. Blichfeldt, 4–10. Lofoten, Norway: High North Alliance, 1995. www.highnorth.no/library/Management_Regimes/IWC/th-in-wh.htm (accessed 16 July 2011).

Dorsey, Kurkpatrick. *The Dawn of Conservation Diplomacy: U.S.-Canadian Wildlife Protection Treaties in the Progressive Era.* Seattle: University of Washington Press, 1998.

Dower, John W. *Embracing Defeat: Japan in the Wake of World War II.* New York: Norton, 1999.

Dunlap, Thomas. *Faith in Nature: Environmentalism as Religious Quest.* Seattle: University of Washington Press, 2004.

———. *Nature and the English Diaspora: Environment and History in the United States, Canada, Australia, and New Zealand.* New York: Cambridge University Press, 1999.

———. *Saving America's Wildlife: Ecology and the American Mind, 1850–1990.* Princeton, NJ: Princeton University Press, 1991.

Ehrlich, Paul. *The Population Bomb.* New York: Ballantine, 1970.

Elliott, Sir Gerald. *A Whaling Enterprise: Salvesen in the Antarctic.* Wilby, Norwich, UK: Michael Russell, 1998.

Epstein, Charlotte. *The Power of Words in International Relations: Birth of an Anti-Whaling Discourse.* Cambridge, MA: MIT Press, 2008.

Evans, Peter. *Ari: The Life and Times of Aristotle Onassis.* New York: Summit, 1986.

FBI. "Aristotle Onassis." http://vault.fbi.gov/Aristotle Onassis (accessed 15 June 2012).

Finley, Carmel. *All the Fish in the Sea: Maximum Sustainable Yield and the Failure of Fisheries Management.* Chicago: University of Chicago Press, 2011.

Flippen, J. Brooks. "Richard Nixon, Russell Train, and the Birth of Modern American Environmental Diplomacy." *Diplomatic History* 32, no. 4 (2008): 613–38.

Francis, Daniel. *A History of World Whaling.* New York: Viking, 1990.

Hardin, Garrett. "The Tragedy of the Commons." *Science* 162, no. 3859 (1968): 1243–48.

Heazle, Michael. *Scientific Uncertainty and the Politics of Whaling.* Seattle: University of Washington Press, 2006.

Hitchcock, William. *The Bitter Road to Freedom: A New History of the Liberation of Europe.* New York: Free Press, 2008.

Hjort, Johan, J. Lie, and Johan Ruud. *Norwegian Pelagic Whaling in the Antarctic.* Hvalrådets skrifter: Scientific Results of Marine Biological Research (Whaling Council pamphlets in English) no. 3, 1932.

Isenberg, Andrew. *The Destruction of the Bison.* Cambridge: Cambridge University Press, 1999.

Kalland, Arne, and Brian Moeran. *Japanese Whaling: End of an Era?* London: Curzon, 1992.

Kellogg, Remington. "Whales, Giants of the Sea." *National Geographic* 77, no. 1 (1940): 35–90.

Krech, Shepard, III. *The Ecological Indian: Myth and History.* New York: Norton, 1999.

LaFeber, Walter. *The Clash: U.S.-Japanese Relations throughout History.* New York: Norton, 1997.

Langewiesche, William. *The Outlaw Sea: A World of Freedom, Chaos, and Crime.* New York: North Point, 2004.

Laws, Edward. *Aquatic Pollution: An Introductory Text.* New York: John Wiley & Sons, 2000. http://books.google.com (accessed 7 August 2011).

Leigh, Monroe. "American Cetacean Society v. Baldrige [*sic*]. 768 F.2D 426. U.S. Court of Appeals, D.C. Cir., August 6, 1985." *American Journal of International Law* 80 (1986): 352–54.

Lowenstein, Tom. *Arctic Land: Sacred Whale; The Inuit Hunt and Its Ritual.* New York: Harvill Press, 1994.

McCracken, David. *Four Months aboard a Jap Whaler.* New York: National Travel Club, 1948.

McEvoy, Arthur F. *The Fisherman's Problem: Ecology and Law in the California Fisheries, 1850–1980.* Cambridge: Cambridge University Press, 1986.

McIntyre, Joan, ed. *Mind in the Waters: A Book to Celebrate the Consciousness of Whales and Dolphins.* New York: Scribner's, 1974.

McLaughlin, W. R. D. *Call to the South: A Story of British Whaling in Antarctica.* London: White Lion, 1962.

McVay, Scott. "Last of the Great Whales." *Scientific American* 215 (August 1966): 13–21.

———. "One Strand in the Rope of Concern." *Mind in the Waters: A Book to Celebrate the Consciousness of Whales and Dolphins*, ed. Joan McIntyre, 225–29. New York: Scribner's, 1974.

———. "Reflections on the Management of Whaling." In *The Whale Problem: A Status Report*, ed. Warren Schevill, 369–82. Cambridge, MA: Harvard University Press, 1974.

———. "Stalking the Arctic Whale." *American Scientist* 61, no. 1 (January 1973): 24–37.

Melville, Herman. *Moby-Dick; or, The Whale.* 1851. Reprint, New York: Modern Library, 1992.

Melvin, Edward, and Julia K. Parrish, eds. *Seabird Bycatch: Trends, Roadblocks, and Solutions.* Fairbanks: University of Alaska Sea Grant, 2001. http://nsgl.gso.uri.edu/aku/akuw99002.pdf (accessed 4 August 2011).

Morikawa, Jun. *Whaling in Japan: Power, Politics, and Diplomacy.* New York: Columbia University Press, 2009.

Mowat, Farley. *A Whale for the Killing.* New York: Little, Brown, 1972.

NOAA Alaska Fisheries Science Center, National Marine Mammal Laboratory. "Bowhead Whales in Alaska" (2007). www.afsc.noaa.gov/nmml/bowhead_iwc.php (accessed 16 July 2011).

Olmsted, Francis Allyn. *Incidents of a Whaling Voyage.* 1841. Reprint, New York: Bell Publishing, 1969.

Payne, Roger. *Among Whales.* New York: Delta, 1995.

Payne, Roger, and Scott McVay. "Songs of Humpback Whales." *Science* 173, no. 3997 (13 August 1971): 585–97.

Perry, Simona L., Douglas P. DeMaster, and Gregory K. Silber. "The Great Whales: History and Status of Six Species Listed as Endangered under the U.S. Endangered Species Act of 1973." Special issue, *Marine Fisheries Review* 61, no. 1 (1999). http://spo.nwr.noaa.gov/mfr611/mfr611.htm (accessed 7 August 2011).

Price, Jennifer. *Flight Maps: Adventures with Nature in Modern America*. New York: Basic Books, 1999.

Rozwadowski, Helen. *The Sea Knows No Boundaries: A Century of Marine Science under ICES*. Seattle: University of Washington Press, 2002.

Scheffer, Victor B. *The Year of the Whale*. New York: Scribner's, 1969.

Scheiber, Harry N. "Historical Memory, Cultural Claims, and Environmental Ethics in the Jurisprudence of Whaling Regulation." *Ocean and Coastal Management* 38 (1998): 5–40.

———. *Inter-Allied Conflict and Ocean Law, 1945–53: The Occupation Command's Revival of Japanese Whaling and Marine Fisheries*. Taipei: Academia Sinica, 2001.

Schweder, Tore. "Distortion of Uncertainty in Science: Antarctic Fin Whales in the 1950s." *Journal of International Wildlife Law and Policy* 3, no. 1 (2000): 73–92.

———. "Protecting Whales by Distorting Uncertainty: Non-precautionary Management?" *Fisheries Research* 52 (2001): 217–25.

Stackpole, Edouard A. *Whales and Destiny: The Rivalry between America, France, and Britain for Control of the Southern Whale Fishery, 1785–1825*. Amherst: University of Massachusetts Press, 1972.

Starbuck, Alexander. *History of the American Whale Fishery*. 1878. Reprint, Secaucus, NJ: Castle, 1989.

Stoett, Peter. *The International Politics of Whaling*. Vancouver: University of British Columbia Press, 1997.

Sullivan, Robert. *A Whale Hunt*. New York: Scribner's, 2000.

Tønnessen, J. N., and A. O. Johnsen. *The History of Modern Whaling*. Berkeley: University of California Press, 1982.

UN Food and Agriculture Organization, Fisheries and Aquaculture Department. "*Euphausia superba*." Species Fact Sheets. www.fao.org/fishery/species/3393/en (accessed 7 August 2012).

Union Whaling Company. *Minutes of Proceedings, 1950*. Durban, South Africa, 28 December 1950.

Walsh, Quentin R. *The Whaling Expedition of the Ulysses, 1937–38*. Ed. P. J. Capelotti. Tallahassee: Florida State University Press, 2010.

Watson, Lyall. *Lifetide*. London: Hodder and Stoughton, 1979.

Watson, Paul. *Ocean Warrior: My Battle to End the Illegal Slaughter on the High Seas*. Toronto: Key Porter, 1994.

White, Richard. "'Are You an Environmentalist or Do You Work for a Living?' Work and Nature." In *Uncommon Ground: Rethinking the Human Place in Nature*, ed. in William Cronon, 171–85. New York: Norton, 1996.

Whitmore, Frank. *Memorial to Remington Kellogg, 1892–1969*. Boulder, CO: Geological Society of America, 1969.

Woebse, Anna-Katharina. *Weltnaturschutz: Umweltdiplomatie in Volkerbund und Vereinten Nationen, 1920–50*. Frankfurt: Routledge, 2012.

Yablokov, A. V., ed. *Soviet Antarctic Whaling Data: 1947–72*. Moscow: Center for Russian Environmental Policy, 1995.

Zelko, Frank. "From Blubber and Baleen to Buddha of the Deep: The Rise of the Metaphysical Whale." *Society and Animals* 20 (2012): 91–108.

———. *Make It a Green Peace! The Rise of Countercultural Environmentalism*. New York: Oxford University Press, 2013.

Index

A

A & M Records, 215

aboriginal rights, 117, 220, 234, 244–52, 270, 272–73, 277

Abraham Larsen, 154

Acheson, Dean, 108, 115–18, 135

Addis, J. M., 95

Aeroflot, 237

Africa, 119, 253

Ahab, Captain, 4, 24, 229

air, compressed, 7

Alaska, 27, 218, 241, 244–52; Game Management Department, 246

Alaskan Eskimo Whaling Commission, 248, 250, 271

Albany, Western Australia, 261

Aléman, Roberto, 149

Aleutian Islands, 234

All Japan Seamen's Union, 281

Allen, K. Radway, 185, 187, 189, 260, 263

American Society of Mammalogists, 41

American Whaling Company, 67, 70–71

Amundsen, Roald, 22

Andersen, H. G., 192

Andersen, Lars, 148–49, 151

Anderson, Frank, 126, 141, 142, 153, 179

Andreas, Wayne, 221

Andrews, Roy Chapman, 6, 9, 10, 281

Angola, 257

Annenberg, Walter, 214

Antarctic Maru, 57, 58, 60, 62

Antarctica, 8, 9; claims to, 10, 27, 60, 81, 137, 141; Norwegian industry in, 11; remoteness from the law, 30

Antarctic Convention, 289

Antigua, 267

anti-war movement, 209

anti-whaling movement. *See* "Save the Whales" movement

Anziani, Paul, 119–20, 126

appeasement, 51

Archer Daniels Midland, 221

Arctic, 244–50

Argentina, 10, 26, 29, 33, 46, 49, 60, 67, 72, 102, 120, 145, 147; builds floating factory, 146; whaling, World War II, 97

Aron, William, 224, 231

Atcheson, George, 138

Atlantic Charter, 139

Atlantic salmon, 226

Attlee, Clement, 106, 142

Audubon Society, 10, 221, 227, 246, 272

Austad, Mark, 274

Australia, 29, 64, 67, 77, 266; Antarctic claims, 137, 141; assessment of ICRW, 125; Department of Primary Industry, 262; desire to expand whaling, 60, 97; diplomats expelled by Soviets, 152; files objection, 126; and Japanese whaling, 136–42, 187, 236; Labour Party, 262; Liberal Party, 262; and moratorium, 225, 240, 260, 262, 267; opposes reduction in quota, 171–72, 179–80; POWs, 137; proposes NMP, 231; reviews whaling policy, 260–62; seeks compromise with Japan, 285; whaling in, 33, 58, 67, 71, 74, 87f, 152, 261; whaling legislation, 54–55
autolysis, 20

B

BBC, 210, 213, 214, 233
Bahamas, 257
Baines, E. G., 101
Balaena, 182, 184, 189
Barbados, 267
Barrow, Alaska, 245
Basque whaling, 4, 32
beluga, 265
Bergersen, Birger, 64, 100, 112, 124, 148; 1937 convention, 66–67; 1938 meeting, 72, 76, 79–80; 1945 meeting, 107; 1946 meeting, 114, 125; on blue whale unit, 104, 123; on cheating, 158; in exile, 102; and extinction, 73, 81; IWC chairman, 121, 168; and objections, 126; optimism about IWC, 125; quota reduction, 126, 170; on whalers' motives, 91
Bering Sea, 29
Berlin, Germany, 41
Bermuda, 103
Bevin, Ernest, 63
bison, 289

Blazing Saddles, 30
Blow, Stuart, 220
blue whale, 3, 4, 9, 18, 19, 31, 34, 39, 54, 64, 171, 209; catch data, 40, 80, 156, 169; decline, 73, 121–22, 287; difficulty of hunting, 5; ease of hunting, 23; fear of extinction, 63, 66, 73; in fiberglass, 213; hunting banned, 163, 189, 190, 195, 220, 224; limits on hunting, 63, 122, 170; sinks after death, 7; sounds, 215; value of one in 1935, 59; weighed, 143; yield of oil, 8
blue whale unit (BWU), 53, 58, 106, 112, 122, 163, 221; criticism of, 123, 172, 188; ended, 189, 220, 224, 230; origins, 52, 104
Bollen, Arthur, 259–60
Bonin Islands, 134
Borley, J. O., 40, 54, 58
bowhead whale, 4, 5, 32, 156, 265, 272, 283, 285; controversy, 1970s, 218, 244–52, 259–60, 263, 270; hunting banned, 43; lost while hunting, 246; population estimates, 246–47, 249, 251–52
boycotts of whalers, 237, 269, 271, 273, 280
Branson, Missouri, 238
Brazil, 157, 160, 208, 223, 253, 267, 273
Breaux, John, 254
Bremerhaven, 149
Bretton Woods agreement, 109–10
British Columbia, 234
British Museum (Natural History), 3, 32, 35, 47, 213
British Petroleum, 65
Brosnan, Pierce, 289
Bruun, Svend Foyn, 56
Bryde's whale, 263
Bryn, Kaere, 284
Buckley, James, 246
Buckley, Leonard, 233

Bureau for International Whaling
  Statistics, 39, 43, 152, 155, 157, 161,
  169, 173, 235
Burgeo, Newfoundland, 216–17
Burnett, D. Graham, 38
Burns, John, 246–47
Busch, Rolf, 270
Byrne, John, 266, 269, 273
Byrnes, James, 114

C

California, 74, 218, 235
Canada, 64, 67, 74, 116, 210, 252; leaves
  the IWC, 264–65; policy toward
  whaling diplomacy, 33, 171, 179, 181,
  225; whaling in, 33, 264
Canberra, 210
Cape Cod, 219
Cape Town, South Africa, 126, 244
Capitol Records, 215
Carson, Rachel, 209
Carter, Jimmy, 248, 250, 254
Carver, Clifford, 67, 122, 147
catch per day's work (CDW), 169, 171,
  183
catch per unit of effort (CPUE), 112,
  116, 191
Chapman, Douglas, 187–88, 192, 276
charismatic megafauna, 213
Cheynes Beach, Australia, 240, 262
Chile, 10, 68, 81, 150, 221, 226, 253, 260
China, 50, 68–69, 133, 141, 253
Chrisp, John, 7, 30
Christensen, Christen, 7
Christensen, Lars, 11, 12, 21, 29, 70, 91;
  makes deal with Unilever, 55–56
Cioc, Mark, 123
civil rights movement, 209
Civil War, American, 5
Clark, G. R., 10, 160, 171, 179, 181
Clement-Davies Edward, 94
climate change, 286

Clive, R. H., 64
closed season, 36. *See also* open season
coastal whaling, 271–73, 275
Committee for Humane Legislation,
  207
Committee of Four. *See* International
  Whaling Commission, Committee
  of Three
Common Ground, 215
conservationists, 9, 41, 59, 74, 131, 184,
  214
Convention for the Regulation of
  Whaling (1931), 17, 28, 47, 54, 56, 57,
  60, 67; completion, 42–44; Japan
  and, 58, 62, 64; regulations, 43, 67;
  violation of, 71
Convention on International Trade in
  Endangered Species, 240
Convention on Whaling (1937), 49, 51,
  80, 94, 144; abrogation discussed,
  94–96, 101; negotiations, 65–67; Pro-
  tocol (1938), 49, 72–80, 82; Protocol
  (1939), 81–82; Protocol (1944), 102–4;
  Protocol (1945), 105, 137; Protocol
  (1946), 121; ratification, 68, 72; regu-
  lations, 67, 97–98, 101; violations, 70
cookers, Hartmann and Kvaerner, 21
Cooley, John, 136
Coonan, Kenneth, 142–43
Cooper, D'Arcy, 46–47
Corcoran Gallery, 115
Cordiviola, Juan del Mar, 256–57
Corner, Frank, 150, 168, 169, 171–74,
  180, 185, 202f
Costa Rica, 254–55
Council for the Conservation of
  Whales, 41
Cousteau, Jacques, 213
Cox, R., 95
cranes, 276
Croker, Richard, 134–35
Cronkite, Walter, 235
Czechoslovakia, 44, 153, 236

D

Dagbladet (Oslo), 268
Darby, Andrew, 282
Davidson, C. Girard, 115–17
Dawbin, W. H., 166, 185
Day, Albert, 148
decomposition, 20
Delmonico's, 20
Dent, Frederick B., 226
Denver, John, 243, 262, 330n1
Diamant, Rudi, 297n23
Dingell, John, 246
Discovery, 37, 38, 74
Discovery Committee, 34, 37, 39, 102, 155; supports post-war restrictions, 99–101
Dobson, Alban, 94, 96, 126, 196f, 240; at 1946 meeting, 115, 118–20, 124; IWC secretary, 121, 167, 168; on post-war whaling, 99, 101; relations with Salvesen, 104, 107; and US government, 102, 108–9, 110, 115
Dobson, Jean, 239–40
dolphins, 219, 237, 249
Domei, 66
Dominica, 282
Dominions (in the British empire), 32, 44, 64, 68
Donoghue, Michael, 251
Don't Make a Wave, 234
Dormer, Cecil, 60
Dot Earth, 279
Dower, John, 133
Drummond, Peter, 261
Dublin, Ireland, 59
Dulles, John Foster, 159, 173
Dunlap, Tom, 209, 260
Dutch East Indies, 135

E

ear plugs, 38
Earth Day, 209
ECO, 263
Ecology Action, 229
economic exclusion zone, 150, 158, 253–54, 256; tied to IWC reforms, 175, 178, 192, 265
Economist, 288
Ecuador, 150, 158, 181, 221
Ehrlich, Paul, 209
Eizenstat, Stuart, 250
El Cerrito, California, 238
Elliott, Gerald, 12, 21, 104, 122, 164
El Salvador, 223
environmentalists, 192, 207–9, 223, 225, 227–28, 233, 236, 241, 261–62, 273, 274, 285; on bowhead whales, 247–48, 251–52; direct action, 258, 279–80; dismayed by 1981 objections, 266–67; fake blood, 260, 263; moratorium campaign, 259–67; on Packwood amendment, 253–54; and research whaling, 275; strategy for success, 244; win court battles, 274–75. *See also* "Save the Whales" movement
Essex, 22
export controls, 107, 110, 253; left out in 1946, 111–12
extinction of whales, fear of, 73, 179, 181, 207, 241

F

Falklands Islands, 7, 21, 23, 32, 37, 49, 257
Far Eastern Commission, 136
fats crisis, 91–92, 98, 104, 107–8, 188. *See also* food, shortage of
Fauna Preservation Society, 192
Fiedler, Reginald, 139

fin whale, 3, 4, 9, 18, 19, 31, 34, 40,
171, 190, 219, 220, 226, 240, 286; in
BWU, 52; catch data, 73, 80, 97,
156, 183, 186, 190–91; difficulty of
hunting, 5; limits on hunting, 63;
population, 287; reproduction,
191; sinks after death, 7; sinks the
Tonna, 258; speed of, 4; trapped in
Newfoundland, 216–18

Finley, Carmel, 100

Fisheries Conservation Act, 253

fisherman's problem, 13

Fishing News, 37

flag of convenience, 27, 28, 29, 32, 35,
44, 49, 56, 68, 149–50

floating factories, 22, 27, 30, 57–58, 60,
62, 70–71, 77, 80, 89, 90, 135, 140,
143, 145, 148–51, 154, 156–58, 161,
174, 177, 182, 184, 189, 192, 197–201f,
211; conditions on board, 24, 25; in
convoys, 95–96; development of,
19–22; impact upon efforts to regulate whaling, 28; as land stations,
77, 126; licenses for, 35; Norwegian
in the United States, 97; numbers,
26, 40, 45, 52; as reparations, 99, 118,
134–37, 144, 146, 152; retired or sold
due to lack of whales, 182, 184, 189;
size of, 26; as targets in warfare, 94,
97, 100

Flory, William, 109–10, 118–20, 122,
134, 271

Folger Library, 115

Food and Agriculture Organization,
109, 111, 121, 125, 192, 194, 240, 266

food, shortage of, 13, 102–3, 105, 106,
109, 117; in Netherlands, 113; in
Japan, 113, 129–35, 138, 145. *See also*
fats crisis

Ford, Gerald, 226

Ford Pinto, 237

Forkan, Patricia, 272–73

Forrest, Western Australia, 261

Fort Knox, 27

Foyn, Svend, 6, 7, 26, 266

France, 10, 26, 40, 49, 77, 97, 119, 124,
263; files objection, 126; nuclear
testing in the Pacific, 234, 235

Francis, H. H., 179

Frango, 27, 70–71, 80

Frank, Richard, 256, 271

Franke, J. A. P., 187

Fraser, Malcolm, 260–62

Freemantle, Western Australia, 239

Free Willy, 327n31

French, Sir H. L., 95–96

French Polynesia, 235

Friends of the Earth, 207, 220, 223

Frost, Sydney, 261–62

Fujita, Iwao, 140, 193

G

Gabon, 126

Gabrielson, Ira, 106, 122

Gambell, Ray, 203f, 238–39, 241, 257,
259

Gardner, Hugh, 193

Garrett, Tom, 207, 221, 238, 242, 247

General Agreement on Tariffs and
Trade, 221, 226

Geneva, 36

Germany, 29, 33, 50, 178; and abrogating 1937 convention, 95; Antarctic
claims, 81; chemical industry in,
47; Drang noch Autarkie, 61–62;
encourages Japan to join 1937
convention, 81; moratorium, 265;
occupies Norway, 92, 96; origins of
whaling industry, 60; policy toward
whaling diplomacy, 51, 62, 64; postwar whaling, 146; whalers work
with Onassis, 147–49

Ghana, 254

Glascott, Joseph, 240

Godzilla, 56

Goering, Herman, 61
Golovlev, I. F., 156–57
Gravel, Mike, 249
gray whale, 74, 146, 218, 245, 247
Great Britain: Admiralty, 34, 35, 36;
    attitude toward whaling diplomacy,
    31, 33–35, 42, 44, 47, 70, 92, 99, 101,
    106; Board of Trade, 35, 44, 59; claim
    to Antarctica, 10; Colonial Office,
    32, 34, 35, 101; concern about IWC,
    164; considers abrogating 1937 con-
    vention, 93–96, 101; considers leav-
    ing IWC, 193; Dominions Office,
    137; Dutch whaling supported, 113;
    German whaling ends, 146; Foreign
    Office, 34, 35, 40, 51, 54, 79, 95–96,
    101, 106, 107, 109; on ICRW, 111,
    124–25; India Office, 34; on Japanese
    whaling, 137–38; Liberal Party, 94;
    Ministry of Agriculture and Fish-
    eries, 34, 45, 57, 94, 96, 99, 101, 107,
    121, 193, 223, 257; Ministry of Food,
    91, 94, 95–96, 101, 103, 105, 107, 109;
    Ministry of War Transport, 96, 101;
    national quota division, 182; Onas-
    sis and, 150; pelagic whaling ends,
    189; Polar Committee, 34–36, 39,
    43–44; pressures the Netherlands,
    186; proposes IWC compromise,
    185; Whaler Section, 102, 104; whal-
    ing industry decline, 121; whaling
    law, 1934, 54, 57
Great Depression, 29, 44, 47
Greece, 147
Greenland, 272
Greenland whale. See right whale
Greenpeace, 203–4f, 210f, 240, 251, 258,
    272, 275, 279, 284; anti-whaling
    campaign begins, 234–35; consid-
    ers compromise with Japan, 285;
    Greenpeace Whale Show, 234;
    ideology, 236; origins, 233–34
Grey, Edward, 33

Gruvel, Abel, 34
Guardian (Manchester), 104
Gulland, J. A., 164, 190, 240
Gulliver, 56

H

halibut diplomacy, 116–17
Harcourt, Lord, 32
Hardin, Garrett, 13
Harmer, Sidney, 3, 4, 8, 9, 14, 39, 40,
    42, 58, 84f, 289; on 1931 convention,
    46; Kellogg and, 69; polar commit-
    tee, 35–36; on Unilever, 45–46
harpoon, cold, 266, 272
harpoon, electric, 26, 80, 211
harpoon, exploding, 8, 86f, 87f, 236;
    brutality of, 211–12, 227; invention,
    6
harpooner, 86f, 87f; confrontation
    with Greenpeace, 235; Norwegian
    dominance, 26, 112; pay tied to size
    of whales, 67; position in expedi-
    tions, 24
Harrison, A. R. W., 107, 117
Harrison, R. L., 135
Hartstein, Philip, 276
Harvey, Martin, 238–39
Hashidate Maru, 135, 140, 142–43
Hector Whaling Company, 182, 184,
    211
helicopters, 159
Herman F. Whiton, 148
Herrington, William, 140, 158, 160,
    178, 218
Hershey bars, 109
Hiroshima, 136
historical data, 239
Hitchcock, William, 113
Hjort, Johan, 38, 84f; dismissed by his
    government, 64; on quota system,
    53, 63; on Suarez draft, 34; works
    with ICES, 36

Hobbs, Horton, 213
Hokkaido, 276
Holt, Sidney, 187, 189, 192, 255, 261, 267, 276. *See also* International Whaling Commission, Committee of Three
Honda Civic, 237
Honduras, 148
Hori, Shigeru, 145
Horizon, 233
Hull, Cordell, 103
human rights for whales. *See* sentience and intelligence of whales
Humane Society of the United States, 227, 233, 272
humane societies, 211
humpback whale, 4, 31, 32, 34, 39, 73, 77, 87f, 126, 141, 152, 162, 171, 206f; in BWU, 52; catch data, 156; controversy, 74; easily hunted, 5; hunted from South Georgia, 9; hunting banned, 79, 96, 189, 195, 220, 224; interstellar communication, 215; migration, 38; population, 287; proposal to hunt, 281; songs, 214–15; sung about, 243; value to New Zealand, 185
Hungary, 236
Hunter, Robert, 234
Hvalrådet, 24, 111, 168, 175, 185, 186

I

Iceland, 192, 219, 230, 240, 266, 267, 272–74, 276–77, 279, 284
import controls, 253
Inagaki, Motonobu, 256
India, 156
Indian Ocean Sanctuary, 280, 282
Indonesia, 253
Initial Management Stocks, 232
Inland Fisheries Treaty, 10
Inoue, Kiichi, 281–82
inspectors on floating factories, 30–31, 35, 63, 71, 81, 125; international system, 156, 158–60, 169, 189, 193; Japanese on Soviet ships, 156; Panamanian, 148–49
International Boundary Commission, 10
International Convention for the Regulation of Whaling, 196f, 225, 228, 271, 284; bans hunting bowheads, 245; criticized, 207; drafted, 110; negotiations, 115–24; objection system, 110–11, 114, 118–20, 124; Protocol (1959), 159; ratification, 120–21; replacement convention proposed, 264, 287; terms, 114, 175, 252, 267, 270, 275, 280; United States as depositor, 148, 159
International Convention on Northwest Atlantic Fisheries, 226
International Council for the Exploration of the Sea, 36, 53
International Fisheries Commission, 33
International Fund for Animal Welfare, 248, 272
International Trade Organization, 110
International Society for the Protection of Animals, 225, 233, 257
International Union for the Conservation of Nature, 126, 189, 192, 220, 240
International Whaling Authority, 193
International Whaling Commission, 66, 92–93, 96, 105; ad hoc scientific committee, 187–88; based in London, 121; bowhead whales, 247; cold harpoon, 266; Committee of Three, 184–85, 187–93, 261, 276; concern about collapse, 111, 160, 256, 264, 284; creation, 106–7, 115–22; criticism of, 163–64, 207–8; dues and budget, 121, 167, 181, 188, 255; efforts to save, 1960s,

International Whaling Commission
(*continued*)
185–94; film footage sought, 214; hamstrung by cheating, 130, 157–58, 161–62; hindered by uncertainty, 166; and IUCN, 126; Japan joins, 144; leadership problems, 167–69; letters inspired by Mowat, 218; move to Cambridge, 121, 237; needed by anti-whalers, 210; and NMP, 232–33; objection system, 165, 167, 214, 224, 230, 248, 250, 254, 261, 267–71, 280; Onassis and, 145, 148–51; optimism about, 124–25; pessimism about, 126, 161, 163–64; protest letters, 237–40; reform, 221; role of science, 107, 124, 210; schedule of regulations, 118, 149, 161, 169, 267; Scientific Committee, 155, 163, 166–67, 168, 170, 172, 173, 179, 185–88, 224, 225, 232, 233, 247, 251, 260, 262, 265, 267, 270, 272, 284; structure and rules, 165, 167; Technical Committee, 166–67, 224; vote to restore whaling, 282; withdrawals and accessions, 160, 176, 178, 181, 186, 188, 194, 208, 226, 229, 242, 252–55, 257, 260, 264–65, 267–68, 284. *See also* objection, filed by; New Management Procedure
International Whaling Commission meetings: 1949, London, 126; 1951, Cape Town, 126; 1953, London, 170–72; 1954, Tokyo, 145, 172; 1955, Moscow, 152–53, 173; 1956, London, 174; 1958, The Hague, 176; 1959, London, 178–81; 1960, London, 185, 187; 1962, London, 188; 1963, London, 190; 1964, Sandefjord, 155, 163–64, 190–94; 1965, special meeting, London, 194; 1971, Washington, 214; 1972, London, 223–25, 247; 1973, London, 230, 255; 1974,

London, 232; 1975, London, 232, 235; 1976, London, 229, 259; 1977, Canberra, 241, 247, 259; 1977, special meeting, Tokyo, 250, 261; 1978, London, 260; 1979, London, 243, 262–63; 1980, Brighton, 264; 1981, Brighton, 266; 1982, Brighton, 265, 267; 1985, Bournemouth, 270; 1994, Puerto Vallarta, 281; 1995, Dublin, 284; 2002, Shimonoseki, 281; 2006, St. Kitts and Nevis, 282; 2007, Monaco, 284; 2008, Oman, 284
Inuit whaling, 205–6f, 218, 241, 244–50; cultural arguments, 245, 248, 255; technological changes, 245
Iran, 254–55
Ireland, 27, 108; 1937 convention, 29, 67, 72; proposed compromise in IWC, 284–85
Isenberg, Andrew, 289
Italy, 50, 146

J

Jahre, Anders, 67, 71, 91, 189, 288
Japan, 50, 221; ambassador to US, 274; Antarctica, 81; asks Britain for information, 1940, 96; attitude toward whales, 212; attitude toward whaling diplomacy, 40, 58, 81, 174; and Australia, 187, 236; backlash against anti-whaling movement, 241, 255–58, 263, 281; on bowhead whales, 249–51; boycotts of goods, 236–37; Bureau of Fisheries, 140; cheating, 146; cold harpoon, 272; conditions after World War II, 133; Conservative Party, 281–82; convention of 1937, 65–66, 68, 69; cooperation with Norway, 256, 281, 284; cooperation with Soviets, 190, 193, 236; defends whaling, 216, 222, 224, 276, 281–82; Diet, 64; division of

national quotas, 182–83; Environment Ministry, 222; environmentalist criticism of, 207; European attempts to limit whaling by, 62; expansion of whaling industry, 58–59, 64, 77, 175; food shortage, 113, 132–33, 138, 145; Foreign Ministry (Gaimusho), 58, 81, 178, 222, 255; hires American consultants, 256; joins IWC, 144; lack of maneuverability on whaling, 285; Ministry of Fisheries and Agriculture, 64, 177, 178, 190, 222, 263, 281; moratorium, 222–23, 230, 244, 255, 260, 264–67, 274; objections filed, 187, 226, 253, 266, 280; objections threatened, 267; occupation of, 129–45; opposes quota deal, 177; pirate whaling, 252, 258–59; proposes to hunt humpbacks, 281; protocol of 1938, 76–80; purchase of Norwegian vessels, 57; reputation for waste, 62, 69–70, 102, 129, 137, 139, 144, 145, 156, 236; response to Irish proposal on RMS, 284; return to whaling, 1946, 69, 109, 113–14, 129–45; returns to IWC, 181, 187; sanctions against, 274; science, 191, 275; scientific whaling, 275–76, 279, 281, 285; small-type whaling, 275; US court ruling, 275; uses foreign aid, 260, 265, 282–83, 333n50; whale meat, 62, 129, 132, 144–45, 194, 255–58, 275, 281, 285; wins vote on whaling, 282; withdraws from the IWC, 160, 176, 178. *See also* Supreme Command for the Allied Powers
Japan Advertiser, 81
Japan Times, 255, 276
Japan Whalers' Association, 256, 263
Jonah, 210, 241
Juan Peron, 146, 316n53

K

Kamenaga, Tomoyoshi, 190
Kellogg, Marguerite, 41
Kellogg, Remington, 96, 100, 102, 110, 112, 121, 149, 184, 190, 196f, 218, 253, 286; at 1945 meeting, 107; appointed to lead US delegation, 103; attends conference in Berlin, 41; background, 41–42; blue whale display, 213; chair of 1946 meeting, 115, 264; chair of IWC, 168, 172–73; on cheating, 158; concern about expansion, 125; criticizes 1937 convention, 72–73, 79–80, 81; global quota, 76, 126, 127, 192; and Harmer, 69; on ICRW, 124, 180, 188; on inspection scheme, 160; interprets Argentine data, 97–98; and Japanese whaling, 102, 129, 178; on land stations, 75; meets Maurice, 91; pessimism about IWC, 164, 180, 188; resolves to lead whaling diplomacy, 91–92, 98; on Salvesen, 92, 104–5, 124; suggests US might leave IWC, 172; supports Lillie, 212; on whale oil, 22; yields to State Department, 109, 112
Kemp, Stanley, 34
Kenya, 254–55
Kiel, Germany 178
King George I (island), 85
Kirk, James T., 215
Kirk, Norman, 229
Kirkesby-Garstad, I., 28
Kodaki, Akira, 77–79, 81, 91
Kokoda Track, 137
Korea, 141
Korvald, Lars, 228
Kosmos IV, 189
krill, 8, 38, 123, 209, 228, 289
Kyoto Protocol, 286

L

lactating whales, protection of, 43
land stations, 5; controversy, 6, 74–75,
    126; convention of 1937, 49, 67;
    negotiations of 1938, 74, 77; outlast
    pelagic whaling, 194; during World
    War II, 97
Larsen, C. A., 7
law of the sea, 150; traditions, 29–30,
    175. *See also* United Nations, Con-
    ference on the Law of the Sea
League of Nations, 17, 18, 34, 36, 40, 44,
    50; Economic Committee, 41
Leith Harbour, South Georgia, 7, 45,
    57
Leitzell, Terry, 271–72
letter-writing campaigns, 209, 218, 221,
    230, 237–40
licenses: floating factory, 43; land sta-
    tions, 27, 32; universal, 43
Lichnowsky, Prince, 33
Lie, Trygve, 63
Lienesch, G. J., 169, 185
Lillie, Denis, Gascoigne, 84
Lillie, Harry, 211–12
Lilliputians, 56
Lilly, John, 237
Lisbon, 287
Lloyd's of London, 150
Lodge, John Davis, 222
London, 25, 49, 79, 103, 125
Long, Breckinridge, 103
Lowenstein, Tom, 245
Lykke, Knut, 119

M

MacArthur, Douglas, 113–14, 129–33,
    135–41, 143
Mackintosh, Neil A., 38, 74, 80,
    99–101, 165, 196f, 286; on falsified
    Soviet data, 155; on lower quota,

172, 173; protection of blue whales,
    121–22; work with Bergersen, 102,
    107
Madagascar, 74, 126
Magrane, Peter, 241
Makah, 279
Malawi, 223
Malbran, Don Manuel, 49–50, 80
Magnuson, Warren, 221, 226, 253–54,
    257
Management Stocks, 232
Manchuria, 65
Marchand, J. M., 170
margarine, 13, 18, 21, 22, 40, 47
marking. *See* whale marking
Maud, John, 103
Maude, E. W, 223–25
Maurice, Henry, 6, 57, 73, 195f; on Berg-
    ersen, 64; chairs 1937 meeting, 66;
    chairs 1938 meeting, 49–50, 77–80;
    on Germany, 63, 65; and Kellogg,
    91; Salvesen and, 70, 91; suggests
    global quota, 75–76; on Unilever,
    45–46
Mauritius, 254
Mawson, Sir Douglas, 60
maximum sustainable yield, 100, 106,
    189–90, 210, 231, 261
McCracken, David, 142
McEvoy, Arthur, 13
McHugh, J. L., 188–89, 207, 214, 221,
    223
McIntyre, Joan, 223, 234, 236
McLaughlin, W. R. D., 212
McVay, Scott, 218, 246
Melville, Herman, 5
Mendocino, California, 235
Merriam, John C., 42
Metropolitan Life, 148
Mexico, 224, 232, 263
Meyer, Armin, 222
Midtlyng, T. R., 71
migration of whales, 32, 34

Migratory Bird Treaty, 10, 245
Mind in the Waters, 234, 237
minke whale, 219, 255, 261, 263, 266,
  267, 270, 271, 274, 276–77, 280
Misaki, Japan, 139
Miss Piggy, 243
Mitsubishi, 78
Mizroch, Sally, 276
Moby Dick, 19, 210
Moby Joe, 216–18
Mogadishu, 257
Monash University, 241
Monitor, 271–72
Montevideo, 148
Morasawa, Motikichi, 256
moratorium, 120, 210, 220, 222–24,
  230–33, 240, 241, 262, 268, 283; and
  bowhead whales, 248, 257; commer-
  cial vs. complete, 234, 244; Japanese
  position, 254, 256, 267; passage,
  259–67; phase-out proposal, 263;
  reaction to, 268–72, 285
Morgenstierne, Wilhelm, 125
Morning Herald (Sydney), 240
Morrison, William, 76–77
Moscow, bugged hotels, 152, 173
Mothra, 56
Mowat, Claire, 216
Mowat, Farley, 216–18
muktuk, 245–46
Munich, 1938, 153
Murata, Ryohei, 222
Murphy, John, 254
Mutual of Omaha's Wild Kingdom, 213

N

Nagasaki, 281
Nakasone, Yasuhiro, 274
Nantucket, 5, 22
narwhal, 194, 265
National Geographic, 42, 215
NATO, 274

Nature, 156
Netherlands, 83, 119, 122, 185; begins
  whaling, 109, 111–13; crew controversy with Norway, 112–13; ends
  whaling, 189; Foreign Ministry, 174,
  186; Ministry of Agriculture and
  Fisheries, 174, 186; and moratorium,
  265–66; outlier in IWC, 167; quota
  demands, 177, 186–87, 192; reputation suffers, 171; withdrawal from
  the IWC, 160, 176, 178, 181, 194, 208
Netherlands Whaling Company, 174,
  186
New Bedford, 5
New Fisheries Times, 182
Newfoundland, 35, 216–18
New Guinea, 137
New Management Procedure, 210, 227,
  230–32, 241, 251, 257, 259–61, 263,
  267, 270, 283
New Orleans, 71
New York, 148
New York Times, 246, 279
New Yorker, 219
New Zealand, 26, 28, 41, 64, 67, 77, 185,
  190; on 1931 convention, 47; Antarctic claim, 10, 60; assessment of 1946
  convention, 110, 119; on bowhead
  whales, 248, 250–51; concern
  about IWC, 164; early interest in
  conservation, 41; environmentalists, 228–29, 239, 263; Ministry of
  External Affairs, 136; moratorium
  debate, 259–60, 262–64,
  opposes quota reduction, 179–80;
  proposes an expedition with
  Australia, 97; reaction to Japanese
  whaling, 136–38, 145, 236; rejoins
  IWC, 229; on scientific whaling,
  277; supports extended season, 108;
  whaling in, 74; on whaling in Ross
  Sea, 34; withdraws from IWC, 194,
  208

Nippon Hogei Kabushiki Reisha, 57
Nisshin Maru, 135, 140, 143, 197–200*f*
Nixon, Richard, 220, 223
"no man's sea," 97
North Pacific Fur Seal Convention, 10,
    29, 31, 74, 116, 245, 298n31
North Pacific Ocean, 26, 78, 141, 152,
    221, 234, 251
Northwest Passage, 283
Norway, 6, 23, 26, 32, 56, 61, 70, 185, 221,
    275; Antarctic claim, 10; attitude
    toward whales, 212; attitude toward
    whaling diplomacy, 44, 63, 92, 99,
    182, 285; boycott of, 237, 271, 273;
    cap on whale catchers, 174; concern
    about IWC, 164; convention of 1931,
    32, 54; cooperation with Japan, 256,
    284; criticizes Scientific Commit-
    tee, 284–85; decline in whaling
    prominence, 56, 60, 112, 121, 130, 163,
    182, 189; delegation meets with US,
    233, 272; embassy in Ottawa, 218;
    Foreign Ministry, 194, 225, 271, 285;
    on ICRW, 111; inconsistency, 225,
    268–69; Ministry of the Environ-
    ment, 225, 233, 262, 269; Ministry of
    Fisheries and Agriculture, 93; minke
    whaling in north, 255, 261, 269,
    271–74, 275, 277; moratorium, 225,
    227–28, 230, 264, 267–70, 285; and
    the Netherlands, 112–13; neutral-
    ity, 93; objection filed, 253, 266, 270;
    occupied by Germany, 92, 96, 102,
    105; Panama and, 160; Parliament
    of, 28, 56, 112; policy coordination
    with Great Britain, 121; reaction to
    Japanese whaling, 138; reaction to
    moratorium, 271; response to RMS,
    284; scientific whaling, 276; whalers
    operate from the US, 97, 105; whal-
    ing law, 1929, 36; 1934, 56; 1945, 112,
    146, 147, 186; withdrawal from the
    IWC, 160, 176, 178, 181, 186

Norwegian Whaling Association, 25;
    cancels season, 1931–32, 45; devises
    quota system, 52–53; on withdrawal
    from IWC, 175, 186
nuclear weapons, 234, 235

O

objection, filed by: Australia, 1951, 126;
    France, 1949, 126; Iceland, 1981, 266;
    Japan, 1960, 187; Japan, 1974, 226;
    Japan, 1976, 253; Japan, 1981, 266;
    Japan, 1988, 280; Japan, 1992, 280;
    Netherlands, 1955, 174; Norway,
    1978, 253; Norway, 1981, 266; Soviet
    Union, 1974, 226; Norway, Soviet
    Union, Japan, and Peru, 1982,
    270–71
Observer, 276
Ocean Fishing Company, 134
oceanaria, 219
Officer, Keith, 60
Ohira, Masayoshi, 258
Okawara, Taichiro, 281
Okuhara, H., 178
Olympic Challenger, 145, 148–51, 201*f*,
    257
Oman, 264
Onassis, Aristotle, 12, 27, 130, 145–51,
    158, 159, 160, 164, 252, 257, 288,
    316n58
open season, 56, 63, 66–67, 107, 121, 187;
    effort to extend, 1940, 94–96, 101,
    106, 108; effort to shorten, 170, 172
orcas, 219
Osborn, Fairfield, 106
Oslo, 257
ovaries, in scientific studies, 38

P

PBS, 210, 213
Pacific Garbage Patch, 283

pack ice, 38, 123, 169, 171, 286
Packwood, Bob, 253–54, 257, 272
Packwood-Magnuson Amendment,
    253–54, 256, 258, 269–70, 275
Pakistan, 254–55
Panama, 27, 68, 173, 260; as flag of
    convenience, 149–50; Onassis' fleet,
    145, 148–51, 160
Pantierre, Hayden, 289
Park Hotel, 163
Payne, Roger, 214–17, 223
Pelikan, 97
Pelly Amendment, 225–27, 253–54, 256,
    258, 269–70
Pelly, Tom, 226
Pentagon, 209
People's Trust for Endangered Species,
    203f, 239–40
Pequod, 22
Perkins, Marlon, 213
Peru, 105, 145, 149–51, 221, 226, 253,
    256–57, 267, 270
Peter I (island), 43
Philippines, 238
Phyllis Cormack, 203f, 235–36
Pinchot, Gifford, 3, 4
pirate whaling, 252, 257–59
plankton, 228
Point Hope, Alaska, 245–46
Pol XI, 88f
Poland, 69
Polar Committee. *See* Great Britain,
    Polar Committee
Population Bomb, 209
porpoises, 42
Portugal, 223, 253, 257–58
Powles, G. R., 118, 119, 138
Pribilof Islands, 246
Procter and Gamble, 71
Project Jonah, 210, 229, 232–34, 236,
    241, 261–62
Protected Stocks, 231
pygmy blue whales, 156

Q

quislings, 113, 147
quota, Antarctic (or global), 75, 80,
    100, 106, 120, 152, 163, 188; concerns
    about, 126, 158; created, 1944, 104;
    division among whalers, 175–78,
    186–87; Dutch demands, 177–78,
    186–87; failure to reach, 170; failure
    to set, 163, 193; fin whales, 190;
    proposals to cut, 165, 170–74, 224;
    proposal to increase, 179; reached,
    156; set at 16,000 BWU, 107, 122;
    Soviet demands, 176–77
quota, bowheads, 250–52
quota, national, 182–83
quota, regional, 223–24, 230
quota, species, 231, 267, 274
quota, sperm whales, 260–61, 266, 267,
    274
quota system, 1930s, 52–53, 55, 59, 60,
    61, 62–63

R

rational, as whaling concept, 11, 52, 76,
    80, 156, 175, 188, 193, 227, 240, 260,
    266. *See also* sustainable use
Rau, Walter, 146
Reader's Digest, 216, 218
recordings of whales, 210, 214–15, 235,
    239
Regenstein, Lewis, 207–8, 222
Reich Defense Council, 61
res communis, 207, 242, 244, 280
res nullius, 207
Revised Management Procedure,
    283–84
Revised Management Scheme, 284
Revkin, Andrew, 279–80
Rhineland, 50
right whale, 3, 4, 5, 32, 74, 281; floats
    after death, 6; hunting banned, 43;

right whale (*continued*)
  illegal catch, 43, 156, 157; minimum
  length, 75; modern threats, 283;
  sounds recorded, 215
Rindal, Inge, 253
Rome, 188
Roosevelt, Franklin, 103
Roosevelt, Theodore, 4
Ross Dependency, New Zealand, 28
Ross Sea, 34, 43, 280
Royal Dutch Shell, 65
Royal Society for the Protection of
  Birds, 10
Rozenthal, Anders, 232
Run, 257
Russia, 252
"Russian Sperm," 154, 317n80
Ruud, Johan, 163, 173

S

Sakurauchi, Yashio, 256
Salvesen, Chr., Ltd. 7, 12, 21, 45, 53, 55,
  59, 90f, 164, 182, 211, 240, 323n69;
  earnings, 183–84, 189; employment,
  184; labor problems, 70
Salvesen, H. K., 11, 12, 27, 29, 100,
  107, 111, 122, 194, 288; assessments
  of, 91, 92, 103–5, 173, 240; attends
  1946 meeting, 110; complains
  about South Africa, 70; complains
  about Moscow, 153; criticizes 1937
  convention, 67, 99, 101–2; feuds
  with officials, 104, 240; gathers
  data on "Russian sperm," 154; hires
  Britons instead of Norwegians, 63;
  opposes quota deal, 177; proposes
  compromise, 185; reaction to
  Japanese whaling, 138; reaction to
  Soviet cheating, 158; relations with
  Dobson, 104, 107, 168; retires, 184;
  skeptical about data, 165; worries
  about whaling, 170, 182, 183–84

Salvestria, 29, 59
sanctions, to regulate whaling, 35, 226,
  253–54, 269, 271, 274
sanctuary, 36, 43–44, 79–80, 106, 124,
  170, 279–80, 282
San Diego, 219
San Francisco, 236
Sandefjord, Norway, 6, 23, 39, 57, 155,
  163
Santa Barbara, California, 6
"Save the Whales" movement, 184,
  239, 255, 269, 289; boycotts and
  sanctions, 271–74, 280; ideology, 216–17, 227, 234, 241; leaders,
  214; lost momentum, 280; meet
  Norwegian officials, 272–73; and
  media, 217, 219, 230, 235–36, 238–40,
  260; science, 217–18; significance
  of whales, 209; works out contradictions, 207–208, 228. *See also*
  environmentalists
Scheffer, Victor, 213
Schenck, Hubert, 131–32, 134, 140, 197f
Schevill, Warren, 217–18
Science, 215, 218
science and scientists: as basis for
  quota reductions, 165; benefited
  from hunting, 10; cetacean brains,
  237, 239; computer models, 190;
  data collected under 1937 convention, 67; divisions among, 214; ear
  plus collected, 38; expertise in the
  IWC, 106, 114, 124, 181, 210; and
  false sense of security, 190; key
  to sustainability, 116; meaning of
  whale noises, 214–16, 218; ovaries
  collected, 38; population estimates,
  8, 100, 112, 189–90, 261, 270, 273,
  280–81, 287; pregnancy increases,
  73; rivalry between Norway and
  Britain, 37; scientific whaling, 275–
  77, 279–81, 285; statistical analysis,
  169, 173; and trapped whale, 217–18;

uncertainty of, 35, 37–39, 116, 123, 164–66, 169, 171, 174, 213, 232, 286; vivisection of porpoises, 42; whaling for research purposes, 117, 154. *See also* International Whaling Commission, Committee of Three; sentience and intelligence of whales

Scientific American, 218

Scott, J. V., 259, 261

Scott, Robert, 22, 37

Sea Shepherd, 258

Sea Shepherd Conservation Society, 279

Sea-Air Seafoods, 272

sealing, 8, 246, 257

Seattle, 188

SeaWorld, 219

sei whale, 52, 156, 191, 220, 226, 257, 263

Senegal, 267

sentience and intelligence of whales, 207, 209, 216, 219, 234, 237, 239, 241, 243–44, 288

Seychelles, the, 255, 263–64, 266–67, 270, 280, 282

Shackleton, Ernest, 22

Shakespeare, William, 115

Shane, 30

Shark Bay, Australia, 71

Shell-Mex House, 49, 65

Shin Suisan Shimbun, 182

ship strikes, 283, 286

Siberia, 156, 245

Sierra, 257–58, 279

Sierra Club, 221, 248

Sigfra, 154

Silent Spring, 209

Singer, Peter, 241

Sioux, 258

Slava, 152–54, 156–58, 177; catch data, 153

slavery, 241

Slijper, E. J., 171–73

Smith, Tim, 276

Smith, W. C., 172

Smithsonian Institution, 41, 42, 92, 129, 168, 212–13

Solberg, W. G., 194

Solyanik, Aleksei, 151, 153–54, 157, 193; admits to cheating, 154

Somalia, 146, 253, 257

sonar, 283

Sørlle, Petter, 19

Sourabaya, 70

South Africa, 26, 32, 52, 61, 64, 67, 70, 74, 77, 126, 170, 223, 230, 257

South American whaling commission, 173

South Georgia Island, 3, 7, 9, 32, 183

South Korea, 226, 253, 258, 260, 267, 276

South Pacific Whale Sanctuary, 282

Southern Harvester, 182–84, 189

Southern Ocean Sanctuary, 279, 282

Southern Ranger, 154

Southern Reaper, 22, 30

Southern Venturer, 182, 184

Southern Whaling and Sealing, Ltd., 45, 53

sovereignty, 75, 114, 120, 124, 243–44, 252, 271

Sovetskaya Hotel, 173

Soviet Russia, 161, 177

Soviet Ukraine, 26, 157, 161, 177, 178, 182

Soviet Union, 26, 78, 178, 182, 275; attitude of other nations toward, 152–53, 236; boycott of, 237; cheating, 131, 139, 146, 151–60, 162, 183, 186, 187, 252; cooperates with Japan, 190, 193, 236, 266; defends whaling, 224; environmentalist criticism of, 207; expansion of whaling industry, 120, 161, 175, 176–77, 186; expels Australians, 152; files objection, 270; inspectors, 157; Ministry of Fisheries,

Soviet Union (*continued*)
157; opposes FAO, 121; opposes
moratorium, 224, 230, 267, 270;
over reporting catch, 152, 154, 156;
sends delegation to ICRW, 118,
122; threat to northern Norway,
274; under reporting catch, 152,
156; uses whale meat, 233; whale
marking, 154–55, 191; whaling data,
156–57
Spain, 253, 257, 258, 266, 267, 273
Speak up America, 239
sperm whale, 4, 97, 105, 126, 194, 213,
220, 226, 229, 235, 251, 257, 260–61,
263, 266, 267, 270, 274
Spong, Paul, 219, 234, 235, 237
Stacey, Reginald, 214
Stanford University, 131
Star Trek, 215
stern slipway, 18, 19, 146, 200–201f
Stevens, Christine, 248, 272
Stevens, Ted, 246, 249
Stewart, I. G., 262
Stockholm. *See* United Nations,
Conference on the Human
Environment
Stowe, Irving, 234
Strong, Maurice, 202f, 223
Suarez, Jose Leon, 34
Sukhoruchenko, M. N., 155, 160, 169
Sundt, Herman, 143
Supernature, 263
Supreme Command for the Allied
Powers (SCAP), 114, 130–45;
Diplomatic Section, 138; Fisheries
Division, 134; Natural Resources
Section, 130–34, 139, 144; remakes
Japanese whaling, 139–44; whaling
expeditions, 139, 142–44; whaling
production, 144
Surplus Shipping Act, 147
sustainable use, 4, 31, 35, 51, 66, 97, 106,
114, 116, 168, 207, 232, 241, 243–44,

268, 281. *See also* rational, as whal-
ing concept
Suzuki, S., 145
Suzuki, Zenko, 256
Sweden, 60, 112, 224, 265, 284
Switzerland, 265, signs the 1931 con-
vention, 17, 18, 44
Sydney, 241; Royal Botanical Garden,
215

T

Taiwan, 258
Taiyo Gyogyo, 140, 144–45
Taylor, Fred, 125
Taylor, Rowan, 229
television, whales on, 210, 213–14, 233,
279
Terry, William, 139, 140, 145
Thanksgiving, 118
Thorshammer, 89f
Three Wise Men. *See* International
Whaling Commission, Committee
of Three
Tikigaq, Alaska, 245
Time, 61
Time-Life, 214
Times (London), 104, 233
Tonan Maru 3, 77
Tonna, MV, 19–20, 258
Tønnessen, J. N, and A. O. Johnsen,
21, 62
Tønsberg, Norway, 6, 23, 61, 70
Train, Russell, 222–24, 228
transfer of whaling equipment, ban,
68
Treaty of Versailles, 65
Tresselt, Per, 272–73
Trouton, Rupert, 101, 182
Truman, Harry, 150
tuna fishermen, 150, 249
Turkey, 223

U

Ulysses, 27, 70–71
UN Relief and Rehabilitation Administration, 102
Unilever, 12, 22, 45–47, 53, 55, 59, 64, 94
Union Whaling Company, 12
unions, 24, 63, 70, 281
United Nations, 109, 139; Conference on the Human Environment, 202f, 209, 221–25, 248, 250, 267, 272; Conference on Law of the Sea, 175, 211, 265; proposed ownership of whaling, 164; Security Council, 111
United States Congress, 121, 167, 207, 225, 246; House Committee on Merchant Marine and Fisheries, 246; Senate, 94, 107, 108, 120, 286
United States National Museum, 42
United States of America, 29; Agriculture Department, 135; attitude toward whaling diplomacy, 33, 40, 44, 74, 99, 105, 117; Biological Survey, 42; bowhead issue, 249–51; Bush Administration, 286; Carter Administration, 249; Commerce Department, 42, 44, 221, 225, 226, 249, 271–73; commercial moratorium, 220–24, 230, 233, 249–51, 264; concern about a return to whaling, 65, 111; convenes meeting of anti-whalers, 266; cooperation with Japan, 222; Council on Environmental Quality, 222; court overturns deal with Japan, 274–75; decision to lead whaling diplomacy, 92, 103, 105, 108; drafts 1946 convention, 109; early interest in conservation, 41; embassy in Buenos Aires, 222; embassy in London, 214; embassy in Tokyo, 222; endangered species laws, 220, 235; Federal Maritime Board, 148; Fish and Wildlife Service, 106, 122, 148, 188; Fishermen's Protective Act, 225; and Greenpeace, 275; history of conservation, 65, 74, 116; Interior Department, 115, 220–21, 247, 249–50, 271; and Kellogg, 103, 109; and MacArthur, 113–14, 134, 136; Marine Mammal Act, 246, 287; and MSY, 106; National Marine Fisheries Service, 247, 250, 271; Navy, 220, 237; and New Management Procedure, 230–31; Nixon Administration, 220–22; NOAA, 273, 276; pressures the Dutch, 174; proposes committee of experts, 179–81, 185; post-war vision, 99, 109, 112, 115–16, 221, 227; Reagan administration, 254, 269, 274–75; sanctions, 226, 269, 274; seeks compromise with Japan, 285; State Department, 41, 74, 91–92, 95, 102, 108, 137, 140, 146, 148, 158, 218; Supreme Court, 283; Treasury Department, 71, 135; whaling off Australia, 70–71, 74; whaling law, 1936, 54; whaling law violation of, 71; works to save IWC, 192, 194
United States Petroleum Carriers, 147, 151
University of California, Berkeley, 41
utilitarianism, 4, 41, 62, 100, 132, 193, 217, 228

V

Van Note, Craig, 271–73
Vancouver, 219
Vangstein, Einar, 235
Vereker, G. G., 51
Vestfold, Norway, 23, 56
Vietnam War, 209
Vlastny, 235, 258
Vogt, William, 106

W

Waalman, M. 61
Wakeham, William, 33
Wall, Ron, 150, 158, 166, 173, 174, 179
Walsh, Quentin, 71, 305n66
Walt Disney, 214
Washington, D.C., 115, 244
waste, 8, 9, 20, 31; Japanese, 62, 69–70; SCAP expedition, 142
water, for processing whales, 18, 19, 21, 142
Watson, Lyall, 255, 263, 334n61
Watson, Paul, 203f, 236, 258, 279–81, 337n1
Watt, James, 271
Wellington, New Zealand, 28, 41
Western Australia, 67, 71, 239–40, 261–62
Western Operating Company, 70
Wetmore, Alexander, 42
Whale and Dolphin Coalition, 262
whale catcher, 24, 57, 87f, 88f, 154; accompanying floating factories, 22, 27; development of, 6, 8, 169; limits on, 63, 80, 174–75; as naval vessels, 97; storage in southern ports, 23
Whale for the Killing, A, 216–18
whale, inflatable, 204f, 209
whale marking, 38–39, 74, 154–55, 169, 191, 300n63
whale meal, 20, 22, 26, 183
whale meat, 22, 164, 186, 257, 277, 286–87; for animals, 194, 214, 233, 241; canned, 212; compared to horse, 20; Japanese desire for, 62, 129, 132, 144–45, 194, 255–57, 275, 281, 285; sperm whale, 235
whale oil, 3, 5, 19, 21, 26, 29, 144, 277; alternatives to, 13, 21, 184, 327n34; confiscation, 71; consumers of and markets, 12–13, 21–22, 40, 45–47, 53, 57, 64–65, 94, 194, 288; Germany, 60, 61, 62, 66; Hjort and, 36; as margarine, 13, 18, 21, 22; in nitroglycerine (explosives), 22; prices, 40, 44, 53, 59, 60, 63, 94, 164, 172, 183; production, 53, 55–56, 76, 144, 151, 153; refining, 18, 21–22; rendering, 20; sperm oil as lubricant, 103, 234; stored by Britain, 95; tariffs and taxes on, 27, 34, 65, 71; units of measurement, 12; per whale, 8, 24; after World War II, 97; in World War II, 94
whale, other products, 241
whale populations, 273, 280–81, 287; pre-hunting estimates, 8, 287; in MSY management, 189–90; in NMP, 261, 270; wartime change, 100, 112
whale pot au feu, 20
Whale Protection Fund, 238
Whale Research Fund, 238–39
Whale Wars, 279
whale watching, 218–19, 283–84
whalers, 18, 90f; conditions on board, 24, 25, 153; dangers to, 21; definition of a whale, 212; employment figures, 113, 184, 323n69; flensing, 20, 21; Norwegians banned from Dutch vessels, 112–13; Norwegians on German vessels, 60; Norwegians on Japanese vessels, 57; Norwegians on Soviet vessels, 152–53; on Olympic Challenger, 148–49; tasks on board, 23. See also unions
whales in museums, 212–13
Whaling Council (Norway). See Hvalrådet
whaling expeditions, 22–23, 191; international nature of, 26–27; number of, 177, 187; sold to Japan, 1934, 57; structure and supplies, 24, 93; weather constraints, 23–24, 25, 106

whaling industry: catch numbers, 73, 170, 183, 187; collapse, 1931, 52; concern about expansion of, 3, 36, 39, 50, 58, 73, 121, 125, 130, 146; coordination within, 25, 45, 56, 167; decline of, 5; differences across countries, 12, 49–50, 61, 74–75; expansion, 60, 161; Japanese losses, 268; nature of, 12, 17, 22; need for restructuring, 100; power in the IWC, 180; struggle with Unilever, 45–47; technology, 6–8, 18–22, 169, 171

whaling, scientific, 275–77, 279–81, 285

whaling season: 1926–27, 28, 45; 1930–31, 39, 44, 45; 1931–32, 45, 53, 73; 1932–33, 53, 55; 1933–34, 55; 1934–35, 58, 60; 1935–36, 29; 1936–37, 43, 77; 1937–38, 67, 72; 1938–39, 59, 64, 72, 169; 1939–40, 94; 1940–41, 97–98; 1941–42, 97; 1945–46, 104, 112, 134; 1946–47, 12, 106, 118, 121, 134, 136, 142, 144, 152–53; 1947–48, 121, 142, 144; 1948–49, 141, 156; 1950–51, 149; 1951–52, 149, 169; 1952–53, 170; 1955–56, 173; 1956–57, 173–74; 1958–59, 183; 1959–60, 177–78, 182–83, 185; 1960–61, 183; 1961–62, 184; 1972–73, 156; 1974–75, 226

whaling, small-type, 271–73, 275

Wikinger, 118, 152

Willcock, John, 67

Willem Barendsz, 157, 174, 182, 189, 192

William Wilson Maru, 57

Wilson, J. Innes, 32

Winnipeg, 210

Winston, Waldon, 142–43

Winter, Paul, 215

Wohlthat, Helmuth, 61, 66, 72, 76, 91

Woods Hole, 218, 276

World Health Organization, 109

World Trade Organization, 110

World War II, 69, 81, 92, 93

World Wildlife Federation, 192

Wounded Knee, 258

Y

Yablokov, A. V., 156

Year of the Whale, 213

Yonezawa, Kunio, 263, 265–66

Yukon, 27

Z

Zelko, Frank, 237

Zodiacs, 235, 258

Zoological Society of London, 91, 195f

Weyerhaeuser Environmental Books

The Natural History of Puget Sound Country by Arthur R. Kruckeberg

Forest Dreams, Forest Nightmares: The Paradox of Old Growth in the Inland West by Nancy Langston

Landscapes of Promise: The Oregon Story, 1800–1940 by William G. Robbins

The Dawn of Conservation Diplomacy: U.S.-Canadian Wildlife Protection Treaties in the Progressive Era by Kurkpatrick Dorsey

Irrigated Eden: The Making of an Agricultural Landscape in the American West by Mark Fiege

Making Salmon: An Environmental History of the Northwest Fisheries Crisis by Joseph E. Taylor III

George Perkins Marsh, Prophet of Conservation by David Lowenthal

Driven Wild: How the Fight against Automobiles Launched the Modern Wilderness Movement by Paul S. Sutter

The Rhine: An Eco-Biography, 1815–2000 by Mark Cioc

Where Land and Water Meet: A Western Landscape Transformed by Nancy Langston

The Nature of Gold: An Environmental History of the Alaska/Yukon Gold Rush by Kathryn Morse

Faith in Nature: Environmentalism as Religious Quest by Thomas R. Dunlap

Landscapes of Conflict: The Oregon Story, 1940–2000 by William G. Robbins

The Lost Wolves of Japan by Brett L. Walker

Wilderness Forever: Howard Zahniser and the Path to the Wilderness Act by Mark Harvey

On the Road Again: Montana's Changing Landscape by William Wyckoff

Public Power, Private Dams: The Hells Canyon High Dam Controversy
    by Karl Boyd Brooks

Windshield Wilderness: Cars, Roads, and Nature in Washington's National Parks
    by David Louter

Native Seattle: Histories from the Crossing-Over Place by Coll Thrush

The Country in the City: The Greening of the San Francisco Bay Area
    by Richard A. Walker

Drawing Lines in the Forest: Creating Wilderness Areas in the Pacific Northwest
    by Kevin R. Marsh

Plowed Under: Agriculture and Environment in the Palouse by Andrew P. Duffin

Making Mountains: New York City and the Catskills by David Stradling

The Fishermen's Frontier: People and Salmon in Southeast Alaska
    by David F. Arnold

Shaping the Shoreline: Fisheries and Tourism on the Monterey Coast
    by Connie Y. Chiang

Dreaming of Sheep in Navajo Country by Marsha Weisiger

The Toxic Archipelago: A History of Industrial Disease in Japan by Brett L. Walker

Seeking Refuge: Birds and Landscapes of the Pacific Flyway by Robert M. Wilson

Quagmire: Nation-Building and Nature in the Mekong Delta by David Biggs

Iceland Imagined: Nature, Culture, and Storytelling in the North Atlantic
    by Karen Oslund

A Storied Wilderness: Rewilding the Apostle Islands by James W. Feldman

The Republic of Nature: An Environmental History of the United States by Mark Fiege

The Promise of Wilderness: American Environmental Politics since 1964
    by James Morton Turner

Nature Next Door: Cities and Their Forests in the Northeastern United States
    by Ellen Stroud

Pumpkin: The History of an American Icon by Cindy Ott

Car Country: An Environmental History by Christopher W. Wells

Vacationland: Tourism and Environment in the Colorado High Country
    by William Philpott

Loving Nature, Fearing the State: American Environmentalism and Antigovernment Politics before Reagan by Brian Allen Drake

Whales and Nations: Environmental Diplomacy on the High Seas by Kurt Dorsey

Tangled Roots: The Appalachian Trail and American Environmental Politics by Sarah L. Mittlefehldt

Pests in the City: Flies, Bedbugs, Cockroaches, and Rats by Dawn Day Biehler

WEYERHAEUSER ENVIRONMENTAL CLASSICS

The Great Columbia Plain: A Historical Geography, 1805–1910 by D. W. Meinig

Mountain Gloom and Mountain Glory: The Development of the Aesthetics of the Infinite by Marjorie Hope Nicolson

Tutira: The Story of a New Zealand Sheep Station by Herbert Guthrie-Smith

A Symbol of Wilderness: Echo Park and the American Conservation Movement by Mark Harvey

Man and Nature: Or, Physical Geography as Modified by Human Action by George Perkins Marsh; edited and annotated by David Lowenthal

Conservation in the Progressive Era: Classic Texts edited by David Stradling

DDT, Silent Spring, and the Rise of Environmentalism: Classic Texts edited by Thomas R. Dunlap

The Environmental Moment, 1968–1972 edited by David Stradling

CYCLE OF FIRE BY STEPHEN J. PYNE

Fire: A Brief History

World Fire: The Culture of Fire on Earth

Vestal Fire: An Environmental History, Told through Fire, of Europe and Europe's Encounter with the World

Fire in America: A Cultural History of Wildland and Rural Fire

Burning Bush: A Fire History of Australia

The Ice: A Journey to Antarctica